Routledge English Language Introductions cover core areas of language study and are one-stop resources for students.

Assuming no prior knowledge, books in the series offer an accessible overview of the subject, with activities, study questions, sample analyses, commentaries and key readings – all in the same volume. The innovative and flexible 'two-dimensional' structure is built around four sections – introduction, development, exploration and extension – which offer self-contained stages for study. Each topic can also be read across these sections, enabling the reader to build gradually on the knowledge gained.

Introducing English Language:

- ❑ is the foundational book in the *Routledge English Language Introductions* series, providing an accessible introduction to the English language
- ❑ contains newly expanded coverage of morphology, updated and revised exercises, and an extended Further Reading section
- ❑ comprehensively covers key disciplines of linguistics such as historical linguistics, sociolinguistics and psycholinguistics, as well as core areas in language study including acquisition, standardisation and the globalisation of English
- ❑ uses a wide variety of real texts and images from around the world, including a Monty Python sketch, excerpts from novels such as Virginia Woolf's *To the Lighthouse*, and news items from *Metro* and the BBC
- ❑ provides updated classic readings by the key names in the discipline, including Guy Cook, Andy Kirkpatrick and Zoltán Dörnyei
- ❑ is accompanied by a website with extra activities, project ideas for each unit, suggestions for further reading, links to essential English language resources, and course templates for lecturers.

Written by two experienced teachers and authors, this accessible textbook is an essential resource for all students of the English language and linguistics.

Louise Mullany is Associate Professor in Sociolinguistics in the School of English at the University of Nottingham, UK.

Peter Stockwell is Professor of Literary Linguistics in the School of English at the University of Nottingham, UK.

The accompanying website can be found at www.routledge.com/cw/mullany

ROUTLEDGE ENGLISH LANGUAGE INTRODUCTIONS

SERIES CONSULTANT: PETER STOCKWELL
Peter Stockwell is Professor of Literary Linguistics in the School of English at the University of Nottingham, UK, where his interests include sociolinguistics, stylistics and cognitive poetics. His recent publications include *The Cambridge Handbook of Stylistics* (2014), *Cognitive Grammar in Literature* (2014) and *The Language and Literature Reader* (2008).

SERIES CONSULTANT: RONALD CARTER
Ronald Carter is Research Professor of Modern English Language in the School of English at the University of Nottingham, UK. He is the co-series editor of the Routledge Applied Linguistics, Routledge Introductions to Applied Linguistics and Routledge Applied Corpus Linguistics series.

TITLES IN THE SERIES:

Introducing English Language
Louise Mullany and Peter Stockwell

Pragmatics
(previously published as *Pragmatics and Discourse*)
Joan Cutting

Global Englishes
(previously published as *World Englishes*)
Jennifer Jenkins

Stylistics
Paul Simpson

Practical Phonetics and Phonology
Beverley Collins and Inger M. Mees

Discourse Analysis
Rodney Jones

English Grammar
Roger Berry

Researching English Language
Alison Sealey

Language and Power
Paul Simpson and Andrea Mayr

Language and Media
Alan Durant and Marina Lambrou

History of English
Dan McIntyre

Sociolinguistics
Peter Stockwell

Child Language
Jean Stilwell Peccei

Language in Theory
Mark Robson and Peter Stockwell

Psycholinguistics
John Field

Grammar and Vocabulary
Howard Jackson

For more information on any of these titles, or to order, please go to www.routledge.com/linguistics

INTRODUCING ENGLISH LANGUAGE

Second Edition

A resource book for students

LOUISE MULLANY AND PETER STOCKWELL

Routledge
Taylor & Francis Group

LONDON AND NEW YORK

Second edition published 2015
by Routledge
2 Park Square, Milton Park, Abingdon, Oxon OX14 4RN

and by Routledge
711 Third Avenue, New York, NY 10017

Routledge is an imprint of the Taylor & Francis Group, an informa business

First edition published by Routledge 2010

British Library Cataloguing-in-Publication Data
A catalogue record for this book is available from the British Library

Library of Congress Cataloging-in-Publication Data
Mullany, Louise.
  Introducing English language : a resource book for students / Louise Mullany and Peter Stockwell. – Second edition.
    pages cm. – (Routledge English language introductions)
  Includes bibliographical references and index.
  1. English language–Grammar.   2. English language.   I. Stockwell, Peter, author.   II. Title.
  PE1112.M78 2015
  428.2–dc23

                                                                                      2014044540

ISBN: 978-1-138-01618-7 (hbk)
ISBN: 978-1-138-01619-4 (pbk)
ISBN: 978-1-315-70718-1 (ebk)

Typeset in Minion
by Graphicraft Limited, Hong Kong

MIX
Paper from
responsible sources
FSC® C013604

Printed and bound by CPI Group (UK) Ltd, Croydon, CR0 4YY

HOW TO USE THIS BOOK

The Routledge English Language Introductions (or RELIs) are 'flexi-texts' that you can use to suit your own style of study. The books are divided into four sections:

A **Introduction** – sets out the key concepts for the area of study. The units of this section take you step by step through the foundational terms and ideas, carefully providing you with an initial toolkit for your own study. By the end of the section, you will have a good overview of the whole field.

B **Development** – adds to your knowledge and builds on the key ideas already introduced. Units in this section might also draw together several areas of interest. By the end of this section, you will already have a good and fairly detailed grasp of the field and will be ready to undertake your own exploration and thinking.

C **Exploration** – provides examples of language data and guides you through your own investigation of the field. The units in this section will be more open-ended and exploratory, and you will be encouraged to try out your ideas and think for yourself, using your newly acquired knowledge.

D **Extension** – offers you the chance to compare your expertise with key readings in the area. These are taken from the work of important writers and are provided with guidance and questions for your further thought.

You can read this book like a traditional textbook, 'vertically' straight through from beginning to end. So you would establish a broad sense of the key ideas by reading through Section A and deepen your knowledge by reading Section B. Section C would then present you with a programme of activities to test out different aspects of your broad knowledge. Finally, having gained a good level of competence, you could read the Section D articles and follow up with the Further Reading section.

However, the RELIs have been carefully designed so that you can read them in another dimension, 'horizontally' across the numbered units. For example, units A1, B1, C1 and D1 constitute a *strand* introducing you to phonetics, then developing your knowledge, then testing out and exploring some key ideas, and finally offering you a key case study to read. The strand across A2, B2, C2, D2, and the other strands, 3, 4, 5, and so on, all work in the same way. Reading across the strands will take you rapidly from the key concepts of a specific area to a level of expertise in that precise area, all with a very close focus. You can match your way of reading with the best way that you work.

The glossarial index at the end, together with the suggestions for further reading for each strand, will help to keep you orientated. Each textbook has a supporting website with extra commentary, suggestions, additional material, and support for teachers and students.

Introducing English Language

This book covers the vast field of the study of the English language. It is broadly arranged across three areas. Strands 1 to 5 cover the structure of English to include sounds, words, meanings, grammar and discourse. Strands 6 to 11 cover the main sub-disciplines within language and linguistics study: acquisition and processing, history and society, the spread of English globally, and the close analysis of literary language. Finally, the last two strands set out some methods of linguistic study and a theoretical review of the field. Every strand is also covered in further detail by a devoted book in the RELI series. If you have read across a strand and found that you want to know more, the corresponding RELI book will pick you up and take you further.

This book is an introduction to the study of the English language: an elementary book on linguistics and discourse analysis, essentially. It is not a book for those beginning to learn English as a second language, and it is aimed at college and university students around the world who are studying language or linguistics, either for their own sake, or as part of a broader study of literature, culture or history. It is also the introductory book for the other, more specialised RELI books in the series.

The RELI books are innovative textbooks in that they do not aim to replace your teacher or lecturer, but instead offer both student and expert a resource to adapt as they think most appropriate. You will want to take issue with what we say, test out our assumptions, and – we hope – feel motivated to read and explore further. We have always left space for tutors to mediate the material and for students to explore beyond the book. Especially in this textbook introducing the study of the English language, there are many routes not taken which we have left for you to explore. The English language in all its rich diversity reveals its deeper complexities and its endless fascination the more closely you look at it and think about it. Welcome to the study of language.

CONTENTS

Contents cross-referenced   x
Acknowledgements   xii

A Introduction: key basic concepts   1
1   Phonetics and phonology   2
2   Morphology and lexicology   6
3   Semantics and pragmatics   10
4   Grammatical parts   14
5   Text and discourse   21
6   Early language acquisition   25
7   Psycholinguistics   29
8   Origins of English   33
9   Sociolinguistics   37
10 World Englishes   41
11 Stylistics   45
12 Methodological paradigms   50
13 Language theories   54

B Development: aspects of English   59
1   Consonants and vowels   60
2   Lexical semantics   66
3   Pragmatic principles   69
4   Syntax   76
5   Conversation   81
6   Literacy   87
7   Schemas and worlds   91
8   Standardisation and language change   95
9   Language attitudes   99
10 Codification   103
11 Stylistic analysis   107
12 Techniques and ethics   111
13 Language and thought   116

C   Exploration: investigating English language   121
   1   Performing accents   122
   2   Word plays   128
   3   Doing politeness   133
   4   Syntactic effects   139
   5   Texts in action   144
   6   Learning to read   150
   7   Exploring the mind   157
   8   Corrections   162
   9   Identify yourself   167
  10   Influencing language   171
  11   Exploring literature   178
  12   Collecting data   186
  13   Theory into practice   194

D   Extension: linguistic readings   199
   1   Articulating masculinity (Kiesling)   200
   2   The search for units of meaning (Sinclair)   207
   3   The speech acts of the in-group (Cutting)   214
   4   Prefabricated expressions in spoken language (Cheshire)   221
   5   Advertising discourse (Cook)   227
   6   Socialisation and grammatical development (Ochs and Schieffelin) 233
   7   Promoting perception (Field)   239
   8   Lexical change (Smith)   245
   9   Social relationships and social practices (Milroy and Gordon) 252
  10   The development of World Englishes (Kirkpatrick)   257
  11   Speech and thought as point of view (Simpson)   263
  12   Qualitative, quantitative and mixed methods research (Dörnyei) 271
  13   Researching 'real' language (Carter and Sealey)   278

Further reading   285
References   289
Glossarial index   305

CONTENTS **CROSS-REFERENCED**

UNITS	**A** **INTRODUCTION** *Key basic concepts*	**B** **DEVELOPMENT** *Aspects of English*
1 Sounds	Phonetics and phonology 2	Consonants and vowels 60
2 Words	Morphology and lexicology 6	Lexical semantics 66
3 Meanings	Semantics and pragmatics 10	Pragmatic principles 69
4 Grammar	Grammatical parts 14	Syntax 76
5 Discourse	Text and discourse 21	Conversation 81
6 Acquisition	Early language acquisition 25	Literacy 87
7 Processing	Psycholinguistics 29	Schemas and worlds 91
8 History	Origins of English 33	Standardisation and language change 95
9 Society	Sociolinguistics 37	Language attitudes 99
10 Globalisation	World Englishes 41	Codification 103
11 Stylistics	Stylistics 45	Stylistic analysis 107
12 Methods	Methodological paradigms 50	Techniques and ethics 111
13 Theory	Language theories 54	Language and thought 116

Further reading

References

Glossarial index

C EXPLORATION	**D** EXTENSION	UNITS
Investigating English language	*Linguistic readings*	
Performing accents 122	Articulating masculinity (Kiesling) 200	**1** Sounds
Word plays 128	The search for units of meaning (Sinclair) 207	**2** Words
Doing politeness 133	The speech acts of the in-group (Cutting) 214	**3** Meanings
Syntactic effects 139	Prefabricated expressions in spoken language (Cheshire) 221	**4** Grammar
Texts in action 144	Advertising discourse (Cook) 227	**5** Discourse
Learning to read 150	Socialisation and grammatical development (Ochs and Schieffelin) 233	**6** Acquisition
Exploring the mind 157	Promoting perception (Field) 239	**7** Processing
Corrections 162	Lexical change (Smith) 245	**8** History
Identify yourself 167	Social relationships and social practices (Milroy and Gordon) 252	**9** Society
Influencing language 171	The development of World Englishes (Kirkpatrick) 257	**10** Globalisation
Exploring literature 178	Speech and thought as point of view (Simpson) 263	**11** Stylistics
Collecting data 186	Qualitative, quantitative and mixed methods research (Dörnyei) 271	**12** Methods
Theory into practice 194	Researching 'real' language (Carter and Sealey) 278	**13** Theory
		Further reading
		References
		Glossarial index

ACKNOWLEDGEMENTS

The English language is too wide a topic even for two authors, and this book has been produced in the productive company of many friends and colleagues. In particular, the School of English at the University of Nottingham is a world-class collection of researchers and teachers whose expertise we have drawn on extensively. We would like to extend our grateful thanks to Svenja Adolphs, Sarah Atkins, Kathy Conklin, Robbie Dewa, Zoltán Dörnyei, Kevin Harvey, Lucy Jones, Dawn Knight, Christina Lee, Mike McCarthy, John McKenny, John McRae, Michaela Mahlberg, Ana Pellicer-Sánchez, Michael Rodgers, Nicola Royan, Norbert Schmitt, Violeta Sotirova and Katie Wales. The incomparable Ron Carter embodies the nearest we can imagine to an expert across the entire field, and his advice throughout the whole writing process has been invaluable. Equally, we would also like to thank Sara Mills for her perceptive and speedy advice, and the numerous authors in the RELI series for their useful comments and for reading through drafts.

We are grateful to Phoebe Lin for her help with translations of the Hong Kong advertising data. The Hong Kong street scene photographs were taken by Matthew Green. Our thanks go out to him for his permission to use these images. We would like to thank Nadia Seemungal, Eloise Cook, Catherine Foley and Louisa Semlyen at Routledge for their perspicacity and patience.

Thanks and love to Joanna Gavins and Matt Green for creating space for yet another project that took longer than planned, to Abbie and Tommy, and to Ada and Edith, whose first adventures in language appear in this book.

Permissions

The authors and publishers would like to thank the following for permission to reproduce copyrighted material:

Scott Fabius Kiesling and John Wiley and Sons publishers for extracts from 'Men's identities and sociolinguistic variation: the case of fraternity men', *Journal of Sociolinguistics* 2/1 (1998);

The estate of John Sinclair and Taylor & Francis publishers for extracts from *Trust the Text: Language, Corpus and Discourse* (Routledge, 2004);

Joan Cutting, the journal editors and Elsevier publishers for extracts from 'The speech acts of the in-group', *Journal of Pragmatics* 33 (2001) © Elsevier 2001;

Jenny Cheshire, the editors Leonie Cornips and Karen Corrigan and Benjamins publishers for extracts from *Syntax and Variation: Reconciling the Biological and the Social* (2005);

Guy Cook and Taylor & Francis publishers for extracts from *The Discourse of Advertising* (Second Edition. Routledge, 2001);

Elinor Ochs and Bambi Schieffelin, the editors Paul Fletcher and Brian MacWhinney, and Blackwell publishers for extracts from *The Handbook of Child Language* (1995);

John Field, the journal editors and Oxford University Press publishers for extracts from 'Promoting perception: lexical segmentation in L2 listening', *ELT Journal* 57/4 (2003);

Jeremy Smith and Taylor & Francis publishers for extracts from *An Historical Study of English: Function, Form and Change* (Routledge, 1996);

Lesley Milroy and Matthew Gordon and Blackwell publishers for extracts from *Sociolinguistics: Method and Interpretation* (2003);

Andy Kirkpatrick and Cambridge University Press publishers for extracts from *World Englishes: Implications for International Communication and English Language Teaching* (2007);

Paul Simpson and Taylor & Francis publishers for extracts from *Language, Ideology and Point of View* (Routledge, 1993);

Zoltán Dörnyei and Oxford University Press publishers for extracts from *Research Methods in Applied Linguistics* (2007);

Bob Carter and Alison Sealey, the editors Bob Carter and Caroline New, and Taylor & Francis publishers for extracts from *Making Realism Work* (Routledge, 2004);

Solo Syndication for 'Birmingham bans apostrophes from road signs' (Metro, 29.01.2009);

Curtis Brown on behalf of Brian Aldiss for an extract from *Barefoot in the Head* © Brian Aldiss 1969;

Neal Stephenson and Penguin publishers for an extract from *Crash* (1992);

Carmen Llamas for the Survey of Regional English (SuRE) Sense Relation Network Sheet diagrams from 'A new methodology: data elicitation for social and regional language variation studies', *Leeds Working Papers in Linguistics and Phonetics* 7 (1999).

Every effort has been made to contact copyright-holders. Please advise the publisher of any errors or omissions, and these will be corrected in subsequent editions.

Section A

INTRODUCTION
KEY BASIC CONCEPTS

PHONETICS AND PHONOLOGY

To begin our study of the English language, we will start off with a consideration of exactly how human beings are able to communicate with one another using speech. The most logical way to begin is by focusing on speech sounds. The study of the sounds that we produce when we engage in spoken communication is called **phonetics**. In contrast with other mammals, the human body contains a complex set of equipment, commonly known as the **organs of speech**, which enables us to produce spoken language. The power for all speech sounds emanates from the lungs, travels up the windpipe, past the vocal cords and then into and out of the mouth or nose.

Individuals who conduct research on speech sounds are known as **phoneticians**. Phoneticians investigate the production of speech in one of three ways: through **auditory phonetics**, which refers to how speech sounds are perceived, through **acoustic phonetics**, referring to how speech sounds are made up of physical properties, and finally through **articulatory phonetics**, the study of how speech sounds are produced by the organs of speech known as **articulators**. The units on sounds in this book (A1–D1) fall under the third category, articulatory phonetics. This is the area of phonetics that has the most applicability in an introduction to the English language, and it is also the most accessible area of investigation within phonetic science.

In order to be able to learn about articulatory phonetics as a foundational area for English language study, it is really important for you to test out speech sounds practically yourself in order to get to grips with exactly how your own articulators work. Though articulating individual speech sounds in isolation, without surrounding sounds to give meaning to the noises that you make, may seem rather strange, as may articulating seemingly random individual words in isolation, it is the most effective way to learn about how your organs of speech work. If you are a little reticent to do this at first, you can always lock yourself away in a private room while reading the units on sounds! Mastering exactly how your organs of speech work is an important step in enabling you to recognise and describe all of the different sound features of the English language.

Another key area of study in the investigation of sounds is **phonology**, which is a very closely related discipline to phonetics. Individuals who specialise in the study of phonology are known as **phonologists**. As a general way of distinguishing between the two disciplinary areas, phonology can be perceived as investigating sounds as an abstract system, whereas phonetics focuses on the actual sounds as they are spoken by specific individuals during particular speech events.

However, as you will find with many areas of the English language which we will study in this book, the boundaries between disciplinary terms can often be fuzzy and clear delineations between phonetics and phonology are frequently difficult to pinpoint. Overall, it is important to bear in mind that in order to produce a phonetic analysis of speech in English you need to draw upon the phonological system of the English language to fulfil this task successfully.

Within phonology, the term **phoneme** refers to a set of abstract units which together form the sound system of a language. Contrasts in meaning are produced through directly contrasting phonemes. For example, if we compare /p/ with /t/, as in *pip* and *tip*, then a different meaning is created by the contrast. Word pairings where there is only one sound change between them, as in this example, are known as **minimal pairs**. Phonemes of the English language, or of any other language for that matter, can only exist as abstract entities. They can never be literally produced by speakers.

The written system of the English language, or its **orthography** as it is technically termed, does not correspond directly with how words are articulated in speech. In order to make a permanent, written record of speech sounds, known as a **transcript**, there is a need to use a separate writing system especially devised for this purpose. This system is known as the *International Phonetic Alphabet*, or the IPA. It provides a much more accurate version of the sounds of the English language as well as those of other language systems.

A distinction can be made between the production of **phonemic transcripts** and **phonetic transcripts**. The former do not demonstrate the actual articulation and instead highlight the contrasts from one phoneme to another. Phonemes are transcribed in slanted brackets, such as /p/ or /t/, whereas actual phonetic realisations, exactly how the sounds are articulated by speakers, are represented by square brackets such as [p] or [t].

There are variants that exist within individual phonemes when these are realised phonetically by different speakers, and they are termed **allophones**. The allophones of a phoneme are concrete entities produced by speakers and can thus be analysed phonetically and recorded in a phonetic transcript. To illustrate, the phoneme /t/ in the word *butter* can be realised as [t] or by the **glottal stop** [ʔ]. The term 'glottal stop' is derived from the **glottis**, the space that exists between vocal cords. It refers to occasions when the vocal cords close and block the air from the lungs – it is a very common speech feature in many regional varieties of English.

The phoneme /l/ can be realised either by the allophone known as **light l**, (sometimes termed **clear l**), when /l/ is produced at the front of the mouth as in the beginning of a word such as *lip*, or by the allophone known as **dark l**, the name given to /l/ when it is produced at the back of the mouth, as in the end of a word such as *pool*. However, realisations of /l/ will vary depending upon the speaker. For instance, if it is uttered by a speaker with a Scottish accent, the dark l quality is articulated at the beginning and end of words, so *lip* and *pool* would be articulated with the same dark l sound.

In contrast with phonemic transcripts, phonetic transcripts will indicate these subtle differences in speakers' articulation of allophones. Phonetic transcription contains additional marks known as **diacritics**, which enable the finer details of articulation to be recorded. For example, we can consider the allophones of the phoneme /l/ highlighted above; if a speaker produces dark l, then this is more accurately represented with the addition of a diacritical mark as [ɫ] – as opposed to [l], which represents light l and which does not have the diacritical mark.

Say the words *pool* and *lip* out loud to yourself concentrating in particular on your realisation of the phoneme /l/. Decide whether your articulations can be represented as having a 'light' or 'dark' quality. Also say the word *butter* out loud to yourself and decide whether you articulate the phoneme /t/ as [t] or as a glottal stop [ʔ].

The glottal stop can also be used by speakers when pronouncing the consonants /p/ and /k/ as well as /t/. Listen out for glottal stop usage in the everyday speech you hear around you, including speech used on the radio, television and Internet. Which speakers tend to use the glottal stop feature? Which speakers do not?

The IPA symbols will be further illustrated in B1.

Articulators and articulation

As we have seen above, articulators are the specific parts of the vocal tract that are responsible for sound production. An individual speaker has a number of articulators:

- ❑ lips
- ❑ teeth
- ❑ tongue
- ❑ alveolar ridge (the ridge in the roof of the mouth, behind the front teeth)
- ❑ hard palate (the hard, bony area behind the alveolar ridge)
- ❑ soft palate (the soft, fleshy part behind the hard palate)
- ❑ uvula (the back of the soft palate)
- ❑ vocal cords

The most important articulators are our lips and tongue. The articulators are listed above in order, starting from the very front of the mouth through to the back of the vocal tract. Trace these different locations in your own mouth using your tongue. Begin with your lips, and then work your way through to the uvula. You can feel where your vocal cords are by placing your fingers on the outside of your windpipe in your neck. Do this and then articulate the phoneme /z/. You should be able to feel your vocal cords vibrating – /z/ is what is known as a **voiced** sound. Other sounds are **voiceless** when articulated – there is no vibration of the vocal cords. To illustrate, articulate the phoneme /s/ with your fingers on your vocal cords. You should not be able to feel any vibration.

All sounds start in the lungs and then get manipulated on their way through the oral cavity. Interestingly, consonant and vowel sounds vary quite significantly in how they are produced. Consonants are formed when the airflow stemming from the lungs is obstructed at some point. The lips and the tongue are most frequently responsible for the obstruction, which then results in consonant sounds being realised.

Phoneticians have devised a three-part system in order to describe consonant sounds:

- ❑ Place of articulation: where does the air stream become obstructed?
- ❑ Manner of articulation: how is it manipulated?
- ❑ Nature of articulation: is the sound voiced or voiceless?

The first place category, which is used in order to describe the place of articulation of consonant sounds, is defined as **bilabial**, that is, as taking place between the upper and lower lips. Make the sounds /p/ and /b/, and you will feel how these sounds are formed through the lips.

The second category is known as **labio-dental**, a term which refers to the lower lips and the upper front teeth. If you make the sounds /f/ and /v/, you will be able to locate the labio-dental positioning in your mouth. The next category is termed **dental**, when the tip/blade of the tongue touches the upper front teeth, as with the sounds /t/ and /d/. Two other consonant sounds that belong to the dental category are the 'th' sounds, one voiced and the other voiceless. The 'theta' (/θ/) symbol is used to represent the voiceless variety, as in words such as *thigh* or *think*. The symbol /ð/ is used to represent the voiced version of this dental sound in words such as *the* or *thus*.

Moving a bit further back in your mouth, the next 'place' category is known as **alveolar**, referring to when the tip or blade of the tongue touches the alveolar ridge, as in the sounds /s/ and /z/. **Palatal** refers to when the central portion of the tongue touches the hard palate, as in /j/, and **velar** refers to when the back of the tongue touches the soft palate, as in /k/ and /g/.

The final place of articulation is the **glottal** category, which we have already come across, and which refers to the glottis. In addition to the glottal stop, /h/ is the only other sound which is made in the glottis area. The /h/ sound is made when the glottis is open.

In terms of the manner of articulation, the first consonant category is called a **stop**, where articulators are closed for a short time and then let go quickly, as with /p/ and /b/. Make these sounds again, this time thinking about the manner in which your articulators are working.

The second category is known as **nasal**, where air escapes through the nose instead of the mouth, as in /m/ or /n/. Try pinching your nose and saying these sounds, and you will find it impossible.

The next category is termed **fricative**, which refers to occasions when the articulators are closed, so the air has to squeeze through a small opening, resulting in a 'hissing' noise, as in /f/ or /v/.

Approximant is the next category, referring to when turbulence occurs due to articulators being close together, as with /j/ or /w/. These sounds are sometimes referred to as **glides**, as they are made with the tongue in motion, gliding between different sounds.

Next is **lateral approximant**, a sub-category of approximant, referring to when air flows out through the side of the tongue, as with /l/.

Finally, the **affricate** category refers to a brief stop followed by a slow release of air, with the speech organs lingering in the fricative position for a time, as in the 'ch' sound in *cheese*, represented by the phonetic symbol /tʃ/ (see B1 for further details).

In contrast to consonants, vowels are not related to obstruction and there is no need to decide whether vowels are voiced or voiceless, as all vowels are voiced – it is impossible to produce a vowel sound without the vocal cords vibrating. Also, all vowels are approximants, so it is not possible to use the manner category for distinguishing between different vowel sounds. In terms of the place of articulation, vowels are always produced in the oral cavity. Different vowel sounds are made by varying the positioning of the tongue and the lips.

Therefore, instead of the system used for consonant description, the identification of vowel sounds focuses upon the following:

❑   the shape of the tongue
❑   the positioning of the lips
❑   whether the tongue and lips are kept still or whether they change position during
     sound production
❑   how long the sound is made for, known as **duration**.

To aid the process of description, phoneticians have devised a diagrammatic map of
the tongue, which is designed to trace these features. Such maps are commonly
referred to as **vowel trapeziums**. We will look at examples of these trapeziums in B1
as part of our more detailed consideration of vowels and consonants.

A2   MORPHOLOGY AND LEXICOLOGY

What is a word?

Most non-linguists would say that a **word** is the smallest chunk of meaningful
language. This is a unit made up only of individually meaningless sounds (if spoken)
or letters (if written). Certainly, most linguists would agree that phonemes (speech
sounds, introduced in A1) and **graphemes** (written letters) in themselves usually do
not have a meaning: the phonemes /t/, /a/, the diphthong /ai/, the cluster /lt/, the
grapheme 'g', and the digraphs 'th' and 'gh' are meaningless in isolation. However,
there are many words in this paragraph that are not neatly unitary. For example, the
word 'themselves' seems to be made up of at least two smaller words, namely, 'them'
+ 'selves' – here, the two composite words are proper words in their own right.
'Certainly', though, seems to be made up of a word in its own right ('certain') and
another odd addition ('-ly') that cannot really stand on its own.

'Meaningless' can similarly be divided into two ('meaning' + '-less'); we could
even go further and divide it into three ('mean' + '-ing' + '-less'), though not four (the
unit 'mean' here is not composed of the senses of 'me' and 'an'). By contrast, again,
'however' can be divided into two other words that can stand on their own ('how' +
'ever'), but it does not seem clear how the meaning of 'however' can exactly be
determined by the meanings of these two words.

Other words in the above paragraph have been formed by hyphenating two
elements together ('non-linguists'), or by taking small chunks that were originally
meaningful in other languages ('phon', 'eme', 'graph', 'para'), or by adapting words from
other meaningful contexts so that they can only be metaphorical (how do words
literally 'stand on' their own?), or by formulaic phrases that seem to mean more than
the sum of their parts ('made up'). If we said that we wrote that first paragraph
deliberately to lead you up the wrong path, to pull the wool over your eyes, to throw
you a red herring, or to convey antinormalisationness, you can probably guess what
we mean. But if you are a beginning learner of English, an elementary word-for-word
translating dictionary will be pretty hopeless in this regard.

Words and their parts

The notion of a word is therefore not particularly straightforward, and linguists prefer to use the term **morpheme** for the smallest meaningful unit of language. 'Certain', 'mean' and 'linguist', in the examples above, are all **free morphemes** – *free* because they can stand on their own as fully fledged words. The others are **bound morphemes** – *bound* because they can only survive meaningfully by being attached to free morphemes: '-ly', '-ing', '-ise', '-ation', '-less', 'non-', 'co-', and so on are all bound morphemes.

You can take any word in English and decide whether it is made up of one or more morphemes. You can also tell a lot about the meaning and use of the word by understanding which of its constituent morphemes are free or bound.

Notice that it is the meaning of these units that is most important, rather than how they look or sound: the written versions of 'phone' and 'none' change their shapes when attached to other morphemes (losing their final 'e' in, for example, 'phonological' and 'nonsense', respectively). Similarly, words can change their sounds (listen to the differences when 'use' is combined to make 'usually' (/s/ or /z/ → /ʒ/), 'composite' to 'composition' (/t/ → /ʃ/), and even 'formula' to 'formulaic' (/ə/ → /ɛɪ/). Clearly, phonetic and graphological quality is secondary to morphology here.

Morphology (the study of these elementary units and their rules of combination) is traditionally divided into two areas: grammatical **inflection** and **word-formation** (the latter area increasingly becoming the concern of the field known as **lexicology**). Inflections are when a bound morpheme is added whose main purpose is to alter the grammatical category of the free morpheme. So the free morpheme 'look' can be connected to other, bound morphemes to produce 'looks' (noun plural), 'looks' (third person verb-form), 'looking' (present participle) and 'looked' (past participle). These additional morphemes are all **suffixes** – they follow the root word.

Most English grammatical morphemes are suffixes, though in the past English has had past-marker **prefixes** ('yronne' = ran), reflexive prefixes ('methinks') and possessive prefixes ('akin', 'afresh'). See if you can find any more of these.

English also used to have a great many **infixes**, where the bound morpheme occurs in the middle of the root word, preserved in modern usage as 'strong' forms of the past tense ('run – ran', 'bring – brought', 'steal – stole'). These three forms of **affix** all serve a grammatical purpose, by contrast with non-inflectional affixes such as 'un-', 'in-', 're-', '-ly', '-ness', '-isation', '-wise', and so on. These last examples of word-forming affixes are very rarely infixed, except for creative oddities like 'absobloodylutely'.

Word-formation is the most productive area of morphology. The addition of non-inflectional affixed morphemes is a form of **derivation**. So from the root word 'help', English has derived 'helpful', 'unhelpful', 'helpless', 'helplessness' and 'helper', and could conceivably derive others with a bit of creativity: 'helperwise' (pertaining to assistants), 'rehelp' (to fill one's plate again), 'dishelp' (to hinder more strongly than being 'unhelpful'), 'helpily' (with cheerful assistance), and so on. The root word ('look', 'help', 'run', 'steal') is called the **lemma** – the form you would look up in a dictionary.

Derivation has produced many new word-forms in English. **Zero-derivation** is where the word does not change shape but nevertheless comes to be used as a new word: **verbification** is particularly common in English, from Shakespeare's first usage of 'knife' as a verb rather than a noun (see B4 for definitions of terms), to more recent '*access* the file', '*chair* the meeting' or '*green* your politics'.

The combination of two or more free morphemes is known as **compounding**, and this phenomenon of word-formation is very common in English – as it is in other basically Germanic languages. Formulaic phrases ('red herring', 'head waiter', 'climate change'), hyphenations ('self-harm', 'role-play', 'after-effects'), true compounds ('horsebox', 'whiteboard', 'sportscar') and lexical blends ('digibox', 'cyborg', 'smog') are all examples of compounding. Notice that the compounded elements can be from different parts of speech (noun + noun, or noun + verb, or adjective + noun, and so on, see A4), and can even be from two different languages ('über-chic' – German and French, 'teleport' – Greek and Latin).

Adopting and adapting words

It should be evident from these diverse sources that English has been particularly open across its 1500-year history to **borrowing** (perhaps better understood as *copying* or even as stealing). English began as a Germanic dialect with Scandinavian contact (so we have 'apple', 'tree', 'sky', 'skirt'), in a Celtic landscape ('tor', 'banner', 'slogan'), followed by Norman French influence and French borrowing over 500 years ('parliament', 'mutton', 'administration'), with Italian, Latin and Greek loans through the Renaissance and continuing into the modern era ('violin', 'oxygen', 'catalyst', 'microcomputer').

French, Latin, and the Germanic languages account in almost equal measures for most common English words, with everyday speech weighted towards Germanic sources and with formal or technical language leaning more towards French and Latin sources. Other borrowings include 'caravan' (Persian), 'juggernaut' (Sanskrit), 'sushi-bar' (Japanese), 'lager' (German), as well as 'safari', 'zombie', 'jumbo' and 'a-go-go' (Bantu languages), 'alcohol', 'algebra', 'zero', 'tariff' and 'magazine' (Arabic), 'teak', 'zebra', 'marmalade' and 'palaver' (Portuguese), and 'papoose', 'shack', 'barbecue', 'canoe' and 'cocaine' (native American languages).

When borrowing from other languages, English has tended to anglicise the pronunciation, which is often reflected in the spelling: 'vindaloo' curry from the Portuguese 'carne de vinha d'alhos'; 'cafe' often appears without the French acute accent on the final letter ('café') and sometimes gets pronounced [kaf] or [kafi], without a French accent at all (see B1 for further details on how to write in phonetic notation). There are some exceptions, of course, such as 'chic', which retains its French sound (perhaps because of both its *haute couture* sense and also because of a clash with 'chick'). When words are borrowed into English, they usually tend to become grammatically fixed for inflections too: so we might order two 'pizzas' rather than 'pizze', eat two mint 'Magnums' (ice lollies) instead of 'Magna', and talk about 'schemas' not 'schemata'. There is even a great deal of debate over whether the plural of the computer 'mouse' is the modern inflection 'mouses' rather than the medieval 'mice'. Words often carry their origins, though, as demonstrated by the fact that a 'wireless mouse' no longer looks like a mouse at all.

When words are borrowed, as in some of the examples above, the source words are often shortened. **Shortening** in itself is also a form of word-formation. We have 'mobs' not 'mobiles', 'fans' more usually than 'fanaticks', and modern life has the 'telly', the 'phone', the 'flu', the 'gym', the 'car', the 'bus', the 'pram', the 'fridge' and many more, all clipped from longer original words. These are all abbreviations of various forms, and often the longer and shorter versions co-exist for a long time in the language, with the shorter form being colloquial and the longer form reserved for formal or technical contexts.

Shortening in the form of **acronyms** is very common especially in technological innovation: the LP was replaced by the CD and DVD, then by the MP3. Acronyms can be **atomic** if each element is pronounced separately (FBI, BBC, EU, RAF) or **molecular** if pronounced as a genuine word ('laser', 'radar', 'NASA'). Occasionally, a combination of processes of word-formation results in historical oddities. The most famous is the 'hamburger', originally invented in Hamburg, New York, and made from beef with coffee and spices between bread. The 'ham' morpheme is wrongly associated with meat and so is regarded as detachable from the whole word, producing the **back-formation** 'burger'. This free morpheme is then available to be compounded with many other prefixes: 'cheeseburger', 'veggie-burger', 'BBQ-burger', 'tofu-burger', plain 'burger' and even the wrongly corrected 'beefburger'.

Similarly, the verb 'to burgle' was wrongly back-formed from 'burglar' in the late nineteenth century (as if the suffix was the morpheme '-er', denoting the doer of the action) probably from the Middle English 'burgh-breche' and 'burgator' (home-breaker). American usage suffixed the morpheme in 'burglarized'. Other back-formations include 'auto-destruct' (rather than 'destroy', from 'auto-destruction'), 'bicep' (from 'biceps'), 'trouser' and 'pant' (from 'pants'), 'peddle' (from 'peddler' or 'pedlar'), 'sleaze' (from 'sleazy'), 'transcript' (from 'transcription'), 'televise' (from 'television'), and many others.

Related to these forms are **retronyms**, which are words created anachronistically in response to later developments. For example, the 'acoustic guitar' was just any old guitar until the invention of the 'electric guitar'. Similarly, 'World War I' was just 'the Great War' until 'World War II'. Others include 'landline' (before mobile cellular phones), 'analogue' (meaning anything pre-digital), 'vinyl' (to describe what used to be simply 'records'), and so on.

New words

Quite unusually, words can be formed simply by creation out of nowhere. Genuinely novel creations are hard to identify, however, since they usually conform to standard phonological rules of English and so will always be suggestive of some source or other, and many **neologisms** (new coinages of words) are formed from other existing words. Literary and science-fictional texts are good sources for creative neologisms, but the origins of 'warp-drive', 'raygun', 'flying saucer' and 'cyborg' are plain or easily deducible. More obscure neologisms might include 'kemmer' (Ursula Le Guin's invention of the reproductive period of an alien race), 'grok' (Robert Heinlein's wide-ranging term for mutual empathy), and Philip K. Dick's very useful 'kipple' (the bits and pieces of detritus that accumulate and multiply over time in drawers and cupboards).

Of course, all the various types and combinations of word-formation can be extended by grammatical inflection as well. So the verb 'to grok' can be inflected to produce 'I grok', 'she groks', 'we grokked', 'they are grokking', and the noun 'raygun' can be inflected as 'two rayguns', as well as expanded by derivation to yield 'raygunner', 'raygunnery', 'anti-raygun', and so on.

Over the course of the development of English, most new words in the language have been free morphemes borrowed from other languages or adapted from existing words as set out above. Innovation in new grammatical bound morphemes is very rare: the Old English third person verb-ending '-eþ' lasted into Middle English (spelled as '-eth', as in 'my cup runneth over'), but the northern dialectal '-s' ending eventually replaced it ('runs over'). There have to be very powerful, longlasting and widespread forces to sustain a new grammatical morpheme. For example, the pronoun 'it' (from Old English 'hit') was originally a useful option between 'he' and 'she' (originally 'he' and 'heo/seo' in Old English), but today 'it' has a sense of inanimacy. It would be very useful in Modern English to have a less clumsy neutral option than 'he or she', the written 's/he', or the increasingly common but odd non-agreement of 'they' in a sentence like: 'when the reader gets to this point, they will have finished the unit'. Transgender people have been struggling to find an alternative for years. Perhaps you might try to invent or import a useful alternative pronoun yourself.

SEMANTICS AND PRAGMATICS

Semantics and pragmatics are closely related terms in language study. **Semantics** refers to the construction of meaning in language, while **pragmatics** refers to meaning construction in specific interactional contexts. Pragmatics is also sometimes referred to as the study of 'meaning in use' or 'meaning in interaction', whereas semantics is concerned with the more abstract study of general, conventional meaning within language structure.

These two disciplines of language study are thus firmly linked, and establishing a clear distinction between the two of them is difficult as they tend to blur into one another. Similarly, in recent years there has also been a blurring of the boundaries between semantics and other disciplinary areas of language study as linguists have increasingly realised that it is misleading to treat sentence meaning in isolation from its surrounding context. One example of such blurring is with lexical semantics (see B2), which illustrates the interrelationship between lexicology and the semantic study of meaning construction. Pragmatics is also heavily interrelated with studies of discourse, as we will see in Strand 5. Elements of pragmatics study are also used within sociolinguistics (see A9).

In this unit, we begin by briefly introducing you to more traditional terms and foundational elements of semantics; we then consider how semantics and pragmatics interrelate with one another; finally we move on to examine some foundational principles of pragmatics study.

Sense and reference

An important distinction in semantics is that between the **sense** and **reference** of linguistic expressions. This distinction is also a useful principle for our exploration of the traditional role of semantics in English language study. Sense and reference are crucial components of language, as they form part of the foundation of every facet of study within semantics. Sense refers to the central meaning of a linguistic form and how it relates to other expressions within the language system. Reference can be defined as characterising the relationships between language and the world, and particularly between language and specific entities that are being focused upon.

A classic example to help illustrate the distinction between the two terms is consideration of the noun phrases 'the morning star' and 'the evening star' (see A4 for a definition of noun phrase). Both can be defined as having the same reference – they both refer to the planet *Venus* – but they clearly have different senses. This example also neatly illustrates the crucial role of context in determining reference. Whilst there are some terms in the English language that have constant reference, such as 'the moon' (at least while on this planet) or 'Great Britain', most often terms which express reference are reliant upon context for their meaning.

Sense is more difficult to define than reference, as it does not refer to a particular person or thing – it is a much more abstract concept. The best way to consider the sense of a linguistic form, and thus define its central meaning, is to compare it with other entities. For example, if we compare a dog to a cat or a giraffe, we get a better understanding of the semantic features of the lexical term 'dog'. By making such comparisons, we are defining the senses of the linguistic form 'dog'. It is important to remember that all expressions which have meaning can be defined as having sense, but not all expressions of meaning will have reference.

A key concept to keep in mind when defining reference is **referring expression**, denoting a word or phrase that specifically defines a particular entity in the world. Noun phrases are classic examples of referring expressions. However, as we have seen above, it is important to bear in mind that reference cannot be ascribed in a vacuum. Reference is context-dependent, and ascertaining the meaning of particular referents depends entirely upon who is speaking, who they are speaking with, and in what setting the interaction is taking place.

Some utterances may be referring expressions in one context but cease to be referring expressions in another. For example, indefinite noun phrases need to be viewed in context – on some occasions, they will be referring expressions, but on other occasions they will not fulfil this function. Compare the utterance 'a woman was just staring at you' with the utterance 'this apartment needs a woman's touch'. In the former, 'a woman' is a referring expression, but in the latter it has indefinite reference: it does not refer to one particular woman, and so it is not operating as a referring expression in quite the same way.

Can you think of other, similar examples where the same phrase has different reference, depending upon context? The contextual difference between the same referring expression can be exploited for humorous purposes. In the Irish television situation comedy *Father Ted*, Father Ted comments to Father Dougal that their parochial house is in need of 'a woman's touch'. Unable to understand the indefinite reference, Father Dougal accuses the only woman who is present, a visiting nun, of physically touching Father Ted – making the accusatory statement 'Ted said you've been touching him'. Dougal has failed to understand Ted's indefinite, metaphorical meaning, resulting in humour through his interpretation of 'a woman' as having literal, definite reference.

The blending between the study of semantics and meaning in context (pragmatics) can be further illustrated by the interrelated concept known as **deixis**. The term deixis is borrowed from Greek and translates as 'pointing'. The English language, along with all other languages, contains a specific set of words known as **deictic expressions**, which will vary in meaning depending upon who is using them, where they are being uttered, and when they are being uttered. The cross-over of deixis between the two linguistic sub-disciplines of semantics and pragmatics results in the term being defined and discussed within both areas of language study.

Deictic expressions always take their meaning from some aspect of the context in which they are uttered. These words all operate as indexes of specific meaning in context and thus belong to investigations of what is commonly known as the **indexicality** of language. Many referring expressions can be seen as belonging within the category of deixis (for example, 'you, we, there, yesterday'). Some modifiers with deictic reference are used alongside referring expressions such as demonstrative pronouns, as in 'this dog, that woman, these tables, those helicopters', in order to help interlocutors identify the particular referents of a referring expression. It is also possible for some verbs to be deictic too. For instance, 'come' and 'go' are good examples of verbs that give evidence of location and thus qualify as deictic expressions.

In order to consider deictic expressions from a more systematic perspective, we can usefully group them into the following categories. The three most common deictic sub-types are as follows:

- ❑ **Person deixis**: *I, you, her, Peter, Louise*
- ❑ **Place deixis**, sometimes referred to as **spatial deixis**: *here, there, this, that*
- ❑ **Time deixis**, sometimes referred to as **temporal deixis**: *now, today, yesterday, tomorrow, next month*

Social deixis is another category that is sometimes used. It includes referring expressions which clearly encode social meaning. In Modern English, this includes categories known as **address terms**, where social status is indexicalised through the linguistic terms that we use – for example 'Madam', 'Sir', 'Professor', 'Doctor' – or through more informal **terms of endearment** such as 'mate', 'love' or 'flower'. Social encoding was once included with English pronoun usage through the use of 'thou/you'. Such pronoun usage is termed the *T/V system* of address (named after the French pronouns 'tu/vous'), and it is still present in many languages other than English, including French and German.

One further deictic category is known as **discourse deixis**. This applies to forms such as 'the former', 'the latter', or 'when I said that . . .', where such expressions are used to point backwards or forwards to particular moments within written or spoken texts.

The number of studies investigating pragmatics in the English language has grown rapidly in recent years. This growth can arguably be traced to a shift in language researchers' focus, from being less interested in language as a theoretical, abstract system with idealised speakers to being more interested in actual language usage. Most recently, this has been dominated by a focus upon the interactions of specific speakers in real-world contexts.

Speech act theory

Speech act theory is a foundational part of the study of pragmatics. It was originally developed by philosopher J.L. Austin (1975) as an attempt to explain the processes of how meanings are constructed within conversation. Speech acts are defined as what actions we perform when we produce utterances.

Austin characterises a three-part system for describing different components of speech acts:

❑ **Locution**: what the speaker literally utters, which – drawing upon semantics terminology – consists of sense and reference.
❑ **Illocution**: the force of what has been said as defined by social convention in the context in which it is uttered. The locutions 'Do that now', 'What time is it?' and 'Buster is six years old' have the **illocutionary force** of a command (an imperative), a question (an interrogative) and a statement (a declarative), respectively.
❑ **Perlocution**: the actual effect of the utterance, that is, exactly how it is interpreted by the hearer(s).

Ideally, the perlocution should match what the speaker intended, but this is not always the case. Unintentional effects may well result, and on occasion this can result in miscommunication or even communication breakdown. Other utterances are ambiguous, and it can be difficult to assign the exact perlocution. Also, if the sincerity of the utterance is called into question, then the perlocution of the utterance can be affected (see below). It is worth noting at this point that the term illocutionary force is sometimes known as **illocutionary force-indicating device**. Examples of illocutionary force-indicating devices are 'I'm sorry' and 'I apologise', operating to signal the speech act of apology (further discussed in C3).

Austin also devised a category known as a **performative** speech act. This term can be applied to an utterance which simultaneously performs and describes the speech act. Most performative speech acts take the form of first person + performative verb, as in 'I promise', 'I apologise', 'I inform you' and 'I warn you'.

In order for all speech acts, including performatives, to be described as successfully produced, then a set of criteria known as **felicity conditions** needs to be fulfilled. According to Austin (1975), there are three different components to felicity conditions. The first is that a conventional procedure should exist for what is being carried out. The second is that participants within the event need to fulfil their roles properly. This can include enacting professional role responsibility appropriately, such as the job of a qualified registrar to perform a marriage ceremony.

The third is that the necessary thoughts and intentions need to be present in all participants. Within this third category lie **sincerity conditions**: a participant must be sincere about the act in order to fulfil this condition. For example, if a speaker utters 'I'm really sorry I disturbed you' when they have woken you up by telephoning, and they are *sincerely* sorry that they have disturbed you, then the sincerity conditions have been met. If they are not genuinely sorry, then this is not a legitimate apology.

These conditions can often be difficult to gauge in everyday conversation due to our inability to read speakers' minds and due to the potential ambiguity of certain utterances. Though speakers often give verbal and non-verbal clues as to whether we can interpret their utterances as sincere or not, including **intonation** (voice pitch) and body language, sincerity will still be ambiguous on some occasions. As interactants, we may well spend time after a speech event has taken place pondering over exactly what someone has said to us in order to try and ascertain their intention.

Speech acts can be further categorised as either direct or indirect. A **direct speech act** is where the meaning of the utterance is literal, so the meaning is the sum of its constituent parts. An example of a direct speech act is when the question 'Are you coming to the theatre tonight?' is uttered by a speaker to his housemate, where the speaker genuinely wants to know whether his housemate is coming to the theatre that evening.

Compare this direct example to one in which the question 'Can you pass the remote control?' is uttered between the same two speakers in their living room while they are watching television. This utterance is also interrogative in form. However, despite its form, the illocutionary force behind this utterance is actually a command, not a question. The speaker wants the remote control given to him – he does not want to know whether the hearer is literally capable of passing the remote control to him. This is an **indirect speech act**, where the meaning of the utterance depends upon context and the hearer's ability to interpret the **implicature** (the indirect meaning) contained within the utterance.

Indirect speech acts regularly occur in everyday conversations. They play an important role in the study of pragmatics in general and in the study of politeness in particular. We will develop this focus on the important interplay between speech acts and linguistic politeness in B3 and C3.

In preparation for this, think of examples of indirect speech acts which have taken place in your everyday conversations. Decide upon the difference between the illocution and perlocution of the indirect speech act. What do you think the consequences would have been had direct speech acts been used instead?

A4   **GRAMMATICAL PARTS**

As native speakers of a language, we all have the rules of that language interiorised in our minds: we know how to express just about any concept, event, state or argument, and we also recognise how *not* to articulate these things. Our interiorised rules are not easy to discover, and there are many dozens if not hundreds of different theories which try to set out precisely what those patterns are. These theories about how language works are called **grammars**, and they can differ from each other quite radically (even talking about the 'rules' of language would be contentious for some grammarians).

We know that English (and every other language) undoubtedly has a grammar, since it is possible to imagine utterances using the vocabulary of the language that are nevertheless badly formed: '?book the table the down put on', '?to to or be be the question not that is', '?was beginning the in word the'. We must already have a set of 'well-formedness' rules in our minds to recognise these as ungrammatical, rather than their resequenced correct forms. Deciding what the constraints are that produce *only* the good sentences is a difficult and debatable matter. There is, then, no such thing as 'the grammar of English', only different grammars of English with different emphases and principles. Grammars are theories about language.

Constituents

Having said all that, there are some broad matters of consensus about what any grammar needs to account for, and these patterns will be described in this unit. First, there are a finite number of words in the language, but a very large number of possible utterances, and native speakers are creative in the sense that it is possible to utter a string of words that has never been uttered previously. You can be novel either by **collocating** two or more words together that do not usually go together, or by extending your utterance with longer and longer material that quickly produces a permutation that must be unique. In spite of this, and in spite of the related problem that language and its rules are constantly changing, communication happens. This astonishing set of facts relies on at least three properties of English that most grammarians would agree on: constituency, dependency and recursion.

When we want to say something, we do not simply reproduce a combination of set phrases in an unstructured way. Every utterance that is well-formed displays **constituency**. Every **sentence** is not simply a list of individual words, but can be seen to be a systemic structure of words in well-formed phrases, and these phrases are in well-formed positions in **clauses**. Further down the grammar system, words are composed of morphemic 'chunks' in the correct pattern and phonologically allowable structures within those morphemes. Further up the grammar chain, the well-formed clauses combine in proper ways in sentences and texts and extended discourse.

If you take the last sentence of the preceding paragraph as an example, the comma marks out a meaningful chunk that goes before it. You could draw lines around other meaningful chunks as follows:

> *The well-formed clauses | combine | in proper ways | in sentences and texts and extended discourse.*

It would be odd to carve up this sentence as follows:

> *The | well-formed clauses combine | in proper | ways in sentences and | texts and extended | discourse.*

The fact that this last version looks odd shows that you have an interior sense that your language has a constituent structure.

Furthermore, that sense of structure can be understood independently of the meaning of the words that are involved. For example, all the following sentences (and many others you might think of) have exactly the same syntactic structure:

*The well-formed clauses combine in proper ways in sentences and texts and
    extended discourse.*
An especially fat man arrives in good time before me and you and almost everyone.
*Some semi-skimmed milk pours without a splash into flour and eggs and the fruity
    mixture.*
*A nineteenth-century traveller moved at top speed by horses and carriages and
    steam trains.*
*The beautifully decorated cakes fit with no difficulty into boxes and cartons and
    little paper cups.*

The boundaries marked by the lines in the first example above show the constituent structure of the sentence. 'The well-formed clauses' is a complete and meaningful unit: in the sentence, this unit stands as the subject of the verb 'combine' that follows it, and 'the well-formed clauses' is the theme of the sentence – the starting argument for the propositional material that attaches to it afterwards. Equally, 'an especially fat man' is the subject of 'arrives'. 'Some semi-skimmed milk', 'a nineteenth-century traveller', and 'the beautifully decorated cakes' are all subjects and themes of their respective sentences. These are all **noun phrases** or **NPs**. Each of the chunks in the first, properly carved-up sentence is a **phrase**, and most grammarians agree that there are five types of phrasal categories in English:

noun phrase	(NP)	*The well-formed clauses*
verb phrase	(VP)	*combine*
adverbial phrase	(AdvP)	*in proper ways*
prepositional phrase	(PrepP)	*in sentences and texts and discourse*
adjectival phrase	(AdjP)	*well-formed*

or,

noun phrase	(NP)	*The beautifully decorated cakes*
verb phrase	(VP)	*fit*
adverbial phrase	(AdvP)	*with no difficulty*
prepositional phrase	(PrepP)	*into boxes and cartons and little paper cups*
adjectival phrase	(AdjP)	*beautifully decorated*

The phrase constituent is defined by its **head**, so an NP is defined by the main headword or **noun** within it: here in the last example, the noun is 'cakes'. Put another way, for a phrase to be an NP, it *must* contain a noun as its head. There might be other words in the NP, but the noun is the essential one. A noun can be an ordinary label for a concept, or a *proper noun* (a name like 'Peter' or 'Nottingham'), or a *pronoun* (like 'he', or 'she', or 'their').

In my last example here, the NP also has two **pre-modifiers**, which are first a **determiner** 'the' and second an **adjectival phrase** 'beautifully decorated'. In many sentences, an NP can consist only of a single noun: the sentence could make sense as 'cakes fit with no difficulty', but not as 'the beautifully decorated fit with no difficulty' (unless you reinterpret 'beautifully decorated' as a noun, which isn't the same sentence at all). The noun in an NP could also be followed by a **post-modifier** or **qualifier** ('the cakes altogether fit'). All the elements apart from the noun are optional, though, so notationally we can formulate this as:

NP → (det) (mod) N (qual)

This means: a noun phrase is constituted by an essential noun as its head, with an optional determiner (such as 'the', 'a', 'some', or 'this'), an optional pre-modifier (such as an adjective), and an optional qualifier (another adjective). In our example NP above, we have (det) (mod x 2) N: *the beautifully decorated cakes*.

The **verb phrase (VP)** in my example consists only of a **verb**, 'fit'. Again, a verb (V) is the essential head in a VP, which can also have an optional **auxiliary** preceding it ('have stolen', 'was caught', 'might have been running'), and an optional **completor** following it (as in the phrasal verbs 'run up', 'cast off', 'look after', 'rabbiting on'). So, notationally, we have:

VP → (aux) V (compl)

Most well-formed, complete clauses or sentences (S) in English consist at least of an NP and a VP. We can show this with a simple **tree-diagram**:

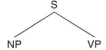

Any clause such as 'Peter writes', 'Louise ran off', or 'The book has appeared' could be placed underneath this tree-diagram. 'Peter' and 'Louise' here are proper nouns under the NP. Under the VP, we would have 'writes' as a simple verb, or 'ran off' as a verb plus a completor, or 'has appeared' as an auxiliary plus a verb. In these cases, the verbs are **intransitive**. If, though, there was a direct object involved (and the verb was **transitive**), then we could show the full constituency like this:

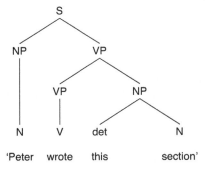

Notice how our intuitions about the constituent parts are captured by the groupings in the tree-diagram.

In the more complex example from above, 'the beautifully decorated cakes fit with no difficulty into boxes and cartons and little paper cups', the constituent 'with no difficulty' is an **adverbial phrase (AdvP)**. This is an adverb because it modifies the verb ('fit'), or describes the manner in which the verb is acted out. Notice that on the surface it looks very much like the **prepositional phrase (PrepP)** that follows it: 'into boxes . . .'. This is because both the AdvP and the PrepP in this sentence are constituted by a **preposition** ('with', 'into') followed by another NP. In the AdvP, the embedded NP is constituted by a pre-modifying particle ('no') and a noun ('difficulty') – the particle here functions just like an adjective in that it pre-modifies the noun. In the PrepP, the embedded NP is constituted by three further NPs, each constituted either by a single noun ('boxes', 'cartons') or a pre-modified noun in an NP ('little paper cups'), connected by the **conjunction** 'and'. The most common AdvP form in English consists simply of a lexical **adverb** – a single word derived from an adjective by ending in '-ly' ('quickly', 'enthusiastically', 'exuberantly'). But 'tomorrow', 'fast' and 'seldom' are also usually adverbs.

The first NP contains an **adjectival phrase (AdjP)** 'beautifully decorated', which is constituted by a modifying **adjective** ('beautifully') and the head adjective 'decorated'. Notice that this phrase is derived from a past participle and an adverb, but in the example sentence it functions grammatically as an adjective (it has been **rank-shifted** there: see B4). The last NP in the sentence ('little paper cups') also contains an AdjP, which this time consists only of an adjective ('little').

Recursion and dependency

The PrepP at the end actually consists of three prepositional phrases: 'into boxes and (into) cartons and (into) little paper cups'. The two last prepositions are omitted because the whole combined phrase is governed by the first preposition 'into'. This can be argued to show **recursion**: a PrepP can contain another example of itself, and that PrepP can contain another example of itself, and so on. The same recursive capacity applies to the other phrases too. In fact, overall in the structure of a **sentence (S)**, though we can say that at the most abstract level a sentence can be constituted by a noun phrase and a verb phrase (S → NP + VP), the VP can be constituted by another VP + S. For example, in 'He said that we must go', the NP is realised by the pronoun 'He', but the VP is realised by a V + S: 'said', with a complementiser 'that', and then another S ('we must go'), consisting of an NP 'we' and a VP as an auxiliary 'must' and a V 'go'. Recursion allows in principle an infinite and everlasting number of novel utterances; even within the bounds of actual communicative practice, this sort of grammatical embedding allows a very large number of possible utterances. You simply have to imagine a sentence such as 'A did B, which did C, which did D, which . . .' and so on. The material in the VP that follows the 'which' begins another recursive S all over again.

The constraint maintained by the systematic constituency is also provided by **dependency**. The grammatical form of phrases is dependent on other nearby phrases. The governing of the two final NPs ('and cartons and little paper cups') by the PrepP ('into boxes . . .') is a type of dependency. The **agreement** of NPs and VPs that relate to each other is another type of dependency: the plural NP 'the beautifully decorated cakes' requires a zero-inflected verb-ending on 'fit' (that is, not 'fits', or 'fitting', or 'fitted'). The verb-ending or auxiliary that expressed tense or aspect would also be governed by this sort of agreement. Furthermore, there is a semantic dependency between this subject and this verb, since 'fit' requires a subject that is fittable, and 'cakes' requires a verb that matches the concept too. Agreement (also called **concord**) includes matching the appropriate forms for person, number, gender, tense and case.

To illustrate the constituency, dependency and recursion of the example sentence, we can draw a complex tree-diagram to show the systematic nature of grammar (see Figure A4.1).

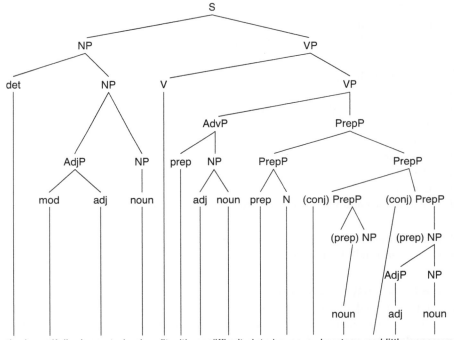

the beautifully decorated cakes fit with no difficulty into boxes and cartons and little papercups

Figure A4.1 A syntactic tree diagram

The upper part of the diagram in Figure A4.1 illustrates the systemic constituent structure very clearly. The right-hand side of the diagram shows the complex embedding of the overall VP, with recurring structures. (Different grammars would draw the diagram a bit differently, and with variable terminology, but the basic constituency structure shown here would be common to most approaches). You can see how the other example sentences given above would also fit into this same tree-diagram:

> *The well-formed clauses combine in proper ways in sentences and texts and extended discourse.*
> *An especially fat man arrives in good time before me and you and almost everyone.*
> *Some semi-skimmed milk pours without a splash into flour and eggs and the fruity mixture.*
> *A nineteenth-century traveller moved at top speed by horses and carriages and steam trains.*

So far in this unit, we have outlined the **phrasal categories** defined by their headwords:

❑   noun phrases
❑   verb phrases
❑   adverbial phrases
❑   prepositional phrases
❑   adjectival phrases

At the bottom of the tree-diagram, each word at the surface of the sentence is labelled in terms of its **lexical category** (the traditional 'parts of speech'):

❑   nouns (including pronouns and proper nouns)
❑   determiners
❑   adjectives (pre-modifiers and qualifiers)
❑   verbs
❑   auxiliaries
❑   completors
❑   adverbs
❑   prepositions
❑   conjunctions and particles ('and', 'but', or, 'not', and so on)

This simple, hierarchical set of categories can account for every possible well-formed example of an English sentence.

The adaptability of grammar

It could be argued that there is a fourth general property of grammar alongside constituency, dependency and recursion: this is **contingency** or adaptation. Since different dialectal speakers of a language can speak to each other, and since a language changes over time, it is clear from these two sorts of evidence that, whatever the interiorised rules of grammar are, they cannot be absolutely fixed.

Innovations and evolution in grammar are handled by individuals on the basis that the normative and expected syntax, vocabulary and morphology are flexible within broad limits. People have no difficulty producing and understanding utterances without verb phrases ('Queues likely', 'No jeans'), or without noun phrases ('Slow', 'Go now'), or with nouns ('knife', 'access', 'host') used as verbs ('to knife', 'to access', 'to host'), and other reversals and shifts. It seems odd to assume that these fragmentary variations in usage are merely incomplete or unrealised versions of properly formed grammatical sentences. Much more likely is the notion that grammar is treated as a set of the best rules that apply for the task in hand, but they are always provisional, adaptable, and contingent on change.

The field of syntax is probably the most hotly and vehemently debated area in modern linguistics. In this unit, we have presented the closest we can get to a broad consensus, but almost every syntactician will want to argue with some, most or all of the concepts we have set out here.

TEXT AND DISCOURSE

In language and linguistics study, it is established practice for the term **text** to be defined as a continuous stretch of written or spoken language. While you may be more familiar with thinking of a text as an object that is written down, *text* should be viewed as inclusive of both written and spoken forms of language. In its broadest sense, the discipline of **discourse analysis** refers to the production of analyses of written and spoken texts.

However, **discourse** is a complex term, and it has been defined in a range of ways across different academic disciplines. The most important, defining characteristic for discourse in language and linguistics is conceptualising it as language above the level of the sentence. While graphemes, phonemes, morphemes and lexemes are the building blocks of language, discourse operates beyond these levels.

Discourse analysis has much in common with pragmatics, as mentioned in A3. Both of these sub-disciplines are concerned with a focus on context, along with the specific functions fulfilled by language as it is used by speakers in real-world settings. Pragmatics also focuses on discourse as language beyond the level of the sentence. The main difference between pragmatics and discourse analysis is that, whereas pragmatics focuses upon the importance of principles governing language usage, discourse analysis instead focuses upon producing examinations of the structure of the text itself.

However, there are still a number of points of cross-over between the two areas. Some of the terminological categories and distinctions that are used in pragmatics are of key importance in discourse analysis and vice versa. English language and linguistics researchers often combine aspects of discourse analysis with pragmatics, and the manner in which this combined focus can be conducted will be illustrated at various points during this strand.

Coming back to the importance of context, one crucial distinction which is made in discourse analysis studies is between **co-text**, the context surrounding the text itself, sometimes referred to as the **linguistic context**, and the context outside the text, sometimes referred to as the **physical context**, the setting where the discourse takes place. In addition, context in this broader sense can also refer to the assumed background knowledge that exists between speakers, or, in the case of written texts, between author and reader. As we have seen in A3 (and B3–D3), context plays a crucial role in determining meaning in interaction. It plays an equally significant role when determining the structure of discourse.

That said, individual discourse analysts will draw upon the importance of context to differing degrees depending upon which particular sub-discipline of discourse analysis they follow (see below). It is important to realise at this stage that 'discourse analysis' is a very broad category – there are a number of sub-disciplinary paradigms which take differing approaches to analysing texts and context.

Cohesion and coherence

In order to produce a thorough analysis of the co-text of a spoken or written text, there are two key categories that can be drawn upon that are known as **cohesion** and **coherence**. We will focus on cohesion first of all and then move on to consider coherence.

Cohesion refers to the parts of the language system which tie sentences and clauses together. Cohesion provides discourse with its structure. Some of the linguistic features which are incorporated with the category of cohesion will be familiar to you already, as they are also a part of semantics and pragmatics: prime examples of cohesion include sense relations and referring expressions as illustrated in B2 and A3, along with deixis, which we also came across in A3.

There is a range of other categories which create cohesion, including **repetition**, **substitution** and **ellipsis**. Repetition is when the same word or phrase is directly repeated within a text. Substitution refers to situations where one word is substituted for another in order to avoid direct repetition. The term *ellipsis* refers to when material has been missed out because it is not essential for the meaning of the text to be conveyed – hearers/readers will be able to work out the textual meaning from the surrounding discourse.

The following example of a short extract taken from a **transcript** of spoken language will illustrate these features of cohesion. The (physical) context will also be detailed for background information. The extract below contains symbols known as **transcription conventions**. These conventions are fully defined in B12, which also includes a discussion on the importance of transcription for the linguistic study of interaction.

> *Two female friends are talking over coffee. Context: the conversation takes place in Jill's living room. The speakers have known each other for 21 years and meet regularly in each other's houses. They are the only two participants present and are sitting next to each other on the sofa. They are talking on the topic of Jill's niece, who has just given birth to her fourth child.*

> 1   Jill: she was eight pounds seven ounces so she was quite big=
> 2   Sue: =is that the biggest baby she's had?
> 3   Jill: yeah all the others were like seven an six so each one's
> 4   Jill: [got bigger]
> 5   Sue: [oh right   ] got bigger=
> 6   Jill: =she said 'I'm not having any more' ((laughs))
> 7   Sue: I was gonna say got to stop ((laughs))

In line 1 there is repetition of 'she', operating as a referring expression to the baby. The other two repetitions of 'she' (lines 2 and 6) have a different referent, the baby's mother, Jill's niece. In line 5 there is more repetition, as Jill repeats 'got bigger'. In addition to adding to the cohesion of the conversation, this echoing is also a classic example of supportive, collaborative talk. This will be discussed further in B5. In line 3 there is an example of substitution, with 'one' being used instead of 'baby'. There are many examples of deixis here too: 'I', 'you', 'she', 'that', and other referring expressions: 'the biggest baby'.

Additionally, there are many illustrations of ellipsis, in line 2 'is that [baby] the biggest baby', in line 3 'seven an six' [pounds and ounces], at the end of line 6 in the reported speech, ' "I'm not having any more" [babies]' and in line 7, 'I was gonna say' [she has] 'got to stop' [having babies].

It is worth commenting on the shift from speech to writing created by the production of a transcript here. The transcription process has transformed what was originally a stretch of spoken language into a stretch of written language. The written transcription has been created by one of the book's authors from listening several times to an audio recording of the above conversation. In order to conduct discourse analysis properly and successfully, the process of transcription is absolutely crucial for language and linguistics study. It is simply impossible to pick up the finer details of spoken discourse just by listening to an audio recording or watching a video, even if you were to do this many times.

In addition to listening and watching on multiple occasions, you also need to produce a written text as a fixed record of the spoken discourse that takes place. The process of transcription for discourse analysis studies is discussed further in C5. The importance of the process of the production of written transcription for spoken data analysis more generally is considered in B12.

Coming back to cohesion, other important terminological distinctions when analysing textual cohesion are **anaphora**, words which refer to preceding text, and **cataphora**, words which refer to something in the following text. Both of these terms are contained within the overarching category of **endophora**, defined simply as when linguistic items refer to other linguistic items *within* the same text.

To illustrate anaphora and cataphora, here are two examples taken from a business meeting interaction. In the first example, the proper noun 'Colin' is then followed by 'he' and 'him', giving anaphoric reference:

```
1   Joan:    but it's up to Colin if he doesn't do it=
2   Steve:   =Have you sent him a gentle reminder?
```

In the second example, we have this the opposite way around, with the pronoun 'he' linking forward to the proper noun 'Steve':

```
1   Julie:   Does he know that it's here?
2   Rob:     Steve knows that it's the meeting room yeah
```

In contrast to endophoric reference, **exophoric** reference is defined as referring *outside* of the text, so not as part of the co-text but instead as a part of the broader, external context. We will leave business meetings behind and go back to our two female speakers to illustrate exophoric reference:

Jill has been talking on the topic of her mobile hairdresser.

```
1   Sue:    bit of pocket money isn't it for her
2   Sue:    [you know]
3   Jill:   [she only ] lives in Green Lane but she said she's eh
4           emigrating
```

In line 3, Jill invokes their shared background knowledge of local geography, external to the preceding text, by uttering the proper noun referent 'Green Lane', a road which is about a twenty-minute walk away from their homes (Jill and Sue live within a five-minute walk of each other).

The category of textual cohesion can be perceived as a component of coherence, but this has to be accompanied by the receiver having a global, unified sense of a language system. So, as well as having a set of identifiable linguistic features, coherence is a broader category which also has a cognitive dimension. Texts may have cohesion but not coherence – just because a text is made up of clauses and phrases that give cohesion does not by default make a text coherent. Deciding upon textual coherence depends to a large extent upon pragmatics, in particular upon the pragmatic principles of cooperation and politeness (B3). These principles can help discourse analysts understand how the unity of the English language system is perceived.

More examples of cohesive devices in action, along with illustrations and discussions of coherence, are given in D5. This includes further consideration of how discourse and pragmatics are linked with one another.

Varieties of discourse analysis

As mentioned above, there are several different paradigms that exist within the overarching category of discourse analysis. We will give a brief introductory overview of the most influential of these in the remainder of this unit.

The first paradigm is **conversation analysis**, which has its roots in the work of Sacks, Schegloff and Jefferson (1974). Conversation analysts focus on establishing patterns such as turn-taking in conversation, and researchers have examined features such as interruptions and topic transitions within this approach. We will focus on conversation analysis in more detail in B5.

The **exchange structure** approach is associated with Sinclair and Coulthard (1975) and focuses upon discourse patterns which can be established in particular contexts. One of the most famous and often cited frameworks from this approach is the **initiation, response, follow-up** (IRF) sequence, best known to characterise the structure of conversation between teachers and pupils in fairly formal classroom contexts. For example:

> Teacher: can anyone tell me what this means
> Pupil: does it mean danger men at work
> Teacher: yes . . .

(Coulthard 1985: 135)

The teacher asks an initial question (the *initiation*), the pupil answers in *response*, and then there is a *follow-up* from the teacher. Not all conversational discourse in classrooms or in other similar settings follows this neat pattern. Nonetheless, the exchange structure is a useful, adaptable concept which forms the foundational basis of the approach.

Look out for the IRF pattern in your everyday discourse. In what kinds of contexts does it occur? Who uses which strategy? What can this tell you about the relationship between the speakers?

Another paradigm for discourse analysis research is the **ethnography of speaking**. This is ambitiously designed to characterise all of the different factors that influence how we speak with one another. The most prominent figure in this field is Dell Hymes (1974). He coined a very useful analytical framework known as the

SPEAKING model, whereby each of the individual letters refers to part of the analytical process:

Setting and scene: time, place and cultural setting of the interaction
Participants: who is taking part
Ends: expected outcomes
Act: form and content of exactly what is said
Key: tone or manner in which it is said
Instrumentalities: choice of channel, such as spoken or written
Norms: established expectations for speaking behaviour
Genre: type of utterance (lecture, formal speech, etc.)

Yet another paradigm of discourse analysis is known as **critical discourse analysis** (CDA), most prominently associated with the work of Norman Fairclough (1995). Researchers who follow a CDA approach have the overall aim of revealing hidden ideological power structures which are contained within discourse. Critical discourse analysts aim to do this by conducting close textual analyses of spoken and written data, which are then analysed as part of the constraints of the wider socio-cultural context where the texts are produced. CDA researchers often have a clearly stated, overt political purpose for conducting their research, such as revealing racist discourses within particular texts. They often integrate techniques from **systemic functional linguistics** into their analysis (detailed in B4) to help reveal hidden ideological meanings within the language system.

This brief overview has presented a range of different areas of discourse analysis, emphasising that it is a wide and varied discipline – dedicated researchers have also used a number of different tools and techniques to investigate a plethora of spoken and written texts. Some researchers mix together different elements of the above approaches, whereas others stick quite rigidly to the specifics of their chosen approach. We will develop these issues in B5 and C5.

EARLY LANGUAGE ACQUISITION   A6

We human beings are all born too early. To be at a comparable stage relative to the adult state of other mammals, human pregnancy should be anything up to double the nine months that it has been for thousands of years. Human babies are born unable to walk, unable to see very far, unable to manipulate their own bodies much at all, and unable to speak or comprehend other humans. We remain in this dependent state for several years, except for the rapid speed with which we acquire language. Babies' large, evolved brains are housed in large skulls, which would kill their mothers during birth if gestation were much longer. These large brains, however, are what allow us to learn language, and language serves to create culture and civilisation to compensate for our dangerously weak physical capacities in our early years.

All humans acquire the language that they are exposed to, and we can acquire several languages at once. The stages which babies go through are broadly the same across the world; there is no such thing as a language that is more difficult to learn than others. The only differences arise where some structural levels are more important in one language than another. For example, English has fewer and simpler inflections (suffixes such as plural '-s', past tense '-ed', present participle '-ing', and some others) than Hungarian (with its eighteen cases and numerous affixes to indicate grammatical function), so Hungarian babies take a short while longer to master the acquisition of inflections than their English counterparts, but overall Hungarian children match their English-speaking peers pretty much equally in language competence and performance. Within English-speaking families, babies acquire aspects of English at varying rates, so the ages of acquisition given below are very broad, but roughly consistent.

Pre-birth

Language acquisition begins in the womb, as sounds from outside begin to familiarise a baby with the tone of speech, especially the mother's and others' voices around during late pregnancy. Babies are born with the human hardwiring in the brain to learn language, and have already begun to recognise the characteristic tonal patterns and rhythm of the language of their particular society. The capacity for hearing sounds and differentiating between them, and the physical practice of moving mouth, lips and tongue are both developing before birth. It even appears to be the case that pre-birth babies are acquiring simple spatial concepts that will develop into the linguistic expressions of cause and effect, action and reaction, and figure and ground later on.

Birth to six months

Practice in the womb means babies can suck and swallow as soon as they are born, and from around the eight-week stage, the oral and vocal tract sounds associated with these actions can be heard as **cooing**. The lip-sounds /mə/ and /bə/ and the swallowing sounds /gə/ and /kə/ involve the physical extremes of the mouth (front and back) and are pronounced with the tongue at rest as the mid-vowel /ə/. Babies play around with these sounds, producing the stereotypical 'mama' and 'gaga' sequences – these cannot yet be said to be words, since the baby has no idea that sound and sense are connected. Over the next few months, babies fill out the consonant sounds between these extremes and vary their vowel quality as they gain more and more control over their tongue.

As the initial occasional cooing gives way to more extensive **babbling**, babies produce playful strings of sounds. At first these range over all the possible sounds that a human mouth can make, but gradually those sounds that are not part of the phonological system of the community's language fall away, and the baby babbles only with the sounds that will be used in their native language. Babbling sequences will often take on the intonation contour of the native language too, so babies sometimes sound like they are asking questions, making assertions, complaining, telling a story, or engaging in question-and-answer with an adult. In all of these cases, they are simply modelling the extended sound pattern on what they hear, without any understanding.

Six to eighteen months

Babbling gradually develops into **holophrastic** speech consisting of one-word utterances. By around twelve months, a baby seems to be able to understand some words spoken by others, especially if they are often-repeated words attached to familiar physical objects. Their own production ability, though, lags far behind their capacity for comprehension. The single-word utterances do at least count as language production, as the child gradually realises that certain words in the right context produce desired effects. Sounds have thus become attached to meanings, in the child's mind, and words are no longer just playful sounds but labels. Intonation patterns – such as those that convey questioning, being stern, being upset, or being excited – are differentiated and understood.

By the end of the holophrastic period, a child's vocabulary might be as large as 150 words, with many of these words having extended meanings and covering whole domains. For example, 'hot' might refer to any dangerous object or situation, including ovens, open fires, radiators, knives and implements in general; 'button' might refer not only to a button on a shirt, but to the shirt itself as well, and clothes in general; and an unusual word that has become a vocabulary item might stand for a particular everyday object ('monkey' as a word for 'banana', for example).

The process of establishing the appropriate range of a word is its **packaging**. This can happen because new vocabulary terms are learned that cover part of the previous domain of an existing word (so 'fire' becomes attached to an open fire, thus removing some of the applicability of 'hot'), or because the child learns that a word that has been metaphorically attached (like 'monkey' for a banana) in fact refers to something else specific (a monkey). All of these words are fixed, though: they do not vary; they do not have plurals or past tenses attached to them; and they are not combined with other words.

Eighteen months to two years

Up to this stage, a child might repeat the same word over and over (**echolalia**). However, once a child learns to combine different words, at first in two-word phrases (**concatenation**), there is an explosively rapid advance in ability. Multiple-word utterances obviously allow sequencing rules to be demonstrated, so a child's syntactic development in terms of her production can be observed. The two words in utterances are almost always connected by some semantic relationship. For example, a child might produce 'baby shoe' (possession), 'get milk' (imperative), 'milk allgone' (negation), 'that car' (nomination), 'byebye teddy' (greeting), but not, say, 'allgone that' (deictic indexing) or 'baby teddy' (to mean a small teddy rather than a possessive like the baby's teddy). Note that words that an adult might perceive as two words ('allgone') are treated at this stage by the child as a single, fixed word: she would never say 'all milk gone' or vary the form and say 'allgo milk'.

Prepositions begin to be acquired, with the literally spatial ones 'in', 'on' and 'under' usually the first to be used. The differentiation of 'I/me' and 'you' marks the beginning of a sense of deictic projection. The packaging of words into domains that begin to match the adult senses of words continues with the child beginning **network-building** of words: those items that are semantically connected ('dog', 'cat', 'pet'; or 'car', 'seat', 'go') are mentally grouped together and are spoken in groups. This process of semantic field learning continues throughout life, but it begins here. By age two, a child has an active vocabulary of around 500 words, but can certainly understand many more.

Action sequences are acquired late in this stage ('fill drink', 'Mammy pick', 'give teddy'), before the child begins to produce three-word, four-word and longer utterances in a rapid period of expansion. It is at this stage that regular inflectional endings will be acquired too. Plural '-s' and past tense '-ed' will begin to appear as the child moves on from the two-word sequence. These are often generalised across irregular forms ('bringed', 'runned', 'sheeps', 'mouses') and are even back-formed on principle (so a single item of 'clothes' is a 'clo', a single chunk of 'cat-mix' food is a 'cat-mic').

Children's pronunciation also develops rapidly. Almost all the vowel sounds that a child will need in her language are available by the age of two, though the acquisition of the complete consonant set is often not finished until age five or above. Specific patterns can be observed, for example omitting final consonants, especially dentals (/ka/ for 'cat', /fuː/ for 'food'); omitting unstressed syllables (/apə/ for 'apple', /nɑnə/ for 'banana'); using /w/ and /j/ variably for /l/ and /r/ (/wɛd/ for 'red', /jɛgəʊ/ for 'lego', /kʊdəw/ for 'cuddle'); and using other systematic consonant mismatches. However, around two-thirds of all the child's utterances in this phase will be articulate enough to be intelligible to an adult.

Two to five years

Through these years, the child's language develops to the point at which it is more or less fully formed. The remaining consonants and clusters are perfected. The appropriate intonations for different speech acts such as questioning, commanding, pleading, being sarcastic, and so on are all mastered. Accent features of the speech community (see A9) are accurately performed. Most morphological patterns are performed accurately, perhaps with the exception of irregular examples such as 'tooken' for 'taken', or 'bringed' for 'brought', and so on. Active vocabulary rises towards 2,000 words and keeps accelerating throughout later childhood towards the adult norm of around 40,000 words.

Once the two-word phrase period has passed, a child's syntactic ability becomes highly complex. The ability to form questions by reversing the verb and auxiliary; the ability to form passives by deleting the subject as agent; the ability to form negations; the ability to create complex phrases using adjectival modifiers and adverbials; the ability to form subordinate and relative clauses; and the ability to conjoin clauses to articulate complex reasoning all appear very rapidly in these years. While they are still not perfected by age six, the basics are usually there.

Conversational and other pragmatic skills also develop fast. Children learn how to hold the floor, how to interrupt appropriately, how to negotiate politeness strategies, how to be rude and insulting with accuracy, how to generate empathy, and how to express abstract concepts and emotions. Children will start to develop the beginnings of narrative skills that allow them to recount a story. In the next few years, they will enrich this skill with the ability to pause the story for asides, explanations, commentary, moralising, and comparison with other stories; they will eventually develop the skill of telling the story out of sequence for literary impact.

Six years old

From this point, something of major significance seems to happen in human brains. Having acquired a rich capacity for language (either one or several languages), the child's brain begins to switch off its acquisition capability. From this **critical age**, any further languages that are to be gained will have to be learned rather than acquired. Though children's minds up to adulthood find it generally easier to learn new languages, nothing compares with the ease of the first language(s) acquisition. Around this point, other cognitive skills also seem to close down: babies and toddlers can differentiate faces of different ethnic and racial origins very easily, but from this age onwards, face-types that the child does not commonly encounter will appear very similar to each other. Preferred smells and tastes will be established at this point that will shape adult preferences.

All of this suggests that there is some reality to the notion that our human brains are genetically hardwired with a **language acquisition device** (which may have a wider scope as a cognitive function setup device), which allows us to acquire any languages we encounter in infant life, and then shuts down. By early puberty (between 11 and 14 years old), our astonishing childhood capacity has gone.

PSYCHOLINGUISTICS

As an interdisciplinary field, **psycholinguistics** draws on many of the experimental scientific methods of psychology as well as the theoretical categories of linguistics. Psycholinguistics touches on several of the topics covered elsewhere in this book, especially language acquisition (A6) and syntax (Strand 4). Of course, for much of its history, linguistics has been implicitly psychological and cognitive in the sense that researchers have tried to formalise rules that are interior in individuals' minds.

Psycholinguists have attempted to test out some of the theoretical models hypothesised in linguistics by using test exercises with small groups of people; by observing physical analogues of mental activity using techniques such as eye-tracking and magnetic resonance imaging (MRI) scans; and by deducing the workings of normal behaviour on the basis of mental disorders or brain damage.

The brain and language

For example, on the basis of evidence from people with lesions or injuries to certain parts of the brain, it is clear that certain areas in the brain are predominantly responsible for different aspects of language. The brain is divided into two hemispheres – the slightly larger left and the right – connected by a bundle of nerve fibres called the *corpus callosum*. The left hemisphere controls the right side of the body, and the right hemisphere controls the left. For most people, the left hemisphere predominantly governs most aspects of language, though rhythm and intonation seem to be produced and processed in the right hemisphere.

In the mid-nineteenth century, two areas of the left hemisphere were found to be particularly important for language, both about half an index-finger's length in from your left ear. These are Broca's area and Wernicke's area (named after their discoverers, Paul Broca and Carl Wernicke). Damage to Broca's area seemed to result in an inability to form proper syntactic sequences, and damage to Wernicke's area seemed to result in problems grasping after specific vocabulary. These two sorts of **aphasia** suggested that the brain worked according to a principle of **localisation**, with particular cognitive abilities located in particular regions.

Today this seems to be somewhat overstated. Again, on the basis of evidence from people with head injuries, it seems that the functions of the two areas are not so clear-cut and also that many language functions can be distributed across large areas of the brain's 100 billion neurons and 10,000 connections. Some people with left-hemisphere injuries have even been observed to be able to learn to speak again by redistributing language processing into the right hemisphere. Two-thirds of left-handed people have their Broca's and Wernicke's areas in the right hemisphere of their brains. Though grammar and vocabulary tend to be lateralised to the left, for most people, and intonation and accent recognition to the right, the nature of **lateralisation** is variable and you will find a lot of nonsense written about its significance for logic and the emotions. Brain function seems to be more plastic and adaptable than was once thought.

Processing

In terms of language processing, we can differentiate two general approaches based on global or **top-down** strategies and particular or **bottom-up** strategies. The former includes the processes by which we make general sense of the world, and can process for significance and coherence: this is addressed in B7. At the particular level, an area that has exercised psycholinguists is the question of how an individual stores their vocabulary (their **lexicon**). For example, it seems clear that our brains do not store lists of words and their meanings like a dictionary. In tests, people who are shown one word (say, 'house') are able to recognise other words from the same semantic domain ('windows', 'doors', 'apartment', 'shed', 'home', or 'family') more quickly than words with no or little association. This suggests a network of connections rather than a straightforward filing system.

Furthermore, it would seem extraordinarily inefficient if we had separate lexical entries for every *inflected* and *derived* form of a word (see A2): the **lemma** or basic form of a word (say, 'interest') plus every one of its grammatical inflections ('interesting', 'interested', third person verb-form 'interests', plural 'interests', 'interest' as verb and as noun), and also all its various derivations ('disinterest', 'uninteresting'). Instead – again on the basis of speed of recognition tests – it seems that we store the lemma forms and the grammatical affixes separately and then assemble them as the need arises.

This capacity for dynamic assembly allows us to work out a lot about words that we have never met before and guess at their meaning on the basis of the affixes that can be attached to them. It also allows us to take a good guess at novel, creative or innovative words, such as George Orwell's (1948) 'doubleplusgood' or 'unperson', and produce such creative words ourselves. There is even a suggestion that sounds or clusters that we customarily find in other words can affect our interpretation of new words: consider a meaning for 'sloopy', or 'grittly', or 'plapped', for example.

Aside from this sort of morphological information, the words in our lexicon also contain syntactic information about the type of word-class that they typically occupy. A **cloze-test** procedure – once very popular as a language-teaching tool in classrooms – involves presenting a sentence with one word missing and inviting the student to supply the missing word:

The reader borrowed the _____ from the library.
This one is mine and that one is _____.
_____ the ball up and put it on the spot.

Sometimes a choice of words and word-forms are also given for the student to choose from. It is clear from such tasks that people have a good sense of the appropriate words to slot in, even if they do not get the exact word that was in the tester's mind. The first example requires a noun, for example, rather than a pronoun 'his', or a verb-form 'running', or an adjective 'bright', or a preposition 'under', and so on. Looking at this from the other side, every word carries a sense of places it can legitimately be used syntactically, and this suggests that grammar and vocabulary are not separate but are very much linked.

Memory and recall

A third property of words is their semantic network information. Though we might not have a dictionary definition as a strict *denotation* (see B2), we seem to have a normative sense of the most pertinent meaning of a word. This is regarded as being more central than any looser *connotations* or personal *associations* of the word. Instead of the meaning of a word being delineated by a set of defining characteristics, we seem to treat the meanings of words as being scaled as good examples of a general category, less good examples, and really poor examples. This is known as a **prototype effect** (in a different context, see also B2).

For instance, asked to give examples of things in the category of 'vegetables', most British people come up with a list that starts with 'peas, carrots, potatoes, cabbage, broccoli, cauliflower, beans' and then progresses to 'onions, garlic, cucumber, peppers' and might end with things like 'herbs, tomatoes, daffodil petals, lettuce', and so on. A key defining feature of vegetables, when people are asked, is that they are green, but several items in the 'best example' list are not green at all. What this sort of listing demonstrates is that people have a very strong sense that there are good examples of a category, less good examples, and poor examples. You could try the same sort of listing with categories like 'birds', 'furniture', 'vehicles', 'democracies', 'things to wear to a job interview', 'methods of getting to work on a Friday', 'greeting behaviour when meeting dictators', and so on.

Prototype effects tell us quite a lot about how our brains store our lexicon. For example, ask yourself which is the better example of a fruit: a potato or a pizza? Of course, neither of these are actually fruit, but you might feel that one is more 'fruity' than the other. The fact that you could have such an opinion shows that the radiating scale of prototypicality outwards from central examples of fruit really has no edges. These are not so much 'not-fruit' as simply very bad examples of fruit. Items on the edges of one category might be central to other categories (vegetables and fruit seem close, for example). This means that words in our lexicon connect with other words in similar semantic domains, and those general domains are related to each other too.

Furthermore, the associations and relations are not fixed, but are fluid and adaptable depending on the circumstances. It is possible to imagine a situation in which a potato seems more fruit-like (potato-wine, sweet-potato salad), and the word's meaning would then be adjusted accordingly. Just as lemmas and their affixes are assembled as required, so it seems that the appropriacy of word meanings are constructed as the situation demands.

It seems to be the case that once a word is **primed**, by being mentioned and thus brought to consciousness, it brings with it other words that are associated with it in a prototypicality network. These other words are available for quick processing as a result. So the mention of 'hungry' will make several of the following available: 'food, restaurant, meal, eat, cook, kitchen, sandwich, snack, pie' and many others. This is useful because any utterance that follows a sentence with 'hungry' in it is likely to feature one or more of these words. Instead of having to process every utterance from scratch, we have several possible lines of processing ready to go in each situation. This is incredibly efficient.

We can see that words are stored in terms of their connections of morphology, syntax and semantics, but it also seems to be the case that linkages are maintained on the basis of their form. Words beginning with 's', or 'sl', or 'sil' are easy to produce in a quick sequence: notice how a 'slip of the tongue' can easily make someone say 'silver' when they meant 'sliver', or 'sliver' when they meant 'shiver', and so on. When you are asked for a word that you don't use very often (perhaps, 'What is the capital of Tibet?'), you might struggle for a second, with the answer 'on the tip of your tongue' – you know it begins with 'l', or 'ly', or is it 'sl', 'los', 'lis' or 'llosa' – until eventually you get 'Lhasa'. You know immediately that you know the word, that it exists in your lexicon, and clearly you have several forms of **access code** in terms of its sound, some elements of its spelling, other words it looks like, and so on.

Psycholinguistic methods

Modern psycholinguistic methods tend to be experimental or quantitative (see A12). For instance, examples of words or sentences are devised and people are invited into a controlled setting and asked fixed questions. Their accuracy, efficiency or reaction times can be measured either by direct observation, by recording, or by using specialist equipment such as eye-trackers which measure the fast movements of the eyes over a text. These measurements are then taken as correlates of mental activity, or as evidence in support of certain theories about the brain. Slow, or repeated, or back-tracked eye-movements across texts are treated as indications of processing effort, for example.

More direct observation has recently become possible with a range of technologies that allow researchers to observe the blood and electrochemical flows through the brain in real time in the form of various brain-scanning methods. People can be given different tasks, or asked to respond to different questions, and their brain activity is monitored and recorded. Finally, of course, the old-fashioned technique of close observation and notation is still highly effective, especially in tracking the linguistic processes performed in child language acquisition, or in second language learning.

ORIGINS OF ENGLISH

The word 'English' (originally spelled 'Englisc' but pronounced the same) predates by several hundred years both the word and nation of 'England'. The language of the Angles was brought to the Celtic islands alongside the other Germanic groups, the Saxons and the Jutes, in waves of immigration and settlement long after the occupying Romans had left by the year 400. The Celtic languages of Britain were pushed north-wards and westwards by the invaders over the next 500 years, leaving 'Engleland' for speakers of different English dialects and allowing the newcomers to refer to the natives in the west as 'wealas' (foreigners), those whom we now call 'Welsh'.

The original Brythonic Celts who had settled the islands from 1500 BC were the ancestral speakers of Welsh, Cornish, Breton and Pictish. Later Goidelic Celts from southern France left their language, which developed into Irish Gaelic, Manx and (following the migration of the Scotti from Ireland to northern Britain) Scots Gaelic. The original Neolithic language spoken by those whom the Celts displaced, the builders of Newgrange in eastern Ireland and Stonehenge in southern England, is lost.

During the 350-year Roman occupation, Latin and the native Celtic languages had co-existed but remained functionally separate. North of Chester and York remained a militarised zone, with auxiliary soldiers drafted into the Roman administration. Even in Romanised Britain south of this line, there is little trace of the two languages crossing. Celtic terms remain for landscape features (*tor, llan, dun, coombe, pen, esk*; hill, church, fort, valley, hilltop, river), but Latin remained the preserve of the elite and it shrank back into continental Europe after direct Roman rule was lost. Only in the Christian Church, which remained, was Latin preserved in England, with Roman rather than Celtic customs agreed by the Whitby Synod (664) and Bede even writing his *Ecclesiastical History of the English People* not in secular English but in scholarly Latin (*Historia ecclesiastica gentis Anglorum*) in 731.

Bede also gives one of the earliest accounts of the Germanic invasions around 449. By his time, 300 years later, West Saxon was spoken across the south of the island (Wessex and Sussex) as far west as the Celtic kingdoms of Cornwall (where a Romanised Celt called Arthur had brief military success against the invaders and spawned a longer-lasting legend). Kentish was spoken across the south-east, where the Jutes had settled. And the Anglian dialects of Mercian and Northumbrian were spoken north of the Thames, as far as the highlands of Scotland. Though all these forms differed in many ways, nevertheless with their common Germanic roots and emerging common histories, by the year 1000 they can be regarded as more or less mutually intelligible dialects of the **Anglo-Saxon** or **Old English** language.

Old English

Though many vocabulary items are recognisable to Modern English speakers, the main striking difference in Old English is the **case** system. In Modern English, the function of words in a sentence is largely indicated by word-order: in 'the old king kisses the good queen', it is clear that 'the old king' is the actor in subject position who does the action and that 'the good queen', in object position after the verb, receives the action. Reverse the order in Modern English and you reverse the sense: 'the good queen kisses the old king'.

In Old English, **inflections** added to the end of nouns indicated their function in the sentence. Since each noun has a little tag (a suffix) to tell you whether it is subject or object, the word-order is much less important. In this example, 'the old king' would be tagged with an appropriate ending to show that it is the subject of the sentence (the **nominative**), and 'the good queen' would be tagged as the object (the **accusative**). Old English had two other cases to mark function in the sentence: the **genitive** case (for possessives) and the **dative** case (for indirect objects and other relationships).

In addition, Old English had grammatical gender for nouns, so a word would be marked as masculine, feminine or neuter. And number (singular or plural) was also marked. For nouns, then, the declensions (that is, the possible inflectional endings) were as in Table A8.1.

'The old king kisses the good queen' would be 'se ealda cyning clippeþ þā godan cwene'. The singular nominative zero-inflection on the masculine noun 'cyning' and the singular accusative ending '-e' on the feminine 'cwene' show which is subject and which is object. So, for example, though the word-order might have sounded a bit odd to an Old English speaker, 'se ealda cyning þā godan cwene clippeþ', or even 'þā godan cwene se ealda cyning clippeþ' both still mean 'the old king kisses the good queen'. This manoeuvrability in phrasing allows for great flexibility, especially in Old English poetry.

You will notice that, although the declension table has 24 permutations, there are in fact only 6 inflectional ending forms: zero, '-es', '-e', '-as', '-a' and '-um'. 'The king kisses the child' would be ambiguous in Old English (with zero-inflection 'cyning' and 'bearn' in both nominative and accusative cases), if it were not for the definite article telling you which was the nominative ('se cyning' rather than the accusative 'þone cyning'). As in Table A8.2, definite articles ('the') are also declined (that is, conform to case).

You will notice some letters that Modern English no longer has: 'þ' (the letter thorn, replaced now with the digraph 'th'), 'æ' (ash, replaced with the 'flat' 'a', not 'ah'), and the length mark over the vowel 'ā'. You might also notice some words which survive in one form or another in Modern English: 'þā' became 'the'; 'þæs' became 'this'; 'þǣm' became 'them'; 'þæt' became 'that'; and 'þāra' became 'their'.

In 'se ealda cyning clippeþ þā godan cwene', the adjectives 'old' and 'good' are also grammatically marked to agree with the nouns that they modify. Since 'se cyning'

Table A8.1 Declension of nouns

		Masculine (king)	Feminine (queen)	Neuter (child)
Singular	Nominative	cyning	cwen	bearn
	Accusative	cyning	cwene	bearn
	Genitive	cyninges	cwene	bearnes
	Dative	cyninge	cwene	bearne
Plural	Nominative	cyningas	cwena	bearn
	Accusative	cyningas	cwena	bearn
	Genitive	cyninga	cwene	bearna
	Dative	cyningum	cwenum	bearnum

Table A8.2 Definite articles ('the')

		Masculine	Feminine	Neuter
Singular	Nominative	se	sēo	þæt
	Accusative	þone	þā	þæt
	Genitive	þæs	þǣre	þæs
	Dative	þǣm	þǣm	þǣm
Plural	Nominative	þā	þā	þā
	Accusative	þā	þā	þā
	Genitive	þāra	þāra	þāra
	Dative	þǣm	þǣm	þǣm

Table A8.3 Adjectives ('old' and 'good')

		Masculine	Feminine	Neuter
Singular	Nominative	ealda / goda	ealda / gode	ealde / gode
	Accusative	ealdan / godan	ealdan / godan	ealde / gode
	Genitive	ealdan / godan	ealdan / godan	ealdan / godan
	Dative	ealdan / godan	ealdan / godan	ealdan / godan
Plural	Nominative	ealdan / godan	ealdan / godan	ealdan / godan
	Accusative	ealdan / godan	ealdan / godan	ealdan / godan
	Genitive	ealdra / godra	ealdra / godra	ealdra / godra
	Dative	ealdum / godum	ealdum / godum	ealdum / godum

Table A8.4 Verbs ('clippan')

Present		Past	
I	clippe	I	clippede
You (sg.)	clippest	You (sg.)	clippedest
S/he	clippeþ	S/he	clippede
We	clippaþ	We	clippedon
You (pl.)	clippaþ	You (pl.)	clippedon
They	clippaþ	They	clippedon

is singular nominative and masculine in the sentence, 'ealda' is also in this form; since 'þā cwene' is the singular feminine accusative, 'godan' is also in this form. Table A8.3 shows the inflections for adjectives.

As in Modern English, the verb-form must also agree for number and person (first person 'I and we', second person 'you' and 'youse' or 'y'all', and third person 'he/she' and 'they'), and tense. Table A8.4 shows the typical verb-endings for the verb 'to kiss' ('clippan').

Towards Middle English

In the Middle English period (from the Norman Conquest after 1066 to roughly 1500), most of the case system was lost. Modern remnants include the nominative pronoun 'I' ('ic'), the accusative pronoun 'me' ('mē'), and the genitive pronouns 'mine' ('mīn') and 'our' ('ūre'). The possessive apostrophe in Modern English ('Peter's book') preserves the genitive singular endings '-es' for masculine and neuter nouns (see Table A8.1 above), with the apostrophe indicating that the 'e' has been omitted. Given this complicated history, it is no wonder the possessive apostrophe is so often wrongly used in Modern English. Even the grammarians of the nineteenth century made mistakes in wrongly deciding that the (traditional) possessive 'it's' should be 'its' because the other pronouns 'his' and 'hers' did not have apostrophes!

The case system was generally lost in favour of a more fixed word-order for several reasons. The gradual influence first of Norman French, and in the later medieval period Orléans French, brought a ruling class speaking a non-case language. A huge number of French words were borrowed by English in this period, largely but not exclusively in the domains of law and administration, cuisine and fashion, education and manners, architecture, and medicine. Many of these words would have seemed odd with inflectional endings.

Furthermore, Danish influence in the form of Viking invasions and settlement in the east of England before the Norman Conquest and the speakers of the diverse Old English dialects produced a contact situation in which many of the root words were very similar but the inflectional endings were variable: it was natural that these different endings tended to be assimilated towards a single form. Given these other factors, the typical Germanic stress on first syllables also meant that inflectional endings came to be assimilated towards an undifferentiated mid-vowel /ə/.

At the same time, many inflectional forms were altering. The northern '-s' suffix for third person verbs began to spread to the south, displacing the original '-eþ', now spelled '-eth'. (Caxton did not in fact have a 'þ' block on his Dutch-imported printing press and used 'Y' with a scraped dot above it instead, giving rise to the 'Ye Olde Englishe' characterisation: 'Ye' was never pronounced /ji/ but always /ðə/). The King James Bible form ('My cup runneth over') was already archaic by 1611. Standard plural '-s' was being used in preference to the Old English '-en' ('children', 'oxen') or zero ('sheep', 'fish'). And weak past inflections ('hanged', 'looked', 'spelt') were more productive than strong forms ('brought', 'ran', 'hung').

Towards Modern English

By the time of the introduction and widespread use of printing presses (generally imported from the Netherlands), Middle English relied more on syntactic word-order than inflection. Dative and other undifferentiated endings tended towards a word-final '-e' in writing. These were still pronounced, and our modern spelling system stands as a frozen representation of Middle English pronunciation – all the letters in the following words would have been sounded: 'name', 'servyse', 'drought', 'knight', 'through', and many others.

Unfortunately for the spelling of Modern English, the language underwent a large-scale pronunciation change in the few hundred years after printing began to fossilise English spelling. This was known as the **Great Vowel Shift** and was generally characterised by the 'raising' of most vowel sounds (that is, the vowel sounds in particular words were replaced by vowels articulated higher on the tongue). So 'name' went from Chaucer's (1400) /naːmə/ to Shakespeare's (1600) /neːm/, and then later in southern English accents to /neim/; 'sweet' went from /sweitə/ to /swiːt/; 'down' moved from /duːn/ to /daʊn/; 'bath' went from /bæθ/ to /bɑːθ/; 'run' from /rʊn/ to /rʌn/ and then /rən/, and so on. The change started in London and spread away northwards and westwards. You will notice from some of the last few examples here that the Great Vowel Shift did not reach as far as some northern English and Scottish accents, which still retain earlier forms of pronunciation.

Changes in vowel quality also caused changes in consonant pronunciation and stress patterns across words and phrases. **Rhoticity** (pronouncing /r/ in words like 'car' and 'farm') was gradually lost from all English and Welsh accents with modern exceptions only in south-west and north-west England, and Scotland and Ireland. The common rhoticity in most American accents is due to the fact that settlers left England largely from rhotic areas and at a time that preceded the general loss of British rhoticity.

The period of Early Modern English is usually taken to begin soon after 1600, and we can see that by this time many of the forms of pronunciation and grammar are recognisable to present users of English. This is not to say, of course, that there has been no historical change in the past 400 years. The spread of English around the world has created many more forms of the language than could have existed only within the British Isles. All of these other World Englishes have diverged along their own historical paths. Many of the speakers of these forms (Americans, Indians, Australians, and others) have returned and changed British English too. The effects of mass migration, globalisation, and the dominance of English as an international language continue to produce innovation and change. It remains to be seen whether diversity or convergence will be the dominating trend in the future.

SOCIOLINGUISTICS

A9

Defining sociolinguistics

Even if this book is the first time that you have ever heard of the term *sociolinguistics*, there is every chance that you will have engaged in conversations upon sociolinguistic topics on many different occasions. Most of us have been involved at some time in a discussion about accent and dialect, or 'correct' English, or the state of the education system, and so on. All of these topics are studied within sociolinguistics.

Broadly speaking, sociolinguistics can be defined as investigating the relationship between language and society. Researchers who work in this field of language study are commonly known as **sociolinguists**. One of the key areas that sociolinguists focus on is how we vary our language use in different social contexts. This is commonly referred to as **variationist sociolinguistics**.

Think about how you vary your style of speaking depending upon what social context you are in, who you are talking to, and other factors such as who could potentially overhear you. Compare the following:

❑ The language that you would use as an interviewee in the public setting of a job interview, whilst being interviewed by a panel of three company directors, versus an informal conversation in the private setting of your home, with three long-term friends from your local regional area.

❑ The language that you would use in a telephone conversation with a close friend in the public setting of the workplace, when you know that you are in earshot of your boss, versus a telephone conversation with the same person in the private setting of your own home, with no overhearers.

Consideration of these different social contexts raises a set of issues which lie at the core of sociolinguistic investigations. The **speech styles** we choose to adopt will be affected by differences in the levels of **formality** of a situation, as will any differences in perceived **social status** and **power** between speakers, along with the closely related issue of how much **solidarity** or **social distance** we perceive there to be between ourselves and other people.

Another area of keen interest for sociolinguists alongside language variation is the study of **language change**, in particular how language changes over time (see B8). You have already come across examples of this in A8, where we set out how some regional and social changes in society have influenced changes in the English language system. These considerations can be viewed as belonging to the sub-discipline of **historical sociolinguistics**.

During the nineteenth century and the first half of the twentieth century, socio-linguists mainly examined **regional variation**, cataloguing differences between speakers in specific geographical areas. There was a focus in particular upon using older speakers from rural locations who had never left the area of their birth, as they were perceived to speak a form of 'pure' dialect. These informants were also all male, as at the time of recording men were perceived to be a more reliable, 'purer' source of language data than women (NORMs – non-mobile older rural males)! The principal aim of this research was to record variations so that dictionaries and grammars of regional varieties of English could be published.

The modern-day discipline of sociolinguistics developed during the 1950s and 1960s, when sociolinguists rapidly expanded their areas of research interest. Instead of limiting investigations to rural locations and NORMs, interest grew in exploring more complex geographical regions in urban areas, where a variety of different speakers had physically moved around, resulting in different varieties of English coming into contact with one another. The study of this phenomenon is called **urban dialectology**.

Furthermore, the traditional focus upon geographical location expanded to include a combined focus upon **social variation**, with the social identity categories of age, gender, socio-economic class and ethnicity being examined for patterns of variation. Younger and older male and female speakers from different socio-economic back-grounds and ethnicities emerged as important subjects of research.

The modern field of sociolinguistics has grown at a rapid rate. There are now a broad range of well-established sociolinguistic sub-disciplines, which sit both within and alongside the more traditional approaches to language variation and language change. These include, amongst others, language and ethnicity, language and gender, language and age, multilingualism, language planning and policy, language attitudes and World Englishes (the subject of Strand 10). Certain areas of pragmatics also cross over into sociolinguistics, as mentioned in A3. A prime example of this is the socio-linguistics of politeness, for instance when linguistic politeness is examined from the perspective of the social variable of gender.

Key terms

Within sociolinguistics, a key distinction is made between the terms **accent** and **dialect**, which is often blurred in everyday conversations, popular culture and journalism. Accent refers to pronunciation. Dialect instead is a more encompassing term which refers to word-choice and grammar as well as pronunciation. Sociolinguistic researchers who explore accent variation thus also tend to be trained phoneticians, or 'socio-phoneticians' (see D1).

Whilst much sociolinguistics has tended to focus upon accent and dialect and thus on investigations at the phonological, lexical and grammatical levels, it is important to emphasise that sociolinguistic study can take place at any level of the linguistic rank scale, encompassing a range of the layers of the language system you will come across in this book. Sociolinguistic studies can be conducted by investigating phonetics, lexis, grammar, syntax, discourse and pragmatics, or a combination of these different elements.

Cutting across these levels, however, we can draw on a very useful set of terms to capture aspects of our own language awareness. These are the categories of *stereotypes*, *markers* and *indicators*, which were coined by North American sociolinguist William Labov (1972c). Labov has played a significant role in the development of modern-day sociolinguistics, and he is commonly accepted to be the most influential founding figure in the discipline.

The first of Labov's categories, **stereotype**, refers to obvious features of language use, such as the use of 'chuck' as a term of endearment in Lancashire, or 'queen', fulfilling the same endearing function in Liverpool, the use of the 'eh' as a tag in Canadian and New Zealand English, or the use of the agreement marker 'och aye' in Scottish English. These features are those that are most obviously noticed and will be those that are most frequently commented upon in everyday conversations and discussions about how language varies between speakers. Stereotypes tend to be associated with vocabulary items and are therefore far easier to spot than phonological or grammatical variations.

What language stereotypes exist in your own local area? Who uses them? Do you use them? Why/why not? In what contexts do you hear them being used/use them yourself? What attitudes do you have towards these stereotypes?

The term **marker**, sometimes called **social marker**, refers to a feature where there is still some conscious awareness of variation by language users, but far less so than with stereotypes. These features may thus still become the topic of everyday conversations about language usage. Markers are very important to academic sociolinguistic study, as they are features with clear social significance that are firmly associated with particular social groups and speech styles. Rhoticity, defined in A8, is a good example of a marker of the social status of the speaker. Some people, for example in south-west and north-west England, regard the pronunciation of /r/ in 'farm' or 'car' as a prestigious feature that marks them out from other groups, while some of those other groups might regard it as a stigmatised feature. Elsewhere, for example in most of North America, this rhoticity is seen as a prestigious variable marking social status; similarly, notable exceptions exist amongst some groups in New York and New England (see A12 and B9 for further discussion).

How many markers can you think of for your own local area? Again, consider who uses them and if you use them yourself. Why/why not? If you use them, in what contexts do you use them/hear them being used? What attitudes do you have towards these markers?

Finally, the term **indicator** refers to features which are below the level of consciousness and can often be spotted only by trained sociolinguists. These features are therefore not expected to occur as topics of everyday conversation about language usage. Crucially, there is no social encoding associated with these variants – individual speakers will use the same language feature regardless of context or who they are speaking with. In certain parts of North America, for example, some speakers will pronounce the vowels in 'cot' and 'caught' exactly the same in all settings, whereas others will not. There is no consequence for speakers either way in terms of any positive or negative social evaluation – merging these vowel sounds is not socially encoded.

It is important to note that there can be slippage between these three different categories over time: indicators can become markers which in turn can then become stereotypes.

Communities, networks and practices

One of the most influential frameworks in sociolinguistic study is that of a **speech community**. This doesn't simply mean a group of people who speak the same language, because such a group is likely to be very disparate and varied. In any case, this definition is an example of a methodological problem known as **circularity**. This arises when *linguistic* features are used to identify a group that the study will then go on to analyse *linguistically*. A category from outside the language system itself is required in order to produce a justifiable and legitimate definition of a group. Labov came up with a useful and influential definition which moves away from the circularity problem. He argued that a speech community can be defined by speakers' participation in a shared set of norms. These norms can be found either by overtly asking speakers for evaluations of one another, or by finding clear patterns of language usage.

In a series of studies in New York City, Labov discovered that a set of shared norms existed between speakers, which helped him define New York City as a speech community. He argued that, whilst there was clear language variation according to different social class groupings, the more formal a situation became, the more members from every social class group in New York City would alter their speech style and use the more prestigious language variants, such as rhoticity. Speakers thus shared a set of norms: they moved closer to prestigious speech variants in more formal situations (see A12 for a more detailed illustration).

The speech community can be seen as a rather abstract concept. Speakers can be geographically disparate, and researchers can have very limited contact with them. In contrast with the speech community are two other approaches, known as **social networks** and **communities of practice**.

The social networks model focuses on the frequency and different types of contact that a specific cluster of individuals share. It then examines how the closeness of the social ties that exist between speakers will influence their language usage. Researchers who follow a communities of practice model examine particular groups of individuals who physically come together to engage in a specific, regular activity. Shared sociolinguistic practices and goals develop over time between these groups of people. Examples of communities of practice can include sports teams, friendship groups, colleagues in a workplace, and students in a seminar. Close-knit communities tend to sustain particular linguistic identities and features.

There are values in all three of these different frameworks for conceptualising groups depending upon what sociolinguists are aiming to analyse. The speech communities approach is useful if analysts want to survey language usage in broad populations of people. The social networks approach is useful for observing how the social closeness or social distance of a particular network affects language usage. The communities of practice approach is useful for observing how a specific group develops shared language practices, as well as how membership categories are co-constructed and how membership can change over time.

WORLD ENGLISHES

A10

World Englishes is a recently emergent area of sociolinguistic study. It is a field which has grown rapidly since the early 1980s, reflecting the spread of English as an international language (initially highlighted in A8). The expansion of different varieties of Englishes across the world has been intensified by English as the global language of the Internet and therefore the dominant form of all different types of computer-mediated communication. Academic courses and degree programmes devoted solely to World Englishes have also emerged along with numerous publications on the topic. World Englishes can thus legitimately be seen as a sub-disciplinary area of English language enquiry in its own right.

The 'circles' model
In the 1980s, Braj Kachru (1986), now commonly perceived as the most influential global figure in the field, produced a framework for conceptualising World Englishes. This has proved to be the most influential approach which researchers use as an entry point to studying World Englishes. Kachru argued that, instead of thinking about 'English' in singular form, the language should instead be seen as a pluralised concept. The sociolinguistic make-up of the whole range of different types of Englishes across the world should be perceived as belonging within one of three concentric circles, which he termed the Inner, Outer and Expanding Circles.

The **Inner Circle** refers to the UK, Canada, the United States, New Zealand and Australia, where the English language has its linguistic basis and where it is associated with longevity, tradition and culture. The Inner Circle loosely corresponds with the acronym **ENL**, English as a Native Language. The **Outer Circle** refers to contexts where English has become an official language due to colonisation, which Kachru maps onto the category of **ESL**: English as a Second Language. Examples of this include Nigeria, Singapore, Malaysia and India. Finally, the **Expanding Circle** refers to situations where English is used as a foreign language, commonly referred to as **EFL** contexts. Prototypical examples of the third circle are the use of English in China and Japan (see D10 for further details on Kachru's model).

World Englishes should thus be viewed as a collective, all-encompassing term which includes all of these different circles. Kachru's model of multiple Englishes poses a range of complex questions, especially when considering issues surrounding the teaching of the English language. These issues gain further prominence when viewed in light of the fact that for well over a decade now it has been consistently reported that there are more 'non-native' English speakers than there are native speakers in the world. Barbara Seidlhofer (2004) reports that the majority of interactions which take place globally in English do not involve native speakers and thus English is being moulded and developed by non-native speakers just as much as it is by native speakers.

Roughly one-third of the world's population now speaks English. So, pertinent questions such as which English(es) should be taught, who should learn them and who should teach them are currently being hotly debated by academics, practitioners and policy-makers worldwide.

English as a lingua franca

One important area of study for World Englishes which is becoming an increasingly popular topic of investigation is how English operates as a **lingua franca**, most simply defined as a common language. The need for a lingua franca arises when individuals who speak different, mutually unintelligible languages come into contact with one another. English has become the world's lingua franca, and the acronym **ELF** (English as a Lingua Franca) is now frequently used. Speakers from any of the three circles, including native speakers, can engage in ELF communication.

Examples of English fulfilling the role of a lingua franca can be found in various locations across the globe. For example, South Africa has 11 official languages, but English operates as the country's lingua franca, functioning as the language of business, government and the mass media. Across Asia, English operates as a lingua franca in numerous countries, including Malaysia, Singapore, Thailand and Indonesia. English is also the most common lingua franca in Europe. While there is variation in terms of the positioning of English within individual European countries, English is the lingua franca imbued with the most importance: more individuals learn English in Europe than any of the other European languages put together. The European Parliament has 23 official languages, but English is the one most commonly used.

English as a lingua franca in Europe can be observed in action in the following report of a short yet revealing interaction which took place in the Czech Republic. While quietly sipping a Budweiser Budvar beer in a café in Old Town Square, Prague, one of your book's authors observed a group of Spanish L1 speakers approach one of the Czech waiters. The group was engrossed in conversation (in Spanish) and was deciding on nominating one of its members to ask the waiter for directions to the famous Charles Bridge. One woman eventually came forward and immediately code-switched from Spanish into English, thus selecting English as the perceived common language in order to communicate with the waiter:

Tourist: Excuse me, where is Carlos Bridge?
Waiter: Straight on then turn left at the corner and follow to the river
Tourist: Thank you

In the tourist's initial utterance, one lexical item, the proper noun 'Carlos' from her native language, was still present. It is clear from the waiter's response that this 'splicing' together of language varieties, known in sociolinguistics as **code-switching**, had not hampered his understanding – the conversation was completed with all relevant information disseminated.

When English is operating in the role of lingua franca, Firth (1996) has argued that, from the perspective of pragmatics, there is a 'let-it-pass principle' in operation: providing that conversationalists can basically understand each other, they will let any mistakes pass without comment in an effort to communicate effectively in a manner that displays consensus and cooperation.

However, despite the successful nature of the above encounter in terms of information dissemination and maintenance of cooperation and consensus between speakers, this did not prevent an aside from a British woman at a nearby table to her companion once the interaction had finished. She clearly would not 'let-it-pass', even though she had played no part in the conversation apart from being another overhearer. She rather sarcastically made the following comment: 'Funny that I thought it was Charles Bridge not Carlos Bridge. Who's this Carlos?'

This British woman's comment, and the rather snide laughter that followed from her and her interlocutor, can arguably be seen as a prime example of native-English-speaker monolingual superiority and a negative attitude towards code-switching. The sharp-eared waiter could not resist responding to this and took great delight in informing the woman (in English of course) that Charles Bridge is actually called 'Karlův Most' in his country's native language.

This brief example illustrates a range of sociolinguistic issues surrounding World Englishes, including insights into language attitudes and stigmatisation associated with code-switching, the maintenance of the pragmatic rules of cooperation by two 'non-native' ELF speakers, and the use of English as a successful lingua franca.

Standardisation of World Englishes

There has been common agreement amongst many World Englishes academics that the increases in the usage of English as a lingua franca within Europe will lead to the future establishment of a variety of 'Euro English' and that such a 'Euro English' could well undergo the process of **standardisation** (see Kirkpatrick 2007). For a variety of any language to become standardised, it needs to undergo some process of **codification**: to be officially recorded. A common manner in which language varieties are codified is through the publication of dictionaries and grammars. Therefore, it is predicted that in the future dictionaries and grammars of a World Englishes variety known as 'Euro English' may well appear.

Once a variety of a language has been codified, norms of usage become established from these sources of authority. A standard language variety can then be formally taught, in part, by drawing upon these resources. In order for World Englishes to ever be properly recognised, varieties need to undergo some process of codification. Codification is often considered to be the most powerful mechanism to enhance the status and prestige of World Englishes varieties. Dictionary publication is crucial in demonstrating that a variety has become properly institutionalised.

The process of codification is the most effective way of cataloguing descriptions of different, emergent varieties of English. In particular reference to English as a lingua franca – though this point applies equally to all World Englishes research – Seidlhofer (2004) argues that one key principle which should be accepted by researchers is an acknowledgement of the need for detailed description and then codification. The cataloguing of descriptions would create a highly useful and much-needed source so that knowledge of the linguistic features including phonological, lexical, grammatical, discoursal and pragmatic features that constitute different varieties of English can be shared.

However, it is important to highlight that once a standard variety develops and undergoes codification, this does imbue **prestige** to this one variety at the expense of all other varieties, which will become **stigmatised** variants in comparison. The standard variety is the one that has the most social, political and economic power attached to it. The standardisation process places an uncomfortable control upon the natural process of language evolution. As emphasised in the previous unit, variations and changes are a completely usual and expected part of the life course of any variety of language, be it a newer variety of English, such as those in the Outer and Expanding Circles, or any other variety of English circulating in the Inner Circle.

Therefore, despite the advantages of codifying particular varieties, it is important to bear in mind that fixing a language goes against its natural evolution. Any standard variety that has been selected by appropriate authorities is not inherently more complex, 'correct' or 'pure' – it is simply the version that has been imbued with the most societal power and prestige.

So, how many different types of World Englishes dictionaries are there, and when did they first emerge? World Englishes researcher Kingsley Bolton (2006) reports that the first was *Webster's Dictionary*, published at the beginning of the nineteenth century (1806) in the United States, followed by a revised and expanded version in 1826. Further versions of American dictionaries were also published during the twentieth century. The first Canadian dictionary was published in 1967, but this has been replaced by the publication of the *Canadian Oxford Dictionary* in 1999; Australia had its first dictionary in 1981, entitled *The Macquarie Dictionary*, and a New Zealand dictionary first appeared in 1997.

India has a history of glossary and word list publications dating back to the late nineteenth century, but as yet does not have an official national dictionary. The Caribbean has twentieth-century dictionary publications of Jamaican English and Bahamas English and a dictionary of English usage published in the late 1990s, but no national dictionary. No other World Englishes varieties as yet have any fully fledged dictionary publications, though there are projects underway to produce dictionaries for East Africa and South-East Asia.

It is immediately noteworthy that the fully fledged codification examples of national dictionaries are from the most established, Inner Circle countries of the United States, Canada, New Zealand and Australia. The only other countries which have had (non-national) reference works published are Outer Circle countries which, like the United States, Canada, Australia and New Zealand, have a lengthy history of English usage through colonisation: English was first introduced in the early seventeenth century in the Caribbean and India. The use of English in these Outer Circle geographical locations thus has much longevity, and, like its former colony counterparts in the Inner Circle, English has had the status of an official language in these countries for a considerable period of time.

Publication of national dictionaries is a part of a country's independence process and clearly demonstrates an official, separate identity from the former coloniser. It is arguably more clear-cut to do this in post-colonial situations than in newer situations in places such as Europe or South-East Asia, where English is used as a lingua franca by speakers across many different nations. These codification issues will be further discussed in B10.

STYLISTICS   A11

All texts, whether spoken or written, display **style**, which can loosely be defined as the recognisable linguistic and discoursal patterns in the text. Since every sound, word, syntactic structure, co-referential link and overall shape of the text exists as a consequence of choice (even if that choice is not highly conscious within the constraints of the language system), style can be regarded as a set of choices. Those choices are significant rather than merely ornamental: comparing the actual form of expression of a text with any of the other numerous possibilities in which it could have been realised quickly reveals differences in meaning, different emphases of meaning, different tones and evaluative shadings, different perspectives, and different senses of emotion, commitment and value. In other words, although it has been convenient in the past to separate form (the linguistic patterning as structure) and content (its interpreted meaning), in practice form and content are indivisible.

The discipline of **stylistics** explores the relationships between language patterns and interpretation. Though stylisticians examine the whole range of texts in the world, stylistics has a particular interest in literary works as the most prestigious examples of language use.

Style as choice

For example, imagine in a literary text a person contemplating whether it would be a good idea or not to commit suicide. The crux of this person's existential dilemma can be articulated in a variety of ways:

❏ 'Should I kill myself or not?' Here, a self-oriented interrogative is framed as a moral imperative in the foregrounding of the modal 'should', and the act of suicide is rendered semantically as a killing. The realisation of 'kill' and the negation and elision of its contrary ('or not') places the act of killing in the foreground – the opposite version would be something like 'Should I carry on living or not?'

❏ 'Euthanasia is an option for me.' Here, the lexical choices are much more formal and emotionally distanced, which is rather odd given the subject-matter. The dilemma is cast in a declarative form rather than as a question.

❏ 'There's no point in going on!' Here the choice is more exclamatory than the last example, and here it captures direct speech more closely (the elided 'There's', the informal lexical choices, and the graphology of the exclamation mark). Furthermore, the grammatical form begins with an existential 'There', which is ironically apt in the circumstances. The negation is by the particle creating a negative noun phrase ('no point') rather than by a verb-negation ('There isn't any point'), which is less negative than this alternative. Equally, the choice of living or dying is positively framed ('going on') rather than negatively framed (something like 'ending it all'). The sentence also draws on a conventional metaphor in which life is cast figuratively as a journey and the end of life, by extension, is an end of motion: here, this finality is captured also by the sentence ending with a strongly final closing exclamation mark.

There are many other possible ways in which this dilemma could be articulated. In Shakespeare's *Hamlet*, most famously, it is cast as follows:

❏ 'To be, or not to be, that is the question'. Here, the action of self-killing is abstracted into an existential verb – the copula 'to be' – which itself is presented non-finitely without a grammatical subject. The existential state is foregrounded by the reversal and clefting of the usual order of the sentence, which might normatively be regarded as 'The question is to be or not to be'. There is no self-reference, no personal pronoun, no subject expressed at all, except implicitly in the speaking voice. This *is* a speaking voice, of course, placed in the mouth of the actor playing Hamlet on a stage. All the utterances around this line are in a regular metrical pattern – an iambic pentameter – with five repetitions of the iamb (an unstressed then a stressed syllable). In this line, though, the established pattern is disrupted. In the first six words, '. . . be, . . . not . . . be' take the stress as you would expect, but few actors sustain the pattern by stressing 'is' rather than 'that' (though either are reasonable intonational options). This begins to undermine the certainty of the metrical patterning already established. Furthermore, there is an extra syllable at the end of the line (making an odd eleven syllables rather than the normative ten), giving the effect of a weakly trailing sense of bathos and indecision to the line and undermining the clear rational articulation that the speaker seemed to start with. Finally, like the second example of the line above, the speaker chooses a form that distances himself from the action of suicide. Like the third example above and contrary to the first example, the positive ('To be') is placed more prominently than the negative and derivative form ('not to be'), which shades the statement marginally positively overall. You could argue on the basis of this stylistic evidence that this is not a person actually intending suicide, but someone contemplating it intellectually and procrastinating.

It should be clear how it is possible to connect these close stylistic observations of this single line with significances of characterisation, theme and motive in the play as a whole, especially if placed into a longer analysis of the entire speech that follows. This is the basic craft of the stylistician.

Of course there are complications to be considered. One difficulty for stylistics is that the literary text does not present all of the alternative versions that were potentially available, as we have rather more usefully done above. Unless numerous drafts and revisions of a writer's manuscript exist, the literary work is singularly what it is. Furthermore, if the subject-matter is fictional or even articulated with poetic licence, there is not in fact any pre-existing event that can be regarded as giving rise to the linguistic articulation: the language *is* the event.

Of course, the exercise we have sketched out above allows a comparison of the possible alternatives that were not taken to illuminate the choices that actually were taken by the writer. This creative intervention as an analytical method is a useful one for the stylistician. And the fact that there is no pre-existing version of a literary articulation is of course actually a powerful argument for the significance of analysing the language of the literary text in detail and in a professional manner.

Style as patterning

It should also be apparent in the very brief stylistic analyses above that an important concept in stylistics is the notion of prominence or **foregrounding**. Texts are not even; some parts are more noticeable than others. This unevenness of texture is a consequence of different linguistic choices: it underlies the existence of style itself, and it is what allows stylistics its validity and power. Foregrounding depends on a sense that the particular feature that you have noticed is doing something noticeably different from the previous co-text or from what you might ordinarily have expected in that context. It thus relies on **deviance** or deviation from a norm. Of course, it is not simple to specify exactly what that norm is – whether in the language system in general or in the prior establishment of the literary work in particular or genre in general. However, we can at least talk of characteristic patterns in texts that are recognisable and available for analysis.

Foregrounding can be analysed stylistically as a feature of textual organisation, but of course it is also simultaneously a readerly and psychological feature. Features which are highly deviant or non-normative (such as when Cathy says 'I am Heathcliff' in Emily Brontë's *Wuthering Heights*, or Roethke's 'the inexorable sadness of pencils', or e.e. cummings' 'pity this busy monster, manunkind') are likely to be regarded as foregrounded elements by most readers, but other patterns can be more subtle and give rise to more disagreement in interpretation. The fact that foregrounding is both a textual and readerly phenomenon is an unavoidable truth that makes stylistics neither purely objective nor purely subjective. Instead, stylistic analysis can be regarded as intersubjective: the arguments and evidence are presented in a systematic and disciplined manner for other researchers to consider.

Since texts are generally uneven in texture and possess variable foregrounding, there is often an organising and prominent feature that appears to be most significant in a literary work: this is the **dominant**. Stylistic analyses tend to focus on this feature in order to get to the nub of the mechanics of the text's technique. For example, the presentation of a heated argument in a play or in a passage of dialogue in a novel could profitably be analysed using frameworks from conversation analysis and the pragmatics of politeness (see B3 and B5). A short lyrical poem with apparent sound effects and a very distinctive rhythm could usefully be analysed from the perspective of phonetics (see A1) and metrics. A poem with odd clashes in meaning would be amenable to a semantic analysis (A3). A poem with syntactic sequencing that did not appear to match everyday language might be interesting under a syntactic exploration (see A4 and B4), and so on.

Of course, almost no literary text is one-dimensional. No doubt, in the semantically odd poem or the phonetically interesting lyric there are also foregrounded patterns at other levels of language. Where these patterns appear in alignment, the **parallelism** itself is noteworthy and significant. For example, in a famous lyric by Robert Browning, words which carry the semantic content of kisses and kissing are arranged so that the phonetic effect of saying the words out loud forces the reader to form kisses with the lips. Try this verse out loud with an awareness of what your mouth is doing:

The moth's kiss, first!
Kiss me as if you made me believe
You were not sure, this eve,
How my face, your flower, had pursed
Its petals up; so, here and there
You brush it, till I grow aware
Who wants me, and wide ope I burst.

(from 'In a Gondola' by Robert Browning, 1842)

In this text, phonetic patterning, lexical choice, semantic meaning, syntactic form, and the selection of verbs, tense and aspect all line up towards the same powerful effect. A detailed and more lengthy stylistic analysis than could be produced here would set out all these parallelisms and demonstrate how they contributed to the significance of the literary work. Where stylistic patterning and interpretative significance are directly aligned and related, stylisticians talk of **iconicity**. So, for example, in the Browning extract, the phonetic articulation that is foregrounded in the text is iconic of the act of kissing.

Stylistic analyses can be conducted, then, across the linguistic rank scale, from phonology, morphology and lexicology, through syntax and semantics, and up to text and discourse levels. A practical constraint often accompanies examples of stylistic analysis, in that exploration of features up to clause level is possible in shorter poems but increasingly difficult and unwieldy in longer poems, prose fiction and plays. In practice, when stylisticians analyse novels, for instance, exemplary passages for analysis are selected on the basis that they represent something important about the novel as a whole, or that they demonstrate crucial points of shift across the development of the whole work.

Furthermore, although stylisticians in general deploy models, frameworks, approaches and the principles of linguistics in exploring literary works, there has also been a great deal of theoretical development within stylistics itself. Take, for example, the way that point of view is articulated in narratives, or the ways that speech and thought are presented in fiction, or the way that mental representations in the form of text worlds are constructed during literary reading – all these are innovations in our understanding of language that have arisen within the discipline of stylistics itself. Stylistics, then, is both a form of literary criticism and a form of applied linguistics, and is at its best and most successful when these can be combined seamlessly.

The stylistic tradition

Stylistics as a discipline has its roots in classical **rhetoric**, especially in the dimension known as *elocutio* or 'style'. It is therefore probably the oldest form of both literary and linguistic study still in operation today. In its modern manifestation, stylistics has closely mirrored developments in applied linguistics while remaining largely separate from the critical debates in literary theory.

For example, the practices of close reading in British universities in the 1930s and 1940s, and the 'New Criticism' in the United States in the 1940s and 1950s led to a renaissance of stylistics in the form of a linguistic account of the phonology, metrics, semantics and syntax of poetry in the 1960s. As applied linguistics developed new insights in pragmatics in the 1970s, and in sociolinguistics and discourse analysis in the 1980s, stylisticians acquired powerful new tools that allowed them to explore the language of prose, drama, and the text and discourse levels of all literary works.

The new century has seen further innovations in linguistics taken up enthusiastically in stylistics. In **corpus stylistics**, the increasing use of large language corpora and computer software to investigate them has revolutionised the scope and detail of what the stylistician is able to do. Patterns in evidence across large expanses of text, or even across different works by authors, or in literary movements can be explored systematically and comprehensively without long and laborious exercise. Computer software can quickly display all occurrences of a certain word or phrase, and the close textual contexts in which they occur. Intuitions and impressions of reading that seemed beyond the reach of traditional stylistic analysis are suddenly made available for explanation.

Second, the influence of cognitive science in arts and humanities has also produced a **cognitive poetic** dimension for stylistics, with a large new set of analytical tools from cognitive grammar to text world representations in the mind. The cognitive turn in stylistics has augmented a purely linguistic analysis with a psychological concern for readers and interpretation.

In literary studies, the influence of stylistics is being felt in a return, 'post-Theory', to attention paid to texts and textuality, and the teaching of literary appreciation alongside literary history. These are old terms rejuvenated with new interest. In applied linguistics, and in fact in many of the other disciplines from which modern stylistics draws its techniques, there is a renewed realisation that it is important to study examples of language in their full context and natural setting, as stylisticians have always done.

A12 METHODOLOGICAL PARADIGMS

In order to consider different methodological paradigms that inform English language study, it is useful to step briefly beyond the disciplines of language and consider its place within social sciences and humanities more generally. Methodological trends can be witnessed as belonging to much broader patterns, and it is beneficial to view these trends in the light of the overarching academic arena where language studies belong.

In recent times, there has been an observable move from **quantitative** to **qualitative** methods in numerous disciplines across the social sciences and humanities. Sociologist Martyn Hammersley (1992) observes that during the 1940s and 1950s quantitative methodology was the dominant approach to social research, but since the 1960s qualitative methods have gained in popularity. Qualitative research has moved from the margins of many social science disciplines to occupy a far more central place. As qualitative methods have grown in popularity, a debate surrounding the relative values of quantitative and qualitative methods has emerged. This debate between the two paradigms is discussed thoroughly in D12. In this unit, we will focus on characterising and then illustrating the different types of paradigms that are followed in English language studies.

Historically, the basic principles of quantitative methods can be summarised as aiming for the following:

- ❑ objectivity
- ❑ neutrality
- ❑ replicability
- ❑ generalisation
- ❑ discovery of laws: in language study, instead of 'laws' quantitative researchers use the terms 'rules' and 'norms' – there are always exceptions to language patterns that can be found, so the term 'laws' is not a wholly accurate representation for language researchers

Classic methods that are typically employed by quantitative language researchers include standardised questionnaires, standardised interviews, where exactly the same set of questions are asked to numerous informants in exactly the same manner, and experimental settings where laboratory conditions are used to elicit spoken or written language data.

In contrast, qualitative research focuses on observing the social world as naturally as possible. From this perspective, the use of any artificial settings, be it through experiments, questionnaires or artificial settings such as interviews, is arguably flawed as researchers instead need to study 'the social world in its natural state' (Hammersley and Atkinson 1995: 6).

The main principles for qualitative methodology are often seen as being based upon a critique of quantitative methodology, in particular, upon survey and experimental methods. The validity of quantitative methods has been challenged by qualitative researchers. For example, any claims to objectivity and neutrality are fundamentally flawed, as quantitative researchers' assumptions and perspectives on the social world *will* be imposed by the structured nature of the data collection, despite any claims to the contrary. This biases research, as it makes it very difficult to discover evidence that does not correspond with these assumptions and perspectives.

To illustrate this point, Alvesson and Deetz (2000: 69) argue that questionnaires entail that informants have no choice but to 'subordinate themselves to the expressions of the researcher's subjectivity', thus making it impossible for alternatives to the researcher's position to be explored. Other criticisms include the following:

❑ Naturally occurring behaviour cannot be analysed by setting up artificial contexts such as experiments or standardised interviews. Therefore, evidence gained in these artificial settings cannot be used to make valid claims about what takes place in naturally occurring situations.

❑ You cannot rely on accounts of what people say they do without observing what they actually do in naturally occurring settings, as this fails to acknowledge that there can be a discrepancy between informants' attitudes and their actual behaviour in specific social situations. Informants therefore need to be observed in their natural environments. If you as a researcher directly observe naturally occurring events, then you are no longer solely dependent on the respondent only.

❑ Quantitative research can imply that the aspects of language usage and social identities are distinctive and fixed. This may draw attention away from the fact that informants' language usage will both change and develop depending upon context.

❑ Quantitative researchers tend to treat informants' behaviour as something which is mechanically produced, thus arguably neglecting individual creativity and cognition. Therefore, the quantitative approach can appear to have a rather static perception of human interaction.

❑ As a social researcher, you are part of the social world you are investigating, and this factor cannot be ignored. Researchers should do everything in their power to reduce bias and the influence of idiosyncrasies in research, but appealing to objectivity or neutrality is problematic because they are both impossible to achieve. Researchers can never escape from their own ideologies as researchers in the social world or the interrelated fact that theoretical presuppositions are involved in all data (see A13–D13).

Such criticisms of quantitative methods reveal the critical principle behind qualitative methods, namely, that the 'nature of the social world must be *discovered*' (Hammersley 1992: 12, emphasis in original). This can be achieved by the method of **participant observation** in order to produce detailed descriptions, sometimes referred to as 'thick' descriptions. Participant observation is generally defined as part of **ethnography**, where researchers physically join in and participate in the social world which they wish to study, so that they can observe it from an insider's perspective.

However, despite historical differences and disagreements between quantitative and qualitative research, more recently social scientists have begun to question the purpose of the arguments between the two paradigms, suggesting that the debate itself is a fruitless exercise, which has resulted in detracting attention away from more important issues of theory and methodology.

We would agree that the dichotomies which exist between qualitative and quantitative approaches, and any dichotomies that exist in social science disciplines in general, are unhelpful and limiting, often resulting in researchers situating themselves in 'armed camps' (Silverman 2000: 11), unwilling to learn from each other. Researchers should instead be seeking common themes between different social science traditions in an effort to move disciplines forward by sharing ideas and expertise. If researchers stop viewing concepts as being in opposition to one another, then more integrated and arguably more sophisticated **mixed-methodologies** can be produced.

Furthermore, contrasting different approaches has led to the assumption that quantitative and qualitative methodologies are themselves harmonious and unified. This is certainly not the case with either paradigm, both of which include many diverse approaches. On some occasions, qualitative methods may be deemed more appropriate by a researcher, but on other occasions, the very same researcher may deem quantitative methods to be more appropriate. In some circumstances, a mixture of the two methods may be used, depending upon the problem or the area of investigation which is at hand. However, this pragmatic, mixed-methods approach is not without its problems. We will explore this further in D12.

Researchers from all paradigms can improve the reliability and validity of their methodology by acknowledging clearly that they are actively involved in the social world in which they are studying. Hammersley and Atkinson (1995: 16) argue for a commitment to producing what is termed **reflexive** research, which is defined as the means by which researchers directly acknowledge that their orientations 'will be shaped by their socio-historical locations, including the values and interests that these locations confer upon them'. This represents a rejection of the idea that social research can be carried out in isolation from the social world in which the researcher is studying and also an acknowledgement that the researcher as an individual in the social world will influence the research project.

Deciding upon which methodology or methodologies to use is a crucial process, which should be thought through carefully, even if you are only conducting a small project. To illustrate these different paradigms, we will now present an example of well-regarded English language studies for each of the different areas, including mixed-methodologies, to show the different approaches in practice.

An illustration: quantitative methods

Sociolinguist William Labov (1966) used an innovative and effective research method for his seminal quantitative study of New York City department stores, which is now commonly referred to as the **rapid and anonymous** method basically because it enabled him to compile sociolinguistic data from a number of different individuals very quickly, without needing to get any personal details from those who took part in his study.

Labov wished to analyse a particular phonological feature as articulated by shop assistants in three different department stores: Saks, Macy's and S. Klein. Labov selected the three stores based upon perceived differences in the targeted socio-economic class groupings of shoppers. He was interested in investigating the popular and highly useful phonological variable of rhoticity, which, as we have already highlighted in A9, is a prestigious speech variant in New York.

He asked many different shop assistants a question about the location of goods in the store, where he already knew the answer to be 'fourth floor'. He pretended not to hear the first time around and got the assistants to repeat their answers. In total, then, Labov ended up with four different examples of /r/ pronunciation per individual informant. He had examples where /r/ appears both in the middle of a word, known as word-medial positioning ('fourth'), and also at the end of a word, known as word-final positioning ('floor'). The phrase 'fourth floor' was ideal for presenting Labov with a number of different realisations of the rhotic pronunciation.

An illustration: qualitative methods

Qualitative or 'thick' descriptions can be basically defined as collecting anything and everything that you can when you are present as a participant observer in a research setting, including audio or video recordings, written documents, field notes containing additional background details or any details that cannot be formally recorded for ethical reasons (see B12). The most productive way of gaining a thick description is commonly thought to be ethnography involving participant observation.

Health communication researcher Srikant Sarangi has conducted a number of studies in the medical profession where he has conducted ethnographic research and become a participant observer. He has then drawn upon his 'thick' descriptions to produce thorough, discourse-based analyses of medical interactions, including work on genetic counselling (see Roberts and Sarangi 2003). The participant observation method has the advantage of enabling researchers to pursue research questions which can be continually negotiated with those being researched, with the intention that the findings can be of practical relevance to those being studied.

An illustration: mixed-methods

The following is a quotation from Penny Eckert's lengthy ethnographic participant observation in a Detroit high school called Belten High. In total, she spent over two years collecting data at this location. Here we have an example of linguistic data which is embedded within a rich ethnographic description of what is going on around the conversation. It gives rich detail to the positioning of the body as well as language – the advantages of which we discuss in D9 in reference to Eckert's notion of communities of practice (see also Wenger 1998). The passage shows the importance of spatial features of context – how standing in specific locations is linked with the performance of identities alongside linguistic features:

> At lunchtime in the spring of 1997, in an ethnically very heterogeneous junior high school in northern California, a crowd of Asian-American kids hangs out in a spot that is generally known in the school as 'Asian Wall'. Girls stand around in their high platform shoes, skinny bell-bottoms, and very small T-shirts, with hips cocked. As they toss their heads, their long sleek black hair (in some cases tinted brown) swishes across their waists, the slimness of which is emphasized by shiny belts. Some of them talk to, some lean on, quiet-demeanored boys with baggy jeans and baggy shirts, with hair long on the top and shaved at the bottom. Linda turns away from her group of friends with a characteristic tilted head toss, bringing her hair around her shoulders; and with an exaggerated high-rise

intonation on the pronoun, she calls to a boy who's standing nearby. 'What are YOU?' Another girl, Adrienne, who happens to be walking by, answers on his behalf. 'He's Japanese-Filipino.' The boy smiles silently, and Linda turns back to her friends.

Eckert and McConnell-Ginet (1999: 185–6)

In addition to these ethnographic observations, Eckert also carries out very detailed quantitative analyses from recorded data of phonological and grammatical linguistic variables from a large number of realisations of phonetic and grammatical features over time. These quantitative studies are statistically tested and enable her to make valid and reliable arguments from her findings regarding language, regional identities, social identities and adolescence.

Eckert (2009) contrasts the ethnographic approach which she took at Belten High with what she describes as a 'quick and dirty' method of briefly going into various other schools in the surrounding area to examine the phonological manifestations of her adolescent identity categories. This method, which shares similarities with Labov's 'rapid and anonymous' method described above, enabled Eckert to place her phonological analysis on a broad geographical continuum for the whole of the suburban region where her research took place.

In a reflexive evaluation of her own methodological practice, she notes that the 'quick and dirty' method lacked the textual detail and access to communities of practice which was so crucial in being able to characterise how adolescent groups use linguistic strategies to signal their identities. She concludes: 'I was never as sure of the status of my data in the other schools as I was at Belten' (2009: 150).

Once the decision regarding methodological paradigm(s) for conducting a particular English language study has been made, there are other decisions regarding data collection techniques and ethics that need to be taken. We will explore some of the most significant of these issues in B12.

A13   LANGUAGE THEORIES

Almost everything we have said about language in the first twelve strands in this book has been contentious at different points in history. The ways that people described language 300 years ago (see B8 and C8) were very different from more recent descriptions. Even observations from only 30 years ago which gradually became the general consensus (the paradigm) have gradually been questioned, rejected and replaced by new perspectives. No doubt our current thinking will also soon be superseded in due course.

This does not mean that linguists are generally incompetent: the fact that the field of study is constantly being revised is a consequence of the fact that language in general is immensely complicated and difficult to study. It ranges from material and measurable phenomena (writing, sounds) all the way to things that are very difficult to get at (meanings, implications). The close connections between language, thought and consciousness also take you very quickly to difficult philosophical considerations. Language covers the things that an individual says and writes, as well as the variations across large groups of people over geographical distances and throughout history. Language itself is a universal capability of all humans, and the particular languages that societies use have always changed over time.

Furthermore, because there are so many different dimensions to language, it is impossible to hold them all in equal and perfectly objective balance at the moment of study – every researcher comes to the study of language with ideas, ideologies, commitments and perspectives that influence which part of language they choose to study, which questions they decide to ask, which methods they decide to employ, and how their findings can best be interpreted from their own angle.

Linguistics as a social science

The objective of language study – like any properly progressive discipline – is to gain a better understanding than the state of existing knowledge. The best way of ensuring this development is to be healthily sceptical of all ideas and ask questions to determine the basis of those ideas. Being critical does not simply mean finding fault and rejecting others' work: there is an ethical imperative on you also to be creative and suggest solutions where you find problems. The general scientific principle – even for a complex social science like linguistics – that underlies all this is the notion of **falsifiability**. Any statement you can make about an aspect of language must be able to be disproven. Consider, for example, the following two statements:

> Language is the blood of the soul into which thoughts run and out of which they grow
>
> (poet Oliver Wendell Holmes)

> Language is always changing
>
> (linguist David Crystal)

Only the second of these can be proven false – for example, you could try to find a living language somewhere in the world that has remained exactly the same for at least three generations. You would only need to find one contrary example to falsify Crystal's general statement – or at least force him to amend the phrase 'always changing' to something weaker, like 'tends to change in general'. The first statement is certainly poetic and certainly meaningful, but it is not possible to disprove it, because as a metaphor it is already literally false, and the range of meanings it might evoke in different interpretations means that it does not say anything precisely. In short, the first sentence is a poetic and expressive statement of an opinion and viewpoint that is untestable, and the second is a scientific statement that is testable and disprovable.

Falsifiability must apply to all assertions in language study, from simple statements like the ones above to entire theoretical frameworks such as the way in which we carved up the constituents of clauses in A4 and B4. All statements about language can then be regarded as theories offered as descriptions of language available to be falsified. They cannot be proven true, since you can never say what new evidence, new techniques or new approaches might emerge in the future to disprove the theory, so the best we can do is to hold a set of theories about language which are as good as we can manage for the moment. This means that in language study, as in any analytical study, everything in this (or any other) book is best thought of as being only provisionally not wrong.

Different approaches to language study

Of course, when a theory receives criticism, or a new perspective is suggested, not everyone always agrees that the original theory is disproven. Some adherents to the original theory will defend it, arguing against the criticism. Others will adapt the original theory to meet the challenge offered by the new proposal. And, of course, some researchers will have their positions changed by the new debate and will work to develop other theories too. This process means that the historical development of modern linguistics has not been a neat march from one descriptive position to another, with everyone in perfect step. If you take a snapshot at virtually any historical moment in linguistics, you will find adherents of several contradictory and complementary theories existing at once and debating with each other. On occasion, this has become so passionate that one spat in the 1970s was even termed 'the linguistics wars'.

For example, the study of language through most of recorded history has been through **rhetoric** (learning the art of speaking and persuading) and through prescriptive treatises on correct grammar and good usage. Through the later nineteenth century, **philology** was the name for language study, with a strong focus on the historical development of languages, the etymology of words, sound-change rules in pronunciation, and literary history.

Around the turn of the twentieth century, linguists began to be interested not so much in these diachronic developments but in more synchronic patterns, looking at a snapshot of the language of the present as a system of structures and symbols. This was **structuralism**, which dominated language study for the first half of the twentieth century. Structuralism shifted the emphasis of study away from historical processes and onto social ones, which meant that links between linguistics and anthropology were easier to make.

In the 1950s, a revolution in language study occurred in the name of **generativism**, which created the discipline of modern linguistics. In some respects, generativism continued the structuralist approach of aiming to discern underlying systematic patterns and structures in language, rather than being interested in language history or social variation. Indeed, generativists explicitly claimed to be interested only in a speaker's underlying **competence** rather than their observed **performance**, though of course their intuitions about well-formedness constituted important information that shed light on deeper structures. In other respects, generativism marked a break with structuralism in the disregard of social, performative aspects of language. Generativists believed that the capacity for language – and even many of its deepest structural patterns – was innate in humans.

Focusing on syntax, constituent structure, and the rules by which different phrases and sequences could be transformed below the surface performance of language, generativism aimed to develop simple mathematical formulae that could account for every well-formed grammatical sequence in English. These syntactic rules, it was argued, could generate any well-formed sentence. Generativism, through its various modifications over the last 70 years, has remained a formal grammar. It distinguishes surface structure (the manifestation of language in the world, actual utterances, part of performance) from deep structure (the underlying patterns and transformations that determine the language). It is the deep structure that this approach has mainly been interested in, to the extent that when people talk about 'theoretical linguistics', they almost always mean generativism, as opposed to other, more applied forms of linguistics.

Alongside this approach, and developing out of anthropological structuralism, a **functionalist** tradition emerged in language study, largely at odds with generativism. Functionalism regarded language as part of social practice rather than a separable module, and so there is no focus on syntax but rather an argument that syntax and semantics are mutually influential, no focus on formal rules but rather an emphasis on systemic descriptions that allow for the variations in actual usage and communicativeness. The most famous functional model of language is systemic functional grammar (SFG). Because of its aim (simply put) of theorising what language does rather than what it is, SFG has proven useful in discourse analysis and the exploration of sociological and political contexts of language use.

Though generativism appears to be a branch of highly abstract psychology, and functionalism a branch of sociology and anthropology, in practice each draws on evidence from all these domains. The intuitive tests applied by generativists to their formal descriptions are placed into the public, social domain for approval (or not) by others. The systemic descriptions produced by functionalist grammarians correspond quite well with psychological matters of cognition, perception and attention.

Generativism takes a **formal** approach to language, assuming that the important facets of language can be represented by notational principles, rules and explicit parameters. One way this assumption can be sustained is to define these important facets of language as including only those aspects of language that can be accounted for in this way. So generativism is often said to be modular, with dimensions such as interpretation and social communicativeness explicitly excluded from the definition of linguistics.

Functionalism takes a **systemic** approach to language, assuming that language is not modular but integrated in principled ways. So, for example, the lexicogrammatical choices made at clause level are implicated in and by the interpersonal situation of the speaker and the sort of text and discourse they imagine they are involved in. A functionalist's view of language is thus broader than a generativist's, including with regard to social symbols and conventional codes, and functionalism is often allied with the social-linguistic field of **social semiotics**. What functionalism gains in a broader definition of language, of course, it loses in a less precisely manageable analytical account, from a generativist perspective.

In recent years, a **cognitivist** approach has developed across the social sciences that has also influenced language study in the form of a cognitive linguistics. **Cognitivism** takes an 'embodied' approach to language, arguing that – far from language being self-contained and modular – there are evolutionary, biophysical and psychologically plausible connections between the material nature of our bodies in the world and the ways we cognise, understand and articulate the world and our experience in language and thought.

Cognitivists argue, for example, that the way our mental attention is deployed across a clause or discourse situation is simply an adapted case of the way our visual attention has worked since the days before we, as a species, developed language. Cognitivism is basically a functional model in that it places communicativeness at the heart of its approach, but it draws heavily on psychology and claims psychological validity for its models – furthermore, many of the proponents of cognitive linguistics in the 1980s were former generativists who were disillusioned as a result of the 'linguistics wars' of the previous decade.

At the moment, you will find the field of linguistics populated by generativists, functionalists, cognitivists and others, all with their own research programmes, books, journals, courses and conferences. From time to time, they will also engage with each other and criticise, review or adapt developments from the others' projects. Underlying each of their approaches are fundamentally different views of the relationships between language, thought and society that are not obviously reconcilable. Though each group would argue that their own paradigm best fits the data as they see it, the fact is that there are advantages and problems with all of these approaches. Their different views will be the field of discussion in Unit B13.

Section B

DEVELOPMENT
ASPECTS OF ENGLISH

CONSONANTS AND VOWELS

In all of the B units, we will offer further discussion and explanation of the areas that we introduced in Section A. Rather than providing extra detail on everything that was introduced, we focus in this section on some of the significant aspects of the English language. In this unit, for example, we examine the nature of consonants and vowels in more detail.

Consonants

In A1, we introduced the three-part categorisation system for characterising the articulation of a consonant: place, manner and voice. To develop our knowledge of this process further, it is helpful to view these three different categorical elements in a systematic format, which is most commonly achieved by viewing consonants in a grid formation. However, before we do this, it is useful firstly to present a detailed list of the range of consonant symbols of the English language so that you are familiar with the symbols that belong to the International Phonetic Alphabet (IPA) for consonant production.

Many of these symbols will be very familiar, as they are the same as traditional English spelling, though there are also some that are quite different. Alongside each symbol is an example of a specific word to illustrate the particular sound quality that is being represented. The exact part of the word which is being represented by the phonetic symbol is underlined.

p	–	pat
b	–	bad
t	–	tin
d	–	dog
k	–	can
g	–	got
ʔ	–	bu'er (glottal stop)
m	–	man
n	–	tan
ŋ	–	sing
r	–	road
f	–	flash
v	–	van
θ	–	thigh
ð	–	the
s	–	sit
z	–	zinc
ʃ	–	sheep
ʒ	–	leisure
h	–	ham
l	–	loft
j	–	yet
tʃ	–	church
dʒ	–	judge
w	–	wipe

While the location of particular sounds within individual words is represented here by underlining, there is a more principled way to characterise this, by referring to **word-initial**, **word-medial** and **word-final** position. For example, with /θ/, the example given above (*thigh*) is word initial. This sound occurs in word-medial position in *author* and word-final position in *path*. With /ʃ/, a word-initial example is given above with *sheep*. It occurs in word-medial position with *fishes* and in word-final position in *dish*. The example of *church* above contains /tʃ/ in word-initial and word-final position within the same word. Such distinctions are important because sounds often change depending on where they occur in a word.

You may have noticed that some consonants that exist in English spelling are not present in the phonetic consonant symbols. The following letters are not listed above: c, q, x and y. They are not required for phonetic representations in the English language. The letter c is most often represented phonetically by either /k/ or /s/. The former is referred to as **hard c** in a word such as *cat*, whereas the latter is referred to as **soft c** in a word such as *cider*. Additionally, in a word such as *cello*, c is represented by /tʃ/. The letter q is not required to be represented phonetically, as it is articulated as [kw].

The letter x is represented by a combination of consonant sounds, either /ks/ as in *ox* or, on rarer occasions and in some accents, as /gz/ as in *exam*. However, there is one exception to this with the letter x. In one particular regional variety of English, Scottish English, /x/ is used as a phonetic symbol to represent the consonant sound in words such as *loch*. We will come back to this below. Finally, the letter y is represented by /j/ as in *yet* as we have seen in the above list.

All of the different consonant symbols listed above can be placed upon a consonant grid which can function as a really useful cross-referencing tool for defining the three-part classification system. Table B1 presents an example of such a grid. The *place of articulation* categories introduced in A1 run horizontally, and the *manner* categories run vertically. You will notice that there are two sounds in some of the squares. Where you have such consonant pairings, the sound on the left is always voiceless, whereas the sound on the right is always voiced. If there is only

Table B1.1 The consonant sounds of the English language

	Bilabial	Labio-dental	Dental	Alveolar	Palatal	Velar	Glottal
Stop	p　　b			t　　d		k　　g	ʔ
Fricative		f　　v	θ　　ð	s　　z	ʃ　　ʒ		h
Affricate				tʃ　　dʒ			
Nasal	m			n		ŋ	
Approximant				r	j	w	
Lateral approximant				l			

one consonant in the box, remember that you can ascertain whether it is voiced or voiceless by performing the vibration test described in A1 – place your fingers on your vocal cords and physically test for evidence of vibration.

Consonant classification tends to take the order of voice, place and manner. Test out the usefulness of the Table B1.1 grid by identifying the IPA symbol for the following consonant descriptions (the answers are at the end of this unit):

voiced velar nasal
voiced velar stop
voiceless dental fricative
voiceless bilabial stop
voiced labio-dental fricative
voiced palatal fricative
voiced alveolar lateral approximant
voiceless labio-dental fricative

Most consonant tables which focus solely on the English language do not tend to include regional variants, but if we were to add the _loch_ sound from Scottish English to the grid, the symbol /x/ would live in the velar fricative cell.

You should now test the usefulness of the consonant grid in reverse by coming up with the three-part description for the following consonant symbols: /m/, /f/, /s/, /tʃ/ and /n/. (Again, the answers are at the end of this unit).

Any speech sound can be symbolised using the IPA and described accurately using the classification system as above. Even some non-speech sounds can be accounted for in this way: a voiceless bilabial released ingressive stop (ingressive refers to when the air in the air stream is pulled into the vocal tract) is a kiss.

Vowels

Before undertaking any formal study of the sound system of the English language, there is a common perception that English has five vowels: a, e, i, o and u. While this is the case for the Roman alphabet and the traditional orthographic written system of Modern English which you are presently reading, there are many more vowel sounds which we make when we engage in spoken communication with one another. These are represented through various symbols within the IPA.

The vowels of the English language can be categorised as **pure vowels** (also referred to as **monophthongs**), or as **diphthongs**. Pure vowels/monophthongs are defined as such, as they have one single sound quality. You may also find these sounds referred to as **steady-state** vowels, reflecting how the tongue and the lips are held in a steady position when the vowel sound is articulated. In contrast, diphthongs have two sounds and the speaker will make a transition from one sound to another in the production of the vowel.

It is important to note that pure vowels can be split into short or long vowels depending upon their duration – how long a sound takes to produce compared with another sound. A long vowel is represented by the diacritic symbol ː which appears directly after the short vowel symbol to signify the vowel length. For example, the short vowel /a/ as in _cat_ has a corresponding long vowel /aː/ as in _car_.

Below is a summary of English language monophthongs and diphthongs. As with the consonant list, the IPA symbols appear directly alongside specifically selected words to illustrate the particular sound quality which is symbolically represented:

Monophthongs

short vowels

ɪ	–	p<u>i</u>t
e	–	p<u>e</u>t
a	–	p<u>a</u>t
o	–	p<u>o</u>t
ʌ	–	p<u>u</u>tt
ʊ	–	p<u>u</u>t
ə	–	batt<u>er</u>

long vowels

ɪː	–	m<u>ea</u>n
ɜː	–	b<u>ur</u>n
aː	–	f<u>a</u>rm
ɔː	–	m<u>or</u>n
uː	–	m<u>oo</u>n

Diphthongs

aɪ	–	b<u>i</u>te
ɛɪ	–	b<u>ai</u>t
ɔɪ	–	t<u>oy</u>
əʊ	–	r<u>oe</u>
aʊ	–	h<u>ou</u>se
ʊə	–	cr<u>ue</u>l
ɪə	–	<u>ear</u>
ɛə	–	<u>air</u>

In A1 we briefly mentioned vowel trapeziums, the diagrammatic way in which vowel sounds can be graphically represented on the tongue, sometimes referred to as vowel quadrilaterals. An example of a vowel trapezium is given below. The eight vowels that appear at specific points on the trapezium in Figure B1.1 are known as **cardinal vowels**.

The cardinal vowel system was devised by phonetician Daniel Jones in the early twentieth century. It has been a highly influential model in aiding the description of vowel sounds, and it is still the dominant model used today. The term *cardinal* was adopted, as the model follows a similar idea to the principle of the cardinal points on a compass (north, south, east and west). The cardinal vowels are fixed points, and the quality of the vowel sounds that are produced by speakers can be identified by reference to these fixed points.

The 'front', 'central' and 'back' categories that run along the top of the trapezium diagram refer to the positioning of the body of the tongue – basically how far forward or retracted it is when the vowel sound is being made. The 'close' through to 'open' categories that run down the left-hand side refer to the positioning of the tongue in

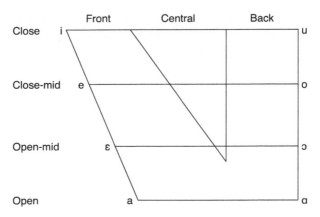

Figure B1.1 Vowel trapezium of cardinal vowels

relation to the roof of the mouth. If the top surface of the tongue is close to the roof of the mouth, then these sounds can be identified as close vowels. If the tongue is far away from the roof of the mouth, then the vowel sounds are termed open.

As we have already seen above, the IPA for English includes a number of other vowels. The vowel sound represented by the symbol /ə/ is known as **schwa**, named after the Hebrew vowel. It is the most frequent vowel sound in the English language. If you relax your tongue, open your lips slightly, and make a vowel sound (usually spelled in writing as 'uh'), that is a *schwa*. The /ɪ/, /ʊ/ and /ʌ/ vowels, together with schwa, are known as **centralised** vowel sounds. They are articulated in a central position in mouth, as illustrated in Figure B1.2.

The shape of the lips is another category which is taken into consideration when characterising vowel sounds. In order to incorporate different lip shapes, phoneticians have identified different shapes within which phonetic symbols can be displayed. A square ☐ is used to indicate that lips are **unrounded**, often termed **spread**, whereas a circle ○ is used to indicate that lips are rounded. Rounded lips tend to be used for

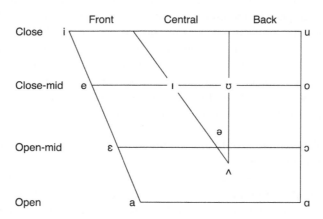

Figure B1.2 Cardinal and central vowels

back vowels, including /u/, /o/ and /ɔ/, whereas other English language vowels tend to use unrounded lips. These shapes can be used on vowel trapeziums to signal lip shape in addition to tongue location.

With diphthongs, some sounds start with rounded lips and end with spread lips, and others start with spread lips and end with rounded lips. For example, /əʊ/ as in *roe* starts with spread lips and ends with rounded lips. The following symbol represents this diphthong lip shape: ◁. Other diphthongs will start off with rounded lips and end up with spread lips, as in /ʊə/ for *cruel*. This transition in lip shape is represented by the following symbol: ▷. Make these sounds out loud in a mirror so that you can physically see the difference with the positioning of your lips.

Accent

Knowledge of phonetics and phonology is crucial for research into accent, the study of pronunciation (see A9). Many phoneticians who work on the English language are interested in describing and cataloguing variations that exist between the accents of groups of English speakers from different regional and social backgrounds. In order to undertake such investigations, a good foundational knowledge of vowel and consonant sounds is essential. Researchers who conduct investigations of accent variations are referred to as **sociophoneticians** or **sociolinguists**, examples of which can be seen throughout Strand 9.

In the list of consonants above, there are 24 sounds plus the glottal stop. **Received Pronunciation**, or RP, the social accent traditionally imbued with the most prestige in England, has 24 consonant sounds, excluding the glottal stop, which is instead traditionally associated with regional accents. Historically, RP has been used as the benchmark reference point for phonetics sounds in many textbooks. However, as we will see in B9, **language loyalty** to RP is dying out. Indeed, some authors have started instead to take what they term **Non-Regional Pronunciation** as their starting point for consideration of phonetics and phonology (for example, Collins and Mees 2013). Non-regional pronunciation can involve the use of glottal stops on occasions for the articulation of certain words (see D1, B9 and C9 for further discussion on language loyalty and particular phonetic speech features).

Furthermore, as we have seen already above, if we want to be inclusive of other varieties then there is a need to include other symbols, such as /x/ to denote the *lo<u>ch</u>* consonant sound in Scottish English. In C1, we will look in more depth at accent variation by focusing on different examples and texts to enable you to explore this important application of phonetics and phonology further.

Consonant classification: some answers

    voiced velar nasal: /ŋ/
    voiced velar stop: /g/
    voiceless dental fricative: /θ/
    voiceless bilabial stop: /p/
    voiced labio-dental fricative: /v/
    voiced palatal fricative: /ʒ/
    voiced alveolar lateral approximant: /l/
    voiceless labio-dental fricative: /f/

/m/: voiced bilabial nasal
/f/: voiceless labio-dental fricative
/s/: voiceless alveolar fricative
/ʧ/: voiceless alveolar affricate
/n/: voiced alveolar nasal

B2   LEXICAL SEMANTICS

A dictionary entry tends to give the meaning of a word as a statement which defines its **denotation**: that is, its precise and narrowest direct and primary meaning. A wide-ranging or detailed dictionary might also give some of the **connotations** of the word – its additional or secondary meanings. So, for example, the *Oxford English Dictionary* defines 'red' first as the spectrum colour that the word denotes, but it also provides some of the different connotations of redness in fire, blood, violence or revolution. A word will also, of course, have very many looser and perhaps more culturally defined **associations**: 'red' and 'reds' associates, in different places around the world, with several British soccer teams wearing red shirts, with communists, with US Republican states, with roads of a particularly high accident rate, with embarrassment, with Marlboro strong cigarettes, with food labelling of a high fat and sugar content, with air squadron identifiers, with ginger hair, with prostitution, with a certain type of civic university, with the car maker Ferrari, and many others. Some associations might be very personal and idiosyncratic. However, all of these senses can be said to be part of the meaning of the word. The study of the meanings of words and their relationships is known as **lexical semantics**.

Words and their meanings

The relationships between the meanings of words can be differentiated and categorised. **Synonymy**, for example, refers to the ideal state in which a word means exactly the same as another. This can be said to be idealised because in practice there are probably no true exact synonyms, since the connotations and associations of the two words are likely to be slightly different. For example, 'book, volume, text, tome' might all be said to be synonymous, but it is easy to see that they have specific and different normal contexts of use. A 'text' sounds more like a book for teaching or analysis, a 'volume' is grander than a book, but not as grand as a 'tome', which also has the suggestion that it might be a boring but worthy read. Other sets of synonyms display similar variations: 'letter, epistle, note, line', or 'clothes, gear, clobber, kit, threads, couture', or 'car, wheels, banger, automobile, motor', or 'dog, doggie, pup, mutt, canine, hound', and so on.

Certain lexical fields can be seen to be **overlexicalised** if they are of particular interest to the speech community, and while the Eskimo/Inuit words for snow are exaggerated, you need only think of the fine gradations in precipitation of 'rain, sleet, wintry showers, hail, snow, rime, drizzle, spitting, bucketing down, downpour', and so on to realise the interest in the temperate climate in British English. Other overlexicalised domains are often taboo or prohibited areas ('toilet, bog, lavatory, bathroom, crapper, netty, loo, cloakroom, WC, restroom, ensuite, shithouse, gents/ladies, little boys'/girls' room, thunderbox', and so on). **Underlexicalised** domains tend to be highly technical, where only one very specific and precisely defined term exists, or areas which the speakers know little about and so use vague or general words. Of course, a domain might only appear underlexicalised when considered relative to another language which has more words in that domain.

Matching up the cultural norms of synonyms and the degree of lexicalisation is an important skill in the native speaker, as is knowing exactly how to disrupt those norms for particular effects. In an email, 'I'll email you' or 'I'll text you' are probably about right; 'I'll drop you a line' sounds a bit old-fashioned now, suggesting paper-based letters; and 'I'll write to you' sounds rather formal in this context, while 'I'll communicate an epistle' is so grand it would almost certainly be taken as an attempt at humour.

By contrast with synonymy, a word is an **antonym** of another if its meaning is almost exactly opposite. Again, we need the 'almost exactly' formula for the same reason that there are no precise synonyms: even 'black and white', or 'up and down' have associations that do not make them exactly equally opposite. These two pairs of examples are binary opposites in that they are usually taken as mutually exclusive and there is no third possibility. Other antonyms are gradable, such as 'big and small' or 'long and short'. The sizes of drink sold by most multinational chains are highly gradable, including 'long, grande, large, regular, straight, super, deluxe, tall', even 'baby' and (quite rarely) 'small'.

Some words have no apparent lexical antonyms: what is the exact opposite of 'table', or 'elephant', or 'fascism'? You might go for 'chair', or 'mouse', or 'communism', but it is easy to argue about these. Some words have opposites that can be imagined but are underlexicalised: is there a single word that is the opposite of 'plain-speaking'; and is the opposite of 'religious' 'agnostic' or 'atheist'? Is the opposite of a word always synonymous with the negated word: is 'black' simply and exclusively 'not white', or is 'female' the same as 'not male'? Are the possible opposites of 'democracy' all 'undemocratic'? These questions demonstrate that there are two distinct types of oppositeness in terms of *contrariness* and *contradiction*.

Some antonyms necessarily involve their other pair. For example, you cannot 'borrow' something without someone else being able to 'lend' it to you. You cannot 'return' from somewhere that you have not 'gone' to in the first place. 'Come and go', 'this and that', 'yesterday, today, and tomorrow' all entail each other as part of their main meaning. A peculiar set of words in English are *contronyms*, words that can have their own opposite meaning. Famous examples include 'fast' (both quickly moving and attached to a stationary object), 'dispense' (give out or give up), 'peer' (your social equal or a member of the aristocracy), 'clip' (attach together or cut apart), 'cover' (conceal or oversee), and many others.

A word is a **hyponym** of another if it is part of the general category and is regarded as more general than the subordinate term. So, 'mammal' is a hyponym of 'dog', and 'dog' is a hyponym of 'terrier', and 'terrier' is a hyponym of 'Yorkshire terrier'. This also means that 'mammal' is a hyponym of 'Yorkshire terrier'. Again, matching up the level of specificity in these words is crucial in communication. 'I'm going to take the terrier for a walk' is only normal if you have several dogs of different types. By contrast, if you are asked at a dog show what a particular animal is, and you reply 'It's a dog', you will likely be taken as being facetious.

The relationship between the things denoted by hyponyms is conceptual, whereas if there is an actual part–whole relationship between the referents of related words, then the relationship between those words is said to be one of **meronymy**. 'Hand and fingers' are in a meronymous relationship, as are 'car and tyres', 'tree and leaves', and 'Washington and the US'. The part–whole relationship is often so culturally naturalised that one can be used for the other: 'Washington condemned the attacks', 'Can I give you a hand?' The extent to which the *meronym* (the most particular word) is a necessary and essential defining part of the *holonym* (the superordinate word) is debatable: is a hand without fingers still a hand? A dog still a dog without a tail? Without legs? Without a head? If the meronym is a defining part, then there should be a necessary logical consequence if anything happens to it: for example, if the tyres are on fire, is it the case then that the car is necessarily on fire?

Polysemy and **homonymy** describe similar effects arising from different histories. A word is polysemous if it has developed two distinct meanings, and it is homonymous when it is the result of two distinct words having converged. For example, 'sole' (the bottom of a shoe) and 'sole' (a type of fish) are polysemes, but 'seal' (the coastal mammal) and 'seal' (a glued interface) are homonyms. The distinction between these two lexical semantic types is often only possible with a knowledge of etymology.

Even more subtle is **plesionymy**. A word is a plesionym if it is a near-synonym, but substitution of the word does not leave the same truth conditions. For example, in 'It wasn't misty, just foggy', the words 'misty' and 'foggy' are plesionyms of each other. Other examples would be: 'He was murdered, or rather executed'; 'He's a farmer, or strictly a stockman'; and 'It's a pie, or actually a savoury tart'. Plesionyms are often used to indicate that the speaker is grappling after precision, but perhaps does not possess the precise vocabulary or technical term for the object in mind. Though subtle, the reality of plesionymy can be illustrated by considering some odd examples that are cast in the right form but that are not lexical plesionyms: '?My brother's a shopkeeper, or more exactly a policeman'; '?She bought a dog, or more exactly, a cat'; and '?It wasn't misty, just sunny'.

In general, all closely located words in coherent discourse exhibit **philonymy**. Two words are philonyms if they collocate in an acceptable and expected way: 'The speaker can speak French'; 'The pregnant woman'; 'fine and dandy'. Antonyms, if used in a coherent sentence, can be philonymous. Two words are **tautonyms** if they merely repeat without adding new value, creating a tautology: 'The speaker is speaking'; 'Boys will be boys'; 'War is war'. Of course, it is easy to imagine contexts in which these tautonymous phrases could be communicatively valid, demonstrating again that connotations and associations are imported along with denotations whenever words are brought together.

Words which are not used philonymously are **xenonyms**, if they create semantic dissonance: 'fat water'; 'the inexorable sadness of pencils'; 'Whispering lunar incantations dissolve the floors of memory'. Such xenonyms are often the ground of creative or literary language (these examples are from a 1970s US west-coast rock and blues band, and the poets Theodore Roethke and T.S. Eliot).

Basic terms and prototypes

In all of these semantic relationships, there is often a notion that there is a basic, normative or default word, against which the related words are measured. For example, 'dog' seems to be a **basic level term** compared with its superordinates 'mammal, animal, creature' and its subordinates 'hound, terrier, collie'. Basicness, here, seems to attach to those concepts that are most familiar or most accessible, most human in size, experience or understanding. Basic terms tend to be etymologically ancient and persistent, even resisting newer and potentially displacing alternatives ('canine', for example). There is even an argument that a conceptually basic term is likely to be phonologically and morphologically simpler than other terms in its semantic domain.

What these arguments are actually demonstrating is semantic **prototypicality** (see also A7). We seem to carry around notions of the best examples of categories on the basis of previous experience and cultural habit: so a dog is a good central example of an everyday and familiar animal, and the conceptual level of 'dogness' is the most familiar and easiest way of thinking about those objects in the world most of the time. Higher-level terms ('mammal', and so on) are too abstract, whereas sub-ordinate terms ('poodle', and so on) are overly specific, most of the time. Sometimes, of course, 'mammal' or 'poodle' will be normal. Within the *dog* domain, a terrier or a collie is, for us, a good example of a dog. A poodle or a dingo is a less good example in terms of our cultural prototypicality judgement. In fact, dingoes and wolves are peripheral examples of dogs for us, moving outwards to hyenas, coyotes, foxes and other dog-like semi-dogs in our minds. Note that these judgements have nothing to do with scientific classification. Next outward along the radial prototypicality structure of dogs would be wolverines, badgers, ferrets and weasels. Beyond them would be very poor examples of dogs, like panthers, cheetahs, lions and other technically non-dog mammals.

If this sounds odd to you, simply ask yourself: which is the worse example of a dog – a ferret or a badger? Or which is worse, a panther or a bicycle? The fact that you can probably answer this, and even defend your decision, shows that category membership is a matter of gradation and prototypicality rather than fixed definition. So it is not that a cat is simply not a dog, it is that a cat is just normally a very poor example of a dog. The prototypicality of categories applies to every semantic type identified in this unit.

PRAGMATIC PRINCIPLES   B3

Alongside the features of speech act theory introduced in A3, there are two principles of pragmatics which have played a significant role in the field. The first is the **co-operative principle**, following the work of Grice (1975), and the second is the **politeness principle**, following the works of Leech (1983) and Brown and Levinson (1987). Both of these principles are still influential today. We will start off by considering the co-operative principle and then move on to examine the politeness principle and the large amount of work which has emerged on politeness in the English language since these initial publications.

Co-operative principle

Grice argued that a basic foundational principle which is followed by all rational adults is to co-operate with one another when engaged in spoken interaction. From Grice's perspective, all interactions can be defined as co-operative efforts to at least some degree. His co-operative principle is as follows:

> Make your contribution such as is required, at the stage at which it occurs, by the accepted purpose or direction of the talk exchange in which you are engaged.
>
> (Grice 1975: 45)

In order to illustrate this further, Grice devised four conversational maxims which logically follow on from the co-operative principle:

> *Maxim of quantity*
> Make your contribution to the conversation as informative as necessary
> Do not make your contribution to the conversation more informative than necessary
>
> *Maxim of quality*
> Do not say what you believe is false
> Do not say that for which you lack adequate evidence
>
> *Maxim of relevance*
> Say only things that are relevant
>
> *Maxim of manner*
> Avoid obscurity of expression
> Avoid ambiguity
> Be brief (avoid unnecessary wordiness)
> Be orderly
>
> (Grice 1989: 27)

Abiding by the above maxims is considered to be the prototypical way of communicating with one another. However, it is not uncommon for one (or more) of the above maxims to be regularly **flouted** in everyday conversation. This does not mean that conversationalists are ceasing to be co-operative. On the contrary, when flouting of conversational maxims takes place, hearers will search for a **conversational implicature** of the speaker's intention precisely because of the co-operative principle: faced with an apparent break with a maxim, a hearer will still assume the speaker is being co-operative and will set off to find a reason why the maxim was deliberately flouted. The co-operative principle is therefore maintained by implicature. There are clear similarities here between Grice's principles and the concepts of direct and indirect speech acts which we came across in A3.

To illustrate this further, it is useful to consider some examples of the flouting of maxims. Similar to an indirect speech act, maxims can be described as being flouted when speakers are conveying a sense of implied meaning. Consider which of Grice's maxims is being flouted in the following examples. Attempt to work out which conversational implicatures can be made from these scenarios:

Between two strangers at a bus stop:
'Lovely weather we're having' when it is pouring down with rain

Conversation between an arguing couple:
'Where are you going?'
'Out'
'When will you be back?'
'Later'

Conversation between two students:
'There are millions of places to eat on-campus if you're starving'

Conversation between a couple:
'Have you finished the laundry yet?'
'The Baxters over the road have bought a new dog'

Conversation between two friends over dinner:
'Do you want some yoghurt?'
'I had yoghurt last week it was strawberry flavour really nice I do like raspberry too though the bits get stuck in my teeth I don't like cherry or natural'

There are many different ways in which the social force of implicatures can be interpreted. They can be used to generate humour, as with irony or sarcasm, or used as expressions of annoyance or exasperation, or as metaphors or as techniques of understatement or overstatement (also known as **hyperbole**), for poetic/creative effects. By flouting a conversational maxim, the speaker is deliberately drawing the hearer's attention to a form of implicit meaning. While abiding by the conversational maxims is conceptualised as the prototypical manner in which conversation takes place, flouting maxims and searching for implicature to arrive at the implied meaning of utterances happens with regularity in everyday conversation.

Consider how often you break Grice's conversational maxims in everyday interaction, using the above examples as a guide.

Politeness principles

Lakoff (1973) was the first to suggest principles of politeness with accompanying rules: showing formality by avoiding imposition, making the hearer feel good by showing camaraderie and showing deference to the hearer by giving options (see D5). However, Leech's principle is the better known and more thoroughly worked-out principle with an accompanying set of maxims. Leech coined the following politeness principle to work alongside the co-operative principle:

Minimise (all things being equal) the expression of impolite beliefs; maximise (all things being equal) the expression of polite beliefs.

(Leech 1983: 81)

The use of indirect speech acts can be frequently attributed to abiding by the principles of linguistic politeness. Following Grice, Leech (1983: 104–5) coined a set of politeness maxims to accompany his principle. The four most significant maxims are as follows:

- tact
- generosity
- approbation
- modesty

Each of these four maxims follows the 'maximise' and 'minimise' style of the politeness principle itself. With tact, speakers should 'minimise cost to other' and 'maximise benefit to other'. With generosity, speakers should 'minimise benefit to self' and 'maximise cost to self'. With approbation, speakers should 'minimise dispraise of other' and 'maximise praise of other'. With modesty, speakers should 'minimise praise of self' and 'maximise dispraise of self'.

Work your way through these four politeness maxims and write down scenarios from your day-to-day interactions where you have abided by these principles. Did these strategies always work in maintaining co-operativeness and harmony? Can you think of scenarios where you did not abide by these politeness maxims? If so, what happened?

By far the most influential theory of pragmatic principles for politeness is Brown and Levinson's (1987) set of politeness universals. Although Brown and Levinson's theory has been criticised, it does provide a systematic account of the crucial role that politeness plays in the conversational strategies we use when interacting with one another. Many pragmatics researchers still draw upon many of the specific principles from Brown and Levinson's work.

Brown and Levinson's (1987) theory is based upon the concept of **face**: the public self-image that all rational adults across all cultures possess. Face consists of two components: **negative face**, the desire to be unimpeded, and **positive face**, the desire to be liked, admired or needed. All participants in spoken interaction emotionally invest in face, and it must be constantly considered. Influenced by Grice's co-operative principle, Brown and Levinson argue that it is in the mutual interests of interactants to maintain each other's face in conversation. Strategies known as **positive politeness** and **negative politeness** are identified to attend to individuals' positive and negative face, respectively (see below). They are designed to enable interactants to abide by the co-operative principle.

If a demand or an intrusion needs to be made on another person's autonomy, then this is identified as a potential **face-threatening act** (FTA). When speakers are posed with performing an FTA, they first have to decide whether it should be performed *on record* or *off record*. The off-record strategy enables a speaker to avoid responsibility for performing an FTA by inviting conversational implicature. Speakers also have the option of not performing the FTA at all.

However, if the FTA is to be performed, then a speaker can do this in one of the following ways:

- Bald on-record, without redressive action: examples are 'Give me that!' or 'Get out!' According to Brown and Levinson, speakers will only perform an FTA without politeness strategies if a situation is urgent or in the interests of efficiency. For example, if the room is on fire, a speaker would be wasting time addressing the hearer's face needs – instead, we would expect the speaker to issue a bald, on-record direct command to stress the urgency of the situation and ensure that the hearer responds accordingly.

❑ Using positive politeness: where the speaker pays attention to the hearer's positive face needs by demonstrating that the hearer's wants or needs are thought of as desirable. Examples are as follows:

- ○ claim common ground
- ○ use in-group identity markers such as nicknames
- ○ express interest in hearer
- ○ seek agreement, avoid disagreement
- ○ exaggerate your interest, approval or sympathy with the hearer

❑ Using negative politeness: where the speaker desires not to impose on the hearer by restricting the hearer's actions, thus paying attention to the hearer's negative face needs. Examples are as follows:

- ○ question/hedge
- ○ indicate pessimism
- ○ minimise the imposition
- ○ give deference
- ○ apologise
- ○ impersonalise: 'patrons are reminded not to walk on the grass'

Negative politeness strategies will often co-occur, as in the following example: 'I'm terribly sorry to bother you, but I don't suppose I could borrow your computer for just a few minutes? I really wouldn't be that long'.

Brown and Levinson's concentration on strategies which avoid the performance of FTAs and their reliance on the co-operative principle has led to criticisms that they leave the area of **impoliteness** overlooked. Researchers have argued that it is impossible to have a comprehensive theory of politeness if impoliteness, a crucial part of the overall theory, is ignored. Culpeper (1996, 2005b) argues that, in order for a theory of politeness to be comprehensive, it is integral for the topic of linguistic impoliteness to be properly addressed and for strategies of impoliteness to be defined.

Culpeper (1996, 2005b) revisits Brown and Levinson's work and devises an opposite parallel strategy to account for impoliteness. Culpeper questions Brown and Levinson's belief that impoliteness is marginal to everyday conversations. He argues that it is far more common in everyday conversation than initially thought (by theorists such as Grice) and that an analytical impoliteness framework needs to be developed.

Culpeper defines impoliteness as follows:

Impoliteness comes about when: 1) the speaker communicates face-attack intentionally or 2) the hearer perceives and/or constructs behaviour as intentionally face-attacking, or a combination of (1) and (2).

(Culpeper 2005b: 38)

He coins the following impoliteness versions of Brown and Levinson's original strategies given above:

❏   Bald on-record impoliteness: this strategy is deployed where there is an intention to attack face, and this is performed in a direct, clear, unambiguous way. Here and in the definition of impoliteness, it is important to note that Culpeper draws upon the concept of a face attack act (FAA), first coined by Austin (1990), as opposed to an FTA, to distinguish clearly a *deliberate intention* to attack face.

In the following example taken from a documentary on parking attendants, the sequence highlighted in italics exemplifies a bald on-record FAA: 'You're a parking attendant act like one okay *shut up and act like a parking attendant*' (Culpeper et al. 2009: 1556).

❏   Positive impoliteness – damage positive face wants:
    ○   ignore/snub the other
    ○   deny common ground with the other
    ○   be disinterested, unconcerned, unsympathetic
    ○   select a sensitive topic
    ○   use inappropriate identity markers
    ○   use obscure/secretive language
    ○   seek disagreement
    ○   use taboo words
    ○   call the other names, etc.

❏   Negative impoliteness – damage negative face wants:
    ○   frighten
    ○   condescend
    ○   scorn
    ○   ridicule
    ○   invade the other's space literally or metaphorically

Additionally, Culpeper (1996, 2005b) inserts the following two categories:

❏   Sarcasm/mock impoliteness: a strategy performed with the use of politeness strategies that are obviously insincere, and thus remain surface realisations
❏   Withholding politeness: the absence of politeness where it would be expected, as in:
    ○   keeping silent
    ○   failing to act

(Culpeper 2005b: 41–2)

One of the main sources that Culpeper examines to demonstrate how his model of impoliteness works is media data – television programmes in particular. He has focused on documentaries, quiz programmes and films, where there is frequently conflict between interactants. Indeed, media data are productive sources to use for examinations of impoliteness, as in recent years there has been an observable move by multiple broadcast networks to produce shows where impoliteness directly correlates with entertainment.

Drawing upon Culpeper's impoliteness strategies listed above, consider how the following television programmes rely upon impolite interactions for their entertainment values – the majority of these programmes are broadcast around the world. Consider how strategies of impoliteness are realised in the shows listed. Add any other examples that you can think of (if you are not familiar with any of these examples, clips can be found online):

> *X-Factor, Pop Idol, America/Britain's Got Talent, Wife Swap, Jerry Springer, The Apprentice, Big Brother, The Weakest Link;*

several shows hosted by TV chef Gordon Ramsay:

> *The 'F' Word, Ramsay's Kitchen Nightmares, Hell's Kitchen.*

Why have these television shows based upon impoliteness become so popular in Western culture? Culpeper (2005b: 45) suggests the following reasons:

1. intrinsic pleasure: the thrill of arguing for its own sake;
2. voyeuristic pleasure;
3. the audience is superior: humour and pleasure can stem from the audiences laughing at others who are in a worse state than themselves;
4. the audience is safe (unlike if you were physically present witnessing a fight in a pub or on a street).

In Gordon Ramsay's television shows recorded and broadcast in the US, taboo words, and certain expletives in particular, are bleeped out. However, when *Ramsay's Kitchen Nightmares USA* was broadcast back in the UK, the expletives were put back in by UK programme producers and the bleeping was removed. This process neatly highlights a cultural difference in the boundaries of 'appropriate' language. The strength of the positive impoliteness strategy of taboo language appears to be evaluated differently in different English-speaking countries, reflected in the different practices adopted by programme producers.

Another criticism which has been levelled at Brown and Levinson's work is that whilst their model claims to be a set of universal principles, there are many differences in politeness norms and conventions across different cultures which cannot be accounted for by their approach. As we can see from the above example, this can happen within the same language and when spoken by the same individual but in a different cultural setting.

As we can see when considering World Englishes (Strand 10), the English language is used in a significant number of countries by a range of speakers from a multitude of cultural backgrounds. Politeness norms and conventions will vary from culture to culture even when the same language is spoken. Investigating inter-cultural and cross-cultural interactions from the perspective of politeness and pragmatics more generally can produce some very interesting findings in terms of cultural differences between different groups.

Maxims answers

At the bus stop: Quality
The arguing couple: Quantity
Student talk: Quality
The couple and the laundry: Relevance
Friends over dinner: Quantity (too much information) and Manner (unnecessary wordiness)

SYNTAX

Aside from labelling the parts of speech (see A4), the components of a sentence can be viewed in terms of what they do. This more **functional** approach to grammar impinges, to a certain extent, on semantics and pragmatics (see A3 and B3), since meaningfulness is being combined with syntactic form. Some grammars of English prefer to remain entirely at a formalist level – the most influential of these are the generative grammars which are exclusively interested in syntactic rules. In that approach, the rules by which allowable syntactic sequences are created or transformed into other well-formed clauses are the focus of formal notation. A famous early example is the rule of 'whiz-deletion', in which the underlying syntactic structure of a clause like 'the man who is fat', can lose the 'wh-' and the 'is', and the adjective moved to a pre-modifier position to produce the roughly equivalent 'the fat man'. This rule thus defines a well-formed pattern in English grammar.

Functional clause structure

However, in this unit, we will be more interested in the functional approach to syntax which tends to be the principle adopted where linguistics is applied to real-world utterances. In general, we can say that a clause can be divided into the operational constituents of subject, predicate, complement and adjunct (SPCA).

- ❏ A **subject** is the thing which enacts the verb in a clause. Subjects are typically agents, topics and the focus of the clause.
- ❏ A **predicate** is realised by the verb material in a clause. A predicate says something about what the subject does.
- ❏ A **complement** completes the meaning of a predication, supplying its objective or scope. Complements include direct and indirect objects (see below).
- ❏ Lastly, an **adjunct** is additional material that specifies the range or circumstances of the predication. Adjuncts can include adverbials, for example, but adjuncts are always removable from the sentence.

Here is a simple example – note that SPCA is the prototypical functional sequence in English:

S	P	C	A
Peter	finished	it	yesterday.

These functional slots can be filled with more complex material, of course:

S	P	C	A
Peter, tired from his exertions,	had finished off	writing the book	only a few days ago.

Here, the subject is a complex of a proper noun ('Peter') plus a qualifier that consists of another verb-phrase ('tired from his exertions') moved (or **rank-shifted**) to operate at a different level. The predicate in the second example is also realised by a more complex verb-phrase. In this example, 'writing the book' is the essential complement, again formed by the rank-shifting of another embedded verb-phrase. The last element, the adjunct, could be omitted from the clause; it merely specifies the predication.

Subjects can take several forms in English. The most common is the noun-phrase, as above. However, the subject slot can also be filled by an infinitive ('To be or not to be, that is the question'), material that is quoted or exemplified ('"I wish I were rich" is unrealistic thinking'), a nominalised gerund, a non-finite verb-form ('Running away is cowardly'), an expletive or dummy subject ('It is 3 p.m.', 'It's raining'), a cleft ('It was her phone that rang', where 'it' is the thing that happened), or a rank-shifted clause ('That I have run a marathon is amazing'). Subjects are usually but not always the **agents** or **actors** of the predication. For example, compare the active form of the sentence 'Louise read the book' and the passive form 'The book was read by Louise'. In the first instance, the subject is 'Louise', and in the second it is 'The book', but in both cases the actor is 'Louise' and the **goal** of the action is 'the book'.

Predicates are realised by verb-forms. Verbs require a subject, to the extent that utterances where a verb appears without a subject are understood as 'subject-less': 'Gone fishing', 'Running out of breath', 'Skipping, laughing, happy'. Some verbs also *require* a complement in the form of a **direct object**, as in 'I found the page', 'He kissed her' – these are **transitive** verbs. Where the verb is a copula (*to be*), as in 'The book was complicated', the complement here ('complicated') that relates to the subject ('The book') is called a **subject complement** or **intensive complement**. Examples like these always accompany the copula verb 'to be' ('am, are, is, was, were') where it is being used as a lexical verb ('He is fat') rather than as an auxiliary ('He is running'), and also with some other verbs such as 'seem, become, appear'. The following all include subject complements: 'That man is a fool', 'She seems strange', 'He is a policeman'. Though adverbial phrases usually operate as adjuncts (see below), sometimes where they follow these sorts of verbs and are not removable without doing violence to the sense, they are **adverbial complements**: 'Peter is in the office', 'Louise appears at the top of the bill'.

We can also talk of **object complements**, where an existing direct object complement is further specified: 'I labelled him an idiot', 'The people elected her president', 'They call the wind Maria', 'She painted the wall yellow'. Predications with object complements have two complementary elements (or two complements, if you prefer). These are different from verbs that have a second complement as an **indirect object**: 'I gave the book to her', or 'I gave her the book', where '(to) her' is the indirect object.

Predicates that do not require a complement at all are **intransitive** verbs: 'She smokes', 'The baby cries', 'The window shattered'. This last verb – 'to shatter' – is one of many examples that can be used intransitively (like it is in this case) or transitively: 'The boy shattered the window'. To illustrate the subject–agent distinction once again, these two sentences have different subjects, but could be uttered with the same agent in mind. In the first example, though, it is as if the event happened without an agent at all. 'The window shattered' is something the guilty boy might say as an account of the event.

Adjuncts are usually adverbial in form. Adverbs are commonly realised with '-ly' suffixes: 'quickly', 'softly', 'indubitably' – though 'yesterday', 'tomorrow', 'here' and 'fast' are also used adverbially as adjuncts. Adjuncts are removable without grammatical damage to the clause, and they establish things like the specification, range or scope of the predication. Examples of types of adjuncts would be 'I went to Nottingham', 'It appears at the end' (locatives), 'It happened one night', 'She arrived two days late' (temporals), 'I ate it because I was hungry', 'In order to get to the end, I worked all night' (causals), 'The book was read by Louise' (agentive), 'If I were rich, I'd travel now' (conditional), 'Although it was already midnight, I went out' (concessive), 'He broke the window with a brick' (instrumental), and 'We wrote the book together' and 'It happened without a sound' (scoping or modifying adjuncts).

Sentence realisations

So far, all the examples mentioned in this unit are illustrations of fully realised, declarative clauses, most of them in simple form. They are **declarative** because they make a statement about an aspect of the world (or another world): 'That man is fat' (or 'The unicorn looks beautiful'). Of course, sentences can appear in other forms too. **Negatives** deny a statement about the world: 'That man is not fat'. **Interrogatives** ask a question about the world: 'Is that man fat?' **Imperatives** give a command to the interlocutor: 'Lose weight!' **Subjunctives** point explicitly to unrealised, speculative or doubtful possibilities in the world: 'If I were fat, I'd be happy'. **Exclamatory** sentences make an intensive expression about the state of the world: 'What a fat man!'

These are simple sentences rather than compound or complex sentences because they consist of one single clause. A **compound** sentence consists of several clauses chained together with a **connective** of one sort or another ('and', 'then', 'but', 'though', 'so', 'because', and so on). The clauses in a compound sentence can stand independently of each other, even though the connective might establish a sequential, causal or blameful relationship between the clauses. Where one clause depends grammatically on another, the multi-clause sentence is then **complex**.

Sentences with relative clauses ('The man who was fat could barely walk') or subordinate clauses ('She told me that he was fat') are chained together with **subordinating conjunctions** ('that') or **relative pronouns** ('who, which'). In complex sentences, one clause is independent and the others are dependent on that main clause. Sentences can be multiply embedded, with an alpha (main) clause, and then beta, gamma, delta, and further Greek-labelled clauses to the point of comedy: 'The man who ate the huge pie which was full of steak that had been cooked by his mother who hadn't realised really how huge he was already, which was quite a mistake, given the fact that her son's health was suffering as a result of his poor diet, was fat'.

Sentences with a great deal of embedded subordination and a great deal of syntactic complexity are very common in legal language, where concepts need to be explicitly connected without the possibility of ambiguous reference across sentences. Surprisingly, complex subordination is also very common in relaxed spoken discourse, where speakers also include lots of meta-talk in order to help the listener keep track (for example, 'as I was just saying', 'so he – that is, the one I was talking about a second ago', and so on). In spoken discourse, conjunctions and relative pronouns often also introduce subordinations, and then the speaker never returns to the main clause level, as the conversation drifts (see B5). Participants in speech tolerate such incompleteness with ease.

When we say that clauses are 'fully realised', this describes their prototypical form. We often say things like 'See you later' (lacks subject), 'Nice-looking boy, on your left' (lacks predicate), and 'Faster' (lacks subject and predicate), but the fact that we can produce and understand these utterances suggests that there is general agreement not only about the fact that something has been omitted, but also about exactly what that something is.

Systemic-functional grammar

A particular approach to grammar that makes the function of the sentence the primary concern categorises clauses on the basis of what they do. This is **systemic-functional linguistics** (see, primarily, Halliday and Matthiesson 2004). For example, a clause expresses a **process** (expressed in a predication) involving one or more participants, whether human or not (carried by the subject and complement), in a circumstance or situation or manner (in the adjunct). This approach is not a purely syntactic one, since deciding what sort of process and what sort of participant is involved will often depend on the meaning of the clause in context. In functional grammar, then, semantics and pragmatics are implicated in syntax. This marks a divergence from many other approaches to grammar that are purely syntactic, but it brings advantages – especially where grammar is being used as the basis for an applied analysis.

For example, all predications are either material (they enact some concrete thing in the world), human (they express behaviour, cognition or speech), or metaphysical (they indicate some existential or relational process). In systemic-functional grammar, these functions of processes can be arranged in a system as shown in Figure B4.1.

Material processes express either something being done (material action) or a happening (material event). Where there is an action, if there is a wilful consciousness as the agent (such as a person), then the action can either be intentional or simply something that occurs to that consciousness (a supervention). So, 'I deliberately broke the glass' is a material action intention process; 'I accidentally dropped the glass' is a material action supervention process; and 'The glass broke' is a material action event process. Material processes have an essential **participant role** of **actor** involved, plus an optional participant of **goal**. In the first two examples here, 'I' is the actor, and 'the glass' is the goal. Other, less direct participants that could appear in material processes include **recipient**, **client**, **initiator**, **attribute** and **scope**.

Behavioural processes express predications which involve both physical material and mental processes, but which will not easily fit exclusively into either category alone. For example, 'He was breathing heavily', 'I dreamed a dream the other night',

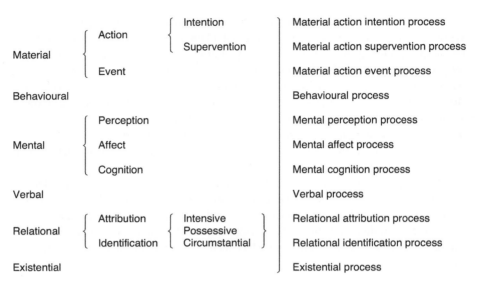

Figure B4.1 Functional processes

'She frowned'. Such processes tend to have only one participant, the **behaver**, though an indirect participant in the form of the behaviour itself could also feature ('She smiled a crooked smile').

Mental processes proper more usually have two participant roles attached, making them more commonly transitive in form. The participants are the **senser** role, typically in subject position, and the **phenomenon** that is sensed by the process. Mental perception processes involve pure sensing ('I saw three ships', 'It tasted fantastic'). Mental affect processes involve feeling ('She touched the rough bark', 'Lucy had the strangest feeling'). Mental cognition processes involve aspects of thought and recognition ('He wondered about her love for him', 'She concluded that it was impossible').

Verbal processes could be regarded as a sub-type of mental processes in that they are the externalised form of interior will, though in the most recent version of systemic-functional grammar they are treated separately. Any speech or writing, or any other communicative exchange (email, semaphore, telepathy), comes under this category. The primary participant roles are thus the **sayer** and the **target/recipient**. Of course, where the hearer or reader of the message is not the intended target of the message, we might want to distinguish them as the **receiver** rather than the target – for example, in an overheard conversation, or reading someone's diary.

The material that is expressed in a verbal process (usually in reported speech realised by a subordinate clause rank-shifted to complement position) is a participant termed **verbiage**. In 'He told me to return the next day', there are the participant roles of sayer ('He'), target ('me') and indirect verbiage (which directly would be 'Come back tomorrow'). Processes can be embedded in one another, of course. 'She overheard him telling me to come back tomorrow' features a verbal process embedded in a mental perception process.

Relational processes concern attribution and identification. The former requires the participants of **carrier** and **attribute**, where the attribute is ascribed to the carrier: 'The band was really good', 'Louise has a brand new Mini', 'The book is on the third shelf up'. Each of these express slightly different aspects: the first involves an **intensive** attributional mode, the second a **possessive** attributional mode, and the third a **circumstantial** attributive mode. Similarly, relational identification processes – where the **identifier** participant identifies the **identified** participant – can be expressed in each of these modes: 'Peter is the professor' (intensive identification, with 'Peter' as the identified), 'The Mini is Louise's car' (possessive), 'Tomorrow is my birthday' (circumstantial). A simple (though not fool-proof) test is that the participants in identifications can be reversed without damage to the identification process, whereas attributions cannot: 'The professor is Peter' (where 'Peter' has become the identifier), 'Louise's car is the Mini', 'My birthday is tomorrow'.

Lastly, **existential processes** account for all those situations in which there is an **existent** participant alone: 'It rained', 'There was a speech at the end'. In this second example, the material after the existential process acts as a circumstance. In general, circumstances are realised in adjuncts. Circumstances are a different sort of participant in the process, answering the following questions:

extent and location	–	where? how long?
manner	–	how?
cause	–	why?
accompaniment	–	with what?
matter	–	what about?
role	–	what as?

Altogether, the functional model of language provides a powerful and comprehensive tool for the analysis of language use in the world.

CONVERSATION

Our development of discourse will focus upon two classic areas of conversation analysis: the turn-taking system and topic.

Turn-taking

One of the most well-known frameworks within conversation analysis is the **turn-taking system**. This model was originally devised by Sacks, Schegloff and Jefferson (1974) and is based upon the norms of spoken American English. They argue that speakers follow an unwritten rule that only one speaker will speak at a time. If there is any cross-over between speakers, then it will be quickly and efficiently rectified.

They detail a systematic process of how a change in speaker turn takes place:

1. The current speaker will select the next speaker.
2. The next speaker will self-select.
3. The current speaker will continue speaking.

These options are presented in hierarchical order: the first option overrides the second, self-selection option, and self-selection overrides the third option of the current speaker continuing.

A basic premise behind the model is that speakers are attuned to particular places where speaker change can be taken. They call these points **transition relevant places** (TRPs). Some good examples of TRPs include pauses that occur at a clause or a sentence boundary, falling intonation, or body language signals such as the relaxation of a hand movement or sitting backwards.

Speaker change and the signalling of a TRP can also be indicated by what are known as **adjacency pair sequences**. These are defined as a set of two utterances whereby uttering the first pair part sets up an expectation of a second pair part. There are many adjacency pair sequence categories, including the following:

- ❑   question–answer
- ❑   greeting–greeting
- ❑   invitation–acceptance
- ❑   farewell–farewell

The second parts of these pairs above can be identified as **preferred responses**. If we ask a question, we expect an answer to be given. If we offer a greeting or a farewell, we expect to be offered one in return. If we give an invitation, a preferred response would be an acceptance. However, **dispreferred responses** may also occur if, for instance, someone refuses to answer a question; you greet someone and they do not reciprocate the greeting; you offer an invitation but the invitee declines; or you say goodbye to someone and they do not reply.

The performance of dispreferred responses such as needing to decline an invitation is heavily interlinked with politeness principles (see B3). The manner in which speakers utter dispreferred responses often involves the use of linguistic politeness strategies if the respondent wishes to pay attention to face and avoid being impolite. If not, then dispreferred responses can often be perceived as impolite behaviour.

Compare the first example below, where a dispreferred response is uttered to an invitation with face redress, with the second example of a dispreferred response without face redress:

Example 1
S1:   Do you want to come to my party on Saturday?
S2:   Oh (-) I'm really sorry. I'd love to be there with you, but erm my parents are coming over.

Example 2
S1:   Do you want to come to my party on Saturday?
S2:   No I don't.

Even if responses are dispreferred, adjacency pair sequences are still completed. However, if someone refuses to respond to a question, greeting or farewell, then there is no closure or completion of the sequence, potentially signalling impoliteness (or possibly humour) by a refusal to participate in turn-taking norms.

The performance of adjacency pair sequences may often be more complex than the above constructed examples show us. Speakers will frequently insert material before completion of adjacency pairs. Such instances are known as **insertion sequences**. Consider the following example taken from a recording in a telephone sales office:

1   Receptionist: Good afternoon {company name}
2   Sales rep.:   Oh good afternoon (.) could I speak to Mr Jones please?
3   Receptionist: May I ask who's calling please?
4   Sales rep.:   Yes certainly it's Steve Smith from {company name}
5   Receptionist: I'm sorry (.) Steve?
6   Sales rep.:   Steve Smith
7   Receptionist: One moment and I'll put you through

Whilst we have completion of the initial adjacency pair greeting sequence in a preferred, reciprocal manner in lines 1–2, the first pair part of the sales representative's question in line 2 is responded to not with an answer but with another question. The role of questioner thus shifts here: until the new adjacency pair sequence has been completed in a preferred way, the sales representative is not going to get his initial question sequence completed. There is then a further question sequence initiated by the receptionist, as she has not heard the caller's surname properly. The sales representative completes this question–answer sequence by repeating his surname. The initial question sequence from line 2 is then finally answered at line 7 with two embedded insertion sequences in between.

Some researchers have used the Sacks, Schegloff and Jefferson model as the basis of their own empirical studies and amended or developed it as necessary. Many have questioned the principle of the one-at-a-time floor. For example, Zimmerman and West (1975) produced a study which focused upon what they termed 'irregularities' with the model, which they classified as **overlaps** and **interruptions**. Overlaps are occasions where there is slight over-anticipation by the next speaker, whereas interruptions represent a violation of the one-at-a-time turn-taking system. Speakers can be witnessed engaging in simultaneous talk, sometimes for prolonged periods, as they battle for the conversational floor. This is simply not accounted for by the one-at-time model.

Holmes (1995: 52) aptly describes an interruption as a 'disruptive turn' in the discourse. In some speech events, interruptions will occur regularly. For example, in political broadcast interviews, where the turn-taking system is very competitive and turns are highly valued, interruptions frequently occur.

Can you think of other contexts where interruptions frequently occur because the turn-taking is competitive and turns are highly valued?

In addition to disruptive turns, simultaneous talk can also play a supportive function in conversational interaction. Edelsky (1981) coined a distinction between a **single floor** (the one-at-a-time model) and what she termed a **collaborative floor**, where speakers talk simultaneously, though unlike interruptions the purpose of this is to engage in the joint production of talk. She found that there were periods within university faculty meetings where the accepted turn-taking norms shifted from the single to the collaborative floor and then back again.

Similarly, Coates (1996) has categorised an **all-together-now** conversational floor (ATN) and a **one-at-a-time** floor (OAT). In the ATN floor, Coates argues that supportive simultaneous talk is very frequent. She characterises this as instances where speakers talk at the same time, producing co-constructed utterances. The voices of different speakers combine together, resulting in the joint production of discourse. Coates has observed this as a frequently occurring feature in research which she has carried out with all-female friendship groups.

To illustrate the all-together-now collaborative floor in action, we will examine an extract taken from an informal conversation between Jill and Sue, two speakers whom we have come across already in A5. On this particular occasion, we have used Coates' convention of inserting dotted lines in the transcription (see B12) to indicate simultaneous talk (these lines are analogous to a musical score in which several instruments play at once):

Jill and Sue are drinking coffee in Jill's living room. They are talking about a man who lives by them who they both frequently see in the neighbourhood.

```
--------------------------------------------------------------------------------
1  Sue:   he spends his life in the shops=
2  Jill:  =yeah (.) yeah I was gonna say whenever I go down to the
--------------------------------------------------------------------------------
3  Jill:  village [I always see you can bet your life you see him]
4  Sue:           [always in the shops there you know (xxx)     ]
--------------------------------------------------------------------------------
5  Jill:  [there (.) I suppose he's lonely isn't he    ]
6  Sue:   [he's in there then he's in the bread shop]
--------------------------------------------------------------------------------
7  Jill:  cos he's on his own like=
8  Sue:   =I ex-expect so yeah
--------------------------------------------------------------------------------
```

Based upon the conversational structure in lines 3–4 and 5–6, it is clear that a categorisation of the one-at-a-time turn-taking system simply does not account for what is taking place in this interaction. Jill and Sue talk at exactly the same time, collaborating and agreeing with one another by engaging in supportive simultaneous talk to produce their discourse jointly. They use repetition and say similar things at the same and at slightly different times.

While supportive simultaneous talk occurs very frequently in private, informal contexts, it can also take place in formal, public contexts. In the following example, which also utilises the 'musical score' style of transcription, we have two male business managers using supportive simultaneous talk during a business meeting:

The meeting participants have been discussing changes to stock ordering.
Rob is the meeting Chair and is drawing the discussion to a close.

---

1   Rob: So we just need to think about how we

---

2   Rob: [(-) how we can categorise] that [how] we look at it separately
3   David: [how we categorise on that]   [yeah]

In lines 2–3, David and Rob utter a remarkably similar utterance, almost saying exactly the same thing at exactly the same time. This is a classic illustration of supportive simultaneous speech and firmly indicates that they agree with one another. David reiterates his agreement by issuing 'yeah' simultaneously here too in line 3, something which is known as a **supportive minimal response**. This short utterance is not an attempt to re-take the floor, but is instead a signal of active listenership and agreement.

Come up with other contexts, either formal or informal, where supportive simultaneous talk takes place, using the above examples as a guide.

Topic

Another area of examination which conversation analysts focus upon is that of conversational **topic**. Again, context is a crucial consideration. In informal settings where conversation is progressing well, topic change usually occurs gradually: there is **topic drift** as speakers gradually move from one topic to another. This contrasts with more formal settings, particularly institutional or organisational settings such as courtrooms or, to a lesser extent, business meetings. In courtroom settings, the turn-taking system is rigidly governed by the judge. In business meetings, particularly formal, pre-planned encounters, it is common practice for a written agenda which formally lists the topics to be covered to be circulated beforehand. It then becomes the job of the meeting chair to ensure **topic shift** during the meeting according to the order of the written agenda text. In contrast to topic drift, successful topic shift should take place swiftly and deliberately. Agenda-based topic shifts can be achieved quickly and concisely, as participants are all aware of what the topics will be beforehand. This is illustrated in the meeting extract below:

Meeting Chair Chris has been discussing financial budgets, a specified topic on the meeting agenda. He is bringing this topic to a close.

1   Chris: Errm I have it on memo I'll get you the information
2   Stuart: Yeah (.)
3   Chris: Okay (.) recruitment
4   Jim: Yeah
              ((Chris talks on the topic of recruitment followed by discussion))
5   Chris: You okay with that Stuart yeah?
6   Stuart: Okay
7   Chair: Okay so if you can work towards that that will be great (-) err
8   a couple of revised store aims (.) at tills . . .

At line 3, Chris initiates topic shift from 'financial budgets' to 'recruitment', the next specified topic listed on the meeting's written agenda. He signals this transition by use of 'okay', a **discourse marker**, marking a transition in the interaction, followed by a short pause and then direct naming of the next agenda item. In line 5, he checks Stuart is happy with what they have agreed to do regarding recruitment, summarises what Stuart needs to do, and then positively evaluates this. The topic shift is then signalled by a lengthy pause, a hesitation 'err'. The next topic is then asserted by a declarative (like 'recruitment', this topic was listed on the written agenda as 'revised store aims') followed by a short pause. The details of the topic then begin with 'at tills'.

Although topic change in informal settings is a much less rigid process, speakers do need to signal why they are introducing a particular topic at a particular moment in time. Even in the most informal of contexts, where speakers know each other very well, there is still a need for new topics to be justified, otherwise speakers run the risk of being negatively evaluated as conversational bores or as individuals who ramble on rather aimlessly, without paying adequate attention to the need for topical relevance. This leads us back to politeness and the importance of paying attention to face needs (B3).

In the following example, Jill introduces a new topic first by carefully ensuring that the previous topic is finished. After two evaluative comments on the previous topic ('oh dear' and 'arrrrr') and a lengthy pause, she then establishes the new topic's newsworthiness, thus justifying why this particular topic shift and why now. As with Jill and Sue's example of supportive simultaneous talk above, this is a rather collaborative enterprise:

> *Jill and Sue are talking about a man who lives by them whom they both frequently see in the neighbourhood.*
>
> 1   Sue: I think his sister nags him so he doesn't stop too long
> 2   Sue: [((laughs))]
> 3   Jill: [((laughs] oh dear (.) arrrrr (-) did I tell you (.) errm my niece
> 4   Jill: had a baby (.) I don't think I did did I? You know I said she
> 5   Jill: was having her fourth baby (.) did I tell you Sue?
> 6   Sue: I said to Suz- to you about Sharon having a baby
> 7   Sue: didn't I=
> 8   Jill: =that's right
> 9   Sue: having a baby daughter and you says 'oh my niece is waiting
> 10   Sue: [to have her baby']
> 11   Jill: [she was   ] due (.) she she had the baby two two
> 12   Jill: weeks old this week

Jill negotiates the newsworthiness of her new topic by asking Sue whether she has told her before that her niece had given birth (lines 3–4). She back-tracks further by asking Sue to confirm that she had told her that her niece was pregnant (line 5). These questioning strategies help Jill ascertain both the newsworthiness of the topic and aid her in confirming exactly where she needs to start the topic, ensuring that she does not repeat any information that may have been given already. Following confirmation from Sue, where Sue recounts one of their previous conversations and reports Jill's previous speech to her (lines 6–7 and 9–10), Jill goes ahead with her topic (lines 11–12).

Consider the last conversation you had which took place in a similar context to Jill and Sue's conversation. What topics did you talk about? Did the topic drift or shift? What does this tell you about your relationship with these speakers?

In overall summary, in this unit the tools and techniques of conversation analysis have been investigated. Producing analyses of the various facets of the turn-taking system and topic can result in fruitful and thorough analyses of discourse being produced in a multitude of different settings.

LITERACY

Writing is not simply speech written down. Though of course there are close connections and influences between speech and writing, it is better to think of writing and speech as two distinct but cognate systems, both of which represent the more abstract system of language. The distinctiveness between speech and writing can be seen right across the structure of language in each case. A simple comparison of a conversation and a passage of written text will quickly reveal significant differences in vocabulary choice, fluency, clause length and complexity, sequencing of the main point, and address forms, among many other variations. To give only a few examples:

❑   Speech is prototypically dialogic; writing is – at least initially – more monologic. So speech tends to have more explicit second-person address forms, imperatives, invitations, and supportive feedback phrases than writing.

❑   The basic unit of speech is the utterance or turn; in writing it is the clause. So speech turns tend to consist of simple clauses, whereas writing often features complex or compound multi-clause sentences.

❑   Speech tends to be spontaneous; writing tends to be planned. So writing is more likely to feature multiple logical relative clauses such as 'if . . . , and . . . , or . . . , then . . .', or 'because of this, which . . . , then . . .', and so on, and speech is more likely to have vague words like 'stuff' and 'thing'.

❑   Speech is tolerated in many accents; writing tends to have a strongly prestigious and standardised form that is socially preferred and sanctioned. So variation in pronunciation is accepted, whereas variation in spelling is not. English spelling largely represents medieval pronunciation at the point at which printing froze many spelling forms ('through', 'knight', 'name'). Even in languages that have a more phonetic spelling relationship (such as Italian), there are still various accents that can be used for a single unchangeable spelling.

❑   Speech tends to be face-to-face; writing tends to be displaced in time and space. So speech tends to consist of two or more people taking turns, asking questions, offering opinion and viewpoint explicitly. Writing tends to be free of the context, whereas speakers can refer to 'this', 'that' and 'those' things that are in their immediate vicinity, without further explanation.

❏ Speech exists in the aural medium, whereas writing is visual. So speech features more sound effects, intonation-effects and emphatic gestures, whereas writing relies more on shape and structure, and is only able to signal sound effects iconically.

Becoming literate

Clearly, we acquire speech before writing (see A6): speech has a 4–5 year head-start on writing in most formal education systems of the world. This means that pre-school children only have one system for representing language (their speech) before they are encouraged to learn another (writing), and so early writing is strongly affected by the child's speech capacities at age 5. Between this point and the early teens, both speech and writing skills continue to develop and influence each other. In this unit, we will outline the stages of the development of literacy in these years.

The general assumption for most people would be that children's writing development begins with learning the alphabet and being able to write the letters – though of course ABC (/aɪ biː siː diː iː ɛf dʒiː/) rather than abc (/æ bə kə də ɛ fə gə/ and so on) are learned first. People might assume that simple phonetic words ('cat', 'dog', 'went') are then learned, followed by words with digraphs ('the', 'ship', 'chop') and non-phonetic words with various irregular or 'magic' rules ('time', 'brought', 'knife'). Then, it might be supposed that sentences are learned with spaces between words, punctuation and capital letters, and that finally sequencing of narratives and other text-level genres are mastered.

In fact, literacy development is much more complicated than this, with several of these processes developing alongside each other. The evolution of narrative skills, for example, can be observed at a very early stage, even if those narratives are very simple or apparently poorly formed from an adult perspective. It is important to realise – as with the acquisition of speech – that child-literacy should not be viewed as an imperfect version of adult writing, with errors and omissions, but as a form in its own right which gradually comes to converge with adult writing. Children's written capacity is usually roughly sufficient at each stage for the level of expression that they require. As these expressive requirements advance alongside their socialisation into a print-rich culture, so their need for literacy development advances too.

Scribble script

Children, especially those with older siblings, will scribble circles and whirls while colouring or drawing that they regard as writing. This initial stage of pre-school 'writing' is important both in mechanical training and in the conceptualisation that marks have representative meaning. In the transition around initial schooling, children will often imitate adults' practices in writing – typically this will involve writing notes or shopping lists. Children's pre-school shopping lists will look like scribbled lines, though (Western) features such as linearity, left to right and top to bottom, and gaps between 'words' can often be noticed even at this stage. Children will 'read' out their shopping lists as genuine grocery items, though of course their spoken list will change each time they 'read' aloud: they do not in fact have their own secretly denotational scribble system.

Naming and captioning

One of the first recognisable words to appear is the child's own name. Being able to recognise your own name (to identify possessions, your coat peg, or just for the fun of it) is a skill that adults encourage at an early stage, and children quickly learn to shape their own name in writing. The letters of the child's own name are often those which are also most strongly learned and recognised in other words. It seems that the first function of this genuine writing is labelling and captioning, with self-drawings of the child being named in writing, and then other family and friends being labelled and other drawn objects similarly captioned. Sequences of captioned drawings, or a network of labels on a page of paper are used narratively – often the story is told as the child draws/writes it radially on the page, rather than in a linear sequence that can be read out afterwards.

In these early stages, children's attention is focused largely on mastering the mechanics of making legible letters of roughly equal size; ensuring that the direction-ality of letters is right (contrasting 'p'/'q' or 'b'/'d' or 'n'/'h'); writing left to right along a line and top to bottom down a page; creating spaces between words by placing a finger after the last letter; and not writing off the margin onto the table-top. This *preparation* stage develops into a *consolidation* stage after a couple of years, at which time children are able to express their speech in writing. Later, they can *differentiate* speech patterning from writing, and lastly – by ages 9–10 – most children possess *integrative* knowledge to be able to choose which blend of patterning is most appro-priate for their communicative purpose.

Pattern-generation

Children begin to experiment with patterns that seem to constitute their own rules and principles as soon as they begin to learn letter shapes, syllable shapes and word shapes. For example, many schools using a 'phonics' approach teach the small letter sounds (/æ bə kə/ not /ai biː siː/) first. Non-phonetic vocabulary is a challenge to a pure phonics approach ('lamb', 'lame', for example), so children will try to create their own pattern: 'lam' for *lamb* and 'lAm' or 'laam' for *lame*. Similar patterns will be applied across a large range of words.

The patterns that children generalise cannot be regarded as rules, though, since they are often highly variable. So 'pole' for target *poorly* does not always get generalised to produce 'hole' for *holy*, though *holly* might be spelled 'hole'. Similarly, a child who uses a capital to signal the vowel shift produced by CVCe (consonant-vowel-consonant-e as in 'name', 'mite', 'fame') as in 'lAm' for target *lame* might on other occasions use doubling 'shiin' for *shine* or a variant digraph 'piel' or 'payl' for *pile*, and so on. Word boundaries are also flexible, so 'wonsa pona taym' for *once upon a time* or even 'wyanetn' for *wire netting* have been observed. Clearly, these are also influenced by pronunciation and accent patterns.

Vocabulary development in writing is obviously dependent on the size of the child's spoken vocabulary. For example, a child whose past tense of 'bring' is 'bringed' will not recognise 'brought' as a genuine word. This is a good example where the experience of the written form is likely to expand the spoken repertoire. In general, though, the influence is the other way around. Early vocabulary (up to age 10) tends to develop by the acquisition of new words and their extension by derivation (plural -s, person agreement, tensing and aspectuals), whereas the adaptation of complex morphology seems to be a late skill: so younger children are unlikely to write 'unlikely' even though they might have 'like' and be able to read and understand the prefix 'un-' and the suffix '-ly'. As vocabulary extends in later years, children make use of synonyms to avoid lexical repetition for aesthetic and cosmetic reasons.

Speech-influence to written conventions

Early examples of coherent writing are often strongly speech-like. Since the sentence is not a unit of speech, children initially do not have a representative model for the main unit of writing, and so their production echoes oral turns very closely. As children develop the ability to chain clauses together in writing, after two or three years of schooling, the clauses are less likely to be connected simply by 'and' and more likely to be related in more logically complex ways using 'though', 'because', 'before', 'while', and so on. Ultimately, the use of conjunctions decreases altogether as clausal apposition, relative clauses, and implicitness in logical argument take a more sophisticated role. At the same time, conversational tags ('like', 'you know'), which might have appeared in some form early on, are discarded. Conversational vocabulary choices ('stuff', 'like that', 'and all') are replaced by more formal choices.

Narrative and other generic discourse patterns emerge, so that the opening of a text will signal (often in a headline title) what the passage is about; the text will begin with orientation to help the reader create the participants and setting; the core of the text itself will feature embedded evaluations and other commentary that digresses from the main line of the story or argument; and the text will end with a reiteration of what the point of the writing was, or some sort of conclusion. Narrative is the most popular form of school text, with the majority of children's writing focusing on recounting experience, and the majority of reading scheme books being narrative in orientation.

Freeing from bound context

Gradually, as literacy develops, children's writing moves from being bound to the context to becoming context-free. In other words, it becomes possible to read children's texts without needing to be in the same surroundings as the child in order to under-stand the referents. 'This', 'these', those' and ambiguous 'it' or 'he' begin to be introduced with full identifications, followed by co-reference: 'There was a boy. He was called Eric'. This shift indicates a growing awareness of the diversity of audience that writing has that speech does not easily have. Children like to write cards or letters to family, grandparents, neighbours and friends who are not immediately in the environment. These developments involve learning about registers and genres.

For example, early children's writing often involves an explicit signal in the begin-ning that the pragmatics of the current situation are suspended ('Once upon a time') and a symmetrical signal at the end that the classroom pragmatics are resumed ('and they all lived happily ever after'). As a child develops the ability to adopt a cognitive stance that is fictional or otherwise projected, the finalising signal is dropped, and then later the opening signal is dropped: story stance comes to be signalled in the shift to other, more subtle and sophisticated features of writing.

SCHEMAS AND WORLDS

Imagine you are walking into what you think is a restaurant on the planet Zog. You think it is a restaurant because you have been directed there by a friendly English-speaking hotel barman, but you do not speak, read or have any telepathic ability in Zogan, the language of Zog. Obviously, it is a problem that you lack the necessary linguistic knowledge, so – Zogan technology being quite advanced – you download the grammar and vocabulary from a free online site directly into your brain. The grammar at least is surprisingly like the Yorkshire dialect of twenty-first-century English. Filled with confidence, you stride into the restaurant. You see no tables or chairs, only tanks of clear pink liquid in which there are either plants or fish – you are not sure which. 'Can I get something to eat here?', you ask the Zogan person who burbles up to you. 'Aye, yer [singular] can', says the Zogan, and slithers away, leaving you standing there. You do not know what to do; all you can think is that you are very hungry and you picture a plate of roast beef, vegetables and Yorkshire puddings with gravy. In an instant, you feel full and not hungry any more, so you leave the restaurant. Later, over a cup of steaming cold ztroob in the hotel bar, the barman explains that in Zogan restaurants your order is taken telepathically and the food is instantly teleported into your stomach. You discover that the exorbitant cost of the food has also been teleported out of your wallet. It was the most expensive restaurant in the whole of Zog.

You might have found yourself in a similar – though probably not identical – situation at some point in your life, where an unfamiliar context caused you communicative problems. In the Zogan restaurant, in spite of possessing well-formed syntax and the right vocabulary, choosing what to say and do has defeated you because you do not have the appropriate frame of knowledge that will allow you to function properly in the situation. Of course, the next time you visit a Zogan eaterie, you will be better prepared: your first-time mistakes constitute a process of learning how this situation works.

Storing linguistic knowledge

In psycholinguistics, any knowledge frame that you need to behave appropriately is a **schema** (plural 'schemata', though the anglicised form 'schemas' is more common). Many approaches within linguistics have required a vague category of 'encyclopedic knowledge' that a hearer or reader has to deploy in order to make sense of what is being said. **Schema theory** is an attempt to specify exactly how this works. Though philosophers have suggested earlier versions of schemas, the theory itself was invented in the 1960s as part of the search for creating artificial intelligence. It quickly became apparent that computers and software needed a sense of experience and context to be able to communicate in anything like a natural human way.

The problem for researchers is deciding which part of the vast array of knowledge is relevant for a particular moment of language use. For example, when we walk up to a (terrestrial) restaurant, it is clear that our knowledge of science fiction stories, beach holidays, dog-walking or the many thousands of other areas of our general knowledge is not likely to be as relevant as our knowledge of restaurants. Although all of our previous experiences of individual restaurants might be stored in memory, when we enter this particular new restaurant, we are drawing on an idealised, distilled representation of all of those experiences: this idealised, *schematic* model is a schema.

We know that we need our restaurant schema because we are standing in front of a restaurant. Where the location defines the appropriate set of knowledge, a **situational schema** is invoked. Where the schema that is required depends on your individual role – such as being a train passenger, being a boyfriend, or being a gardener – you will draw on a **personal schema**. And where you need operational knowledge and skill to be able to do something – such as drive a car, write an essay, or mend a chair – you will use an **instrumental schema**.

These different sorts of schemas tell you what to expect, and how to behave, including how to behave linguistically (and the prominence of language behaviour in schemas led to an earlier version in the theory being referred to as **scripts**). Your choice of words will be different when you are in different schemas with different expectations of formality, for example. Your choice of syntax will vary, your sense of pragmatic requirements like interruptions, politeness or rudeness norms, your sense of turn-taking in conversation – all of these features of language will vary depending on the schema you think is most appropriate. Misjudging the schema can lead to confusion, hostility, rudeness, or just a plain failure of communication.

Using linguistic knowledge

A particular schema is invoked by various forms of **header** that trigger the most appropriate set of knowledge and behaviour. Being physically in the location where a particular schema usually occurs is an obvious trigger for that schema: examples such as standing in front of a restaurant, or being at a football game, or attending a family party would all instantiate the restaurant, football or party schemas by a **locale header**. Where the schema is prepared by some gesture or reference in advance, this is a **precondition header**. So being hungry, or driving past a restaurant, or receiving an invitation to a meal would all act as triggers for the restaurant schema.

Where the trigger is primarily an action which is a means of realising the schema, such as booking a table at the restaurant, this is an **instrumental header**. Lastly, and especially in written texts which displace your thinking to some other, virtual schema different from the here-and-now, an **internal conceptualisation header** is where some element from within the schema is mentioned or encountered. For example, a scene from a film that opens at a restaurant table, or in a hotel kitchen, is likely to instantiate the restaurant schema.

Once the schema is running, definite references can be made without sounding odd. For example, in a narrative with a restaurant schema in operation for the hearer, the storyteller can say things like 'The waiter arrived', 'The food was cold' or 'The tip was generous' without you becoming confused ('Oh, was there a waiter?', 'What food?', 'You didn't say they left a tip') and without the storyteller having to set out all of the objects in the situation ('There was a waiter', 'Some food was brought', 'We left a tip').

There usually needs to be more than one header to trigger a schema, unless the header is especially prominent or central to the schema in question. So being hungry might not invoke the restaurant schema by itself, but entering a restaurant by itself would. Where a single header belongs to a schema, but is not enough to trigger the schema fully, the script or schema is said to be **fleeting**. For example, passing by a restaurant on the road (a single locale header) might create a fleeting restaurant schema, but not stopping would cause that frame of reference to fade quickly from consciousness. Different types of headers often combine, and of course the more that are combined, the stronger the likelihood that a particular schema will then be instantiated. For example, having booked a table, you are welcomed by a waiter at the entrance to a restaurant just as you are really hungry – it is almost inconceivable that at this point you would be running anything other than a restaurant schema.

A schema, by definition, is a schematised representation of an ideal experience, but it is possible to examine the compositional elements that make up a schema. Any such frame of knowledge will consist of various **slots** that are filled out to create a rich representation of the situation at hand. Examples of these slots include **props** (all the objects that usually occur in the schema scenario) and **participants** (the expected people in the situation). So strong is the inventory of props and participants in a schema that the word 'but' in the sentence 'We went into the restaurant but it was empty' seems entirely natural, while in the sentence 'We went into the restaurant but there were waiters and tables there' it seems odd.

It is this sort of example that demonstrates the centrality and importance of schemas when considering how language works.

Aside from the preparatory headers that instantiate a schema, the schema itself will often have a narrativised sequence of further slots that is normal and expected. The restaurant schema typically has **entry conditions** involving walking into the restaurant, sitting down, and ordering food. There is an expected **sequence of events** within the narrative of the schema, involving eating, drinking and conversation, and completing the restaurant schema has **results** that are usually satisfaction, or food poisoning, or going home. Even non-situational schemas (personal and instrumental scripts) possess typical props and participants, and are often conceptualised in narrative terms with opening, sequential and resulting features.

Adapting linguistic knowledge

Restaurants without central slot elements are a challenge to comprehension that might motivate an enrichment of the schema on the one hand, or confusion on the other: a restaurant without tables, chairs or a menu (a tapas bar, for example); a restaurant without waiters (a self-service joint); a restaurant with nothing and nobody there (closed down?).

Most everyday discourse consists of the normal and expected application of schema knowledge without problems. This confirmatory experience is **schema preservation**, and it can even be seen on repeated exposure as being **schema reinforcement**. However, we occasionally encounter scenarios in which the schema is disrupted to a minor extent: there was a restaurant chain called 'Dans le Noir', in which diners ate in complete darkness, for example, which represents a conceptual as well as practical challenge. One way in which these disruptions can be resolved is by **schema accretion**, or the enrichment of an existing schema. So rather than create a new 'sensory deprivation restaurant' schema, you simply expand your existing schema to include this new aspect of the frame of knowledge. Your schema acquires a richer inventory and complexity of slots, or you establish a greater number of **tracks** through your schema.

Where the challenge is more radical (you might find yourself transported in a science fictional scenario to a 'restaurant at the end of the universe', for example), there might be a complete retuning of the schema so that the schema itself is radically reconceptualised: this is **schema refreshment**. Where your past conception of a schema turns out to have been completely wrong (sailing towards the edge of the flat Earth, you discover the planet is actually a globe), this is a thorough **schema replacement**: fundamental shifts in knowledge and understanding are involved here.

Schemas, then, are experiential frames for understanding concepts, situations and the discourse that accompanies them. They can be highly conventional and fixed, or adaptable and flexible, or very provisional and transitory: one of your book's authors once deployed a very sketchy schema for assisting a vet at the delivery of a calf, a schema that he possessed largely through television and books rather than any direct experience. For the vet, this schema was a very rich and fixed one; as an Arts Faculty academic, it is highly unlikely that Peter will ever need it again.

Schemas display prototype effects (see A7) in the sense that there are central parts of the schema and more peripheral aspects of the schema. Furthermore, some schemas will be regarded as central parts of our lives, and these will tend to be the most fixed domains with which we feel most comfortable. Others will be relatively sketchily formed or even barely existent. For new experiences at these edges of our lives, we will need either to create new schemas, or adapt very heavily schematic knowledge that we already possess.

Text-worlds

It should be apparent from the examples above that our understanding and per-formance of language is intimately related to the setting or **world** that pertains at the time. Noun-phrases can successfully refer to entities that are in our schematic knowledge, regardless of whether the referent objects are physically in front of us, elsewhere in time or location, or are fictional, imaginary, supposed or non-existent. You could argue that 'The unicorn is beautiful' can have a truth-value, but only if it is uttered within a world (a non-actual one, in this case) in which unicorns exist. Our ability to invoke a schematically appropriate world to deal with utterances like this seems to develop at a very early age.

The notion that we run a schematised set of world-knowledge in every linguistic encounter explains how our mental representation of a situation is usually richer than the bare words themselves would allow: essentially, we 'fill in' the details from our experience. This experience does not have to be personal and first-hand – as a result of reading this unit, you would be better equipped to deal with a Zogan restaurant, for example. Since we are talking about a schematic world which is text-driven and helps us process language, we can refer to this mental representation as a **text-world**.

A text-world is placed in mind by *world-builders* (all the references to objects and people), and runs in our minds by *function-advancers* (typically, verbs and other markers of events and processes). Of course, we can also follow conversations or texts in which other possibilities are built for us (speculations, imagination, jumps in time, fictions, and so on), and these can be captured as *world-switches*. So, for example, with the utterance 'Don't think of an elephant', what we would typically do is construct a matrix text-world in which someone has said that sentence to us for a particular purpose. We would need to imagine a world-switch in which there is an elephant, but recognise that this elephant was in a negational sub-world. This neatly captures the sense that a negation foregrounds the thing that is supposed to not be there!

The linguistic features that trigger world-switches are:

- ❑ negation
- ❑ modalisation ('might', 'could', 'should', 'ought', 'may', 'believe that', 'want', and so on)
- ❑ flashbacks and flashforwards
- ❑ metaphors (literally true in the sub-world, but not in the text-world)
- ❑ direct speech (that is, into the perspective of a text-world character)

So, for example, saying that something 'ought to be' the case creates a modal sub-world in which that thing *is* the case – and we can then think of it and understand it while bearing in mind that it is not really in the focus of attention.

Text-worlds are useful not only for thinking about fictional and speculative scenarios; they also seem to be the mechanism by which we keep track of different versions of characters and people, how we follow narratives and accounts of experience, and how we understand the relations between things that are referred to in language.

STANDARDISATION AND LANGUAGE CHANGE

All languages that have living speakers change over time. That change is unevenly distributed, so at any one moment there are always several varieties of the language in existence in different places. **Diachronic** change over time and **synchronic** variety across a point in time, then, are the proper and natural states of all living languages. Language change happens for many reasons, mostly a product of subconscious individual shifts or general drifts across large swathes of population that are too enormous to be perceived at any one moment. However, one of the reasons for change is an awareness that language is changing, which sometimes leads to a deliberate intervention by some people to prevent what they see as undesirable changes in the patterns of language. It is ironic that all of the attempts by everyone who has ever tried to stop language changing have ultimately failed and have often resulted in further and faster changes in the language.

Stability and change

In general, diachronically then, there are two contrary forces of *impulse* and *drag* operating on language across time. Impulse is given to language by the inexorable evolution of societies requiring new forms of expression for all the social complexities and fluid relationships that move over time. Drag acts as a brake on change in the form of types of expression that resist change: printing, the education system, governmental and administrative structures, and the desire for mutual intelligibility.

Synchronically, there are also two contrary forces of *diversity* and *homogenisation* operating on language across its territory of usage. Homogenisation is the tendency to converge all forms of the language together into a single variety, often by allocating **prestige** to the approved version and **stigmatising** the others. It is a tendency aimed for either intentionally or coincidentally by governments, the education system, and commentators on language such as journalists, academics and professional writers. Diversity is the opposite social force which resists language becoming monologic: language loyalty and innovation are the keys to diversity. In this unit, we will explore all of these ideas.

The historical forces acting to change language are largely social and economic. For example, the Great Vowel Shift (see A8) can be seen as a consequence of migration towards London from the East Midlands of England in the Middle Ages. As people from the wool villages and market towns moved to the capital in search of commercial wealth, they adopted the accent patterns of the Londoners in order not to appear too regional. This happened over many decades of migration. Unfortunately, whenever a person tries to pick up another accent deliberately, they often **hypercorrect** its features. Even more unfortunately, new waves of migrants to London set about imitating the hypercorrected accents of those recently arrived, adding their own accentuation again. The result was a general raising of vowel sounds that then became associated with the emerging middle class and that began to spread northwards and westwards throughout England.

In this case, geographical mobility reinforced by social mobility led to a major change in pronunciation patterns in English. Other social and economic events have led to changes in English. The colonial settlement of America, Australia and East Africa led to those parts of the world taking the accents and dialects of their settlers and beginning a new history that eventually diverged from the varieties of language spoken in Britain. Wars like those against France in the Middle Ages led to an adoption of English by the ruling class rather than French, and an expansion of vocabulary. Diseases like the great medieval plagues made English-speaking labour more scarce and thus more highly valued. Diseases worsened by economic policy, as during the potato famines of Ireland in the nineteenth century, led to mass migration of Gaelic and English speakers to America, where the common language was another form of English. The Industrial Revolution led to a clearance of the countryside towards the factories, mills and slum housing of the towns and cities, and new urban accents and dialects emerged.

Against these forces of language change, the contrary process of **standardisation** worked towards fixing the language. From the time of King Alfred in the ninth century, through the Tudors' nation-building policies of the later Middle Ages, to the education reforms of the nineteenth century and the national school curriculum of the late twentieth century, British governments have been interested in standardising the English language for ideological and political ends. The major tools of standardisation are in the domain of writing. The gradual replacement of manuscripts with printed books, leaflets and newspapers led to fixed spellings of words. Though Shakespeare, for example, was comfortable with variable spellings across the same text, these days spelling has become so standardised that poor spelling is even taken as a sign of a general lack of intelligence, or moral sloppiness.

When highly prestigious texts – such as Shakespeare and other literature, the Bible, government documents, announcements, laws and national newspapers – all adopt a particular variety of the language, this is known as codification (see A10 and B10). In medieval English, the East Midlands dialect from Nottinghamshire across to Cambridgeshire and down to London came to be adopted as the prestigious dialect of English for the same social reasons as set out above. Once codified in prestigious texts, it becomes the required norm in other texts. Dictionaries and grammars appear which treat the selected dialect as **Standard English**, to the extent that people no longer even call it a dialect. Other varieties of English come to be regarded as 'dialectal' and sub-standard. This codification is then preserved and promoted through the education system, so that the use of Standard English comes to be seen as the mark of the educated person, and it attracts even more prestige.

Standardisation, then, can sometimes be an accident of history as well as a deliberate act of **language planning**. In the later twentieth century, Standard English has very much been promoted as the 'correct' form of English, with many people becoming absurdly and hysterically outraged at any deviation from this standardised norm. 'Rules' of writing which are quite arbitrary, matters of fashion, or the idiosyncracies of influential people come to be treated as sacred:

❑ Double negation (properly 'negative concord') is condemned as if language worked by logic. 'I ain't never been there' is just emphatic. 'No no' does not mean 'yes'. Negative concord was standard until the nineteenth century.
❑ Preferring 'different from' to 'different to' is entirely wrongly argued by extension from the verb 'to differ'.
❑ Sentences like 'Hopefully the car will start' are condemned based on an incorrect model of grammar that does not recognise the pragmatic function of the adverb here.
❑ The rule against splitting an infinitive ('To boldly go') is a ridiculous imposition of Latin grammar (where it is impossible to do it anyway) onto English.
❑ Avoiding ending a sentence with a preposition ('Where are you from?') is also an import from Latin and would create bizarrely convoluted and obscure sentences: how odd does 'From where are you?' sound? Since English – unlike Latin – also has phrasal verbs in which the completors can be moved into final-sentence position, the pedantic rule has also been levelled at useful everyday idioms such as 'Turn the light off'.
❑ Complaining about abbreviations is simply a matter of taste. The eighteenth-century writer Jonathan Swift disliked these especially, condemning 'mob' (mobile), 'fan' (fanatick) and 'rep' (reputation), but shortening has been a continuing useful feature of English since its origins.
❑ Preferring '10 items or fewer' to '10 items or less' is an affectation based on an arcane grammarian's knowledge of count nouns that places pedantry over communicativeness.

Letters to the newspapers and fussy complaints about many of these cause them to find their way into the education system and become part of the standard written language.

The standard language ideology

Where this **prescriptivism** occurs throughout history, it is often accompanied by conservative moral politics and a nostalgic 'golden age' sense of history: language is always seen as becoming debased, distorted and corrupted. The slippage between language and moral judgement is often an easy one. Prescriptivism can be very powerful because prescriptivists are often in influential positions. Jonathan Swift set out a proposal for correcting and 'ascertaining' (that is, fixing forever) the English language. Samuel Johnson's *Dictionary* also had an improving aim and was sold alongside popular rules of grammar. In the UK, Prince Charles has made connections between slovenly grammar, slovenly appearance and lawlessness.

The elevation of one dialect as the prestige standard usually also involves the relative disparagement of the other varieties of the language. So, for example, writing in any dialect other than Standard English in anything but a very informal context would be regarded as improper, ignorant or even humorous over the last century. Of course, there are huge advantages in having a standard written form, since no accent or region is privileged. Any English user from any region or any part of the world can read this book – even read it aloud in any accent – without a hint of the Birmingham or Teesside accents of its two British authors.

Nevertheless, the tendency of much standardisation is towards the **homogenisation** of English. Traditional dictionary-writers and grammarians up until modern times, devisers of educational tools and curricula, and governments looking for national pride and cost-efficient schooling all dislike multiple possible versions of what needs to be taught. Testing and the awarding of qualifications is difficult if there is no standard answer. Dialectal variations are regarded as quaint curiosities, worthy of study for their 'folk' origins. The apparently reasonable position that encourages Standard English as a written norm which can be realised in any accent tends, in practice, towards a more sinister position in which an accent tending towards an educated south-eastern middle-class variant is held up as the 'natural' spoken form of Standard English. This used to be called Received Pronunciation or BBC English, though as mentioned in B1, even this has changed enormously over the last century and is currently in the process of being casualised towards the accents of other large cities (see B9 for further discussion and illustration).

Working against the processes of standardisation and homogenisation is what seems to be the natural condition of **diversity** in language use. Local innovations and changes in linguistic fashion, the movement of people into different contact situations, and the natural creativity of individuals and groups all produce a constant stream of new forms of English. Most innovations flutter and die, of course. Current faddish phrases will go the way of 'fab', 'groovy', 'ace' and 'so long daddy-o', but they will surely be replaced by hundreds more. Occasionally, when an innovation is particularly apt, or the user is particularly influential, or the use is especially persistent, the innovation will diffuse more widely through the local social culture and then into the language system in general. It will become standard and will eventually lose its innovative, non-standard origins.

Local innovations and non-standard varieties are sustained by language loyalty. Ironically, this can be seen as the local form of standardisation, which resists national standardisation of the language. People who speak with a Welsh, Northern English, or American or Australian accent, or who use Hiberno-English, West Midlands English or Geordie dialects don't simply do so because they have not yet got around to learning more standard forms: they maintain their variety as a matter of identity, both individual and cultural. It is virtually impossible to get a northern English person to say /kɑːsəl/ for /kasəl/ ('castle') or /rʌn/ for /rʊn/ ('run') or /fəʊn/ ('phone') for one of the several northern variants of that diphthong, and the reason is not inarticulacy or (primarily) hostility to southern forms, but rather a language loyalty to their own vernacular. Language loyalty maintains regional accents and dialects against national standardisation and homogenisation, but of course those local varieties are also subject to just as much change over time as the language as a whole.

LANGUAGE ATTITUDES   B9

Prestige, stigmatisation and language loyalty

As members of different speech communities, social networks and communities of practice, all of us have deeply ingrained attitudes towards language varieties which are learnt during the socialisation process. One of the most crucial topics of sociolinguistic **language attitudes** research centres on the notions of prestige and stigmatisation which we have already come across in A10 and B8. It is important to bear in mind that, while official language varieties such as Standard English are those imbued with the most power and prestige within societies, speakers from particular social groupings may find prestige in non-standard varieties. Attitudes towards prestige and stigmatisation are fundamentally dependent upon speakers' positive and negative perceptions of relations between different groups, which are significantly interrelated with perceptions of individual and group identities.

Sociolinguist Peter Garrett (2007: 116) gives a useful summary of the three different categories that are commonly thought to make up language attitudes:

❑ cognitive: beliefs and stereotypes
❑ affective: evaluations of one another
❑ behavioural: how we behave towards each other based upon our beliefs, stereotypes and evaluations

With the behavioural category, it is important to acknowledge that we cannot escape stereotyping one another on the basis of the language we use – we all have linguistic prejudices; they are unavoidable. However, it is crucial to recognise this and realise that our judgements about language usage are based upon linguistic prejudice – there is nothing inherent within the English language system (or any other language system for that matter) that makes one variety better or superior to another variety. The varieties encoded with the most social, political and economic power are those that become the most prestigious varieties. One key principle of sociolinguistics is that all language varieties are, and should be seen as, equally complex.

To explore this further, we will again consider Received Pronunciation (RP), which we came across in B1 and B8. RP is traditionally seen as the accent imbued with the most social, economic and political power in England, thus, historically at least, the accent with the most prestige and status. However, there is nothing *inherently* superior about this particular accent. RP is simply the variety that has come to be associated with the most social, political and economic power. Value judgements of 'correctness' and 'purity' are completely arbitrary. Additionally, RP is a phenomenon attached to the English spoken in England. It does not exist in Scotland or any other country in Great Britain, and it does not exist in other languages, such as German.

A classic illustration of the arbitrary nature of prestige is the example of rhoticity, which we have already come across in A8 and A9 – an accent feature positively evaluated and imbued with prestige in New York, yet associated with the non-standard, stigmatised varieties in south-west England and the north-west of the country in the county of Lancashire.

Our individual perceptions of which varieties have prestige and stigmatisation crucially depend upon our own accent and dialect and any **language loyalty** that we have towards particular varieties. As speakers, we also shift our speech styles depending upon context, as we have already seen in A9. We all regularly alter our styles along with a whole range of indexes that encode our social identities depending upon whom we are interacting with and in what specific setting the interaction is taking place.

These style shifts between different varieties can be either conscious or unconscious. For example, many of our students consciously report a change in accent and dialect from when they are at university to when they go home and interact with family and friends from their local or regional area. This is a result of individuals' conscious and subconscious awareness of beliefs and stereotypes of language usage and how people evaluate and judge one another on the basis of such language choices.

Interrelated with this is the fact that we frequently change our sociolinguistic speech styles in order to engage in a process of what is known as **accommodation**. The term accommodation is primarily associated with the work of Howard Giles (1973), who devised **speech accommodation theory** (SAT). The crucial notions within SAT are **convergence** and **divergence**. Convergence refers to how individuals build a sense of solidarity and collective group identity within particular speech communities, social networks or communities of practice by converging language practices such as adopting similar dialect features. Divergence describes the process by which we may differ our speech styles to signal social distance or the existence of an asymmetrical power relationship between ourselves and others.

In one of Giles' (1973) seminal speech accommodation works, he conducted a study on British schoolchildren's perceptions of particular character traits and accents. He discovered that speakers with an RP accent were perceived to be the most intelligent, whereas speakers with a Birmingham accent (a city in the West Midlands of England) were perceived to be the least intelligent.

SAT has been broadened out and renamed **communication accommodation theory (CAT)**. CAT includes the additional investigation of convergence and divergence in the form of fellow interlocutors' body language and gestures, as well as their spoken language styles.

Legitimate group membership of a speech community, social network or a community of practice is crucial in order to claim convergence with others in speech, body language and gesture. The following example illustrates the consequences of what can happen when legitimate group membership is not the case. Experimenting with different speech styles and producing a style that is deemed to go against fellow speakers' expectations can be very revealing in terms of pointing to the norms of accommodation, convergence and divergence.

Based on an activity devised by Ronald Wardhaugh (2009), sociolinguistics students at Nottingham were set the task of deliberately changing one small aspect of their speech style in particular contexts in order to reveal how communicative norms are deeply encoded with levels of formality and perceptions of speech community membership. They were asked to assess the consequences of their deviation from the expected norm on the basis of what happened subsequently in the interaction and then post a report of their findings on an electronic discussion board.

One student reported the following encounter, which focuses in particular upon the local Nottingham term of endearment 'duck'. She had conducted the small shift in speech style experiment in a café in the University's Students' Union building:

> After having a cup of tea in the Portland building a cleaner came to remove my cup. 'Have you finished with that Duck?' he asked. My natural response was to say, 'Yes thank you.' However I knew it was a perfect situation to put this task into practice and employ real informality where it is not appropriate, 'Yeah, cheers Duck' I said. The worker glared at me, picked up my cup, frowned and walked away . . . If I had used another term of endearment such as 'luv' it perhaps would not have been as offensive, but the fact that I repeated his term, which is also very much a feature of his Midlands dialect and therefore clearly uncommon to me, made it appear that I was mimicking and insulting rather than engaging in friendly exchange.

Individuals who are legitimate members of the Nottingham speech community and thus who share its speech norms can use 'duck' as a reciprocal term of endearment to one another, regardless of age and gender. However, on the basis of the cleaner's body language and gesture, he clearly did not perceive the student to be a legitimate member of the local speech community.

The **paralinguistic** features of the cleaner, the glare and frown, along with a lack of any further spoken communication after the student called him 'duck' appear to be clear signs that the student had broken the expected norms of this context, particularly in terms of lacking the required speech community membership to share legitimately in such solidarity-building behaviour in an asymmetrical power relationship. Thus, her reciprocal repetition of this lexical item, which would be evaluated as an in-group identity marker in other situations where membership is legitimate, fails.

Can you think of similar situations where reciprocal usage of a dialect feature has failed due to lack of speech community membership?

Attitudes in court

Negative attitudes towards language varieties based upon stereotyping and prejudice can potentially have very serious consequences, particularly in formal, institutional settings. A good example of this is how the language of the courtroom is assessed and evaluated. Sociolinguists have found that usage of certain regional accents and dialects in courtroom settings can lead to witnesses and suspects being treated as less trustworthy and less reliable. In an Australian courtroom context, Diana Eades (1992) has examined a difference in cultural interactional norms which leads to evidence presented by Aboriginal individuals to be perceived as unreliable.

Eades reports that a respectful silence is typically observed after a question is asked in Aboriginal communication. However, in a White Australian courtroom setting, Eades found that these silences have been viewed with a great deal of suspicion. They are negatively evaluated as strategic devices used to buy time in order to concoct an alternative version of the truth. Any evidence produced following such silences is subject to question, reinforcing the White Australian stereotype that Aboriginals are not to be trusted and thus are unreliable witnesses or guilty suspects.

Similarly, Dixon et al. (2002) discovered that there was a higher conviction rate for defendants with Birmingham accents in courtrooms in England than defendants with RP accents. The stigmatisation of the Birmingham accent originally found by Giles is still subject to linguistic prejudice.

Changing attitudes

Despite the persistent negativity associated with the Birmingham accent in England, it is important to highlight that certain stereotypes and language attitudes can change over time. Contrary to populist beliefs and stereotypes, often perpetuated by mostly right-wing elements of the mass media who bemoan language innovation, as we have seen already in A9 and B8 the English language (and any other language system) is not static or fixed – it is constantly changing and evolving. To illustrate this point further, it is observable that language loyalty to RP has been dying out in England for several years now. Newer varieties, including the aforementioned **Non-Regional Pronunciation** (NRP, see B1), along with a variety that has come to be known as **Estuary English**, have been empirically observed as taking the place of RP.

Estuary English takes its name from the Thames Estuary in south-east England, and it is a term that became popularised in the 1980s. An effective way to conceptualise Estuary English is to view it as located at a mid-point on a continuum, with RP at the one end and Cockney, the local variety, at the other. One popular explanation for the development of Estuary English put forward by linguists including David Crystal (1995) is that RP is going through a process of casualisation at the same time as Cockney speakers are experiencing social mobility and thus moving away from the most stigmatised variety.

Estuary English is seen by sociolinguists as evidence that a process known as **dialect levelling** is taking place, as certain features from this south-east variety have been witnessed spreading across the country. Crystal suggests that the spread of Estuary English can be attributable to a number of factors, including commuting patterns, with far more people now taking advantage of relatively straightforward commutes to the capital; the mass media, particularly high-profile celebrities on television and radio who speak a form of Estuary English; and the building of new cities outside the capital after World War II. The spread of people from the capital who moved to these new towns, along with their social and economic mobility, resulted in modification of their accent and dialect, as well as influencing individuals who were already residents in these locations.

Crystal (1995) characterises some of the key features associated with this variety. These include glottal stops (also discussed in A1 and B1), especially in word-final position or before a consonant, though glottal usage is variable, and only Cockney speakers would use a glottal stop before a vowel. From a grammatical perspective, Estuary English speakers will omit the '-ly' adverbial ending as in 'You're moving too quick', but they are far less likely to use the **double negative**, where more than one negative word occurs within the same clause, which is firmly associated with non-standard variants including Cockney, such as 'I never did nothing'.

There is also usage of what is known as the confrontational **tag question**, (a construction added to a statement), in this case to add negative evaluation to a statement, such as 'I told you that already didn't I'. Crystal points out that 'innit', the well-known Cockney tag, frequently cited as an obvious stereotypical feature, can only be found in jocular Estuary speech, though he does point out that this tag may well become part of Estuary English in the future.

It is still too soon to see what the overall impact of Estuary English will eventually have on the population of England as a whole. Evidence of dialect levelling has been found in many different locations within England, though regional variants are still going strong. Dialect levelling, and resistance to it, is further explored in D9.

CODIFICATION

The development of corpora of World Englishes can be a great aid to the description and eventual codification of varieties (the term **corpus**, along with its plural, 'corpora', is defined as a body or a collection. In specific reference to language study, **corpus linguistics** refers to a collection of a body of texts used for linguistic description and analysis). While a handful of World Englishes corpora were in existence by the early 1990s, including Australian and New Zealand varieties (based at Macquarie University and Victoria University of Wellington, respectively), in 1990, an *International Corpus of English* was proposed by Sidney Greenbaum at University College London (UCL). He had previously worked on one of the first ever linguistic corpora, the *Survey of English Usage*, a collection of British English compiled in conjunction with his UCL colleague Randolph Quirk.

Greenbaum's vision was to compile parallel corpora in different countries where English is used as either a first or second official language. The aim was thus to collect data from Kachru's Inner and Outer circles. Each group of researchers has been presented with the task of compiling a one-million-word corpus recorded after 1989.

To date, the following countries have been involved in this international corpus: Australia, Canada, Ghana, Great Britain, Hong Kong, India, Ireland, Jamaica, Kenya, Malaysia, New Zealand, the Philippines, Singapore, South Africa, Sri Lanka, the United States, Tanzania, and Trinidad and Tobago.

The corpus design is identical and therefore full comparability can be achieved across the different data sets. Each individual country's corpus consists of 500 data samples, of which 300 instances should be of speech and 200 instances should be of writing. A wide range of samples should be collected by research teams from a range of different contexts to give good coverage of language usage in a variety of situations.

Each corpus should be composed of private and public dialogues as well as scripted and non-scripted monologues. In terms of written material, this should consist of the following:

- ❏ non-printed, non-professional writing, including student work
- ❏ printed materials including academic writing
- ❏ non-academic writing
- ❏ reportage (news reports)
- ❏ instructional writing (including administrative writing and writing on skills and hobbies)
- ❏ persuasive writing

Several sets of corpora which have already been completed are freely available online for research and teaching purposes (see www.routledge.com/cw/mullany for further details).

A range of different levels of linguistic detail can be described and compared across the corpora due to the systematic manner in which the data have been collected: researchers can examine and compare morphology, lexis, grammar, syntax, discourse and pragmatics. The results that emerge from this project will represent a big step forward to improve our knowledge of World Englishes varieties and thus improve our abilities to describe, compare and codify varieties of World Englishes. This could eventually lead to outcomes such as a suite of new teaching materials being developed using authentic language data.

Alongside these highly effective attempts at data uniformity, it is important to also bear in mind that data collection needs to be viewed in the light of the particular historical time period in which it has been recorded. For example, the Hong Kong English samples were taken both before and after the British handover to China, thus recording a particularly prominent time in the history of Hong Kong, where corpus compilers accurately predicted that the status of English would change, with Chinese becoming more prominent post-handover.

Another example of a more recent collection is the VOICE corpus, based in Europe. VOICE stands for the *Vienna and Oxford International Corpus of English*, collected by a research team at the University of Vienna, with initial funding from Oxford University Press, headed by Barbara Seidlhofer. The corpus is the first of its kind devoted to English as a lingua franca. It currently stands at one million words and comprises naturally occurring face-to-face spoken language interactions. Within the corpus, native speakers from all of the major first languages in Europe are represented. There are approximately 50 different first languages spoken in total, including some non-European languages. The contexts where data have been recorded include educational contexts, informal leisure settings and various professional environments including spoken communication within businesses and organisations.

Early findings from the corpus analysis of VOICE include the following list of initial patterns of typical ELF 'errors'. Seidlhofer (2004) reports that language teachers will often spend considerable periods of time trying to redress these 'errors' in the classroom. However, the corpus data analysis from VOICE has demonstrated that the 'error' features listed below do not provide any obstacle at all to communicating successfully:

- ❑ Dropping the third person present tense -*s*
- ❑ Confusing the relative pronouns *who* and *which*
- ❑ Omitting the definite and indefinite articles when they are obligatory in ENL and inserting them where they do not occur in ENL
- ❑ Failing to use correct forms in tag questions (e.g. *isn't it?* or *no?* instead of *shouldn't they?*
- ❑ inserting redundant prepositions, as in *We have to study about*
- ❑ Overusing certain verbs of high semantic generality, such as *do, have, make, put, take*
- ❑ Replacing infinitive constructions with that-clauses as in *I want that*
- ❑ Overdoing explicitness (e.g. *black colour* rather than just *black*)

(Seidlhofer 2004: 220)

In contrast, the corpus has provided evidence that certain metaphors, idioms, phrasal verbs and fixed expressions from native English varieties (ENL) do cause communicative problems and can result in miscommunication. Typical examples of this include sequences such as 'This drink is on the house' or 'Can we give you a hand?' These findings provide vital information in terms of intelligibility and question the communicative effectiveness of how the English language is currently being taught.

As a future direction for World Englishes, Seidlhofer argues that the deference which is shown to teaching native varieties of language needs to be seriously re-evaluated in the light of emergent findings from descriptive lingua franca work. The majority of English language interactions globally are now taking place between non-native speakers where English is being used as a lingua franca. This raises the crucial question: why should native-speaker models of English from the Inner Circle still dominate classrooms?

Seidlhofer draws attention to the idea that intelligibility should be prioritised by English language teaching instead of an insistence on 'correctness' and that this be done while developing students' competence in terms of reading and writing skills. She argues that the aim of trying to get learners to speak perfectly like 'natives' is a completely unrealistic, unobtainable and questionable goal that should be abandoned. It is the intention that evidence from corpus studies can help to reinforce these points and that the wealth of description produced by such work can, in turn, influence codification processes so that a much more accurate portrayal of real-life World Englishes usage emerges.

Dictionaries and World Englishes

In order to consider the issue of codification and World Englishes further, one good place to explore is the *Oxford English Dictionary* (OED). We have already made reference to 'Oxford' dictionary titles in A10. The OED bills itself and is arguably widely accepted as 'the world's leading publisher' of reference works, providing 'the definitive record of the English language' (OED 2009). Oxford University Press, the publishing house that owns all Oxford English dictionaries, has, since the 1980s, produced what they have termed 'World English' dictionaries. At present, there are Oxford University Press World Englishes dictionary publications for the United States, Canada, Australia, New Zealand, South Africa and a dictionary of English Usage for the Caribbean.

A key part of the publicity material for these 'World English' dictionaries on the commercial webpages of the Oxford University Press website is a quotation from the Chief Editor of the OED, John Simpson. This operates as a manifesto and rationale for the publication of the OED's World English dictionaries. He states: 'A nation needs a dictionary for much more than finding the meaning and pronunciation of words. The best dictionaries are a record of a nation's history and culture.' This quotation draws upon the unity of an individual 'nation' which often is not the case in multilingual situations where World Englishes varieties are currently thriving, particularly when varieties of Englishes are used as a lingua franca, where individuals from different nationalities come together and use English as a strategic communicative method.

Oxford University Press are keen to highlight that the development of World Englishes is not a new phenomenon. They draw attention to the fact that their 1884–1928 multi-volume version of the OED was not just restricted to British English but also included lexis from varieties of English in North America, Asia, Africa, the Caribbean and Australasia. They argue that it was not until towards the end of the twentieth century that enough information was finally available to publish stand-alone publications/versions of the OED for Australia, Canada, the United States, New Zealand, South Africa and the Caribbean, hence the publication of their own, independent volumes.

The overall number and different types of dictionaries/reference works which Oxford University Press publishes for 'World English' varies from country to country:

❑ The largest number of versions are in American English (there are currently seven different publications available, including thesauruses, desk editions, paperback editions and mini/pocket versions). American English has had a major global impact, and significant numbers of language learners of English worldwide are taught American English.

❑ Australia currently has five varieties of publications.

❑ Canada, New Zealand and South Africa have three different publications, all including one official 'national' Oxford dictionary.

❑ In the Caribbean, so far there has only been one Oxford title – not a fully fledged 'Oxford Dictionary', but instead the *Dictionary of Caribbean English Usage*, compiled and edited by Richard Allsopp, a scholar at the University of the West Indies.

The process by which the only *Dictionary of Caribbean English Usage* was compiled gives an interesting insight into the painstaking production of the codification process in general and of this variety of World English in particular. Robert Allsopp had studied at UCL in the 1960s under the famous corpus compiler Randolph Quirk. In the 1970s, Allsopp was provided with the required funding in order to begin the data collection for his dictionary of usage. Allsopp carefully contemplated naming and identity questions in terms of the book's title during the data collection process. He eventually decided that 'Caribbean' was preferable, and this replaced 'West Indian', his original title, in order to escape the fragmented 'island' connotations that accompany this term.

He adopted the data collection method of setting up workshops with local teachers and eventually he and his research team managed to collect data from all of the different Caribbean islands. Allsopp selected a wide range of topics through which to elicit data at these workshops. These topics included, amongst many others, hairstyles, bush medicines, folk remedies, lizards, insect pests, birds, flowers, fishing, trees, superstitions – including legendary figures relating to deaths, births and marriage – house-building styles, religion and belief systems, and coconut, banana and sugar industries. This whole process was incredibly lengthy and continued well into the 1980s. It was then followed by the complex process of compilation. The dictionary eventually appeared in 1996.

STYLISTIC ANALYSIS   B11

In this unit, we present an extended example of a complete stylistic analysis of a whole literary text. It should be clear from our comments throughout that there are many features of language that could have been explored in what follows that we have not pursued, but the account below is intended to be exemplary and illustrative of a simple sort of stylistic practice.

She walks in beauty

She walks in beauty, like the night
    Of cloudless climes and starry skies;
And all that's best of dark and bright
    Meet in her aspect and her eyes:
Thus mellowed to that tender light
    Which heaven to gaudy day denies.

One shade the more, one ray the less,
    Had half impaired the nameless grace
Which waves in every raven tress,
    Or softly lightens o'er her face;
Where thoughts serenely sweet express
    How pure, how dear their dwelling-place.

And on that cheek, and o'er that brow,
   So soft, so calm, yet eloquent,
The smiles that win, the tints that glow,
   But tell of days in goodness spent,
A mind at peace with all below,
   A heart whose love is innocent!

George Gordon Byron (1815)

Context and commentary

This poem, written by Byron in June 1814 after a party at which he observed his cousin, Mrs. Anne Beatrix Wilmot, in a black and sparkling dress, was published the following year as one of several songs to be set to Jewish tunes in *Hebrew Melodies*. Almost all the literary criticism of the poem mentions these facts in one form or another. The text is regularly listed amongst the most popular poems in English, and it has been much anthologised.

Almost all commentaries on the poem (despite insisting on the historical circumstances of production) declare that it is a poem of praise of an ideal of beauty rather than a description or praise of a particular person. All agree on its poise, balance, elegance and positive outlook. Some commentaries even support these conclusions with stylistic evidence such as the highly regular rhyme scheme (*ababab* in each stanza, including the last with 'brow' close to 'glow' and 'below' in Byron's Scottish accent), or the close internal rhymes ('like the night', 'dear their', 'win . . . tints'), and the alliterations ('cloudless climes', 'starry skies', 'gaudy day denies').

The poem is consistently in iambic tetrameter (four repetitions of an iamb foot comprising an unstressed followed by a stressed syllable), with the sole exception of the fourth line: 'Meet in her aspect and her eyes'. Here, the first two words form a trochee (a reversed iamb, with 'Meet' stressed and 'in' unstressed). The phonetic emphasis on 'Meet' emphasises the notion of blending and balance and also hints at the older adjectival meaning of 'meet' as just and proper, a sense that was still common in the early nineteenth century, though it was even by then becoming archaic.

Sensual phonetic iconicity

A more detailed stylistic analysis would set out further the numerous highly wrought poetic effects in the text. The dominant pattern is a sense of calmness and balance, and this is carried iconically in the prosodic features mentioned above.

There are, further, even more subtle patterns here too. Each stanza might be seen as developing a theme – physical appearance in the first, introspection in the second, moral goodness in the third – and these are accompanied by certain sound effects. For example, the first stanza details the outward senses of visual description and touch ('eyes' and 'tender'), and the phonoaesthetics of the stanza is dominated by alveolars (voiced /d/ and unvoiced /t/, see A1 and B1 for a reminder of phonetic terminology). There is a related emphasis on voiced /g/ and unvoiced /k/. There are sibilants (fricatives with added turbulence) in striking places, beginning with a single /ʃ/ in 'She', then dominated by /s/ (with even the voiceless /k/ in 'skies' serving to devoice what would otherwise be a voiced final /z/). The sibilants end the stanza being voiced: /z/ in 'denies'. It could be argued that this tip-of-the-tongue sensation and this combination of sounds encourage a careful enunciation of the first stanza.

This delicateness is supported by the careful balance between the regular rhythm (which encourages pauses at the end of lines) and the enjambed syntax (which encourages the running-on from one line to the next). So most readers like to pause after 'like the night', but in fact the next line is an essential continuation of the sense. Similarly, even the two lines that are not enjambed begin with connectors ('And' and 'Thus'). The overall effect, encouraged by the lexical semantic content in the stanza, is of a tactile and sensual experience of reading. Remember, too, that the poem was published as a song (iambic tetrameter is the common form of English song), and also that all poetry before the mass literacy of the twentieth century was primarily there to be read aloud.

The second stanza offers a frame of the woman's hair, then face, then interior thoughts. The sense of delicacy here is even greater, with explicit syntactic balance given to 'one shade the more, one ray the less', combined with the balanced semantic binaries 'shade/ray', 'more/less'. There is a sense of diminishment and quietness: 'half', 'softly', 'serenely'. The stanza is phonetically dominated by sibilants; in context, this stanza whispers. In order not to disrupt this gentle quietness, the other main sounds are not noisy dentals or other types of stops, but the approximants or 'liquids' (an aesthetic term for approximants) /w/, /r/ and /l/: 'which waves in every raven tress', and so on. Even where dentals occur, they are placed in phonetic positions which diminish, devoice, destress and de-emphasise them and where sibilants overwhelm them: 'shade the', 'impaired', '-less grace', 'sweet express'. By the time the voiced dentals of the last line appear, the cumulative effect plus the pause and breathy repetition of 'how pure, how dear' has reduced the line to a whisper.

The third stanza blends outward physical experience and interior contemplation in a combined theme that claims an inward moral centre is indicated by the outward appearance. Appropriately, the sound effects that have been established by the first stanza on the one hand and the second stanza on the other are all combined too in this final stanza. Voiced and unvoiced consonants, sibilants and stops, liquids and dentals all appear. In parallel, where the first and second stanzas are filled with emphasised verbs ('walks', 'meet', 'mellowed', 'denies', 'had . . . impaired', 'waves', 'lightens', 'express'), the final stanza seems to be almost verbless. In fact, there is only one main verb ('tell'), and even that is lost after the negational 'But' and is preceded by two 'false' verbs ('win' and 'glow') embedded as qualifiers of the nouns 'smiles' and 'tints'. 'Spent' is a similar qualifier. The final line presents what looks in isolation like a main assertive verb 'is', but this whole line is in fact in apposition, parallel with the previous two lines. The phrasal syntax of the stanza, with lines broken up by commas piling up verbless noun-phrases, also aligns with this verbless sense of stasis. It is finally as if qualities and virtuous properties are more significant than actions and assertions.

Semantic complications

All of this account matches quite well with the standard literary critical and popular view of the poem as a balanced work of art in praise of idealised beauty and good-ness. However, further stylistic exploration reveals other possibilities that are difficult to reconcile with this view. Another way of looking at the balance of semantic contraries ('dark' and 'bright', 'heaven' and 'gaudy day') is as an admission and invocation of negativity rather than positivity. The poem even encourages this in the surprising number and types of negations it contains. For example, the lexical choice 'cloudless' (rather than 'clear', say) brings to mind – however fleetingly – the obscuring gloom of clouds; 'heaven' could have simply denied a 'tender light' to 'day', but instead the day is brash and 'gaudy'; even some of the verb choices that dominate the first two stanzas ('denies', 'impaired') are unnecessarily negatively oriented.

Where presenting the two sides of a balanced view necessarily invokes the negative ('dark' as well as 'bright', 'less' as well as 'more'), the effect when only one side is presented is to encourage thoughts of the unsaid opposite ('best' then hints implicitly at the worst). The choice of register is not just simply poetic, but highly self-consciously poetic. The poem even begins with a semantic and syntactic trap for the reader: 'She walks in beauty' is semantically odd, and its oddness is partly what causes the vast majority of people reading the whole line out loud to pause at the end of the line. 'She walks in beauty, like the night' is then ambivalent between beauty being like the night or she being like the night, and the night is conventionally the time of mystery, edginess, danger and illicitness. Though the next line rescues the sentiment, the fleeting effect has already occurred.

Similar suggestive effects permeate the poem, as in the invocation of darkness and shadow. There is a sense of vagueness and underspecificity in lexical choice ('nameless grace', 'dwelling-place', and especially suggestively 'all below') – these are taken as idealisations of beauty in the traditional interpretation, but they could equally be read as being euphemistic and evasive on the part of the writer. The writer's voice and perspective provide the content of the first two stanzas, but the observing consciousness is not foregrounded. However, this changes in the final stanza, with the distal deictic 'that' ('that cheek . . . that brow') signalling strongly – again by implicit contrast – the deictic centre of the writer, where 'this' would be located. He draws attention to the inarticulacy of his viewpoint ('so soft, so calm') and even highlights the issue itself in invoking the word 'eloquent'. The writer, in fact, enters into the poem towards the end as more than a mere neutral observer, but as an evaluator with his own agenda. The iambic tetrameter, which looks so innocuous, was also prototypically the form of ancient Greek dialogue, and the most famous example of the form is the dialogic and seductive opening to Christopher Marlowe's *The Passionate Shepherd to His Love*, 'Come live with me and be my love' (c. 1585).

Dialogue and viewpoint

The foregrounding of the poem as a dialogue, in which only the writer speaks and the woman is abstracted and silent, seems to evoke a viewpoint with his own agenda. 'The smiles that win' could be read as false, tactical smiles (and the definite article serves to heighten this sense of disembodied artifice); 'the tints' are even more cosmetic and superficial. 'But tell of days in goodness spent' can of course be read as 'merely tell of a life passed in goodness', but it could equally be read as 'instead confess a life with all goodness spent and used up'. In this reading, the sudden shift to indefinite universal sentiment, 'A mind at peace with all below', appears ironically overstated, and the ironic intent of the final line can be strongly inferred in the closing exclamation mark. (It is noticeable that many editors, perhaps intuitively mindful of the undermining potential here, delete the original punctuation in favour of a simple full stop.)

We are suggesting that the idealisation presented on the surface of the poem is too good to be true, and the poem is also more concerned with the writer than might appear at first glance. What might at first appear to be a joyful celebration can under analysis look more sinister and cynical. There are several subtle stylistic cues that might invite this reading, and if the reading is there at all impressionistically, a detailed stylistic analysis can help to reveal it clearly. Whether it can be considered valid or not is a matter for your own judgement and your own production of evidence.

TECHNIQUES AND ETHICS

B12

One of the most important methodological techniques that needs to be acquired for English language study is the ability to record and then transcribe spoken language data. The need for transcription sets the discipline of language and linguistics apart from others in the social sciences. A number of transcription extracts are used in this book, particularly across the discourse strand, in A5, B5 and C5, as well as in D3, on pragmatics and discourse.

Whilst traditional quantitative methods such as experiments which take place in language laboratories are always recorded, other social scientists who conduct qualitative research through participant observation rely solely on a notebook and pen to record their observations. However, to produce a systematic study of any stretch of language data, it is important, wherever possible, for recordings to be made and data transcriptions to be produced. Our memories cannot record accurately the details of exactly who said what, when they said it, and how they said it.

As far as very short exchanges are concerned, researchers may produce a written transcription of the spoken data from memory, writing it down as a record of what took place at the very first opportunity to do so. Of course, if we had a recorded version, we could check and double check it for accuracy, but on some occasions really fruitful examples of language data will present themselves when we do not expect it. For example, there are occasions when we overhear very short exchanges when we are not in any 'official' language-gathering capacity, as in the 'Carlos Bridge' example in A10, where recording is not taking place. Ideally, all language data should be recorded, though exceptions are generally made for very short, spontaneous exchanges when analysing discourse features.

However, if you were wanting to analyse phonetic language variation, then it is essential that you have a recording of your spoken data – you need to be able to listen to recordings of phonetic features on a number of occasions to obtain any accuracy in your analysis. Likewise, any longer stretch of discourse or any discourse where there are multiple speakers would also be impossible to transcribe without a recording being made.

There is no standard system of transcription conventions for English language study, and conventions can vary quite dramatically depending upon which particular aspects of the English language researchers are aiming to analyse. Probably the largest and most comprehensive set of transcription conventions are followed by hard-core conversation analysts, and these conventions were originally designed by Gail Jefferson (see Jefferson 2004).

While the lack of a standardised system can be frustrating when you first start off as a fieldworker and analyst in English language studies, the flexibility with developing your own conventions is really useful, as it gives you the freedom to choose the conventions that are most important and most relevant to the study which you are conducting. For instance, if you are not examining accent variation, then you do not need to transcribe phonetically.

Transcription conventions

Here are the transcription conventions which we have followed in this book. These have been blended together from across the disciplines of sociolinguistics and discourse analysis:

(.)	indicates a pause of two seconds or less
(-)	indicates a pause of over two seconds
(xx)	indicates material that was impossible to make out
{xx}	indicates material that has been edited out for the purposes of confidentiality
[ ]	closed brackets indicate the starting and finishing points of simultaneous speech
%word%	percentage signs indicate material that was uttered quietly
WORD	capital letters indicate material that was uttered loudly
((laughs))	material in double brackets indicates additional information
=	equals signs indicate no discernible gap between speakers' utterances
------------	all materials contained within double dotted lines should be read
------------	alongside each other, as in a musical score.

The observer's paradox and ethics

Should spoken language data be video-recorded or audio-recorded? A newly emergent research focus in discourse analysis is on **multi-modal communication** – where a full range of communicative behaviour, including gesture, is analysed in conjunction with the more traditional approach of investigating spoken discourse by the production of written transcripts. If you are taking a multi-modal approach, then you cannot do this without video recording. However, one disadvantage of multi-modal studies at present is that they tend to be restricted to artificial, experimental settings, due to the number of video-recording devices that are required in one room at any one time in order to make accurate recordings of gestures (see Knight 2009).

It is also well established that video recording is more likely to trigger the effect of the **observer's paradox**: that the act of observing (through the researcher's physical presence and/or recording equipment) is likely to change what it is that you want to observe. Permission for gaining access to data generally becomes far more difficult if you want to use video, as many individuals are far more reticent to be video-recorded than audio-recorded (Duranti 1997). However, with audio recordings you are restricted to gaining 'a filtered version of what happened whilst the tape was running', though this method still has 'the power to capture social actions in unique ways' (Duranti 1997: 119). The inescapable fact remains, however, that the presence of any recording equipment, be it video or audio, can change participants' behaviour.

Duranti (1997: 117) argues that the problems raised by the observer's paradox, if they are carried to their logical conclusions, suggest that 'it would be better to *not to be there* at all'. There are two ways in which such a proposition can be realised. The first option is to throw in the towel and completely abandon the study of people altogether, whilst the second option is to record covertly, not informing participants that their behaviour is being recorded, which raises considerable ethical problems:

> The first option is self destructive [as] . . . it implies that we should not improve our understanding of what it means to be human and have a culture (including a language) simply because we cannot find the ideal situation for naturalistic-objective observation. The second proposal is first of all unethical and, second, impractical under most circumstances outside of laboratories with two-way mirrors.
>
> (Duranti 1997: 117)

The unethical nature of covert recording is also highlighted by Milroy (1987), who argues that it is now essential for language studies to be carried out overtly, so recording covertly and then asking for permission afterwards is no longer a viable option. Milroy points out that, as a tape is a permanent record of behaviour, those being recorded are entitled to know that such a record is being made. As a person's voice is an important part of their self-image, they may often be unhappy with being recorded without their knowledge. Covert recording can also result in serious practical disadvantages. Surreptitious recording, when revealed, can result in future access being denied. Furthermore, the quality of recording is usually poor if the equipment is concealed, and therefore data cannot often be properly transcribed. Codes of ethics are now being established by recognised organisations (such as the British Association for Applied Linguistics) to establish ethical guidelines for data collection.

Whilst the observer's paradox is a problematic concern, this does not mean that researchers should abandon analysing naturally occurring data. For the vast majority of the time, 'people are too busy running their own lives to change them in substantial ways because of the presence of a new gadget or person' and 'neutral' observation is an illusion anyway (Duranti 1997: 118). By arguing this, Duranti is not advocating that the observer's paradox be ignored. Rather, he is quite rightly suggesting that researchers should approach it in full awareness that it is completely unavoidable.

Any language student or researcher should include a discussion in their method-ological rationale on how they have tried to minimise the effects of the observer's paradox, but ultimately acknowledge that it is impossible to get around. A direct and transparent acknowledgement of the observer's paradox, followed by a reflexive account of how you have attempted to minimise its effects and then how it may have affected the data collection, is an acceptable way forward.

In the vast majority of cases, research subjects forget that they are being recorded, as they become absorbed in what they are doing, particularly after the first few minutes that the recorder has been running. Many researchers have interviewed participants afterwards to ask whether they thought the recording equipment had affected their behaviour. The consensus tends to be that after the initial few minutes, they did forget that they were being recorded as they became focused upon the topic and/or task at hand.

However, there are exceptions, and the following examples illustrate occasions where the presence of the tape recorder was noted and actually became part of the topic of the conversation outside of the first few minutes of these business-meeting interactions:

Sharon is talking on the topic of a difficult customer.

1   Sharon: They're banging on that we're always late
2   shove that up your arse
3   ((laughter)) that's recorded
4   ((laughter from many))

Meeting-Chair Amy, who is the line manager of all meeting participants, is running through a staff rota to confirm employees' working hours.

1   Mary: Oh excuse me ((yawning))
2   Amy: What are you laughing at? ((laughter from many begins))
3   Mary: [I've (xxx) been taped (-) taped yawning ((laughs))
4   [((laughter from many))
5   Mary: sorry about that
6   Amy: It's really boring this meeting is it?
7   Mary: [No I just need some food]
8   Karen: [I I   ]

The reference to the tape-recording equipment here appears to take place when speakers become very self-conscious about what they are saying. In the first example, this is related to using the word 'arse' by Sharon in line 2 in a formal business meeting, where the established speech norms of this community of practice do not normally include expletives. In the second example, Mary has become self-conscious, as she has committed a social faux pas by yawning in a meeting. Part of her embarrassment about this is caused by the fact that her yawn has been recorded on tape and is thus permanent.

One of the ethical considerations of recording your own friends is that if you have to leave the room for any reason then it is possible that they may talk about you as they forget the tape recorder is running. So, whilst the example below is a good illustration of participants forgetting that the recorder is on, it presented researcher Jennifer Coates with the ethical dilemma of being able to hear her friends talking about her on the rather sensitive topic of her ex-husband:

Discussing Jen's arrangements to get her ex-husband to help with her move to London

---

MEG: I mean I wouldn't rely on him for something as vital as that/

[. . .] *[Jen leaves the room to answer phone]*

SALLY: Your faces when Jennifer said that- that Paul was going to do
MEG: {LAUGHS}-

SALLY: the move/ .hh I wish I'd got a camera/ {LAUGHING} ((it)) was
MEG: {LAUGHS}

SALLY: sort of- ((xx)) in total disbelief/ I think the most difficult
MEG: mhm/

SALLY: is- is that when you've loved someone / you- you half the time you

---

SALLY: forget their faults [don't you? and still maybe love them/ . . .
MEG: [yeah/

(Coates 1997: 298)

Alongside ethics are also practical considerations of gaining access to language data. Data collection can become difficult, for example, at times due to political and social unrest/upheaval: some social settings can also be really problematic, if not downright dangerous to enter. It is really important that you do not put yourself in danger whilst collecting fieldwork data!

Sociolinguist Miriam Meyerhoff (2006) reports on a case where an individual named Anibal Otero was arrested and imprisoned for being a spy during the Spanish Civil War (1936–1939) because he was discovered with strange 'codes' in a notebook. Assuming he was a spy, he was charged with treason. However, the codes were actually phonetic transcriptions, as he was employed as a fieldworker to work on the *Linguistic Atlas of Iberian Spanish*. As a truly dedicated linguistics researcher at heart, he turned his plight to his advantage by collecting data from his fellow prisoners.

In C12, you will come across an activity that asks you to think about these access issues in more detail and decide whether in some scenarios data collection should not be attempted at all – for instance, studying the language of drug dealers or criminal gangs.

LANGUAGE AND THOUGHT

Do we think in language or do we speak after verbalising our thoughts? One of the main reasons why the study of language has proven so enticing and tantalising for thousands of years is that it appears to be intimately bound up with our thought processes and consciousness itself. Indeed, until the most recent years of psychological experiments, eye-tracking devices, MRI scans and the clinical observation of those who have suffered head injuries, the main window onto the human mind consisted of the patterns of language through which we, as humans, articulated our thoughts. Though the observable tip of language can be seen and heard in writing and speech, we can talk to ourselves sub-vocally and think silently in our own language inside our heads. Whether explicitly or implicitly, much of the modern linguistic study of language has also been a study of the mind.

Determinism and language

Therefore, it is not surprising that the main movements in modern linguistics – generativism, functionalism and cognitivism (see A13) – have all become engaged with philosophical discussions concerning the status of what the mind is, what consciousness is, what reality is, and whether the observable patterns of language can tell us anything about our inner lives, our genetically inherited lives, our determination or free will, our adaptability or how far we are constrained within our social systems, and the human condition.

For example, in the Appendix to his 1948 novel *Nineteen Eighty-Four*, George Orwell set out the principles of 'Newspeak', the fictional language of his imagined totalitarian state. The compilers of the 11th Newspeak Dictionary aimed to reduce the number of words available to the population. The lexicographer, Symes, says:

> Don't you see that the whole aim of Newspeak is to narrow the range of thought? In the end we shall make thoughtcrime literally impossible because there will be no words in which to express it. Every concept that can ever be needed will be expressed by exactly *one* word, with its meaning rigidly defined and all its subsidiary meanings rubbed out and forgotten [. . .] It's merely a question of [. . .] reality-control.

Most words in Newspeak are removed by selecting a basic term ('good', rather than the possible range of 'fine', 'nice', 'excellent', 'ok', 'well', 'lovely', 'pleasant', 'superb', 'brilliant', and so on) and then allowing a small set of very regular inflections ('gooder', 'ungood', 'goodest', 'plusgood', 'doubleplusgood'). The idea on which this is based, as Symes explains above, is that language and thought are directly and causally connected, so reducing the language will reduce the capacity for thinking freely.

This strong linkage between language and thought is a highly deterministic view. It asserts that thought is purely linguistic and that mental operations are conducted in terms identical or very close to the surface structure of language. It also suggests that ideas are literally unthinkable, or at least very difficult to imagine, without the linguistic means of articulating them. Such a view has been called the **Sapir-Whorf**

hypothesis, named after Edward Sapir and his student (and his eventual colleague) Benjamin Lee Whorf. In fact, their theory of **linguistic relativity** was not as deterministic as has been characterised, and 'Sapir-Whorfianism' is largely a misapplied term. However, Sapir certainly took the view that language and what he called our 'thought-grooves' are very closely related and that a culture's perspectives and preoccupations can be discerned in its linguistic patterns. This can be seen, for example, in the overlexicalisation of certain domains (kinship terms for family relationships, technical terms or jargon in certain occupations) where there is a particular cultural interest. Whorf developed his position after noticing, when working as a fire insurance investigator, that people would throw cigarette ends into gasoline barrels labelled 'empty', when in fact they were 'full' of explosive petrol vapour.

Cognition and language

Though fictionally terrifying, Newspeak and its extreme determinism could not possibly work as described in the book. People commonly demonstrate an astonishingly creative capacity for articulating new thoughts either by coining and spreading new words and phrases, by shifting the meanings of existing words and phrases, or by extending metaphorically the meanings of words and phrases. If the deterministic shackling of language and thought were true, it would be impossible to invent any new object or concept before inventing the word for it. Translation between languages would be impossible. Miscommunication and the exaggerations and hypercorrections caused by social diffusion are also a challenge to absolute determinism, since accidental innovation is often taken up and made meaningful. And of course, words convey more than they simply denote, and meanings are conveyed by collocations and syntax as well as simply by words.

Nevertheless, a weaker form of linguistic relativity, closer to Sapir and Whorf's actual work, can be discerned in generativism, functionalism and especially cognitivism. For example, the claims in the first of these for universal deep structures in human language and innate constraints on what can be well formed are both relatively deterministic assertions. Generativists suggest a deepest form of interior language as a sort of 'mentalese', which determines all the various surface languages of the world. In the functionalist tradition, too, there is an acknowledgement that some form of linguistic relativity operates through the social practice of language.

For example, one of the most powerful applications of systemic functional grammar is in critical discourse analysis (see Strand 5), which typically explores the discursive patterns in politically and socially significant and influential texts. Of course, those texts can only be significant and influential if you first acknowledge the power of their language to manipulate, constrain and alter the thoughts of the readers or hearers to a large extent. The claimed power of advertising, the moving power of political speeches, and the resonant power of literary works depend on a degree of mind-manipulation by authors through language.

Lastly, cognitive linguistics is perhaps the closest relation to Sapir and Whorf's work in this area. Some of the earliest work in this tradition in the 1980s was in the large-scale **conceptual metaphors** that underlie not only many common expressions but every part of speech as well: even prepositions ('in', 'over', 'through', 'with', 'amongst', and so on) were shown to be spatially metaphorical and schematic of our early infantile manipulations of objects (see Lakoff and Johnson 1980). Some conceptual metaphors (such as LIFE IS A JOURNEY or LOVE IS WAR) seem to be almost universal across all language cultures of the world. Other powerful conceptual metaphors, such as the following, provide a structuring frame through which we commonly understand and recognise the world:

IDEAS ARE OBJECTS
COMMUNICATION IS A CONDUIT
IDEAS ARE PLANTS
TIME IS MONEY
ATTENTION IS MONEY
ANGER IS HOT FLUID IN A CONTAINER
KNOWING IS SEEING
CAUSES ARE FORCES
CATEGORIES ARE CONTAINERS
IMPORTANT IS BIG
GOOD IS UP

and many others. The following phrases exemplify each of these: 'We can share that idea', 'Do you get what I'm saying?', 'He's been nurturing that notion for a while', 'She just wasted an hour of her life', 'Pay attention', 'He blew his top', 'It's clear', 'She made me do it', 'It falls into the category of an accident', 'It's a huge development', 'Things are looking up'.

The cognitive linguistic research into conceptual metaphor is not absolutely deterministic: no one says that it is impossible to conceptualise LIFE in many ways other than as a JOURNEY, for example (though trying to conceptualise TIME in any ways that are not spatial is very difficult for non-physicists). However, researchers have shown that the extended and habitual usage of a particular conceptual metaphor pushes people towards that form of thinking as the most natural, conventional and easiest form, to the point where they don't even notice the metaphorical nature of the concept any more.

For example, to say that something is 'in front of' something else requires a metaphorical sense of the front and back of objects and your perceived reality of which you are probably not consciously aware. And politicians use metaphors of family, the schoolyard and village communities to articulate their views of international forces and politics in ways that in fact are highly selective and manipulative, but seem entirely appropriate and natural.

Indeed, much of our linguistic life happens below the level of conscious awareness. It seems that we do many things and even say things and then report them to our conscious brain, which then reflects on them and claims ownership and motivation for them. This means that – unless we have had our intensity of awareness raised by very close attention or by the sort of analytical training offered throughout this book – we normally don't even notice the patterns of language that are subtly structuring our perspective and thinking.

Means of access through language

Of course, researchers in language face a significant difficulty because of the fact that language is the material to be observed that gives insight into how language works, and almost our only access to the linguistic workings of the mind is through that same medium. There are several swirls of circularity here that cause real methodological problems for investigators of language in its broadest sense. It is an extreme example of the observer's paradox, which, as we have seen in B12, is the notion that the object of investigation changes by the very act of the observer being in the context. Since language is so bound up with consciousness itself, the problems posed by the observer's paradox for linguists are particularly thorny.

In general, there are three broad means of trying to investigate the nature of the language/thought continuum as practised by the three broad movements in modern linguistics. Generativism for most of its history has relied on the **intuition** of the theoretical linguist or a group of informants to make judgements on the outcomes of predicted rules. Intuition is problematic, of course, from the point of view of transparency and falsifiability, since there is a large element of subjectivity in it that is particular to the circumstances, and the particular circumstances might not be easily repeatable. However, intuitive judgements have the advantage over almost all other methods except neuroanatomical ones of offering a direct means of investigating cognition and perception in language. Aside from the possible interference of false self-awareness – the phenomenon of watching yourself while you are doing something – intuition is very direct.

The second broad method is discourse analysis, discussed throughout Strand 5. This includes not just the analysis of spoken events as discourse analysis is traditionally understood, as conversation analysis or analysis of exchange structure (outlined in A5), but also such methods as stylistics (Strand 11), where linguistic frameworks are used to explore textual patterning; corpus linguistics, where computational power is used to explore large bodies of language data (see B10); and critical discourse analysis, where public, corporate and institutional registers are explored (introduced in A5).

Discourse analysis, in this broad, inclusive sense, aims to add to our understanding of language/thought by investigating its traces left in texts and textuality. Though more indirect than intuition, the analysis of discourse that the analyst has not had a hand in producing serves to minimise any influence on the data, other than the fact that it has been selected for analysis (see A12 and B12). Furthermore, the development of a linguistic framework in relation to one domain of language, which then seems to work also by application to another domain, suggests a general validity for the framework.

Finally, **empiricism** of various kinds can be used to prise open the nature of language and thought. In general, any method which involves the analysis of evidence is empirical, and so there is a sense in which both intuitions about language data and the systematic analysis of language data are both empirical too. However, truly empirical exploration includes things like psycholinguistic experiments in which informants are presented with a linguistic task and their responses are recorded and then analysed in order to establish the truth or falsity of a hypothesis about language processing. This form of investigation tends to be conducted with a close attention paid to the verifiability of the method and the transparency of the data, so it is highly open to falsifiability. However, it is the most indirect means of investigating language and thought, and analysts must be constantly on guard for complicating and interfering factors in complex situations, and aware of the dangers in treating statistical results with more symbolic importance than they merit. These issues are also discussed in A12 and D12.

Section C

EXPLORATION
INVESTIGATING ENGLISH LANGUAGE

C1   **PERFORMING ACCENTS**

Accent keywords

A **word list** refers to a collection of specially selected lexical items that are used as a toolkit by phoneticians to test for variation in individuals' pronunciation. They are commonly given to speakers in the constructed context of a data collection interview, where individuals will be asked to read words out loud whilst being audio-recorded (see B12).

The word-list technique was developed by the highly influential phonetician John Wells in the early 1980s. Word lists have been used by a number of sociophoneticians including Paul Foulkes and Gerry Docherty for their volume *Urban Voices*, an examination of accent variation in urban areas of the British Isles just before the turn of the twenty-first century. Foulkes and Docherty's word list is given below to test for the articulation of vowel sounds.

As we highlighted in A1, the best way to learn about phonetics is to articulate the speech sounds for yourself.

Activity

❑   Read the word list that appears below out loud to yourself whilst looking in a mirror to monitor the shape and positioning of your mouth, lips and tongue.

❑   Try and work out which vowel sounds are being tested for phonetic variation by each individual word.

❑   Distribute the word list to a small group of friends or classmates and, if possible, record them reading this out loud (first refer to B12 for a consideration on **ethics** in relation to recording language data). Ideally, you should give the list to a group of people who are from different geographical locations.

❑   Listen for any examples that are different from your own and each other's pronunciations. Try to account for any recognisable differences in vowel sounds by drawing upon the knowledge you have gained in A1 and B1.

❑   The list of IPA vowel symbols given in B1 is accompanied by an individual word to illustrate its sound. You should now line up each one of these keywords with the most appropriate symbol in the B1 vowel list. When you have finished, you should have examples of two different words to represent each vowel symbol.

KIT
CLOTH
GOOSE
NORTH
DRESS
NURSE
PRICE
FORCE
TRAP
FLEECE
CHOICE
CURE
LOT
FACE
MOUTH
HAPPY
STRUT
PALM
NEAR
LETTER
FOOT
THOUGHT
SQUARE
HORSES
BATH
GOAT
START
COMMA

Foulkes and Docherty (1999: 7)

Representing accent in poetry

In the following two poems, the authors have used a technique known as **eye dialect** in order to represent phonetic variation. As only a very small proportion of members of society are trained to understand and write in phonetic notation, it is common practice for deviant spelling and punctuation marks to be used to represent different accent features in literary texts as well as other text types such as advertisements.

Through the technique of eye dialect, the first poem, written by an anonymous author, represents accent variation of a regional English variety from an area of the British West Midlands commonly known as the 'Black Country', which was so named for its polluted blackened skies from the heavy industry which dominated the area during the Industrial Revolution. Folklore has it that the poem below would often be orally 'performed' by local drinkers in organised entertainment evenings at public houses within the Black Country area. The second poem is a famous Scottish verse by Robert Burns entitled *Ode to a Haggis*. As with the anonymous Black Country poet, Burns also uses the technique of eye dialect to represent features of Scottish English pronunciation.

❏ Read both of the poems out loud either on your own or in a small group.

❏ Can you and members of your group understand them? Which parts are the most difficult to understand? Why do you think this is the case? Attempt to find the meanings online of any words that you cannot understand. To give some contextualisation, for the Black Country poem, its title, 'The Nit Nurse' refers to nurses who travel around primary schools (elementary level) in the UK and inspect children's hair for head lice, also called 'nits'. 'Sulio' (line 4, stanza 3) was the name of medication (a lotion) given to treat an infestation of head lice. (For contextualisation of the Burns poem, see the commentary provided by Smith 1996.)

❏ You should then attempt to pinpoint the specific Black Country and Scottish accent features that the poets are drawing attention to by drawing upon the knowledge of phonetics and phonology which you have gained from A1 and B1.

❏ Record these features using phonetic notation from the IPA given in B1.

❏ Finally, attempt to translate both of these poems into Standard written English and then read them out again in your own accent. What is gained/ lost by engaging in this re-writing process? Note how the apostrophes are used to suggest that particular sounds are 'missing' from a standard version.

The Nit Nuss

It was fower o'clock an' time ter goo 'um
But we just sot theer lookin' glum.
On the taycher's werds we 'ung in 'orrer
The nit nuss comes termorrer.

Ar run 'um fast yo' bet Ar did
Ter raych the toothcum afowa aer kid.
When 'e atter wait 'e was nearly in fits
'Urry up yo; Ar've got nits!'

'Ar short' Ar said 'Ar was 'ere fust
Thuz summat in mar yed an' it ay just dust.
But Ar'll tell yer worr Ar'll dew wi yo'
Ar'll lend yer me bottle o' Sulio'.

Ten ter nine the follerin' mornin'
A sight confirmed the taycher's warnin'.
Cuss raernd the corner fer all 'er was wuth
Pedalled the dreaded skewl nit nuss.

'Er bike 'ad a chainguard an' lights Ar recall
an' brakes that werked an' mudguards an' all.
An' on the frunt a little wire basket
In which 'er kept 'er nit catchin' kit.

They called aer names we all lined up
Between 'er bowsums aer yeds 'er'd cup.
Threw yer 'air 'er'd flick the cum
An' that was it; yo' was done.

Aer kid day 'e 'alf loff an' gloat
When the nit nuss sent me 'um wi a note.
Ar felt ser bad Ar wanted ter cry
Ar'd 'ad a note an' day know why.

Then aer kid gid me some advice
As ter wheer Ar'd catched this yedful o' lice.
'E'd 'ung abaert till Ar was in bed
Then secretly 'e'd toothcummed 'is yed.

Ar'd picked 'em up an' Ar day know wheer
Then aer kid loffed said wi a jeer:
'Thuz summat as yo've just gorrer know
Ar catched all mine an' gid 'em yo'.'

Anon (www.pant.co.uk/potluck/humour/nitnuss.htm)

Ode to a Haggis

Fair fa' your honest, sonsie face,
Great chieftain o'the puddin-race!
Aboon them a'ye tak your place,
Painch, tripe, or thairm:
Weel are ye wordy o' a grace
As lang's my airm.

The groaning trencher there ye fill,
Your hurdies like a distant hill,
Your pin wad help to mend a mill
In time o' need,
While thro' your pores the dews distil
Like amber bead.

His knife see rustic Labour dight,
An' cut you up wi' ready sleight,
Trenching your gushing entrails bright,
Like ony ditch;
And then, O what a glorious sight,
Warm-reekin', rich!

Then, horn for horn, they stretch an' strive:
Deil tak the hindmost! on they drive,
Till a' their weel-swall'd kytes belyve
Are bent like drums;
Then auld Guidman, maist like to rive,
Bethankit! hums.

Is there that owre his French ragout
Or olio that wad staw a sow,
Or fricassee wad mak her spew
Wi' perfect sconner,
Looks down wi' sneering, scornfu' view
On sic a dinner?

Poor devil! see him owre his trash,
As feckless as a wither'd rash,
His spindle shank, a guid whip-lash,
His nieve a nit;
Thro' blody flood or field to dash,
O how unfit!

But mark the Rustic, haggis-fed,
The trembling earth resounds his tread.
Clap in his walie nieve a blade,
He'll mak it whissle;
An' legs, an' arms, an' hands will sned,
Like taps o' thrissle.

Ye Pow'rs, wha mak mankind your care,
And dish them out their bill o' fare,
Auld Scotland wants nae skinking ware
That jaups in luggies;
But, if ye wish her gratefu' prayer
Gie her a haggis!

Robert Burns (1786)

Phonetician Gerry Knowles (1987) points out that by studying phonetics and phonology much can be learnt about the aesthetics of sound in poetry (and see B11 for a detailed analytical example). Knowledge of phonetics and phonology enables us to examine **sound parallelism**. Parallelism refers to when two or more linguistic features occur alongside each other for stylistic effect. In specific relation to sound parallelism, this involves phonemic patterns that are at least **syllable** size: bigger than a phoneme but smaller than a word, and usually inclusive of a vowel. Rhyme is the most prominent example of sound parallelism, where two syllables have the same closing syllable sequence (but a different opening sequence). **Alliteration**, similarity between consonant sounds, and **assonance**, similarity between vowel sounds, are also key examples of sound parallelism. Both of the above poems display syllable rhyme.

Activity

❑   Attempt to characterise the rhyme using the phonetic symbols outlined in B1.
❑   Analyse both poems for any evidence of alliteration and assonance.
❑   Consider how the accent features that are represented affect the sound parallelism in both poems. Would all lines in the poems rhyme if they were not written in eye dialect?

Disastrous sound effects

Another Scottish poet, William McGonagall, helps to illustrate another key point made by Knowles (1987). Knowles argues that in order for sound parallelism to be effective and for a poem to be positively evaluated, the parallelism must be seen to have arisen accidentally. Rhyme that appears to be forced runs the risk of being subject to negative evaluation. Knowles cites one example of McGonagall's work, *The Sprig of Moss*, as an example which suffers from an inappropriate, forced rhyme. Knowles argues that this work is a pretty feeble attempt at poetry, though he is clear to emphasise that there is nothing inherently wrong with the rhyming of the phonemic syllables – the rhyme works fine. The issue instead is related to the linkage between the sound and the meaning.

To consider these points further and to make your own mind up about William McGonagall's poetry, an example of another of his works, a 'disaster' poem written after a Scottish train crash in 1879, is given below.

Activity

❑   Conduct an analysis of sound parallelism in the poem. First, identify the phonetic features of the rhyme by reading the poem out loud.

❑   What happens if you attempt to read the poem out loud in a Scottish accent? Do you need to read the poem in a Scottish accent for the rhyme to work?

❑   Now consider its overall effectiveness as a piece of poetry. Is it susceptible to Knowles' criticism of inappropriate, forced rhyme? Do you think that these verses are successful examples of poetry? Why/why not?

The Tay Bridge Disaster

Beautiful Railway Bridge of the Silv'ry Tay!
Alas! I am very sorry to say
That ninety lives have been taken away
On the last Sabbath day of 1879,
Which will be remember'd for a very long time.
'Twas about seven o'clock at night,
And the wind it blew with all its might,
And the rain came pouring down,
And the dark clouds seem'd to frown,
And the Demon of the air seem'd to say-
'I'll blow down the Bridge of Tay.'
[. . .]
It must have been an awful sight,
To witness in the dusky moonlight,
While the Storm Fiend did laugh, and angry did bray,
Along the Railway Bridge of the Silv'ry Tay,
Oh! ill-fated Bridge of the Silv'ry Tay,
I must now conclude my lay

By telling the world fearlessly without the least dismay,
That your central girders would not have given way,
At least many sensible men do say,
Had they been supported on each side with buttresses,
At least many sensible men confesses,
For the stronger we our houses do build,
The less chance we have of being killed.

William McGonagall (1879)

Activity

As your next activity, you should attempt to build an archive of similar examples of poems, cartoons or any other textual forms that you can find, where the different sounds which represent features of accent variation are represented using the technique of eye dialect. Local newspapers or websites dedicated to the area where you live are often good places to start your search, as are literary texts.

The written recording of representations of different accents in texts is a common way of establishing **solidarity** amongst individuals who share such features, as well as simultaneously acting as a **social distance** mechanism for those individuals who do not share the same pronunciation features. These issues of solidarity and social distance are crucial to the discipline of sociolinguistics, and phoneticians play a very active role in producing sociolinguistic studies. This will be explored further in D1 and throughout Strand 9.

C2   WORD PLAYS

In this unit, you will be able to realise how deeply embedded your rules of morphology and semantics are by trying out the following activities.

Past and future

In Old English (500–1100), the past tense of verbs was commonly formed either *weakly* by adding a dental suffix ('-ed' in 'lifted', '-t' in 'spelt', or '-ed' in writing – even where /t/ was pronounced as in 'walked'), or *strongly* by an alteration in the root vowel ('sing – sang', 'run – ran', or 'bring – brought'). In Modern English, the weak form is now standard, so new coinages are tensed with dentals: simply, 'accessed', or 'hosted', and we have 'sprinted' not 'sprount', for example. There are British and American variations that have diverged over the years, reflecting the state of the dialects of American settlers at the point at which they left regions in Britain: in the UK, meat is 'hung' but criminals were 'hanged', a British swimmer 'dived' into the pool, but an American swimmer 'dove' into the water.

Old English probably had around 300 strong past tense forms; Modern English has less than 100, so the form seems to be dying out. We can imagine a twenty-second-century text as follows, that might capture for us how an Anglo-Saxon person might regard our own English:

> I runned through the woods, catched some sunshine, and goed for a paddle in the river. When I was weared out, I swimmed to the shore and eated my lunch. That evening, we lighted a fire and singed, before we all goed to bed. We waked up in the morning to find that the farmer had bringed us some eggs so we had a big breakfast before we setted off and drived home.

Try to continue this story in twenty-second-century English!	**Activity** ★

A popular anonymous rhyme exploits the comical potentials of the strong and weak past tense systems as follows:

> Forth from his den to steal he stole
> His bag of chink he chunk
> And many a wicked smile he smole
> And many a wink he wunk.

Try to write a second verse on the same principles.	**Activity** ★

How would you render unusual past forms of 'foot the bill', 'a bring-and-buy sale', 'kiss and tell' or 'hit and run driver' without sounding odd?	**Activity** ★

A cautionary tale: a friend staying at her prospective parents-in-law was kept awake all night by the birds tweeting outside her window. Asked in the morning by her prim host whether she had slept well, and a bit nervous, she unfortunately exclaimed: 'not really, the birds twat all night'.

Activity

New words for old

Connect the following affixes together randomly and then try to imagine a meaning for the resulting word. Then try to use the word in a sentence.

-ness	-less	-ish	-ful	-wise	-y
pre-	un-	dis-	re-	bi-	intra-

For example:

'nessless' – the desire for material things rather than abstractions;
'nesslessness' – the philosophy arguing for the desire for material things rather than abstractions;
'ishful' – extreme vagueness;
'ishy' – a bit vague;
'pre-wise' – sometime in advance.

(We are treating bound morphemes as if they were free morphemes here, of course). Make up your own examples and definitions.

What is semantically odd about the following words which are in fact very commonly used?

pre-warn	reconfirm	pre-book	pre-order	re-check	remove	interlink

What is the difference between 'flammable', 'inflammable', 'inflammatory' and 'non-flammable'? Compare your first intuitions with dictionary definitions.

Imagine meanings for the following illegitimate back-formations:

'effable' or 'to eff' (from 'ineffable');
'couth' or 'couthy' (from 'uncouth');
'cessor' or 'cession' (from 'intercessor');
'monstrate' (from 'demonstrate' and 'remonstrate');
'turb' (from 'disturb').

Try and think of other similar examples. Why are these illegitimate?

Why can we be 'grateful' but not 'grateless'? Why can we 'inquire' but not 'quire'? Why are 'outlaws' not the opposite of 'in-laws'? Having been in a relationship, you now have an 'ex'; can you have a 'pre'?

Can you think of any other oddities like these?

You might also investigate the histories and usages of: 'self-harm', 'air-condition', 'curate', 'spectate', 'sculpt', 'surveil', 'gestate', and 'edit', or find other similar curiosities.

How do the following break morphological rules: 'borg' (from 'cyborg' from 'cybernetic organism'), 'boyf' (from 'boyfriend'), 'earfro' (meaning excessive ear hair), 'textrovert' (someone who can only emote by email or text), 'emote' (to express emotion), 'dotcomrade' (an online friend).

Activity

Cartoon wordplay

The song-lyrics of animated family-movie musical cartoons are fertile ground for discovering clever wordplay, often based on semantic ambiguities or syntactic manipulation. Consider the following:

> 'I seen a peanut stand, heard a rubber band, I seen a needle that winked its eye' (from the song 'Did You Ever See An Elephant Fly?' from the film *Dumbo*, which also contains many other smart examples you might look up for yourself.

> 'You think you own whatever land you land on […] You can own the Earth and still all you'll own is earth until you can paint with all the colours of the wind' (from 'Colours of the Wind' from the movie *Pocahontas*)

> 'Numbers are the only thing that count' (song title from the movie *The Phantom Tollbooth*)

Can you explain the nature of the humour or wit here in linguistic terms?

Can you think of other similarly witty uses of wordplay in song-lyrics?

Activity

Mean meanings

Consider the potential semantic confusions present in the following. Can you explain in each case what is going on?

> The bandage was wound around the wound.
> The farm was used to produce produce.
> The dump was so full that it had to refuse more refuse.
> We must polish the Polish furniture.
> He could lead if he would get the lead out.
> The soldier decided to desert his dessert in the desert.
> Since there is no time like the present, he thought it was time to present the present.
> I did not object to the object.
> The insurance was invalid for the invalid.
> There was a row among the oarsmen about how to row.
> You must bow to the woman with the bow, under the bough of the tree.
> They were too close to the door to close it.
> The buck does funny things when the does are present.
> To help with planting, the farmer taught his sow to sow.
> Upon seeing the tear in the painting, I shed a tear.
> I had to subject the subject to a series of tests.
> We can dispense with dispensing the punishments, as a special dispensation.

Can you think of any other similarly ambiguous phrases?

Rewriting Blake

Here is a table summarising many of the common lexical semantic relationships in English.

synonymy	a word is a synonym of another if its meaning is almost exactly the same	*book, volume, text; letter, epistle, note, line*
antonymy	a word is an antonym of another if its meaning is almost exactly opposite	*black, white; up, down*
hyponymy	a word is a hyponym of another if it is part of the general category	*dog, mammal; poodle, dog*
meronymy	where an actual part–whole relationship exists between the meanings of two words	*hand, fingers; car, tyres*
polysemy / homonymy	a word is polysemous if it has developed two distinct meanings, and a homonym where two distinct words have converged (often only distinguishable with a knowledge of etymology)	*sole* (shoe/fish); *seal* (animal/glue)
plesionymy	a word is a plesionym if it is a near-synonym but substitution of the word does not leave the same truth conditions	*it wasn't misty, just foggy; he was murdered, or rather executed*
philonymy	two words are philonyms if they collocate in an acceptable and expected way	*the speaker can speak French; the pregnant woman*
tautonymy	two words are tautonyms if they merely repeat without adding new value, creating a tautology	*the speaker is speaking; boys will be boys*
xenonymy	two words are xenonyms if they create semantic dissonance	*fat water; the sadness of pencils*

Activity

> Now take the following famous poem by William Blake, and systematically rewrite the nouns and verbs by applying one of the lexical semantic relationships listed above. For example, a synonymic version of the poem might be entitled 'That Diseased Flower', and an antonymic version might be 'A Healthy Sink' (you have to be quite imaginative and lateral-thinking). Try to complete the entire poem.

The Sick Rose

O Rose thou art sick.
The invisible worm
That flies in the night
In the howling storm,

Has found out thy bed
Of crimson joy:
And his dark secret love
Does thy life destroy.

Discuss the effects of each change.

Then make a list of every occurrence in the original poem where Blake does not employ a simple philonymy (i.e. every example of deviant language use). You will notice that Blake uses a lot of surprising xenonyms. Note that the personification of the Rose ('O' and 'thou') is a form of semantic xenonymy. Are plants usually 'sick', or rather 'diseased' (plesionym)? Is 'worm' the same as 'serpent' or 'snake'? And what are the semantic resonances in interpretation of this image, from the Garden of Eden myth to a rather nasty phallic suggestiveness? What are the interpretative effects of Blake's actual stylistic choices?

Aside from the *denotational* values (the narrow definitional meanings) of Blake's choices, what are the *connotational* (conventional secondary meanings), *associative* (more personal conventional meanings) and *resonant* (loose atmospheric and tonal) effects of the style of the poem?

DOING POLITENESS

C3

Activity

Both authors of this book have delivered courses as MOOCs (free Massive Open Online Courses) over the Internet to many thousands of students. We used the delivery platform FutureLearn (www.futurelearn.com). When a student signs up for one of the courses, the following page appears:

Code of conduct

As a FutureLearner:

○ I will not use FutureLearn unless I am aged 13 or older.
○ I will register for one account only, using my real name.
○ Answers to all quizzes and tests will be my own work, unless directly instructed otherwise by the educator.

○ I will not share answers to quizzes and tests unless invited to do so as part of the assessment.

○ I will not take part in any activity that dishonestly enhances my own results, or dishonestly affects the results of other learners.

○ I understand that there are large numbers of people on my course, and that I won't be able to personally correspond with the educators, other than within the FutureLearn website.

○ I may engage in robust debate where appropriate to the learning experience, but I will not deliberately personally attack or offend others.

○ I will not use racist, sexist, homophobic, sexually explicit or abusive terms or images, or swear words or language that is likely to cause offence.

○ I will not participate in, condone or encourage unlawful activity, including any breach of copyright, defamation, or contempt of court.

○ I will not use FutureLearn to advertise products or services for profit or gain, nor will I use it as a platform for campaigning.

○ I will not 'spam' other FutureLearners by posting the same message multiple times or posting a message that is unrelated to the discussion.

○ I will not share my personal contact details on the FutureLearn platform.

○ I understand that I am a FutureLearner and do not have access to the same resources and services as a student attending the university that is running my course.

○ As the FutureLearn community's first language is English, I will always post contributions in English to enable all to understand, unless specifically requested to do otherwise.

http://about.futurelearn.com/terms/code-of-conduct/

❑ What politeness difficulties are being anticipated here? And how has the writer suggested linguistic and pragmatic ways of dealing with these?

❑ Do you think that online politeness has different norms from face-to-face politeness? Do different online settings have different politeness rules?

Political apologies

Apologies provide good exploratory data for examining speech acts and politeness in action. We can draw attention to the performative speech act of 'I apologise', through use of the performative verb, and the use of 'sorry-based units', as in 'I'm sorry', as explicit illocutionary force indicating devices (IFIDs) for apologies, introduced in A3.

In collaborative work, Harris, Grainger and Mullany (2006) have presented a taxonomy for defining apologies, focusing upon apologies that take place in the public sphere, and the political arena in particular. Apologies in political contexts have proved to be a fruitful area of data collection in recent years. Harris, Grainger

C3

and Mullany (2006: 716) argue that we may well be living in what has been described in the mass media as the 'age of the apology'. They start by drawing attention to the following text:

> ***S o r r y***
> >   ***E v e r y b o d y***
> >   ***(we tried)***
> >   ***(signed)***
> >   *--- half of America*

This message was posted by James Zelten on a website entitled sorryeverybody.com after George W. Bush was re-elected as President of the United States in 2004. The website became so popular that Zelten published a book of responses using a range of apologies from individuals worldwide. Interestingly, the book's title, *Sorry Everybody: An Apology to the World for the Re-election of George W. Bush*, includes the two explicit IFIDs.

Harris, Grainger and Mullany go on to present the following list of strategies which constitute apologies:

1. An illocutionary force indicating device (IFID) token: ('sorry', 'apologise')
2. An expression which indicates acceptance of responsibility and/or blame
3. An explanation or account
4. An offer of reparation
5. A promise of future forbearance

(Harris, Grainger and Mullany 2006: 721)

The first two elements in the list, the IFID tokens and expressions of responsibility and/or blame, are regarded as compulsory.

Activity

❑ Compile a list of recent occasions when you have apologised in your daily spoken interaction, online communication or written communication using the IFIDs of 'apologise' and/or 'sorry', and when you have received apologies from fellow interactants using these tokens.
❑ How many of the above strategies were used?
❑ Were you always to blame?
❑ Did you always accept responsibility?
❑ How many of the strategies in points 3–5 were present?

Now consider the following examples, particularly from the perspective of point 2, responsibility and/or blame:

❑ Bill Clinton apologising for the United States' involvement in the slave trade;
❑ Tony Blair apologising for the Irish potato famine when he was British Prime Minister;
❑ Queen Elizabeth II apologising for the seizure of Maori land.

Committing offences

In the above activities, you may have found that apology performance can be difficult to assign to these categories, including the 'compulsory' strategy of responsibility and/or blame. This complexity is related to an ambiguity that exists between strategies 1 and 2. 'Sorry' is frequently used to express regret without any sense of responsibility, as in 'I'm sorry your dog died' (providing that you did not in fact kill the dog!).

In terms of the political apologies given above, we have illustrations of Bill Clinton, Tony Blair and the British monarch apologising for historical events that took place long before they took office, events for which they bear no personal responsibility or blame. These public figures appear to be using apologies as moral acts. The notion of morality is related to what constitutes the need for an apology in the first place.

How do we decide which actions warrant an apology? Politeness researcher Janet Holmes (1995) has devised a useful list of categories of 'offences', often caused by speech acts, along with other actions associated with potential impoliteness or rudeness. Following Brown and Levinson's (1987) strategies, Holmes identifies apologies as forms of negative politeness which attend to negative face needs, characterised as follows:

1. Space offences: e.g. bumping into someone, queue jumping
2. Talk offences: e.g. interrupting, talking too much
3. Time offences: e.g. keeping people waiting, taking too long
4. Possession offences: e.g. damaging or losing someone's property
5. Social gaffes: e.g. burping, coughing, laughing inappropriately
6. Inconvenience offences/inadequate service: e.g. giving someone wrong items

(Holmes 1995: 167)

 Activity

☐   Revisit your list of occasions when you have apologised and received apologies.
☐   Which of the above 'offences' did you commit/had the apologiser(s) committed?
☐   Are all of these 'offences' covered by the above list? Does the list need any additional categories?

Another crucial area that needs to be considered alongside offence is level of seriousness, which is crucial in determining how apologies are made. Attempt to rank the 'offences' on a scale of seriousness, utilising the scale below. Then, ask a group of other individuals to give rankings to these offences. If possible, select people from a range of social and cultural backgrounds. Do you all agree? Can any social or cultural differences be identified?

1. *Light offences*: e.g. bumped into someone accidentally, forgot to return a library book on time.
2. *Medium offences*: e.g. broke someone's stapler, kept someone waiting so they were late.

3. *Heavy offences*: e.g. knocked someone over so they were hurt, inflicted serious damage on someone's car, insulted someone in public.

(Holmes 1995: 171)

To assess the effectiveness of an apology, it is essential to examine what happens next in an interaction. In reference to the instances you have been discussing above, consider the following:

❏ Did the hearer/reader accept/reject the apology?
❏ How many times did you apologise using IFIDs/how many apology tokens did you receive?
❏ What happened in the remainder of the interaction?
❏ Consider the effectiveness of the apologies that you have discussed above in light of the hearer's reaction and any subsequent communication with the apologiser/'apologisee'.
❏ Has the relationship between interlocutors been damaged?
❏ How frequently do 'light' or 'medium' apologies occur in everyday life in your culture?

Activity

Political apologies in the public eye

In order to explore the complexities of political apologies further, conduct an analysis of the following media data utilising the above taxonomy of apologies and the categories of offence and seriousness. The data include an 'apology' uttered by Geoff Hoon, the then Defence Secretary in Tony Blair's Labour Government, regarding a soldier who had been killed as a result of not having the appropriate body armour. This 'apology' was originally broadcast on BBC Radio 4's news programme, *Today*. It was extensively debated within the mass media immediately after broadcasting, where discussion focused upon whether or not Hoon had actually apologised:

> I am extremely sorry that Sgt Roberts did not have the enhanced body armour which we expected that he would receive. Some 38,000 sets of that enhanced body armour was sent to theatre. We wanted him to have that equipment. I'm extremely sorry that he did not have it. But – I think this is a crucial issue – ministers were assured that our armed forces were ready for battle. . . . It is a military judgement as to whether soldiers are ready for battle. You would rightly criticise any minister who interfered in such a judgement.

> Hoon apologises over soldier's death, but sidesteps blame (*The Guardian*)
> Grieving widow still waits for Hoon apology (*Daily Mail*)
> Hoon is shamed into an apology to widow: Nine months to say 'sorry' (*Daily Express*)

(Harris, Grainger and Mullany 2006: 721)

The ambiguity surrounding whether Hoon had apologised or not seems to lie in the area of responsibility and/or blame, explicitly pinpointed by *The Guardian* headline. Although the IFID tokens are present, pre-modified by an intensifier, 'extremely sorry', and repeated on two occasions, Hoon does not admit any responsibility or blame, and thus this is not enough to consist of a 'proper' apology according to some media sources. The ultimate offer of reparation (point 4 on p. 135) for politicians is to resign. If they admit responsibility and/or blame, then it is extremely difficult for them to continue in office. Hoon survived this incident, despite some calls for him to tender his resignation.

A larger-scale scandal surrounding a number of British MPs and their abuse of the parliamentary expenses system gripped British politics in 2009. This resulted in a significant number of apologies being issued by politicians from all political parties – a data treasure trove for speech act researchers. One of the most high-profile cases involved the Speaker of the House of Commons, Michael Martin. He issued the following apology in what turned out to be an infamous speech:

> We have let you down very badly indeed. We must all accept the blame and, to the extent that I have contributed to the situation, I am profoundly sorry.
>
> (Michael Martin, House of Commons, 18 May 2009)

❑ Analyse this apology according to the taxonomy of apologies and scales of offence and seriousness listed above.
❑ Can this be classified as an apology?
❑ How does this differ from Geoff Hoon's apology?
❑ Are there any elements missing?
❑ Collect your own set of political apologies and judge whether an apology has taken place according to the above taxonomies and scales.

Unlike the Geoff Hoon example, there was general agreement within the mass media that Michael Martin had apologised. However, as there was no 'offer of reparation' by Martin, this served only to exacerbate such a high-profile situation (in conjunction with a less-than-convincing display of his linguistic ability to keep the House of Commons under control). Less than 24 hours later, he handed in his resignation following significant pressure from the media, other politicians and the general public. The apology simply was not enough as an offer of reparation, and he thus became the first Commons speaker to be forced out of office in over 300 years.

❑ Consider the point made above, that we are currently living in the 'age of the apology'. Politicians are by no means the only public figures who are frequently called upon to apologise in the public sphere.
❑ Come up with a list of other professionals, organisations and institutions that are frequently called upon to apologise in public life.

C4

❑ Can the taxonomy that is applied to classifying politicians' apologies also be applied in these cases, or does a new/revised model need to be developed?

To summarise our data exploration of politeness and speech acts, it is worth highlighting Harris, Grainger and Mullany's (2006) conclusion that Brown and Levinson's (1987) politeness categories of offending negative face and the need for face repair fall short, given the seriousness of some political 'offences'. To state that the face needs of a bereaved partner have been offended, or the face needs of the British public have been offended by politicians' expenses scandal or by Tony Blair's decision to take Britain to war with Iraq does not seem to cover the seriousness of these offences.

According to Mills (2003: 112), apologies should be analysed as 'judgement[s] made about someone's linguistic performance'. If political apologies are to be *judged* by the media and the general public as valid and acceptable, they at least have to contain an explicit IFID, as well as an acceptance of personal responsibility and/or blame. Even then, this may not be enough to avoid the need for resignation.

SYNTACTIC EFFECTS

C4

Activity

The 11 hads
Here is a famous riddle:

How could you punctuate the following sentence to make it make sense?

> James, while John had had had had had had had had had had had a better effect on the teacher.
>
>   (Answer at the end of the unit)

Once you have worked out (or seen) the answer, can you explain the syntactic function of each occurrence of 'had' to show that they are not in fact identical instances? Try to draw a tree diagram of the sentence.

Can you devise another sentence similar to the '11 hads' above with as many uninterrupted repetitions of the same word? How about the similar example:

> The teacher said that that that that that man wrote should have been underlined.

Here, there is 'that' as a subordinating conjunction, then 'that' as an intensifying demonstrative determiner, then 'that' as a piece of quoted material (this exploits the distinction between *use* (as in the other examples of 'that') and *mention*), then 'that' as another subordinating conjunction, and finally another demonstrative determiner in 'that man' to indicate a specific man. Can you repunctuate the sentence to show this before you look at the answer at the end?

Can you devise an even more difficult sentence with more than 5 'thats'?

 Activity

Analysing ambiguity

Using what you know about constituent structure and phrases, can you explain as systematically as possible how the following genuine sentences could be interpreted in more than one way?

> Flying planes can be dangerous (sign at a model-aeroplane event in a park)
> Three-legged iron dog toaster (label on a toasting fork in the rough shape of a dog)
> I once shot an elephant in my pajamas. How he got in my pajamas I'll never know (Groucho Marx).
> It said 'For the sick' (child's explanation for vomiting in the collection box at the back of a church)
> I'll bring the picnic if it looks nice (the problems of an existential 'it')
> Dogs keep off the grass (addressed to literate dogs?)
> Please remove your clothes when the cycle is complete (at a coin-op laundry)
> Nothing works faster than Anadin (overly honest drug company advertising slogan)
> Child teaching expert to speak (university seminar notice)
> No smoking rooms available (hotel sign)
> Slow children ahead (sign near school, Nottingham)
> This door is alarmed! (bus notice, Nottingham)
> Dogs Trust Rehoming Centre (signpost in Cambridgeshire)
> Cat's eyes removed (Yorkshire roadworks sign)

Explain (i.e. spoil) this old joke using a tree diagram:

> 'I once knew a man with a wooden leg called Eric'.
> 'What was his other leg called?'

Explain how the similar patterns in the following pairs are actually more different syntactically than they appear on the surface:

C4

She decided on the apple pie.
She decided on the way home.

I ran up a huge hill.
I ran up a huge bill.

The shop was closed by midnight.
The shop was closed by the manager.

With a stick

Here is an odd but not impossible account of a story:

In the gallery, there were two paintings both called 'I hit the man with a stick with a stick': one was propped up on a chair, and the other was propped up with a stick. I thought the whole idea was absurd, so I hit 'I hit the man with a stick with a stick' with a stick with a stick.

Draw a tree diagram of the final sentence.

Sonnet 116

Let me not to the marriage of true minds
Admit impediments. Love is not love
Which alters when it alteration finds,
Or bends with the remover to remove:
O no! it is an ever-fixèd mark
That looks on tempests and is never shaken;
It is the star to every wandering bark,
Whose worth's unknown, although his height be taken.
Love's not Time's fool, though rosy lips and cheeks
Within his bending sickle's compass come:
Love alters not with his brief hours and weeks,
But bears it out even to the edge of doom.
    If this be error and upon me proved,
    I never writ, nor no man ever loved.

Identify the types of processes in the predications of this poem by William Shakespeare (material, mental, existential, relational, and so on – see B4). Then analyse the clause levels (the main 'alpha' clause, subordinate or relative 'beta' clause levels, 'gamma', 'delta', etc. clauses). Is there any correspondence between the type of process at alpha level and the types of processes at the other, embedded levels?

How can you use what you have discovered in your analysis to support an interpretation of the meaning of the poem? Crudely, is it mainly a poem about feeling, being or doing? Is it mainly about love or mainly about the power of writing?

Activity

Alien action

The following is a passage from the last few pages of the science fiction novelisation of the film *Alien*. Ripley, the last survivor of a deep-space cargo ship, and her cat Jones confront the monstrous alien creature that has killed the rest of the crew.

She did not see the massive hand reaching out for her from the concealment of deep shadow. But Jones did. He yowled.

Ripley spun, found herself facing the creature. It had been in the shuttle all the time. Her first thought was for the flamethrower. It lay on the deck next to the crouching alien. She hunted wildly for a place to retreat to. There was a small locker nearby. Its door had popped open from the shock of the expanding gas. She started to edge towards it.

The creature started to rise as soon as she began to move. She leaped for the locker and threw herself inside, one hand diving for the handle. As she fell in, her weight pulled the door shut behind her with a slam.

There was a port in the upper part of the door. Ripley found herself practically nose-up against it in the shallow locker. Outside, the alien put its own head up next to the window, peered in at her almost curiously, as though she were an exhibit in a cage. She tried to scream and couldn't. It died in her throat. All she could do was stare wide-eyed at the apparition glaring back at her.

[. . .]

Taking a deep breath, she slowly unlatched the door, then kicked it open.

The alien turned to face the locker, caught the steel shaft through its mid-section. Ripley had run with all her weight behind it, and it penetrated deeply. The alien grabbed at the shaft as yellow liquid began to spill outward, hissing violently where it contacted the metal.

Ripley fell back, grabbed a strut support while her other hand flailed at and contacted an emergency release. That blew the rear hatch. Instantly, all the air in the shuttle and anything not secured by bolt or strap or arm was sucked out into space. The alien shot past her. With inhuman reflexes it reached out an appendage . . . and caught hold of her trailing leg, just above the ankle.

She found herself dangling partway out the hatch as she kicked desperately at the limb locked around her leg. It wouldn't let go. There was a lever next to the emergency release and she threw it over. The hatch slammed shut, closing her in, leaving the alien outside.

(Alan Dean Foster, *Alien*, 1979: 249–51)

Sketch out the processes and participants involved across this passage. How does the text encode the relative positions and power of Ripley and the alien at each stage in their confrontation? How is the excitement and suspense maintained syntactically?

Activity ⭐

Completing the vision

The following is extracted from the final pages of Virginia Woolf's novel *To the Lighthouse*.

> 'He must have reached it,' said Lily Briscoe aloud, feeling suddenly completely tired out. For the Lighthouse had become almost invisible, had melted away into a blue haze, and the effort of looking at it and the effort of thinking of him landing there, which both seemed to be one and the same effort, had stretched her body and mind to the utmost. Ah, but she was relieved. Whatever she had wanted to give him, when he left her that morning, she had given him at last.
>
> 'He has landed,' she said aloud. 'It is finished.' Then, surging up, puffing slightly, old Mr. Carmichael stood beside her, looking like an old pagan God, shaggy, with weeds in his hair and the trident (it was only a French novel) in his hand. He stood by her on the edge of the lawn, swaying a little in his bulk, and said, shading his eyes with his hand: 'They will have landed,' and she felt that she had been right. They had not needed to speak. They had been thinking the same things and he had answered her without her asking him anything. He stood there spreading his hands over all the weakness and suffering of mankind; she thought he was surveying, tolerantly, compassionately, their final destiny. Now he has crowned the occasion, she thought, when his hand slowly fell, as if she had seen him let fall from his great height a wreath of violets and asphodels which, fluttering slowly, lay at length upon the earth.
>
> Quickly, as if she were recalled by something over there, she turned to her canvas. There it was – her picture. Yes, with all its greens and blues, its lines running up and across, its attempt at something. It would be hung in the attics, she thought; it would be destroyed. But what did that matter? she asked herself, taking up her brush again. She looked at the steps; they were empty; she looked at her canvas; it was blurred. With a sudden intensity, as if she saw it clear for a second, she drew a line there, in the centre. It was done; it was finished. Yes, she thought, laying down her brush in extreme fatigue, I have had my vision.
>
> (Virginia Woolf, *To the Lighthouse*, 1927: 197–8)

Sketch out the processes and participants involved across this passage. What are the dominant types of processes?

How is this passage from a novel which is often called 'impressionist' different syntactically from the action-adventure passage from *Alien* above?

Had that answer

James, while John had had 'had', had had 'had had'; 'had had' had had a better effect on the teacher.

The teacher said that *that* 'that' that that man wrote should have been underlined.

TEXTS IN ACTION

Analysing text messages

The individual creativity that the medium of texting allows can be of significant value, as it can enable trained language experts, known as **forensic linguists**, to establish the authorship of particular messages. Drawing upon the tools and techniques of discourse analysis, forensic linguists can ascertain a 'texting identity' for particular individuals by establishing patterns from banks of text-messaging data. They can then compare this texting identity profile with any other messages where authorship has been viewed with suspicion.

In 2001, discourse analyst Malcolm Coulthard was appointed by British police officers to investigate the authorship of two text messages which had allegedly been sent by a missing 15-year-old girl to her favourite uncle. Coulthard (2008) emphasises that producing forensic analyses of text messages represents a particular challenge, as text messaging discourse is generally short and thus there is limited language data that can be utilised to profile individual authorship. Using linguistic techniques, Coulthard came up with a projected 'texting' identity profile for the missing teenager from a sample of 65 of her messages. Here is one of the final two messages which had been sent from her phone, which had aroused suspicion:

> HIYA STU WOT U 2.IM IN SO MUCH TRUBLE AT HOME AT MOMENT EVONE HATES ME EVEN U! WOT THE HELL AV I DONE NOW? Y WONT U JUST TELL ME TEXT BCK PLEASE LUV DAN XXX
>
> (Coulthard 2008: 153)

Coulthard questioned the authenticity of authorship in this message, as he found the following discrepancies from the girl's proven text messaging style, ascertained from his detailed linguistic analysis of her 65 messages. Compare these features with the text message above:

❑ She used sentence case, not full capitalisation.
❑ Her abbreviation of 'what' was 'wat' not 'wot'.
❑ Her abbreviation of 'have' was usually 'ave' though she did use 'av' on occasions.
❑ Whenever she used the homonym 'one', as either a pronoun or cardinal number, she always used the numeral 1.

- Her abbreviations of prepositional phrases did not omit the article 'the', but instead she used the abbreviation 'da'.
- There was an actual example of the phrase 'at da mo' in a previous message.
- Whilst 'text back' was used in every message, it was always written as 'textb'.

The inconsistencies of the final two messages on her mobile phone demonstrated to police that these had been sent by someone attempting to perform her identity, rather than being from the missing girl herself. This changed the time of day when she had actually gone missing. The police consequently discovered that her uncle had been involved in her disappearance and that it was he who was the actual author of this message. He was eventually charged with her murder.

Activity ✪

- Based upon the techniques of analysis which Coulthard used, in conjunction with any other applicable linguistic features that you can add, create a linguistic profile of your own text messaging style. You should base your identity profile on a collection of no less than 50 messages from your 'sent items' and observe what language patterns emerge from this.
- Are you always consistent in your texting style?
- Compare your text identity patterns with those of your friends. How idiosyncratic is your own texting style? And can you see any similar patterns that might be regarded as your own group 'textolect'?

Overhearing

In the vast majority of cases, when we interact with one another in spoken discourse we generally tend to be aware of our surroundings at least to some degree, particularly in terms of who we are talking to, where we are talking, and who could potentially overhear us. For example, consider how many times you may have warned a fellow conversationalist that someone who you do not want to be an overhearer is in earshot, or have been warned yourself that someone is approaching.

It is not unheard of to be caught unaware – we have probably all experienced a situation from time to time in our conversational histories where we have uttered something that someone who was not the direct addressee may have overheard and we as speakers sorely wished they had not. It is one thing when this happens in informal contexts where conversations are not being recorded. But what if this happens to high-profile individuals in a public context with the mass media and their recording equipment present?

The following stretch of conversational data is taken from a 'private' inter-action which took place between the then British Prime Minister Tony Blair and the then US President George W. Bush during a lunch break at the G8 Summit held in Russia in 2006. Neither of the political leaders were aware that the microphone in front of them was switched on, nor that their conversation was being recorded.

This conversation provides a fascinating example of the differences between expected spoken discourse styles of particular individuals with specific professional roles in formal, public spheres and actual spoken discourse strategies that take place between such individuals when they think they are not being overheard.

The transcription presented below is our own version, which we have produced from listening to the recordings, initially broadcast many times on the BBC and CNN on 17 July 2006. Although some media outlets produced written 'transcripts', these lacked the detail required to be able to perform a linguistic discourse analysis. There was also considerable variation between them. The quality of the recording is quite poor in places, as there is a good deal of background noise. Where there is uncertainty over the accuracy of the speech, this is marked using the appropriate transcription conventions (see B12).

Produce a detailed analysis of the conversation between Tony Blair and George W. Bush, focusing first of all in particular upon the following frameworks covered in A5 and B5:

❑   the turn-taking system
❑   topic
❑   question–answer sequences
❑   simultaneous speech.

((George Bush has been talking to China's representative Hu Jintao about how long it will take him to fly home))

Bush: ((leans over to Russian President)) It takes him eight hours to fly home
Putin: (xxxxx xxxxx)
Bush: Eight hours
Putin: {I bet} (xxx xxxx xxxx)
Bush: Russia's big and so's China
Putin: {xxxx xxxx}
         ((Tony Blair approaches George Bush. He puts his arm on his chair and leans towards him))
Bush: {Yeah} Blair what are you doing?
Blair: I'm just (xxxx)
Bush: Are you leaving?
Blair: No no no no no yet on this trade thingy {I've been meaning to
Blair: say}(xxxxxxxxxx) [something like that or]
Bush: [Yeah I   ] told that to {xxxx}

Blair:	And are you planning to say that here or not?
Bush:	If you want me to=
Blair:	=Well it's just that if the discussion [arises]
Bush:	[I just want] some movement
Blair:	Yeah
Bush:	Yesterday I didn't see much movement
Blair:	No no but it may be there's not (.) it may be that it's
Blair:	[impossible but]
Bush:	[I'm prepared to say it]
Blair:	But it's just (.) I think that we need to be is in
Blair:	[a position]
Bush:	[Who's introducing] the trade?
Blair:	Angela (.)
Bush:	Tell her to call on me=
Blair:	=Okay
Bush:	Tell her to put me on the spot (.) and thanks for the sweater awfully
Bush:	thoughtful of you
Blair:	((laughs)) It's a pleasure ((laughs))
Bush:	I know you picked it out yourself=
Blair:	=Oh absolutely in fact I knitted it
Blair:	[((laughs))]
Bush:	[((laughs))]
Bush:	What about Kofi then? what sort of xxxx {I don't xxxxx ceasefire} plan
Bush:	his attitude's basically ceasefire and everything resolves (.) but (-) you
Bush:	know what I'm saying
Blair:	Yeah no I think the the really important thing is and it's really difficult
Blair:	is that (.) you can't stop this unless you get this
Blair:	international business agr[eed]
Bush:	[Yeah]
Blair:	I don't know what you guys have talked about about Israeli er but as I
Blair:	say I'm perfectly happy to try to (.) see (.) what it what the lie of the
Blair:	erm I- land is but you need that done quickly
Blair:	[because otherwise it will spiral]
Bush:	[yeah she's going]
Bush:	I think Condi's going to go pretty soon
Blair:	Right well that's (.) that's that's all that matters but (.) i- if you (.) you
Blair:	see it will take some time to get that to[gether] (-)
Bush:	[yeah]
Bush:	yeah
Blair:	But at least it gives people at sh[ot]
Bush:	[It's] a process, I agree
Blair:	at which [she an an]
Bush:	[I told her] your offer too to{xxx xxx}
Blair:	Well it's it's only if it's I mean you know if she's got a (.) or if she
Blair:	needs the ground prepared as it were (.) cos obviously if she goes out
Blair:	she's got to succeed as it were whereas I can go

```
                ((Bush starts eating a cracker))
Blair:   out and just      [talk    ]
Bush:    ((Whilst eating)) [you see] the irony is what they need to do is get Syria
Bush:    to get Hezbollah to come and stop doing this shit and it's over
Blair:   [(xxxxxxx) ]
Bush:    [{(who is}  ]
Blair:   (xxx) {Syria}
Bush:    {Why?}
Blair:   Because I think this is all part of the same thing=
Bush:    =Yeah
Blair:   What does he think? He thinks if Lebanon turns out fine if you get a
Blair:   solution in Israel and Palestine (.) Iraq goes in the right way
Bush:    Yeah yeah he's {through}
Blair:   He's had it and that's what the whole thing is about it's the same with
Blair:   Iran
Bush:    I felt like telling Kofi to call to come get on the phone to (xxx) as-
Bush:    Assad and make something happen
Blair:   Yeah
Bush:    {Because then Israel} (xxxxxxxxxxxx)
Blair:   (xxxxxxxxxxxxx)
Bush:    We are not blaming (.) the Lebanese government
                ((Blair touches the microphone in front of him and the sound is cut))
```

To expand your analysis, you should now bring in the principles of pragmatics and their accompanying linguistic frameworks which were introduced in B3 and C3. Analyse the overheard conversation from the perspectives of the following:

- ❏ Grice's co-operative principle and conversational maxims;
- ❏ Leech's politeness principle and politeness maxims; and
- ❏ Brown and Levinson's concept of face and positive and negative politeness.
- ❏ Discuss how you think the informal terms of address that both Bush and Blair use would be used differently if the two politicians were talking to a public audience through the mass media. What does this reveal in terms of levels of formality for conversations that take place in public versus private spheres?
- ❏ Using the above data as a guide, discuss how the role of an audience or any other potential overhearers governs the discourse strategies that we select when we interact with one another.
- ❏ Compare the spoken discourse that is used here with a formal speech made by either of the two politicians or a press conference where both of these politicians make a speech. What differences can you find? How important is written scripted discourse to politics?

Bush's use of the expletive 'shit' attracted a great deal of media attention. In an exact mirroring of the Gordon Ramsay examples in B3, when shown on US television networks the word 'shit' was bleeped out, but when shown on British networks the word was not censored. In fact, on the BBC, the news reporter actually uttered the word 'shit' himself, in the form of reported speech, quoting exactly what Bush had said, when introducing the story. This adds weight to the view that cultural differences exist between perceived politeness and impoliteness norms and conventions when comparing the editorial decisions taken by British and US broadcasting networks.

There was also much media attention focused upon the greeting sequence initiated by Bush. The following is a typical example of the media reaction:

> Forget prime minister, Mr Blair, or even plain old Tony. The new way to address the prime minister, we learn, is 'Yo Blair'.
>
> (James Wheatdale, BBC Website, 17 July 2006)

Despite doubts about the accuracy of the transcription of 'Yo Blair', particularly due to background noise (as you have seen, after listening several times we decided upon 'yeah Blair'), the term 'Yo Blair' has stuck regardless of whether it was actually uttered or not.

It has been used as the title of a book by British journalist Geoffrey Wheatcroft: 'Yo, Blair!': Tony Blair's Disastrous Premiership (2007). One clothing company produced 'Yo Blair!' t-shirts, and it described this merchandise as 'the new must have political t-shirt' (concepttshirts.co.uk). It was also possible to purchase t-shirts with the Bush expletive: 'Get Syria to get Hezbollah to stop doing this shit and it's over' followed by the satirical caption 'Mid East Politics by G W Bush' as well as a third design, simply the quotation 'On this trade thingy' with the caption underneath reading: 'G8 diplomacy 2006'.

Activity

❏ Consider occasions where you or a friend/family member have been caught out by the presence of overhearers.
❏ What kind of communicative problems did this cause?
❏ What happened next in the discourse?
❏ Were these situations easy to resolve? Why/why not?
❏ Drawing upon what you have learnt during the discourse and pragmatics strands in this book, discuss the overall importance of formality and informality, along with the differing norms and conventions of 'appropriate' discourse in public and private spheres. Consider how this differs in various cultural contexts where the English language is spoken.

LEARNING TO READ

Activity ⭐

Learning to spell

Ada is 5 years old. She is in her first year at school in Yorkshire in the UK and is learning to read and write. Here are some examples of her spellings and the standardised versions in italics (derived from her reading her own writing out loud):

swiintcarn	*sweetcorn*
roobarbAndcosdud	*rhubarb and custard*
ttatos	*tomatoes*
tmortoss	*tomato sauce*
golicbreb	*garlic bread*
piica	*pizza*
milc	*milk*
sosajis	*sausages*
oneeuns	*onions*
chicin	*chicken*
potoes	*potatoes*
fishfingrs	*fish fingers*
soop	*soup*
sbgetee	*spaghetti*
oringepier	*orange and pear*
bingbo	*bingo*
breb	*bread*
bred	*bread*
cupandsorss	*cup and saucer*
sorsa	*saucer*
telee	*telly*
dibr	*dibber (=television remote control)*
teef	*teeth*
plAts	*plates*
AYsgreem	*ice cream*
sosijsAndmAsAnmichdvedg	*sausages and mash and mixed veg*
Once A pon A taym	*Once upon a time*

❑ On the basis of just this limited data, can you speculate on some of the patterns and principles of spelling that Ada uses?

❑ Can you identify regular patterns (where a rule seems to be applied consistently) and variable patterns (where different versions are allowed)?

❑ Can you identify spellings where her pronunciation of the word is influential, and others where the spelling departs from the way the word is pronounced?

❑ What is her system for using capital letters, and what do they signify?

❑ When does she use doubled letters ('ii', 'oo'), and what are they being used for?

Learning to write stories

Age: 60 months
Here is a story that Ada wrote around her fifth birthday (a standardised version is given in italics from her reading aloud):

OnceA ponAtaYm	*Once upon a time*
therwosAcatthe	*there was a cat. The*
cAtmetAbogthee	*cat met a boy. The*
bogsebheLow	*boy said, 'Hello'.*

Age: 62 months
Here is another story she wrote two months later. Again, the standardised spelling and punctuation are given in italics. The story is written 'upside down', beginning at the bottom of the sheet of paper with the top half blank, so a normal sequence is given afterwards.

with the teecup the End	*with the teacup. The end.*
the sarsa plAd gAms	*the saucer played games*
frend wos a sirsa	*friend was a saucer.*
hadafrenb the teecops	*had a friend. The teacup's*
coRb speec the teecop	*could speak. The teacup*
ther wos A teecop hoo	*there was a teacup who*
Once A pon A taym	*Once upon a time*

Once upon a time
there was a teacup who
could speak. The teacup
had a friend. The teacup's
friend was a saucer.
The saucer played games
with the teacup. The end.

Age: 63 months
Here is a story Ada wrote one month after the last example. Her own writing is reproduced in Figure C6.1.

the End	*The End.*
plAd withht eechuth	*played with each other.*
woscold sdon theA	*was called spoon. They*
hAdAFrend hisFrend	*had a friend. His friend*
hors the rocnhors	*horse. The rocking-horse*
ther wos A rocen	*there was a rocking-*
Wo	*(Once)*
Once A pon A tim	*Once upon a time*

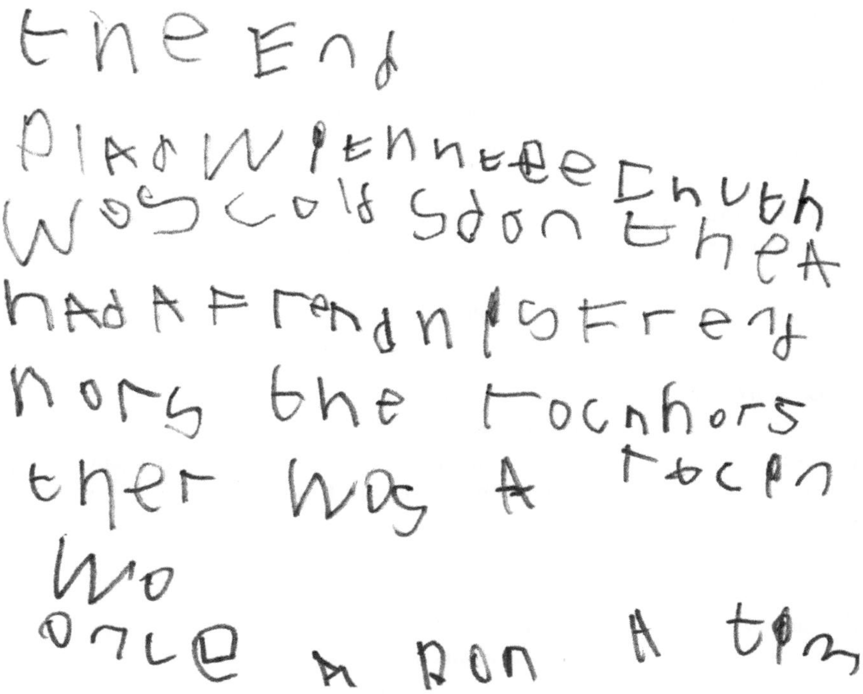

Figure C6.1 Ada's story at age 63 months

> Once upon a time
> there was a rocking-
> horse. The rocking-horse
> had a friend. His friend
> was called spoon. They
> played with each other.
> The End.

Age: 65 months

Finally, here is a story Ada wrote two months after the last one. Again, it is inverted so a reversed-order sequence is also given. See Figure C6.2 for Ada's own writing.

Enb	End.
b offthiA boocs the	(ed) off their books. The
the hAws AndFinish	the house and finished
thien thiA went intoo	then they went into
thia mAd lots ov boocs	They made lots of books
go intot dades booc	go into Dad's book.
And bid A buc too	and did a book to
plAb onthe peeAno	played on the piano
the somhAwsAnd	the summer-house and
Ada and bad went intoo	Ada and Dad went into
Once Apon A tAYm	Once upon a time

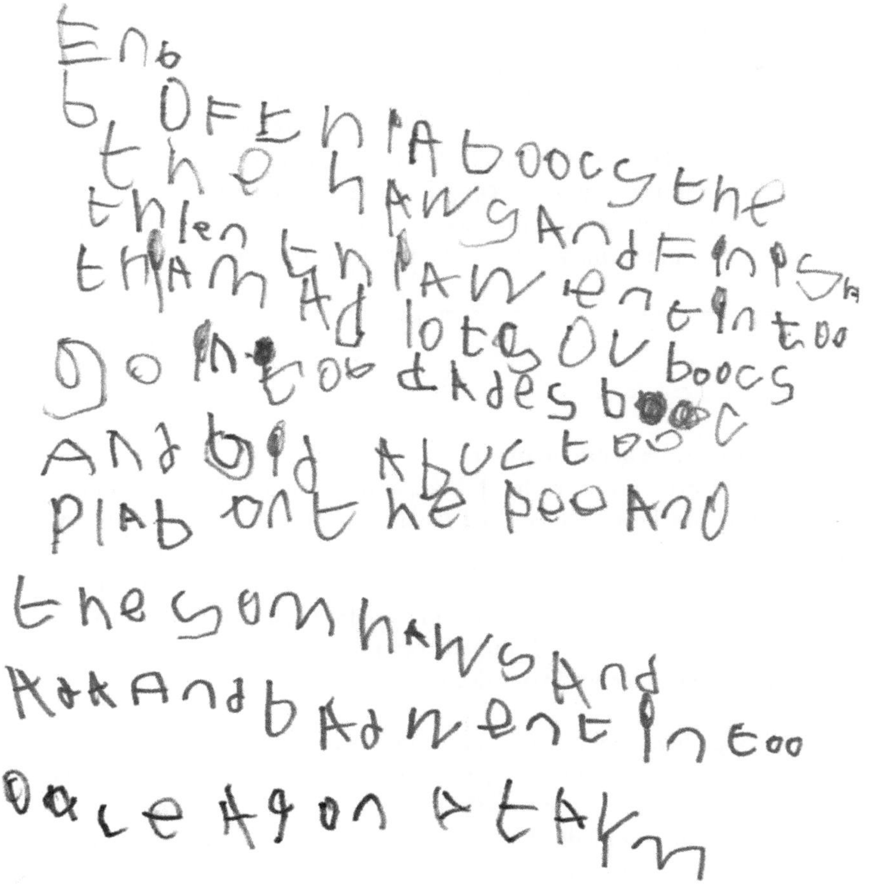

Figure C6.2 Ada's story at age 65 months

*Once upon a time
Ada and Dad went into
the summer-house and
played on the piano
and did a book to
go into Dad's book.
They made lots of books
then they went into
the house and finished
off their books. The
End.*

Activity

- ❑ Examine Ada's spelling patterns again. What is consistent in her system and what is changing? Look closely at her letter shapes.
- ❑ Looking at the content of the stories, how are her narrative skills developing? How does she connect events? What evidence is there that her pronoun usage and reference chaining are developing?
- ❑ Rewrite her final story above, keeping the content but expressing it in a more mature form. What have you added and changed?

Activity

Developing narrative literacy

Here are six stories produced by children at different ages between 2 and 7 (the spelling has been standardised from their originals). Try to put the narratives in chronological sequence based only on the style and organisation evident in the texts. In other words, put them in the right developmental order. (Answers are at the end of the unit.) Before you look at the answers, make a note of why you placed your choices in your sequence: which features of the narratives influenced your decision?

1. The bugs live under the carpet. Bugs like dark. Bugs come out at night. Owls come out at night. Sleeping is at night. Owls don't like sleeping.
2. We went to Grandad's. We went to the seaside. We had ice-cream. The ice-cream was too big. There was a car coming the other way and coming fast but we jumped out of the way because Grandad shouted 'Look out!'. So we went home then.
3. Alan lost his dog. He came back and opened the door and the dog ran out. We helped him look for it. It was called Yo-yo. We looked in the woods and drove around in the car, but we couldn't see it. So we went to wait at home. And Yo-yo was waiting in the house all the time.
4. My friend likes chocolate. That baby is good. They don't want to play with us.
5. Once upon a time Ada and Dad went into the summer-house and played on the piano and did a book to go into Dad's book. They made lots of books then they went into the house and finished off their books.
6. She doesn't like me. She throws things and cries all the time. Today she wanted the thing I was playing with. She said it was hers. It was not hers. We all have to share. She shouted and didn't get it.

Rewind your literacy

Once you have learnt to read fluently (as you, the adult reader of this book, must be doing right now), it is very difficult to remember what it felt like not to be able to read. Even looking at a different linguistic script such as Chinese, Greek, Thai or Cyrillic (if you are not a native of those countries where they are used) is not quite the same as knowing the words of a language like English but not being able to read the letters that form its writing system. It is virtually impossible for you to look at a piece of English writing and somehow switch off the learnt cognitive faculty that insists you read it as meaningful – to see it again as a set of difficult shapes that require a great deal of effort to decode and speak aloud.

 Activity

In order to try to recapture what it feels like to be a 5- or 6-year-old, here is a passage for you to read aloud. Just as young readers have an undeveloped sense of genre and register, we are not going to tell you what sort of passage it is, because that would help you to predict some of the words. Just like a 5-year-old, you must work this out for yourself. Read it aloud once, and then – without looking back at the passage, try to answer the questions that follow.

Finland hosted the 17th most international association meetings in the world in 2007. Among congress cities Helsinki ranked 20th. Other Finnish cities to be included in the top 100 included Turku (72nd) and Espoo (84th). Finland was also the highest ranking Nordic country.

The survey, which was carried out by the Union of International Associations (UIA), covered 176 countries and 1623 cities. Last year Finland hosted a total of 438 congresses, including 200 that qualified according to the UIA as international meetings. Of these, 79 were held in Helsinki.

The rankings of both Finland and Helsinki dropped as expected compared with 2006, which was the busiest congress year ever thanks in no small part to the large number of meetings related to the EU Presidency.

1. Can you name the three cities that are mentioned in the passage?
2. Can you recall any of the rankings or scores of those cities in the survey?
3. Is Finland doing well as a conference destination or not?
4. Why was 2006 a very good year for conference meetings in Finland?
5. Is the article generally optimistic or pessimistic?

The original passage is taken from the business magazine *Meet in Finland* (issue 3, 2008, page 6). You will have realised by now that the text has been mirror-reversed. You can make this exercise even more difficult by also turning the book upside-down. The effect is to present you as a reader with letters that you have to decode into words. The unfamiliarity of the letter shapes means that you have to devote a great deal of cognitive effort simply for the decoding process, so there is relatively little working attention left for processing meaning. This is what it is like to be 5 years old.

You might have found it reasonably easy to answer the name-recall in question 1. Most people find the numbers in question 2 harder to remember, but again this is simply a recall of information that you have just spoken out loud. (If you read the passage out loud to a group of other people, you might be surprised how much easier they find it to answer the questions than you.) Questions 3 and 4 rely on some inferences that you have to draw from complete sentences in the passage, and question 5 is the most cognitively complex of all, as you have to make an evaluative judgement about the perspective of the writer across the whole text. It is highly likely that your entire attention has been so greatly preoccupied with decoding the words that you cannot answer these later questions with much confidence. This effort and uncertainty is also what it felt like when you were learning to read.

Answers

The correct developmental order is 4, 1, 6, 2, 5, 3.

Narrative 4: *Heaps*. This is the earliest formal type of narrative, produced from 2 years old and onwards. Simple present tense is used instead of the adult normative past tense. The ideas expressed tend to be unrelated and unconnected.

Narrative 1: *Sequences*. This type of narrative is typical of 2–3-year-olds. There is a cohesive theme repeated, often following a person or animal, or focused in a particular place. However, there is often no explicit cohesive links, and the whole narrative might consist of several separate events.

Narrative 6: *Primitive narratives*. These tend to develop between 3 and 4 years old. Here, there is cohesive reference chaining ('she'). The crucial advance from simple sequences is an element of narratorial evaluation or a mention of emotion or the state of mind of one of the characters.

Narrative 2: *Unfocused chains*. 4-year-olds tend to produce these. There is cohesive chaining, but the connection is more likely to be focused on the place or the nature of the event rather than on a character, as in primitive narratives. 4-year-olds produce both unfocused chains and primitive narratives, but they generally stop producing heaps and sequences by now. Conjunctions begin to appear to mark out cause and effect, to give explanations, or to draw attention to climactic points in the account.

Narrative 5: *Focused chains*. This is what 5-year-olds do, alongside unfocused chains, while primitive narratives dwindle away. There might be multiple characters and a sense of relationships between them. The sequence of events makes sense and has a 'tellable' point. Often these narratives simply stop without a resolution or round-up.

Narrative 3: *Full narrative*. By age 7, most children can tell full narratives. The stories have become longer, a range of tense and aspect is deployed, and evaluations are embedded in the narrative. Above all, such narratives have 'tellability' and often have an explicitly marked climax, moral, punch-line, or other manifest finale.

EXPLORING THE MIND

Prototypes

Here are some games that demonstrate the reality of prototypicality in language.

Which is more fruity?

- ❑ an apple or a banana?
- ❑ a blueberry or a kiwi?
- ❑ a cabbage or a potato?
- ❑ a stick of rhubarb or a walnut?
- ❑ a plastic apple or a real pumpkin?

Try to make snap decisions and then examine your justifications for your answers.

You can see the patterns in radial structures by writing down as fast as possible 30 examples of the following categories:

- ❑ fruit
- ❑ furniture
- ❑ girls' names
- ❑ flavours of ice-cream
- ❑ things to sit on
- ❑ American presidents
- ❑ alcoholic drinks
- ❑ holiday resorts
- ❑ things to wear to class/college/school/seminar
- ❑ routes from your house to work/school/college

It is likely that the later items in the list of 30 are the more peripheral and marginal ones. Can you arrange each set of 30 in a radial pattern, with a central group and less central clusters? You are unlikely to have written them down immediately in strict sequence.

Now try to think of situations in which your three most peripheral items are treated as more prototypical members of the category. For example, a 'durian' (a large spiky oriental fruit with an indescribably bad smell – so bad it is banned on the Singapore transit system) is a very poor example of a fruit to British minds. However, in the Singaporean context, it is a good example of a fruit – and it is a good example of an 'exotic' fruit – and it is an especially good example of a bad-smelling fruit.

Alternatively, you can record someone trying these same tasks aloud without pausing. Examine the items that appear early in the sequence and then later in the sequence: what patterns emerge? Are there any semantic connections or common features in items that are close together? Towards the end of the sequence, are there any items for which there is disagreement about whether they should be included at all?

For a less disciplined version of this exercise, record someone saying out loud and without pausing the first 100 words that come into their head. Are there any semantic connections between items in this free association? Do you notice any patterns, any clusters around certain semantic domains, and any phonological or morphological repetition that might show the way your mind is chaining concepts together? For example, are the items things in the room, parts of objects, concrete or abstract, within one semantic domain or randomly distributed, swear words, signs of current preoccupations, and so on? What does all this data tell you about thought processes and language?

Activity

Aphasias

Aphasias are disabilities with language usually caused by brain damage, such as stroke or physical injury (see A7). Two general types have been known about for a while. Broca's aphasia is also called expressive or production aphasia: speech is characterised by a disordered syntax, repetition and halting articulation. Wernicke's aphasia is also called receptive or fluent aphasia: it has apparently well-formed grammar, but odd or inappropriate word-choices. Sufferers from Broca's aphasia tend to retain their capacities for comprehending the speech of others, but those suffering from Wernicke's aphasia find this much harder. Given this brief distinction and definition, can you identify which of the following two famous passages is an example of Broca's aphasia and which is an example of Wernicke's aphasia? (Answer is at the end of the unit.) In each, identify the specific features and consider the differences between each example and a more 'normal' speech pattern.

Passage A

'I am a sig . . . no . . . man . . . uh, well . . . again.' These words were emitted slowly, and with great effort. The sounds were not clearly articulated; each syllable was uttered harshly, explosively, in a throaty voice. With practice, it was possible to understand him, but at first I encountered considerable difficulty in this. 'Let me help you,' I interjected. 'You were a signal . . .' 'A sig-nal man . . . right,' Ford completed my phrase triumphantly. 'Were you in the Coastguard?' 'No, er, yes, yes . . . ship . . . Massachu . . . chusetts . . . Coastguard . . . years.' He raised his hands twice, indicating the number nineteen.

Passage B

'Boy, I'm sweating, I'm awful nervous, you know, once in a while I get caught up, I can't get caught up, I can't mention the tarripoi, a month ago, quite a little, I've done a lot well, I impose a lot, while, on the other hand, you know what I mean, I have to run around, look it over, trebbin and all that sort of stuff. Oh sure, go ahead, any old think you want. If I could I would. Oh I'm taking the word the wrong way to say, all of the barbers here whenever they stop you it's going around and around, if you know what I mean, that is tying and tying for repucer, repuceration, well, we were trying the best that we could while another time it was with the beds over there the same thing.'

Activity

Schemas

Consider the following passage first from the point of view of a description in an estate agent/real estate office (which is its actual origin) and second from the point of view of a burglar. Which different elements are fore-grounded for your attention in each case?

> Undoubtedly, one of the finest examples of this type of property currently on the market; this truly outstanding, beautifully presented and superbly appointed, four bedroomed detached house has been comprehensively refurbished to an exceptionally high standard and forms part of this small cul-de-sac within this popular and established residential area, well served by local amenities and affords excellent access to the motorway network. Plans have been submitted to extend the already spacious accommodation to provide a double storey extension with a proposed large family room and bigger third and fourth bedrooms together with an en-suite shower room. Currently having a gas fired central heating system, Upvc leaded double glazing with ground floor locks and comprising: cellar with built-in safe, hall with solid oak flooring that extends through into the living room with contemporary style recesses to the chimney breast for an LCD/plasma screen, dining room again with solid oak flooring, kitchen being beautifully fitted out and recently refurbished, with excellent high quality integrated appliances, fitted utility, downstairs W.C., landing, master bedroom with impressive views across the fields and woodland, excellent built-in wardrobes, superb en-suite luxurious shower room, three further bedrooms and exemplary family bathroom again beautifully fitted out. One bedroom has second phone landline and broadband computer connection. Driveway, separate garage with space for two cars plus workshop area for tools and bicycles and mainly lawned rear garden, secluded by a high laurel hedge. Security lighting and alarm is fitted. Furniture and appliances are included for viewing and may be purchased by arrangements, but property is available for vacant possession. Viewings by appointment with the agents only.

Activity

Read the following recipe. An absolutely literal-minded robot who follows instructions to the letter would not be able to produce a lemon muffin after reading this. (See what the robot would not do at the end of this unit!) What schematic information and activities do you bring to the reading that the automaton could not possess?

Lemon Muffins

1 egg	1/2 cup sugar
1/2 cup vegetable oil	grated rind of 1 unwaxed lemon
3/4 cup milk	juice of 1 to 2 lemons

Preheat the oven to 200°C (gas mk 6, 400°F). Place the egg, oil, milk and sugar in a mixing bowl and beat together until sugar has dissolved. Add the lemon rind and lemon juice and mix.

2 cups plain flour
3 tsp baking powder
1 tsp salt

In another large bowl, thoroughly mix the flour, baking powder and salt.

Add the liquid mix to the dry, and roughly mix it in – it does not have to be absolutely smooth.

Fill a muffin tray with paper muffin cases, and then fill each case approximately two thirds with the muffin mixture. Bake the muffins for 25 minutes.

Makes approximately 12 muffins.

(www.muffinrecipes.co.uk)

Activity

Riddles

Riddles (of the 'What am I?' sort) have been popular in English since the earliest form of the language. They deliberately obscure or delay the application of the correct organising schema in order to provide a puzzle. What are the following describing? (Answers are at the end of the unit.) If you guess them correctly, can you account for how they try to distract you towards the wrong answer?

- ❑ Poke it with your right foot and it moves. It growls when it does this. Poke it again a bit to the left and it stops. It never gets hungry, but if you don't give it liquids it won't work for you at all. What is it?
- ❑ John looked through the dirty window on the 30th floor of the office building. Overcome with despair, he decided to pack in his job and everything there and then. He slid open the window, jumped through, and fell all the way to the floor. How did he survive?
- ❑ What goes up the chimney down, but cannot go down the chimney up?
- ❑ One of several rather rude riddles from the tenth-century *Exeter Book* – what is this?

Wrætlic hongað bi weres þeo,	A curiosity hangs near a man's thigh,
frean under sceate. Foran is þyrel.	Full under folds. It is pierced in front,
Bið stiþ ond heard, stede hafað godne;	Is stiff and hard, and stands in a good place.
þonne se esne his agen hrægl	When a young lord lifts his shirt
ofer cneo hefeð, wile þæt cuþe hol	Over his knees, he wants to greet
mid his hangellan heafde gretan	With the hard head of this hanging creature
þæt he efenlang ær oft gefylde.	The hole it has often filled.

- ❑ If you don't know what it is, then it is what it is. If you do know what it is, then it is not what it was. What is it?

Can you write your own distracting riddle?

Activity

Not Snow White

Here is an extract from John Lennon's *A Spaniard in the Works*, a collection of writing which features some free word association, close semantic and phonetic echoes, creative spellings, and malapropisms. As you read, try to work out the source words and phrases alluded to in the text. Can you rewrite the story in a more standard form, and if you do, how is it different in tone?

Snore Wife and Some Several Dwarts

Once upon upon in a dizney far away – say three hundred year agoal if you like – there lived a sneaky forest some several dwarts or cretins; all named – Sleezy, Grumpty, Sneezy, Dog, Smirkey, Alice? Derick – and Wimpey. Anyway they all dug about in a diamond mind, which was rich beyond compere. Every day when they came hulme from wirk, they would sing a song – just like ordinary wirkers – the song went something like – 'Yo ho! Yo ho! it's off to wirk we go!' – which is silly really considerable they were comeing hulme. (Perhaps ther was slight housework to be do.)

One day howitzer they (Dwarts) arrived home, at aprodestant, six o'cloth, and who? – who do they find? – but only Snore Wife, asleep in Grumpty's bed. He didn't seem to mine. 'Sambody's been feeding my porrage!' screams Wimpey, who was wearing a light blue pullover. Meanwife in a grand Carstle, not so mile away, a womand is looging in her daily mirror, shouting, 'Mirror mirror on the wall, whom is de fairy in the land' which doesn't even rhyme. 'Cassandle!' answers the mirror. 'Chrish O'Malley' studders the womand who appears to be a Queen or a witch or an acorn.

'She's talking to that mirror again farther?' says Misst Cradock, 'I've just seen her talking to that mirror again.' Father Cradock turns round slowly from the book he is eating and ex-plains that it is just a face she is going through and they're all the same at that age. 'Well I don't like it one tit,' continhughs Misst Cradock. Father Cradock turns round slowly from the book he is eating, explaining that she doesn't have to like it, and promptly sets fire to his elephant. 'Sick to death of this elephant I am,' he growls, 'sick to death of it eating like an elephant all over the place.'

[. . .]

A few daisy lately the [woman] comes hooting aboon the apples for sale with a rarther more firm aproach saying 'These apples are definitely for sale.' Snore Wife, who by this time is curiously aroused, stick her heads through the window. Any-way she bought one – which didn't help the trade gap at all. Little diggerydoo that it was parsened with deathly arsenickers. The woman (who was the wickered Queen in disgust) cackled away to her carstle in the hills larfing fit to bust.

[. . .].

John Lennon, *A Spaniard in the Works*, 1965

Answers

Aphasias

Passage A is an example of Broca's aphasia and Passage B is an example of Wernicke's aphasia, both from Gardner 1974 (60–8).

Muffins

Among many other possible gaps, the robot would not know that the list of noun-phrases is a list of ingredients. It might try to unwax a lemon. It might not use the de-rinded lemon also for its juice, but would waste the lemon. It might add up the cup amounts and conclude that 1 and ¾ of a cup cannot fit into a cup. It might throw some cups into the mixture. It would not break the egg. It would not know to be in a kitchen, nor which oven 'the' oven referred to. It would have to know which of the two bowls was the 'liquid mix' and which was 'the dry'. It would not have a muffin tray ready and would not know that 'the muffin mixture' is what is produced from the previous activity. It would not know to 'Bake the muffins' because as yet there are no muffins, only mixture. It would not remove the muffins from the oven after 25 minutes because it is not told to do so. It would have needed the information about how many muffins the recipe makes much earlier on when it was deciding on how many paper cases to use.

Riddles

It's a car.
John is a window-cleaner.
It's an umbrella.
It's a key.
It's a riddle.

C8   **CORRECTIONS**

Activity

Swift's proposal for correcting, enlarging and ascertaining our language

The following extract sets out Jonathan Swift's objections to the degeneracy of English writing and his suggestions for remedying the situation. What do you think of his arguments?

The Period wherein the *English* Tongue received most Improvement, I take to commence with the beginning of Queen *Elizabeth*'s Reign, and to conclude with the Great Rebellion in Forty Two. 'Tis true, there was a very ill Taste both of Style and Wit, which prevailed under King *James* the First, but that seems to have been corrected in the first Years of his Successor, who among many other qualifications of an excellent Prince, was a great Patron of Learning. From the Civil War to this present Time, I am apt to doubt whether the Corruptions in our Language have not at least equalled the Refinements of it; and these Corruptions very few of the best Authors of our Age have wholly escaped. During the Usurpation, such and Infusion of Enthusiastick Jargon prevailed in every Writing, as was not shook off in many Years after. To this succeeded that Licentiousness which entered with the *Restoration*, and from infecting our Religion and Morals, fell to corrupt our Language; which last was not like to be much improved by those who at that Time made up the Court of King *Charles* the Second; either such who had followed Him in His Banishment, or who had been altogether conversant in the Dialect of those *Fanatick Times*; or young Men, who had been educated in the same Company; so that the *Court*, which used to be the Standard of Propriety and Correctness of Speech, was then, and, I think, hath ever since continued the worst School in *England* for that Accomplishment; and so will remain, till better Care be taken in the Education of our Nobility, that they may set out into the World with some Foundation of Literature, in order to qualify them for Patterns of Politeness. The Consequence of this Defect, upon our Language, may appear from Plays, and other Compositions, written for Entertainment with the Fifty Years past; filled with a Secession of affected Phrases, and new, conceited Words, either borrowed from the current Style of the Court, or from those who, under the Character of Men of Wit and Pleasure, pretended to give the Law. Many of these Refinements have already been long antiquated, and are now hardly intelligible; which is no wonder, when they were the Product only of Ignorance and Caprice.

I have never known this great Town without one or more *Dunces* of Figure, who had Credit enough to give Rise to some new Word, and propagate it in most Conversations, though it had neither Humor, nor Significancy. If it struck the present Taste, it was soon transferred into the Plays and current Scribbles of the Week, and became an Addition to our Language; while the Men of Wit and Learning, instead of early obviating such Corruptions, were too often seduced to imitate and comply with them.

There is another Set of Men who have contributed very much to the spoiling of the *English* Tongue; I mean the Poets, from the Time of the Restoration. These Gentlemen, although they could not be insensible how much our Language was already overstocked with Monosyllables; yet, to save Time and Pains, introduced that barbarous Custom of abbreviating Words, to fit them to the Measure of their Verses; and this they have frequently done, so very injudiciously, as to form such harsh unharmonious Sounds, that none but a *Northern* Ear could endure: They have joined the most obdurate Consonants without one intervening Vowel, only to shorten a Syllable: And their Taste in time became so depraved, that what was at first a Poetical Licence, not to be justified, they made their Choice, alledging, that the Words pronounced at length, sounded faint and languid. This was a Pretence to take up the same Custom in Prose; so that most of the Books we see now a-days, are full of those Manglings and Abbreviations. Instances of this Abuse are innumerable: What does Your Lordship think of the Words, *Drudg'd*, *Disturb'd*, *Rebuk't*, *Fledg'd*, and a thousand others, every where to be met in Prose as well as Verse? Where, by leaving out a Vowel to save a Syllable, we form so jarring a Sound, and so difficult to utter, that I have often wondred how it could ever obtain.

Another Cause (and perhaps borrowed from the former) which hath contributed not a little to the maiming of our Language, is a foolish Opinion, advanced of late Years, that we ought to spell exactly as we speak; which beside the obvious Inconvenience of utterly destroying our Etymology, would be a thing we should never see an End of. Not only the several Towns and Counties of *England*, have a different way of Pronouncing, but even here in *London*, they clip their Words after one Manner about the Court, another in the City, and a third in the Suburbs; and in a few Years, it is probable, will all differ from themselves, as Fancy or Fashion shall direct: All which reduced to Writing would entirely confound Orthography. Yet many People are so fond of this Conceit, that it is sometimes a difficult matter to read modern Books and Pamphlets, where the Words are so curtailed, and varied from their original Spelling, that whoever hath been used to plain *English*, will hardly know them by sight.

[. . .]

In order to reform our Language, I conceive, My Lord, that a free judicious Choice should be made of such Persons, as are generally allowed to be best qualified for such a Work, without any regard to Quality, Party, or Profession. These, to a certain Number at least, should assemble at some appointed Time and Place, and fix on Rules by which they design to proceed. What Methods they will take, is not for me to prescribe. Your Lordship, and other Persons in great Employment, might please to be of the Number; and I am afraid, such a Society would want Your Instruction and Example, as much as Your Protection: For, I have, not without a little Envy, observed of late, the Style of some great Ministers very much to exceed that of any other Productions.

The Persons who are to undertake this Work, will have the Example of the French before them, to imitate where these have proceeded right, and to avoid their Mistakes. Besides the Grammar-part, wherein we are allowed to be very defective, they will observe many gross Improprieties, which however authorised by Practice, and grown familiar, ought to be discarded. They will find many Words that deserve to be utterly thrown out of our Language, many more to be corrected; and perhaps not a few, long since antiquated, which ought to be restored, on account of their Energy and Sound.

But what I have most at Heart is, that some Method should be thought on for *ascertaining* and *fixing* our Language for ever, after such Alterations are made in it as shall be thought requisite. For I am of Opinion, that it is better a Language should not be wholly perfect, that it should be perpetually changing; and we must give over at one Time, or at length infallibly change for the worse. [. . .]

The Fame of our Writers is usually confined to these two Islands, and it is hard it should be limited in *Time*, as much as *Place*, by the perpetual Variations of our Speech. It is Your Lordship's Observation, that if it were not for the *Bible* and *Common Prayer Book* in the vulgar Tongue, we should hardly be able to understand any Thing that was written among us an hundred Years ago. [. . .]

(Letter to the Earl of Oxford, 22 February 1711)

Can you find an equivalent example of infuriation at the use of poor English from the last few years? Try searching the letters pages of newspapers, especially those of a politically conservative outlook.

Activity

A modern coda

The following article appeared in the free British commuters' newspaper *Metro* on Thursday, 29 January 2009. What do you think of the issue at the centre of the report?

Birmingham bans apostrophes from road signs

Councillors in Birmingham have walked into a punctuation storm after deciding to scrap apostrophes from the city's road signs.

England's second city has removed the possessive punctuation mark from street names, saying it aims to avoid confusion.

One councillor even went so far to say he did not 'see the point' of the possessive apostrophe in place names.

'If it was to give more clarity to the people of Birmingham it might be something we would look at, but I see no benefits at all,' cabinet transportation member Len Gregory told the *Birmingham Post*.

The decision, which the council hopes will draw a line under decades of dispute, follows a review to establish whether the possessive punctuation mark should be restored to place names such as Kings Heath, Acocks Green and Druids Heath.

Councillor Martin Mullaney said the decision not to reintroduce apostrophes, which began to disappear from Birmingham's road signs in the 1950s, had been taken in light of several factors, including the need for consistency and the cost of changing existing signage.

'We are constantly getting residents asking for apostrophes to be put back in and as a council we have got to make a decision one way or another,' said the chair of the city's transportation scrutiny committee.

The ruling will also mean that Birmingham's well-known St Paul's Square, in the city's Jewellery Quarter, will soon be known as St Pauls.

But grammarians have attacked the decision as 'dumbing down'.

John Richards, the founder and chairman of the *Apostrophe Protection Society*, said: 'It seems retrograde, dumbing down really'.

'It is setting a very bad example because teachers all over Birmingham are teaching their children punctuation and then they see road signs with apostrophes removed. I think the council would be better advised to make sure the right apostrophes are in rather than removing them'.

'It's a bad example to children and teachers. It's a simple rule and so many people get it wrong'.

Activity

Alternate language history

Using your knowledge of what actually happened over the history of English, try to speculate on what Modern English in the world would look like if the following historical moments had been different:

❑ The dominant Anglo-Saxon capital of Winchester remained the capital of England after 1066, with the Normans deciding not to reinforce their hold on London.

❑ The European renaissance in arts and science in the Middle Ages drew more on Arabic culture than the ancient Greek and Roman cultures.

❑ The Spanish Armada initiated the first attack of a successful Spanish invasion of England in 1588, establishing a Spanish-speaking court and restoring Catholicism to the country.

❑ Britain lost the Seven Years' War (1754–1761) in North America against the French, leaving Canada and the north wholly French-speaking and most of Florida, Texas and the south Spanish-speaking.

❑ The Napoleonic Empire succeeded after 1814 in unifying the whole of Europe west of the Urals, from the British Isles to Iberia, Russia to Greece and the Turkish Ottoman region. French-speaking administrators and army officers were stationed in the regions and French law was applied to the entire Empire.

❑ China embarked on a mid-nineteenth-century period of exploration and expansion, annexing much of Asia including India and establishing Chinese protectorates along the entire east coast of Africa.

❑ The old science fiction favourite: Nazi Germany succeeded in defeating Britain in 1940, and then together Germany and Japan, with the aid of a domestic American fascist movement, overthrew the US government.

IDENTIFY YOURSELF

Loyalties and stereotypes

The linguistic features that belong to Labov's 'stereotype' category outlined in A9 are heavily indexed with regional and social identities, and thus data analysis of these features will provide fruitful examples of how constructions from different language varieties are used as overt in-group identity markers to signal language loyalty and membership of particular speech communities.

We will start by focusing upon the burgeoning industry of consumer goods emblazoned with language stereotypes, including clothing. Identity performance through representations of the body – encoded by wearing particular forms of merchandise decorated with regional language variants – provides clear evidence of stereotypes of particular lexical items and phrases. These items provide insight into the indexes that individuals use to display and perform their regional identities. This demonstration of group membership through written text, often in conjunction with particular visual signs, gives insight into how bodily representations index particular sociolinguistic group identities, often directly alongside the individual's spoken language style.

There are a number of t-shirt companies based in the West Midlands region of England that take full advantage of the local lexical item 'bostin' (meaning 'good', 'great' or 'brilliant'). 'Bostin' is a typical example of an obvious, stereotypical dialect feature. One company produces t-shirts with 'Bostin' simply printed across the chest. As well as neutral colours, these can also be purchased in colour-coded form to represent the local football teams of the West Midlands (for example, there are gold and black versions for supporters of the Wolverhampton Wanderers, who play in these colours). To be a legitimate wearer of such shirts, individuals must first identify with the region of Birmingham and the Black Country encoded through language loyalty to the term 'bostin'. They can then add an additional layer of regional identity encoded semiotically through their football team's colours.

Other phrases which appear on Black Country t-shirts include 'Yowm saft yow am', which translates as 'you are silly you are'. This includes use of eye dialect to signal non-standard pronunciation of 'soft' as 'saft' [saft] and 'yow' for 'you', realised as [jau], as well as elision between the pronoun and non-standard singular form of the **copula** verb (the verb 'to be') realised as [jaʊəm].

A further example is a long-sleeved variety with local phrases printed on each arm: It has 'Ow am ya?' ('How are you') on one sleeve and 'Tara-a-bit' ('Goodbye') on the other. The 'sleeves' texts represent a conversational opening and closing, providing good examples of well-known stereotypical phrases which imbue a sense of solidarity and in-group identity when used in informal conversations between members of the same speech community.

> ❑ Compile a similar list of particular words, phrases, symbols, signs and images that are or might be found on consumer goods, including clothing merchandise, to signify language loyalty from your own local or regional area.
>
> ❑ Consider how in-group solidarity is created, but also how this simultaneously creates social distance by contrasting with 'out-groups'.

National identities

The performance of identities using language stereotypes and bodily representations via clothing is by no means restricted to regional identities. There is a 'Shamrock' 'Bostin' edition, presumably targeted at the large number of individuals in the English West Midlands of Irish heritage. The Shamrock symbol represents the 'o' in 'Bostin', and thus the t-shirt producers have chosen to blend together semiotic and visual dialectal representations of regional and national identities. In Canada, there are numerous examples of t-shirts with the slogan 'Canada eh' or some variant on this theme highlighting the Canadian conversational tag. This text is practically always accompanied with an image of the Canadian national flag.

Sociolinguist Miriam Meyerhoff (2006) draws attention to how Canadian and New Zealand speakers often get offended if they are mistakenly referred to as American or Australian, respectively, due to accent similarities. Symbolic resources (such as flags or other national identity symbols), in conjunction with language features specific to these countries, are frequently used as tools for signalling social distance from the American and Australian out-groups, whilst simultaneously displaying a positive group identity for those who are legitimate members of the speech community.

In addition to being found in Canadian English, use of the conversational tag 'eh' is also a very frequent feature of New Zealand English. As with Canada's direct contrast with the United States, 'eh' is a speech feature associated with New Zealand English, and it is not found in any Australian varieties. Although it can serve other functions, 'eh' in both countries primarily invites supportive feedback. It can thus be seen as an interactive, solidarity-building strategy that strengthens in-group membership (and emphasises contrasts with out-groups), and is thus a key part of linguistic politeness (Meyerhoff 2006; Holmes 1995; see also B3 and C3).

> ❑ What kind of words, phrases, symbols, signs and images can be used to signify language loyalty to your nation?
>
> ❑ How difficult is it to define the term 'nation' clearly?
>
> ❑ Again, consider how in-group solidarity is created, but also how this simultaneously creates social distance by contrasting with 'out-groups'.

Name-calling

Analysing the names of sports teams is an interesting way to assess identities encoding through language. For instance, the *National Hockey League* in North America now comprises teams in Canada and the United States, having been previously based in Canada only. Three Canadian team names overtly signal their national identity in their team's name, though there are interesting differences between them:

- ❑ In Vancouver, the ice hockey team is known as the 'Vancouver Canucks' with 'Canucks' being a slang term for 'Canadians'.
- ❑ In Toronto, the 'Toronto Maple Leafs' get their national identity reference from the maple leaf symbol. The team was renamed the 'Maple Leafs' in 1927 following the maple leaf symbol appearing on Canadian World War I uniforms (the maple leaf did not become the emblem on the Canadian national flag until 1965). The irregular plural (not 'Maple Leaves') is also part of this identity.
- ❑ In Montreal, the 'Montreal Canadiens' adopt the French spelling to simultaneously signal language loyalty to French, the other official language of bilingual (especially Eastern) Canada.

The nicknames of football teams in the UK often have clearly traceable regional associations, as in the following:

- ❑ West Ham United's nickname 'The Hammers' originates from the fact that the team started life as 'Thames Ironworks'.
- ❑ Motherwell are nicknamed 'The Steelmen' due to the steelworks located just outside the grounds.
- ❑ Stoke City, nicknamed 'The Potters', are so named after the pottery industry based in Stoke-on-Trent.
- ❑ The 'Saddlers' nickname of Walsall Football Club originates from industry, with Walsall historically being a centre for the manufacture of saddles.

Activity ★

- ❑ Consider the official names and unofficial nicknames of sports teams, clubs or any other sporting and non-sporting associations of which you are either a member or which exist in the area where you live. Also consider specific terms of address which are used to refer to people from the different regions around where you live.
- ❑ Research the etymologies of these names and address terms to find out how they have originated.
- ❑ Explain how sociolinguistic identities have been encoded through such naming strategies over time.

Online identities

The recent explosion of a range of websites which promote themselves as 'social networking' sites pose some interesting questions for sociolinguists in terms of defining and redefining how individuals interact with one another in groups. Whilst most interaction on these sites takes place via the medium of *written* language, the hybrid form of online discourse and the dialogic aspects of discussion boards, blogs and forums have led to many of the linguistic features of *spoken* language, including those associated with collective group identities, being seen online.

With more and more individuals spending huge swathes of time interacting on these virtual social networking sites, it is interesting to consider how collective sociolinguistic identities manifest themselves, particularly in terms of how group memberships emerge online.

 Activity

> The following examples from Facebook illustrate how individuals who share particular interests join groups which demonstrate how they are unified by sharing the same speech norms. Members can thus be classified as belonging to the same speech communities, according to Labov's definition outlined in A9.
>
> The first example of group membership relates to one very specific feature of lexical variation. In England, different regional lexical items are used to refer to a certain type of bread. Shared speech norms within regions have led to the development of a range of groups that members can join on this particular topic. These groups name themselves according to the particular lexical variant they use. They then rival one another in terms of arguing about which is the 'correct' term. Some examples of group names are:
>
> ❑ *It's called a COB!!!!* 23,372 members from the Midlands.
> ❑ *It's a barm cake!* 70 members in Manchester and Central Lancashire, though there can be variation within a region and an additional layering of identity.
> ❑ *It's not a cob, roll, barm cake or anything else . . . it's a BATCH!* 1,347 members from Coventry in the West Midlands, proving that there is variation within the Midlands region.
>
> The second example is a selection of 'test' statements for individuals to use to assess whether they share the language norms of the online groups. There are several of these groups, and they tend to be identified by their group name following the pattern of: 'You know you're from X when'. Again, there is clear evidence of speech communities in existence here, with shared language norms, often language norms at the level of stereotypes, explicitly highlighted. These groups draw attention to sociolinguistic regional language features, language attitudes, and specific cultural knowledge, often utilising deictic expressions with local reference. Selected examples of some of these listings are as follows:

You know you're from Nottingham when:
- ○ you know what a cob is and love mushy peas and mint sauce
- ○ it's a personal attack when northerners call you southern and southerners call you northern
- ○ you call everyone 'duck' or some form of the word 'duck'
- ○ meeting place is the lions and always the left one [in Market Square]

You know you're from Canada when:
- ○ you know what a touque is [it's a winter hat]
- ○ 'eh' is a very important part of your vocabulary and more polite than 'huh?'
- ○ you know that the last letter of the English alphabet is always pronounced 'Zed' not 'Zee'
- ○ you pity people who haven't tasted a 'beaver tail' [a fried dough pastry]
- ○ you pay your bills in 'loonies' and 'toonies' [one- and two-dollar coins]
- ○ you know that 'eh' is the 27th letter of the alphabet

Unless you are from Nottingham or Canada, or you have spent time living in either of these locations, it is unlikely that these defining characteristics of group membership will apply to you.

- ❑ Compile a list of similar categories of language usage and language attitudes for your own region/nation.
- ❑ How inclusive/exclusive are your categories?
- ❑ Search online within social networking sites for similar groups and compare and contrast your own examples of language stereotypes, again considering how solidarity and social distance are established through notions of in-groups and out-groups.

INFLUENCING LANGUAGE   C10

In our consideration of World Englishes, so far we have spent a good deal of time examining how new varieties can be described, catalogued and standardised. This tends to lead to a focus upon how the emergence of *one* World Englishes variety comes to be associated with *one* country or nation. However, as soon as one variety establishes itself, other varieties begin to emerge. We will now explore how a range of different English varieties co-exist *within* one location by looking at language data. We will then explore real-life World Englishes data from the mass media.

Singlish
Singapore provides a good case study for examining different varieties of English. Within Singapore, these varieties exist along a continuum. Standard Singaporean English (SSE) sits at the most prestigious end of the continuum and is often referred

to as the **acrolect** or 'educated' variety. The mid-point on the continuum is known as the **mesolect**, or 'general' variety: Singapore 'Dialect' English. At the other end of the continuum is the least prestigious category, furthest from the standard. This is referred to as the **basilect**, or the 'broad' category, known as Singlish. Singlish contains the mixing of English with other official and local language varieties including Hokkien, the dominant Chinese regional language, Cantonese and Malay.

In 2000, the Singaporean Government launched a 'Speak Good English Movement', which continues to exist today. It is a prime example of an official language planning campaign (there has also previously been a 'Speak Mandarin Campaign' aimed at eradicating different dialectal varieties of Chinese in the 1980s). The aim of the Speak Good English campaign is to rid Singapore of Singlish.

In response, a pressure group known as the *Society for the Preservation of Authentic Singlish* (SPAS) has emerged. The society aims to celebrate and preserve Singlish as a legitimate variety. One of the key principles of SPAS is that Singaporeans are well aware of how to communicate appropriately in different contexts – they do not need the government to tell them how to do this.

Singlish is perfectly acceptable in informal, casual contexts with friends, intimates and family. Speakers will switch from Singlish towards Standard Singaporean English in more formal situations as and when required, such as when interacting within the workplace or writing a formal letter. This argument is fully supported by empirical sociolinguistic evidence and directly accords with Labov's findings, discussed in B9, that all speakers will shift styles towards the standard variety when contexts become more formal.

Activity

Below are textual extracts from the Manifesto of the *Society for the Preservation of Authentic Singlish*. Analyse the language used and the arguments given in favour of Singlish as a legitimate variety. Consider the following:

❑ What does your analysis reveal in terms of the linguistic construction and the linguistic creativity of Singlish as a variety of World Englishes?
❑ How is humour used in the text?
❑ What does the text reveal in terms of language attitudes and resistance to language planning from proponents of Singlish?

THE S.P.A.S. MANIFESTO

[. . .] The government (pronounced 'gah-men') says that we must stop using Singlish otherwise we cannot compete with ang-mors. And because of this, all our TV shows, and preferably other media as well, must stop using Singlish.

But why not ask the ang mors to learn to speak like us? What makes them so atas?

Not only that, now all our shows will have these bleddy chia'h kantang drama club types that we used to hantam in school! Who wants to see? Why can't we have shows where the actors speak like normal people?

Those who argue that our shows will sell better if they are in standard English [. . .] should be reminded who their immediate audience is. What kind of message will this kind of argument send to Singaporean viewers? 'We're not really interested in making shows for you; what we really want is to sell overseas.' [. . .]

And what's wrong with Singlish anyway? It's how Singaporeans speak in casual company. If Londoners can speak Cockney or Liverpudlians can speak Scouse, why can't we speak Singlish? [. . .] Surely we Singaporeans are not so stupid that we cannot tell the difference between the kind of language acceptable in casual settings and the kind expected in business or official correspondence. (When was the last time you used 'lah', 'leh' or 'wah piang eh' in a formal letter or report?)

After all, the British still write grammatically despite watching programmes like Eastenders, which use colloquialisms. Are Singaporeans less sophisticated than the British? Also, why do we accept programmes from the USA, with their own deviations from standard English? Why are Americanisms acceptable, but not Singlish? [. . .]

S.P.A.S. has been set up to promote art that is relevant to Singaporeans, not just propaganda! Singlish is a language that is unique to us and we should celebrate it:

SAVE OUR SINGLISH! Say it, LAH! And say it proud!

Society for the Preservation of Authentic Singlish (2002)

Key:

ang mor	Hokkien for 'red-haired monkey', a reference to Caucasians
atas	Malay for 'upstairs', meaning snobbish or arrogant
bleddy	bloody
chia'h kantang	speaking Asian with a Western accent
hantam	Malay for 'beat' or 'hit'
lah, leh	sentence tags
wah piang eh	Hokkien term – loosely translates as 'oh penis' and is used in the same way as 'oh my goodness', 'wow' or 'damn'.

The main publicity vehicle for SPAS is a website intriguingly titled TalkingCock.com, founded by Singaporean journalist, screenwriter and cartoonist Colin Goh. Despite the range of sexual connotations of 'cock' as a slang term in other varieties of English, 'cock' in Singlish is not slang for male genitals, but instead means 'rubbish', 'non-sensical' or 'not up to standard'.

One of the main features of the Talking Cock website is online access to the *Coxford Singlish Dictionary*, a rather blatant pun and parody of the *Oxford English Dictionary*, as well as further word play on the idea of 'talking cock'. The *Coxford Singlish Dictionary* is also published as a paperback book. Whilst a primary motivation was for a satirical publication to demonstrate the linguistic creativity and originality of Singlish, it also simultaneously functions as an example of textual preservation and thus codification of Singlish, though not with the prestige of a real 'Oxford' dictionary version! Singlish speakers are encouraged to add their own entries to the online dictionary to enhance the lexicon of Singlish, so there is a sense of collective ownership of this ongoing codification process.

Like traditional, mainstream dictionaries such as the *OED*, the *Coxford* version does attempt to document the etymology of a lexeme's origins. For instance, the *Coxford* authors speculate that 'cock' and the popular Singlish phrase 'talking cock' may have its origins in the terms 'cock and bull' and 'poppycock' from British English.

The *Dictionary* has the following advertising slogan:

> Buy the Coxford Singlish Dictionary, before the gahmen bans it!

This text is accompanied by a comedic-looking cartoon cockerel brandishing a loudspeaker. As in the manifesto above, we can observe the use of eye dialect here as a technique to represent the Singlish pronunciation of *government*. Eye dialect is frequently within the dictionary to denote Singlish pronunciations.

In the dictionary's introduction, the Editor-in-Chief, presumably Colin Goh, refers to himself via the spoof satirical job title of 'Supreme Cock' employed at 'Coxford University'. He provides the following summary of why speakers feel a great sense of language loyalty to Singlish:

> Singlish is unique to Singapore . . . contrary to popular belief, it is not merely badly spoken English. There is a conscious art in Singlish, a level of ingenious and humorous wordplay . . . Singlish is to be celebrated as a cultural phenomenon, not buried, as some misguided people have been trying to do.
>
> (Supreme Cock 2002: x)

World Englishes and the mass media

Materials from the mass media provide a plethora of sources of English language data for students and researchers to analyse, and World Englishes is no exception to this. The majority of World Englishes research on mass media to date tends to focus either upon news broadcasting (TV, radio and written media), or the language of advertising, as reported by Elizabeth Martin (2006). She also draws attention to other fruitful sources that have yet to be examined from a global World Englishes perspective, including the film and music industry, along with text messages, email, chat room discourse and music download technology.

In particular reference to the film industry, the dominance of Hollywood and the negative portrayal of characters who speak non-standard English from the Inner, Outer and Expanding Circles is worthy of investigation. Focusing on an example from the Outer Circle, Tej Bhatia (2001) has examined how Indian English speakers and the Hindu religion are frequently negatively portrayed in Hollywood blockbuster films such as *Indiana Jones and the Temple of Doom*.

Bhatia and Martin both draw attention to the international success of the Bollywood film industry as one answer to this. In the recent Bollywood film *Monsoon Wedding* (2001), Martin (2006: 588) reports that Director Mira Nair stated her aim for the film's dialogue to be the appropriate mixture of Indian English, Hindi and Punjabi 'to imitate as closely as possible the language mixing that occurs in everyday life'.

Singapore Dreaming (2006) is another Outer Circle film produced solely by the Singaporean film industry. It was co-written by Colin Goh, founder of TalkingCock. com, and Woo Yen Yen. Like Nair in *Monsoon Wedding*, they aimed for their dialogue to reflect the authentic language used in everyday, real life. This includes a mixture of Singlish, Singaporean English, Hokkien, Malay and Mandarin. This aim for authenticity was far from positively evaluated by the Singaporean authorities, who banned the official trailer for its code-switching and 'promotion' of 'non-standard' language through the inclusion of Singlish and Hokkien.

Activity

Scriptwriters' language variety selections can be very revealing in terms of investigating individual and cultural identities and stereotypes through language usage. The following is an oft-cited quotation from sociolinguist Rosina Lippi-Green (1997: 81):

> Film uses language variation and accent to draw character quickly, building on established preconceived notions associated with specific regional loyalties, ethnic, racial or economic alliances.

With this quotation in mind, consider the portrayals of film characters based upon the varieties of English they speak. What does this reveal in terms of attitudes towards these varieties of English? Use the following as starting points and also come up with your own examples:

❑ The *Star Wars* series
❑ *The Lord of the Rings* series
❑ The *Indiana Jones* series
❑ Walt Disney films
❑ James Bond films
❑ *East is East*
❑ *Bend it like Beckham*
❑ *The Color Purple*
❑ *Monsoon Wedding*
❑ *Singapore Dreaming*

World of advertising

World Englishes researcher Tej Bhatia draws specific attention to Guy Cook's work on advertising discourse (an extract of which appears as D5), and places it within Kachru's circles model as a successful example of advertising analysis within the Inner Circle. He then observes that, since the 1980s, advertising research has also begun to enter the Outer and Expanding Circles.

One area of advertising language which Bhatia focuses on is product names. He draws attention to the dominance of Inner Circle names, particularly from the United States and the UK, such as *Coke* and *Pepsi*, over varieties in other circles. Even in non-English-speaking locations, product names are very frequently given in English. Bhatia cites the examples of soap names in rural India, where knowledge of English is minimal – products including *Palmolive* and *Ponds* go only by their English names. Similar trends with a range of products can also be observed in Pakistan, Russia and in parts of Europe.

Within rural markets in developing countries, *Coke* and *Pepsi* have both been adopted in local, non-Western forms of advertising by painting on walls and other objects. Bhatia reports that when rocks in the Himalayas were recently painted with *Pepsi* and *Coke* ads, environmental groups filed lawsuits against both companies for conservation violation.

Bhatia (2006: 614) also points to occasions when slogans and names have not been translated properly, or when connotations have been missed:

❑ Scandinavian company Electrolux's slogan 'Nothing sucks like an Electrolux' launched in the United States, where the advertising producers were clearly unaware of the pejorative connotations of 'sucks' in American English.
❑ Japanese drink products 'Calpis Water' and 'Pocari Sweat'.
❑ A 'Sex Shop' in China is a perfectly legal, legitimate shop selling herbal teas and other health food products.

A one-size-fits-all model clearly is not applicable for World Englishes advertising, and there are careful cultural sensitivities that need to be taken into account by translators to guard against these problems.

The photographs shown in Figures C10.1–C10.3 were all taken in Hong Kong in 2008.

Figure C10.1   Hong Kong street scene

Figure C10.2   Hong Kong hoarding

Figure C10.3   Bank of East Asia street sign

In Figure C10.1, on the right-hand side the global English acronym KFC for the United States fast food giant *Kentucky Fried Chicken* can be seen, along with multiple images of the global iconic cartoon image of its founder, Colonel Sanders. Directly below the larger KFC signs is the global English *7 Eleven* convenience store logo. *7 Eleven* is currently the world's largest convenience chain, again originating in the United States. The other advertising signs that sit right alongside these are in Chinese. The shop to the left of the bilingually marked 'Police' van is *Maxim's* 'Western style' cakes. The two rectangular signs hanging high in the street in the background are adverts for an estate agent, on the left, and on the right for a well-known Hong Kong food chain which translates as the 'Little Fat Calf' Hot-Pot Restaurant.

Figure C10.2 illustrates bilingualism on an individual advertising sign (as well as how this bilingualism operates officially on all street names and road signs). The advertising sign in Figure C10.3 is for the Bank of East Asia and represents mixing within the same sign, with English utilised for the bank's acronym, followed by Chinese script directly below.

These three photographs represent typical street views for product advertising and reflect the bilingual nature of street advertising in Hong Kong eleven years after the 'handover' to China.

Activity

- ❑ Collect examples of advertising language in the region where you live.
- ❑ Try and find as many examples as you can that are specific to that region.
- ❑ Compare these with global examples (global English product names can be checked online). Also, look for examples where English is mixed with other varieties. For example, consider the use of Italian drink sizes in Starbucks: you might compare the terms used by different coffee chains.
- ❑ Assess why you think advertisers and retailers have chosen to adopt these strategies and consider how effective they are in promoting their products/services.

C11   EXPLORING LITERATURE

The first five threads in this book provide a grounding in phonology (Strand 1: A1, B1, C1, D1), lexicology (Strand 2), semantics and pragmatics (Strand 3), syntax (Strand 4) and discourse analysis (Strand 5). This coverage of the linguistic rank-structure provides you with the basic tools to do stylistics: all you need to do is explore a literary text along one of these dimensions to reveal how the mechanics of the text works.

Rather than offering further examples of full stylistic analyses in this unit, we suggest several literary texts below that you might investigate using the tools you have collected from elsewhere in this book. Remember though, in each case, that identifying, labelling and describing the language of the literary text is only the first step; in order to produce a proper stylistic account, you also need to connect your observations and evidence with a literary critical argument and interpretation.

Also, though we have provided each text under a heading of a linguistic level, this is only because we think that this points to the dominant and foregrounded feature of the text. Of course, you might disagree and find that the work organises itself around a different prominent pattern. And also of course in each case there will be other linguistic features at other levels that work in parallel with the main stylistic feature. For each literary text, sketch out a stylistic analysis and explore the patterning to discover the iconicity of the work.

Activity

Phonoaesthetic singing

Investigate the sound-patterning in this poem by Rudyard Kipling. How do the sound effects and the metrics help to create the sense of the text? How does the syntactic arrangement of the lines contribute to these effects? How do the word choices parallel these patterns?

Harp Song of the Dane Women

What is a woman that you forsake her,
And the hearth-fire and the home-acre,
To go with the old grey Widow-maker?

She has no house to lay a guest in —
But one chill bed for all to rest in,
That the pale suns and the stray bergs nest in.

She has no strong white arms to fold you,
But the ten-times-fingering weed to hold you
Out on the rocks where the tide has rolled you.

Yet, when the signs of summer thicken,
And the ice breaks, and the birch-buds quicken,
Yearly you turn from our side, and sicken —

Sicken again for the shouts and the slaughters, —
And steal away to the lapping waters,
And look at your ship in her winter-quarters.

You forget our mirth, and talk at the tables,
The kine in the shed and the horse in the stables —
To pitch her sides and go over her cables!

Then you drive out where the storm-clouds swallow,
And the sound of your oar-blades, falling hollow,
Is all we have left through the months to follow.

Ah, what is a Woman that you forsake her,
And the hearth-fire and the home-acre,
To go with the old grey Widow-maker?

(Rudyard Kipling, 1906)

Find a poem or transcribed song lyric that seems to you intuitively to have a strong or unusual sound. Try to describe it as accurately as possible, and then try to work out how the sound-patterning is significant in your interpretation of the text.

Activity

Pseudo-lexicology

The satirist Jonathan Swift wrote many punning verses and dialogues that he called 'Anglo-Latin' or 'Latino-Anglicus'. Try to read the following two poems out loud, and then work out how Swift has made English look like Latin. Can you rewrite the passage with conventional word boundaries and spellings in English?

Mollis abuti,
Has an acuti,
No lasso finis,
Molli divinis.
Omi de armis tres,
Imi na dis tres
Cantu disco ver
Meas alo ver?

(Jonathan Swift, c. 1735)

I ritu a verse o na molli o mi ne,
Asta lassa me pole, a lae dis o fine;
I ne ver neu a niso ne at in mi ni is;
A manat a glans ora sito fer diis.
De armo lis abuti hos face an hos nos is
As fer a sal illi, as reddas aro sis;
Ac is o mi molli is almi de lite;
Illo verbi de, an illo verbi nite.

(Jonathan Swift, c. 1735)

(Swift did not provide a 'translation', so the answer at the end of this unit is our best guess.)

Can you find other literary texts in which the disruption or exploitation of morphology and word choice is a major organising feature (see for example the John Lennon passage in C7)?

Activity

Semantics in the head

The following passage is from near the end of Brian Aldiss' 1969 psychedelic novel *Barefoot in the Head*. Set in a post-apocalyptic future in which psychotropic bombs have poisoned the food-chain, the novel describes Colin Charteris' road trip across Europe, in which he gathers a convoy of vehicles and crazy travellers in a series of multiple crashes and confrontations. The style of the novel clearly aims to represent the states of mind of the war's victims. Examine this passage closely to see how Aldiss achieves this iconicity:

> Sparkily flinging up stones from the tired wheels the gravelcade towed darkness, headlights beams of granite bars battering the eternal nowhere signposting the dark. The cuspidaughters of darkness somebody sang play toe with the spittoons of noon the cuspidaughters of darkness play toe with the spittoons of noon the cuspidaughters of darkness play toe with the spittoons of noon. Only some of the blind white eyes of joyride was yellow or others but altirely because the bashing the cars the jostling in the autocayed. And hob with the gobs of season.
>
> In these primitive jalopsides herding their way like shampeding cattletrap across the last ranges of Frankreich that square squeezing country sang the drivniks. Cluttering through stick-it-up-your-assberg its nasal neutral squares its window-bankage to where the Rhine oiled its gunmottal under the northstarbarrels and a wide bridge warned zoll. Break lights a flutter red I'd ride the rifled engines ricochetting off the tracered flow below.
>
> Cryogenetic winds bourning another spring croaking forth on the tundrugged land doing it all over and bloodcounts low at a small hour with the weep of dream-pressure in the cyclic rebirth-redeath calling for a fast doss all round or heads will roll beyond the tidal rave. RECHTS FAHREN big yellow arrows splitting the roadcrown. Writhing bellies upward large painted arrows letters meaningless distant burriers seducing him to a sighfer in a diaphram.
>
> Clobwebbed Charteris stopped the Banshee. He and Angeline climb out and he wonders if he sees himself lie there annulled, looks up into the blind white cliffs of night cloud to smell the clap of spring break its alternature. About him grind all the autodisciples flipping from their pillions and all shout and yawn make jacketed gestures through their fogstacks.
>
> They all talk and Gloria comes over says to Angeline, 'Feels to me I have bound the hound across this country before'.
>
> (Brian Aldiss, *Barefoot in the Head*, 1969: 193)

Stylisticians have particularly been interested – for obvious reasons – in linguistically deviant texts like this. Can you find any others to explore? In particular, look for experimental and avant-garde writing: how are the styles of such movements deployed in the service of their politics or ideological programmes?

Activity

Syntactic imagining

There are apparently only two sentences in the following poem. How does the arrangement of syntax contribute to the sense of the text?

When You are Old

When you are old and grey and full of sleep
And nodding by the fire, take down this book,
And slowly read, and dream of the soft look
Your eyes had once, and of their shadows deep;

How many loved your moments of glad grace,
And loved your beauty with love false or true;
But one man loved the pilgrim soul in you,
And loved the sorrows of your changing face.

And bending down beside the glowing bars,
Murmur, a little sadly, how love fled
And paced upon the mountains overhead,
And hid his face amid a crowd of stars.

(W.B. Yeats, 1891)

Find two passages from different novels which are markedly different syntactically (see, for example, the two passages from a science fiction novel and a modernist novel in C4). How is the syntactic form significant in each case?

Activity

Discourse (oh no it isn't)

The following is a sketch by Monty Python first broadcast on the BBC on 2 November 1972. It clearly presents a surreal, absurd, or at least unusual dialogue. Can you identify what is strange about it from the perspective of normative patterns of everyday conversation? Can you also identify what is conventional about it in order to get a sense of how it balances oddity and normality for its humorous effects?

The Argument Clinic

[A man enters an office].

Man: Good morning, I'd like to have an argument, please.
Receptionist: Certainly, sir. Have you been here before?
Man: No, this is my first time.
Receptionist: I see, well we'll see who's free at the moment. Mr. Bakely's free, but he's a little bit conciliatory. No. Try Mr. Barnhart, room 12.
Man: Thank you.

[Enters room 12].

Angry Man:	WHADDAYOU WANT?
Man:	Well, Well, I was told outside that . . .
Angry Man:	DON'T GIVE ME THAT, YOU SNOTTY-FACED EVIL PAN OF DROPPINGS!
Man:	What?
Angry Man:	SHUT YOUR FESTERING GOB, YOU TIT! YOUR TYPE MAKES ME PUKE! YOU VACUOUS STUFFY-NOSED MALODOROUS PERVERT!!!
Man:	Yes, but I came here for an argument!!
Angry Man:	OH! Oh! I'm sorry! This is abuse!
Man:	Oh! Oh I see!
Angry Man:	Aha! No, you want room 12A, next door.
Man:	Oh . . . Sorry . . .
Angry Man:	Not at all! [Under his breath] stupid git.

[Man enters room 12A. Another man is sitting behind a desk].

Man:	Is this the right room for an argument?
Other Man:	[pause] I've told you once.
Man:	No you haven't!
Other Man:	Yes I have.
Man:	When?
Other Man:	Just now.
Man:	No you didn't!
Other Man:	Yes I did!
Man:	You didn't!
Other Man:	I did!
Man:	You didn't!
Other Man:	I'm telling you, I did!
Man:	You didn't!
Other Man:	Oh I'm sorry, is this a five-minute argument, or the full half hour?
Man:	Ah! [taking out his wallet and paying] Just the five minutes.
Other Man:	Just the five minutes. Thank you. Anyway, I did.
Man:	You most certainly did not!
Other Man:	Now let's get one thing perfectly clear: I most definitely told you!
Man:	Oh no you didn't!
Other Man:	Oh yes I did!
Man:	Oh no you didn't!
Other Man:	Oh yes I did!
Man:	Oh no you didn't!
Other Man:	Oh yes I did!
Man:	Oh no you didn't!
Other Man:	Oh yes I did!
Man:	Oh no you didn't!
Other Man:	Oh yes I did!
Man:	No you DIDN'T!

Other Man:	Oh yes I did!
Man:	No you DIDN'T!
Other Man:	Oh yes I did!
Man:	No you DIDN'T!
Other Man:	Oh yes I did!
Man:	Oh look, this isn't an argument!
[Pause]	
Other Man:	Yes it is!
Man:	No it isn't!
[Pause]	
Man:	It's just contradiction!
Other Man:	No it isn't!
Man:	It IS!
Other Man:	It is NOT!
Man:	You just contradicted me!
Other Man:	No I didn't!
Man:	You DID!
Other Man:	No no no!
Man:	You did just then!
Other Man:	Nonsense!
Man:	[exasperated] Oh, this is futile!!
[Pause]	
Other Man:	No it isn't!
Man:	Yes it is!
[Pause]	
Man:	I came here for a good argument!
Other Man:	AH, no you didn't, you came here for an argument!
Man:	An argument isn't just contradiction.
Other Man:	Well it CAN be!
Man:	No it can't! An argument is a connected series of statements intended to establish a proposition.
Other Man:	No it isn't!
Man:	Yes it is! 'tisn't just contradiction.
Other Man:	Look, if I *argue* with you, I must take up a contrary position!
Man:	Yes but it isn't just saying 'no it isn't'.
Other Man:	Yes it is!
Man:	No it isn't!
Other Man:	Yes it is!
Man:	No it isn't!
Other Man:	Yes it is!
Man:	No it ISN'T! Argument is an intellectual process. Contradiction is just the automatic gainsaying of anything the other person says.
Other Man:	It is NOT!
Man:	It is!
Other Man:	Not at all!
Man:	It is!

[The Arguer hits a bell on his desk and stops].

Other Man:	Thank you, that's it.
Man:	[stunned] What?
Other Man:	That's it. Good morning.
Man:	But I was just getting interested!
Other Man:	I'm sorry, the five minutes is up.
Man:	That was never five minutes!!
Other Man:	I'm afraid it was.
Man:	No it wasn't . . .
Other Man:	I'm sorry, I'm not allowed to argue any more.
Man:	WHAT??
Other Man:	If you want me to go on arguing, you'll have to pay for another five minutes.
Man:	But that was never five minutes just now! Oh Come on! Oh this is . . . This is ridiculous!
Other Man:	I told you. . . I told you, I'm not allowed to argue unless you PAY!
Man:	Oh all right. [Takes out his wallet and pays again]. There you are.
Other Man:	Thank you.
Man:	[clears throat] Well . . .
Other Man:	Well WHAT?
Man:	That was never five minutes just now.
Other Man:	I told you, I'm not allowed to argue unless you've paid!
Man:	Well I just paid!
Other Man:	No you didn't!
Man:	I DID!!!
Other Man:	YOU didn't!
Man:	I DID!!!
Other Man:	YOU didn't!
Man:	I DID!!!
Other Man:	YOU didn't!
Man:	I DID!!!
Other Man:	YOU didn't!
Man:	I-dbct-fd-tq! I don't want to argue about it!
Other Man:	Well I'm very sorry but you didn't pay!
Man:	Ah hah! Well if I didn't pay, why are you arguing??? Ah AAHHH! Gotcha!
Other Man:	No you haven't!
Man:	Yes I have! If you're arguing, I must have paid.
Other Man:	Not necessarily. I *could* be arguing in my spare time.
Man:	I've had enough of this! [leaves]
[Door slams]	
Other Man:	No you haven't.

Find other dramatic scripts in which there is an argument or confrontation. How are the power relations signified in the play?

Answer

Versions of Swift

Moll is a beauty,
Has an acute eye,
No lass so fine is,
Molly divine is.
O my dear mistress,
I'm in a distress,
Can't you discover
Me as a lover?

I writ you a verse on a Molly o' mine,
As tall as a May-pole, a lady so fine;
I never knew any so neat in mine eyes;
A man, at a glance or a sight of her, dies
Dear Molly's a beauty, whose face and whose nose is
As fair as a lily, as red as a rose is;
A kiss o' my Molly is all my delight;
I love her by day, and I love her by night.

C12   COLLECTING DATA

Sociolinguist Carmen Llamas devised the following innovative multi-methodological framework for language data collection. This approach has been very influential both inside and outside of academia. In addition to being a seminal methodological approach within studies of language and linguistics, it has also been successfully utilised by the BBC for a large-scale project they conducted in the UK entitled *Voices*, where they used an adapted version of her multi-methodological approach in order to conduct a broad quantitative survey of accent, dialect and attitudes towards different language varieties across the British Isles.

Llamas devised a multi-layered methodological package designed specifically to elicit sociolinguistic language data. One of its most significant innovations lies in the fact that it can be used to assess sociolinguistic language variation across three different levels of the language system: it can examine **phonological**, **lexical** *and* **grammatical** variants.

The foundational part of Llamas' approach to data collection is what she termed *Sense Relation Network* sheets (SRNs). Selected informants from a particular geographical location which the fieldworker wishes to study are given a pre-interview pack which is partly made up of these SRNs. This is then followed up a few days later by a face-to-face informal audio-recorded interview with the fieldworker.

The interview is often conducted in the informant's home or within surroundings with which they are familiar and thus most likely to be more relaxed. The gap between delivery of the pre-interview pack and the interview encounter itself is designed to give informants a good period of time to think about different dialectal variants in order to maximise the amount of data that is collected. Such an approach has the distinct advantage of avoiding elicitation problems such as a participant's mind going blank, as can be the case if interviewees do not know what to expect in the interview and are then asked for an instantaneous, on-the-spot response.

The SRNs have been carefully designed by Llamas (1999: 98) following Aitchison's (1997) principle that a 'web of words' exists within speakers' minds. Additionally, the visual design of Llamas' SRNs has been influenced by the tools and techniques frequently used in English language teaching, where visual learning aids such as word field diagrams often feature.

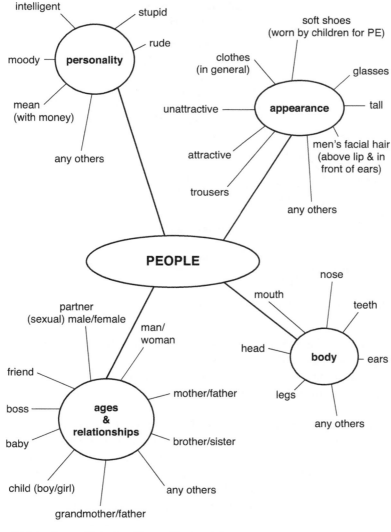

Figure C12.1 Sense Relation Network sheet 1

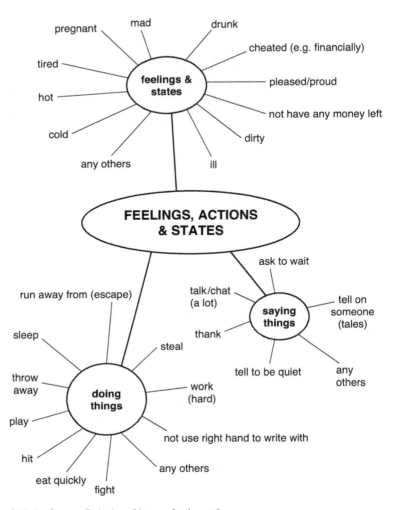

Figure C12.2 Sense Relation Network sheet 2

The centre of the SRN contains a set of **semantic fields**, which in this example are: 'People', 'Feelings, Actions and States' and 'The Outside World'. The 'networks' of words branch out from the different semantic fields, with the standard notional word appearing in the sub-sections of the SRNs. We have reproduced the three SRNs in Figures C12.1–C12.3.

Informants are given an instruction sheet as part of the pre-interview pack so that when the interview takes place they have a good idea of what to expect. This form also acts as a record of the biographical details of the participants. Figure C12.4 is an example of a completed form from one of Llamas' studies conducted in the north-eastern English town of Middlesbrough (Llamas 1999: 110).

Another part of the pre-interview pack is a questionnaire (Figure C12.5) designed to test participants' awareness of non-standard grammatical usage in their local area. The rationale behind this is that the results of this questionnaire can then be compared

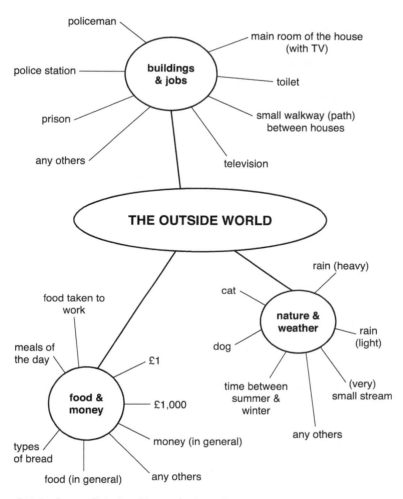

Figure C12.3 Sense Relation Network sheet 3

and contrasted with the grammatical variants that participants use in conversation within the interview.

In interview, the words on the SRNs are read aloud, thus eliciting a more formal speech style from informants. Participants are then encouraged to think and note down other words during the interview encounter itself through more informal conversation. The successful nature of the SRNs as a lexical data elicitation technique was proved in an early pilot study (see Llamas 1999), where, in interview, from the 80 standard notion words on the three SRNs, 272 lexical dialectal variants were produced and recorded, thus showing the fruitfulness of adopting such a multi-methodological approach for lexical variation alone.

After the informant has read out the words they have recorded on the SRNs around the standard notion word, the interviewer then guides an informal conversation around the specific lexical variants that informants have written down, with the overall aim

First Name _Jenny_

Place of birth _middlesbrough_

Other places you have lived and for how long

Teesdale   1 year

Durham   3 years (College)

- Please complete the sheets with words you think are **dialect** words or are local to the area you are from.

- Try to put down the first thing that comes to your mind, words you use every day when talking with friends, for example.

- After that, think about it for a while and note down any other examples of words local to the place you live which come to mind.

- Feel free to discuss the words with other people from the same area as you. But try to keep a note of who you discuss the words with (especially if you note down their suggestions).

- Put down more than one word, if you like. Also, feel free to use expressions as well as single words.

- Use the sections called 'any others' to note down any extra words or expressions you think of (yourself, or in discussion with others). If these are words for things not listed on the sheet, please put down what you think they mean, or what someone not necessarily from your area would understand by them.

- Have a look through the questions about your language and your area, which we'll also be talking about (there is no need to answer these questions on the sheet).

- Complete the Language Questionnaire by putting ticks in the appropriate boxes.

Figure C12.4   Pre-interview instruction sheet

of eliciting a more informal phonological production, as well as grammatical language variation and attitudinal information.

If conducted effectively, these informal interview conversations can also produce a wealth of information on language attitudes, including attitudes relating to the crucial sociolinguistic variables of speaker age and gender as well as participants' views on word etymologies and their own perspectives on language change over time. A whole range of different sociolinguistic aspects of language study can thus be elicited by utilising this multi-methodological approach.

Language Questionnaire

Tick (✓) the first box if you would hear this where you live

Tick (✓) the second box if you would use this type of sentence yourself in speech

Tick (✓) the third box if you would use this type of sentence when writing to a friend.

☐ ☐ ☐   1. He was just sat there by himself.
☐ ☐ ☐   2. They can't do nothing without you saying.
☐ ☐ ☐   3. There's a job going at our place if youse two want to go for it.
☐ ☐ ☐   4. We all talk different.
☐ ☐ ☐   5. You weren't stood there, were you?
☐ ☐ ☐   6. Just say what you want, innit?
☐ ☐ ☐   7. They said they were coming back on Monday and they never.
☐ ☐ ☐   8. That's the best one what she's got on.
☐ ☐ ☐   9. You're insured on them items for 80 days.
☐ ☐ ☐ 10. He's working 9 while 6 this week.
☐ ☐ ☐ 11. I'm going down London next week.
☐ ☐ ☐ 12. I don't fancy going up Stockton.
☐ ☐ ☐ 13. The sharks were only two foot long.
☐ ☐ ☐ 14. I seen Sarah at work yesterday.
☐ ☐ ☐ 15. I knew a bloke who were doing speech therapy.
☐ ☐ ☐ 16. We was walking along the road when it happened.
☐ ☐ ☐ 17. It were too cold to go out.
☐ ☐ ☐ 18. We usually gan down the pub on Thursday's.
☐ ☐ ☐ 19. I bet she was sick as.
☐ ☐ ☐ 20. They give me it the same day I opened the account.
☐ ☐ ☐ 21. I should've went to the medical really.
☐ ☐ ☐ 22. You wasn't listening to what I said.
☐ ☐ ☐ 23. She come in at 12 o'clock last night.
☐ ☐ ☐ 24. She don't like that sort of thing.
☐ ☐ ☐ 25. There's no Electron signs on any doors.
☐ ☐ ☐ 26. I'm not cooking for them, they can do it theirselves.
☐ ☐ ☐ 27. Lend us your catalogue, I want to have a flick through it.
☐ ☐ ☐ 28. There was kids there.
☐ ☐ ☐ 29. I've never heard of him like.
☐ ☐ ☐ 30. He said it wasn't scary but, mind you, he is about 45.
☐ ☐ ☐ 31. They proper hurt you when you crash.
☐ ☐ ☐ 32. The cops ain't gonna do anything.
☐ ☐ ☐ 33. They in't gonna pull you up.
☐ ☐ ☐ 34. It's the only like decent night out we have, isn't it?
☐ ☐ ☐ 35. He wouldn't could've worked, even if you had asked him.
☐ ☐ ☐ 36. Will I put the kettle on?
☐ ☐ ☐ 37. My hair needs washed.
☐ ☐ ☐ 38. I'm opening another account me.
☐ ☐ ☐ 39. If you're left-handed, you're more cleverer.
☐ ☐ ☐ 40. I've forgot my money, can you buy me a pint?

Figure C12.5 Pre-interview questionnaire

Activity

Using SRNs

❑ To get a good sense of how an SRN works, take time to fill in your own words or phrases in the three SRNs given above.

❑ In order to test the potential usefulness of the multi-methodological approach described in this unit, select two informants from a particular geographical area (use friends or family members if you wish) and apply the SRN data collection method (also including the questionnaire above in your initial, pre-interview data pack). Ensure that you give your informants the required time before the interview takes place and conduct the encounter in an informal setting where they will feel most comfortable. Ensure that you audio-record your interview (see B12).

❑ Once you have completed the data collection process, assess the effectiveness of the method by answering the following questions:

   ○ How much language data have you managed to collect?

   ○ How many different lexical variants have you elicited?

   ○ Have you managed to elicit phonological variation in both formal and informal speech styles?

   ○ Have you found data where you can compare and contrast grammatical language variants?

   ○ Have you managed to gain details of language attitudes?

   ○ Critically consider your role as interviewer and how the formality and informality of the interview shifts.

❑ In addition to distributing the language questionnaire to your two informants as part of your pre-interview pack, devise a sampling technique for distributing this questionnaire to a larger group of individuals. You should then send this out (you can either use the questionnaire as it stands, or adapt it for the local area where you are planning to use it).

❑ How successful is your rate of return?

❑ How useful are your findings?

❑ On the basis of your practical experiences, consider the advantages and disadvantages of questionnaires as a data collection technique for eliciting English language data, both as a stand-alone method and as one part of a multi-methodological approach.

Activity ⭐

Different data collection scenarios

Consider how you would attempt to collect data for an English language project from the contexts listed below. Make a note of your responses, as you will need to refer to these later on in D12. When developing your response, ensure that you have thoroughly addressed the following questions, drawing on the knowledge you have gained from A12 and B12:

❑ Would your study be quantitative, qualitative or mixed-method?
❑ What access problems could you potentially face? Would you be able to resolve these problems?
❑ What recording equipment would you use and where would you locate it?
❑ What ethical barriers/dangers could be faced?
❑ Do any ethical permissions need to be gained?
❑ Are there any of these situations where you would not attempt data collection?
❑ Would you consider participant observation?
❑ Would the observer's paradox be an issue?
❑ If so, how would you try and minimise its effects?
❑ Could an experimental setting be created to elicit similar data?

Language in informal settings
a) A conversation between your friends in your living room
b) A conversation between your friends in a café or pub
c) An intimate conversation between lovers on the telephone
d) An intimate conversation between lovers in their own home
e) An argument between a couple in a supermarket
f) An argument between a couple in their own home

Language in online settings
a) Email correspondence between friends
b) Email correspondence between an intimate couple
c) Facebook public 'wall' message postings
d) Facebook private email postings
e) Discussions in chat rooms with friends
f) Discussions in chat rooms between lecturers and students
g) Blog postings on a national newspaper website
h) Blog postings on a specialised website for members only

Language in educational settings
a) The language of primary school children in the classroom
b) The language of primary school children in the playground
c) Teacher–pupil classroom interaction

d) Teacher–pupil playground interaction
e) The language of teachers in a staff meeting
f) The language of teachers in the staff room

Language in judicial settings
a) Police–suspect interview
b) Police–suspect arrest on the street
c) The language of witnesses in a courtroom trial
d) The deliberations of a jury when discussing a verdict

Language in healthcare settings
a) Nurse–patient interaction on a hospital ward
b) Nurse–patient interaction in a private consultation
c) Chaplain–patient interaction on a hospital ward
d) Doctor–doctor interaction in the canteen

Language in the workplace
a) The language of corporate managerial business meetings
b) The language of emails in a multinational company
c) The language of factory floor workers on a production line
d) The language of a sales representative to customers in a retail outlet

Language in the media
a) The language of radio broadcast interviews
b) The language of televised political debates
c) The language of men's lifestyle magazines
d) Letters to a local newspaper
e) The language of advertising billboards
f) The language of radio commercials

C13   THEORY INTO PRACTICE

A neurolinguistic virus

Language was one of the first and probably the most important enabling technologies that humans acquired. It has been the focus not only of analytical linguistic study but also of fantastical and science fictional speculation. Of course, any perspective on language is a *view* of language, with inbuilt assumptions about the nature of language itself. Much science fictional discourse on language (such as in Orwell's *Nineteen Eighty-Four*: see B13) is deterministic in its assumptions, expressing a strong Sapir-Whorfianism and a hard linkage between expression and thought.

In Neal Stephenson's *Snow Crash*, speculation about the historical evolution of languages leads eventually to this conversation:

'I'm here on the Raft looking for a piece of software – a piece of medicine to be specific – that was written five thousand years ago by a Sumerian personage named Enki, a neurolinguistic hacker.'

'What does that mean?' Mr. Lee says. 'It means a person who was capable of programming other people's minds with verbal streams of data, known as namshubs.'

Ng is totally expressionless. He takes another drag on his cigarette, spouts the smoke up above his head in a geyser, watches it spread out against the ceiling. 'What is the mechanism?'

'We've got two kinds of language in our heads. The kind we're using now is acquired. It patterns our brains as we're learning it. But there's also a tongue that's based in the deep structures of the brain, that everyone shares. These structures consist of basic neural circuits that have to exist in order to allow our brains to acquire higher languages.'

'Linguistic infrastructure,' Uncle Enzo says. 'Yeah. I guess "deep structure" and "infrastructure" mean the same thing. Anyway, we can access those parts of the brain under the right conditions. Glossolalia – speaking in tongues – is the output side of it, where the deep linguistic structures hook into our tongues and speak, bypassing all the higher, acquired languages. Everyone's known that for some time.'

'You're saying there's an input side, too?' Ng says.

'Exactly. It works in reverse. Under the right conditions, your ears – or eyes – can tie into the deep structures, bypassing the higher language functions. Which is to say, someone who knows the right words can speak words, or show you visual symbols, that go past all your defenses and sink right into your brainstem. Like a cracker who breaks into a computer system, bypasses all the security precautions, and plugs himself into the core, enabling him to exert absolute control over the machine.'

Neal Stephenson, *Snow Crash* (1992: 369)

❏ What do you think of the assumption that the brain and language are analogous to a computer and its software program?
❏ Is there any validity in thinking about language as programming?
❏ What other assumptions about language underlie the discussion articulated here, and what do you think of these assumptions?

The Babel fish

For many years, science fiction has made convenient use of the imaginary gizmo of the 'universal translator' – which will allow spacefaring humans to converse with aliens in their own languages. In practice, of course, it is difficult to imagine how the universal translator machine could ever work. There are three big problems. First, it would have to work out the grammar on the basis of hearing only a small selection of utterances that it encountered. Second and similarly, it would only be able to build a lexicon of the words which were used in its presence, so it would take a while to be exposed to a wide vocabulary. Third, it would only be able to understand pragmatic matters and other non-denotational utterances involving, for example, metaphor, irony, jokes and politeness by having an extensive understanding of the alien culture encountered.

Activity

> In *The Hitchhiker's Guide to the Galaxy*, Douglas Adams evades the universal translator problem by having his characters wear Babel fish in their ears:
>
> > 'The Babel fish', said *The Hitchhiker's Guide to the Galaxy quietly*, 'is small, yellow and leech-like, and probably the oddest thing in the Universe. It feeds on brainwave energy received not from its own carrier but from those around it. It absorbs all unconscious mental frequencies from this brainwave energy to nourish itself with. It then excretes into the mind of its carrier a telepathic matrix formed by combining the conscious thought frequencies with nerve signals picked up from the speech centres of the brain which has supplied them. The practical upshot of all this is that if you stick a Babel fish in your ear you can instantly understand anything said to you in any form of language. The speech patterns you actually hear decode the brainwave matrix which has been fed into your mind by the Babel fish.'
> >
> > Douglas Adams, *The Hitchhiker's Guide to the Galaxy*
> > (1979: 49–50)
>
> ❑   Why is the Babel fish as far-fetched and impractical as the universal translator?
> ❑   You might consider the theoretical assumptions that Adams makes about the pre-linguistic nature of consciousness and thought. Do you think in language? Do you feel emotions, moods and dispositions in language? Can one language be translated exactly into another (even when both languages are terrestrial rather than alien)?

Some cogitations

Consider the following questions, which draw on the material presented across this book. Discuss your thinking with your friends and colleagues.

❑ The different general approaches to language (structuralist, functionalist, generative, cognitivist, and so on) all have their advantages and disadvantages. Each prioritises different facets of language. Do you think it will ever be possible to produce a definitive and comprehensive model of language, or is there a defining limitation on linguistics for two main reasons? First, language is too complex and multifaceted to be accounted for by one perspective. Second, it is impossible to take a view of language without *taking a view* of it, and so it is impossible to be objective. Even if you agree with these arguments, why might linguistics still be worth doing?

❑ It is said (by cognitive linguists) that language is the way it is because of our embodied human condition. In other words, we articulate and understand language as extensions of our physical circumstances: our sense of spatial and visual orientation is the basis for abstract relationships as expressed in prepositional phrases; our capacity for finding our way around a room is drawn on when we need to find our way around a text; our view of the world is mediated through underlying conceptual metaphors that structure our understanding. Assuming this is the case, how might different bodies (male, female, child, elderly, disabled, Black, White, tall, small, fat, skinny) embody language differently? Or is the notion of embodiment more abstract than this – and if so, how useful is it then? Put facetiously, do fat people have a different articulation of the world?

❑ Some linguists (structuralists and generativists) insist that the only thing that can be studied is language without regard to the interfering complexities of society, context and performance. Do you see an advantage in this position which makes a principled virtue of necessity? Do you think the object of study of a formalist linguistics can still be said to be *language* in any communicative sense?

❑ The main conceptual metaphors that have delineated thinking about language consist of the following:

  ○ LANGUAGE IS A SET OF LAWS
  ○ LANGUAGE IS A COMPUTER PROGRAM
  ○ LANGUAGE IS A GAME
  ○ LANGUAGE IS A VIRUS OR DISEASE
  ○ LANGUAGE IS A BUILDING OR TERRITORY
  ○ LANGUAGE IS A FAMILY

Can you think of examples for these, from the work of linguists that you know? Which metaphor seems to you to be the most productive and offer the most useful insights?

❑ Much of the difficulty in theoretical linguistics is a consequence of the observer's paradox. In other fields of investigation, it is possible to minimise the observer's paradox by replicating experiments on the object, by engaging in several different approaches to the same object, or by using a system of measurement that is universally accepted. When the object of exploration is language itself, however, the difficulty is that the object changes with any form of contact. Furthermore, the means of thinking about language is articulated in language itself. In linguistics, then, is the observer's paradox insurmountable?

❑ Is linguistics a science or an art?

❑ You have been reading a textbook, in which we have mainly and necessarily presented 'facts' about language in an authoritative way. We have suggested in various places that there are different and contentious views on what the facts of language are and whether there are in fact any facts at all. Even where we have presented as straightforward a picture as possible, in almost all cases there are debates and discussions in the field, and all statements in language study should be treated with proper scepticism as being provisional. For each unit and across each strand, explore the Further Reading we provide at the end of Section D and decide for yourself whether you agree with our assumptions about language.

Section D
EXTENSION
LINGUISTIC READINGS

D1 ARTICULATING MASCULINITY

In the following journal article extract, Scott Kiesling reports his study of the (ING) variable in the vernacular speech of male American fraternity (college society) members. He begins from the longstanding sociophonetic observation that men use vernacular variants of stable speech patterns more than women as a sign of their gender identity. For example, men – particularly in social class groups in the band between working and middle class – often use a variable of (ING) word-endings that is mainly associated with the lower-class speakers.

Scott Fabius Kiesling

Scott Fabius Kiesling (reprinted from 'Men's identities and sociolinguistic variation: The case of fraternity men', *Journal of Sociolinguistics* 2/1 (1998): 69-99)

(ING) Patterns in the fraternity

(ING) is perhaps the most studied variable in the English language (if not in all linguistics), because it is variable in all varieties of English and is sensitive to most of the factors sociolinguists have considered: phonology, morphology, syntax, dialect, style, class, ethnicity and sex. Moreover, the general picture is essentially the same across dialects for most factors, so that even in places as far apart as Los Angeles, Norwich, and Australia, men tend to have a higher rate of the alveolar variant [ɪn] than women. This regularity and stability is attractive for analyzing language use in the fraternity, where members are not all from the same dialect area.

Fischer's classic (1958) study of (ING) and Trudgill's (1972) study both focused on male behavior. Fischer's differentiation between the 'model' and 'typical' boy shows that differences among men may be due to a speaker's orientation to authority. Similarly, Trudgill claimed that the 'covert prestige' he found among men in Norwich reflected their identification with the 'roughness and toughness supposedly character-istic of [working class] life which are . . . considered to be desirable masculine attributes' (1972: 182).

Coding

Each token of (ING) was coded as alveolar and preceded by an untensed vowel (N), or velar (G). Each token was also coded for the independent variables of speaker, activity type, following phonological environment, and grammatical category. Speakers were coded individually.

Activity type is similar to the style factor in Labov (1966) and other studies. Most variation studies are based on interviews, and therefore do not have the possibility of coding for activity type. Activity type is defined both emically and etically [from within the group and as the observing analyst sees it]; members themselves recognize a difference between 'hanging out' and meetings, the two main types on which I have focused. 'Meetings' simply involve tokens of (ING) spoken during the full weekly meetings. A random sample of meetings was coded. Socializing takes place at a number of locations and with differing numbers of participants; however, dividing this activity type would not yield comparable results, because each speaker was not recorded in all socializing contexts. Tokens for the socializing activity type were exhaustive for each speaker, because this activity type was the most difficult to tape, and therefore

Scott Fabius
Kiesling

fewer tokens were available. I also coded interview tokens. All interviews were not identical in setting; not all were private, and I did not have a close relationship with all interviewees. Interviews were coded for the first 45 minutes, or the complete interview, if shorter. Because of the volume of talk in interviews, they comprise over half of the total tokens. Some word lists and reading passages were recorded with some speakers.

Internal factors coded included following phonological environment and grammatical category. In addition to grammatical categories outlined by Houston (1985), the marker *fuckin'* was included as a separate category. This word functions as several different grammatical categories, but is almost categorically pronounced as N.

Results

Tokens were analyzed using the IVARB variable rule multiple regression analysis program for DOS [a form of *variable rules analysis, or VARBRUL*]. All factor groups were selected as significant at the .05 level in the step-up-step-down procedure. Table D1.1 lists the results for all factors from a single run, including probabilities and percentage of N.

The non-discrete differences of probabilities in the grammatical status factor group roughly match Houston's (1985) findings for grammatical category, although I have not analyzed the results in detail, since this issue has no bearing on my research question (except to account for any interaction between factors). For the same reason, I will not speculate on the striking differences between my results and Houston's for the following phonological environment. The only similarities between the results are the effect of a following velar consonant (favors G), and [-back] consonants, which slightly favor N.

The results for the speaker factor group are reproduced graphically in Figures D1.1 and D1.2.

In Figure D1.1, the percentages of N use are shown, yielding a range from 80 percent for Speed to 22 percent for Ram. Note the gradual slope; there are no clear groupings among speakers. This situation changes for the variable rule results in Figure D1.2. Although the distribution still appears smooth, notice that Pete is not highly likely to use N (compared with his percentage of 73%), while Saul is very unlikely to use N (compared with his percentage of 51%). The disparities between percentages and probabilities suggest that there is an interacting factor that gives these men higher percentages than would be expected from their probability scores. The probabilities also suggest a way of grouping the speakers: two speakers favor N, but to differing degrees (Speed and Mick), another group disfavors N (Pencil, Hotdog, Saul, Mack, and possibly Ram), while the other speakers form a middle group (Pete, Art, Waterson, and Tommy) who neither strongly favor nor disfavor N. These groupings were for the most part ratified through further Varbrul analysis, which returned nonsignificant (p>.05) differences among Pete, Tommy, Art, and Waterson in one group, and Pencil, Hotdog, Mack, and Saul in another. However, Speed and Mick were significantly different from each other (p<.05), and Mick could not be combined with the middle group. Similarly Ram could not be placed with the group including Pencil. Table D1.2 shows the combined grouping. There is no common social factor uniting these groups; all show differences in the length of time they have been members of

D1

Scott Fabius
Kiesling

Table D1.1 Varbrul probabilities and percentages of alveolar (N) application of (ING) for all factor groups

Speaker	p	%	N
Speed	.91	80	130/162
Mick	.63	66	84/128
Pete	.55	73	100/137
Tommy	.51	55	16/29
Art	.47	62	40/65
Waterson	.45	62	23/37
Pencil	.36	45	50/111
Hotdog	.33	44	77/175
Mack	.31	38	32/84
Saul	.29	51	59/116
Ram	.15	22	12/54
Input/total	.62	57	623/1098

Activity type	p	%	N
Socializing	.72	75	180/240
Interview	.54	53	294/550
Meeting	.30	47	124/264
Reading	.10	54	25/46
Input/total	.62	57	623/1098

Following environment	p	%	N
[–back] cons.	.57	63	291/465
Vowel	.51	58	226/391
Pause	.36	41	75/184
[+back] cons.	.35	53	31/58
Input/total	.62	57	623/1098

Grammatical status	p	%	N
'Fuckin''	.97	97	86/89
Progressive	.60	69	356/513
Preposition	.55	60	9/15
Participle	.48	54	47/87
Noun	.42	49	49/99
Participial modifier	.26	36	15/42
Gerund	.16	24	59/242
Adjective	.11	18	2/11
Input/total	.62	57	623/1098

Scott Fabius
Kiesling

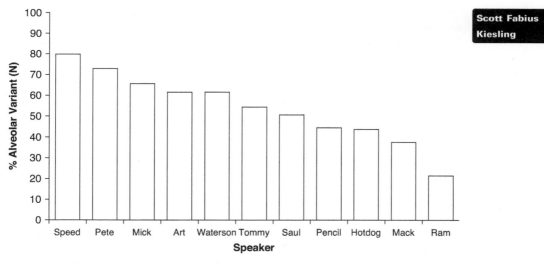

Figure D1.1   Percentage of alveolar variant for speakers

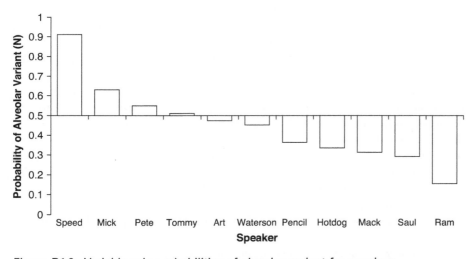

Figure D1.2   Variable rule probabilities of alveolar variant for speakers

the fraternity, geographical origin and class. Ethnicity does not explain any differences, since all the men are white except Saul, whose family is Afghani. There could be a combined age and region effect, with Pencil, Hotdog, Mack, and Ram all being older members from the Washington, D.C. area (but Saul is from Rochester, New York), while Tommy, Art, and Waterson are younger members from the Washington, D.C. area (but Pete is from Virginia Beach, Virginia). These possibilities cannot, however, be investigated without a larger sample of speakers from regions other than Northern Virginia.

**Scott Fabius
Kiesling**

Table D1.2 Probabilities and percentages of alveolar (N) application of (ING), for the combined speaker factor group

Speaker	p	%	N
Speed	.91	80	130/162
Mick	.63	66	84/128
Pete Tommy Art Waterson	.51	67	179/268
Pencil Hotdog Mack Saul	.33	45	218/486
Ram	.15	22	12/54
Input/total	.61	57	623/1098

However, speaker was not the only external variable that affected the use of (ING); activity type was also significant (Table D1.1). Socializing highly favored N at 75 percent (.72 probability), while meetings disfavored N strongly at 47 percent (.30 probability). Interviews fell in between at 53 percent (.54 probability).

The variable rule analysis does not tell the whole story, however. As Labov (1972c: 240) eloquently noted, the interaction between style (activity type) and class (speaker) is one of the interesting aspects of this variable. Thus it is important to investigate the interaction patterns through a cross tabulation. [...] Across activity types, the pattern of speaker stratification changes dramatically; most speakers move in the same general direction, but they do not move in lock-step. Moreover, the differences between speakers increase from socializing to meeting. In the socializing activity type, most of the speakers congregate in a 67–88% range (21 percent difference). This clustering is found again in the interview results, with a group congregating in a 36–60% range (24 percent difference). In the meeting activity type, however, there is no such 'core' middle group; the speakers are spread out almost evenly. [...] Speed continues his outlier status in all three activity types.

I also performed a Varbrul analysis in which the speaker and activity type factor groups were combined into one group. A single factor thus consisted of a speaker and an activity type (e.g., Saul in meeting activity type). This factor group was selected as significant in a step-up-step-down procedure (p<.05). The probability weightings are shown in Table D1.3. [...] The speakers [here] are ordered as they were in Table D1.1, with Speed, the most likely to use N overall, at the top.

The probabilities in this chart show an even more striking interaction. Note that almost all speakers favor N in the socializing activity type, in a range of .50 to .84, and no speakers disfavor N. In further Varbrul analysis, all speakers except Speed were able to be combined into one group in the socializing activity type. In the interview activity type, speakers exhibit the largest range of weightings. This is probably due to the fact that the interviews varied in style, so that some speakers considered them

Table D1.3 Probabilities and percentages of alveolar (N) application of (ING) for speaker/activity type combined factor group

Speaker	Socializing			Interview			Meeting		
	p	%	N	p	%	N	p	%	N
Speed	.84	95	19/20	.97	95	52/55	.79	82	33/40
Mick	.70	67	16/24	.61	60	37/62	.60	71	24/34
Pete	.70	82	31/38	.64	72	34/47	.30	67	26/39
Art	.52	67	10/15	.58	60	24/40	.33	60	6/10
Waterson	.59	71	10/14	.46	47	9/19	knockout: categorical N		
Pencil	.50	53	16/30	.51	48	31/64	.09	18	3/17
Hotdog	.70	83	25/30	.35	43	39/90	.16	24	13/55
Mack	.66	73	16/22	.35	39	12/31	.11	13	4/31
Saul	.62	76	29/38	.29	38	22/58	.16	38	3/8
Ram	.65	88	7/8	.09	10	3/29	.10	12	2/17

more like socializing, and others more like meetings. Speed and Ram were the high (.97) and low (.09) outliers, respectively, while the rest of the men split into two groups, one disfavoring N (.32), another slightly favoring N (.56).

The meeting also shows a split in speaker groups, as confirmed through further Varbrul analysis: a large group who strongly disfavor N, in a range of .09 to .16, and two speakers who strongly favor N in meetings: Speed (.79) and Mick (.60). Note that Waterson's weighting is effectively 1.0; his meeting tokens were excluded from the Varbrul analysis because they were categorically N. Moreover, Pete and Art (.21 combined) do not disfavor N to the same degree as the biggest group (.11). These figures show a clear differentiation among speakers within the meeting activity type, a fact that is more significant when we consider that the meeting is a relatively public activity type, while the interview is not, so that the men have access to models in the meetings, but not in the interview. The Varbrul analysis confirms the view that the men tend to use N more alike in the socializing activity type than in the meeting activity type. By investigating the differences in how the men talk in meetings, then, we should be able to understand more about the 'meaning' of this variable.

The speaker factor group also interacts with the language internal factor group of grammatical category [...]. [We can] see the strong effect of the discourse marker *fuckin'*: almost all speakers use N categorically with *fuckin'*. All speakers except Speed use less N in progressive than in *fuckin'*, and even less in gerund. The results indicate that *fuckin'* tokens may interfere with the regularity of the results (although *fuckin'* is an important part of using language to create identity, and a clue to the meaning of the variable). Therefore, removing it from the analysis may yield more informative results.

[If we consider] the cross tabulation of speaker and activity type without *fuckin'* tokens, [t]he picture now becomes much more regular, because of changes in the meeting activity type. The speaker stratification without *fuckin'* tokens is almost identical in the socializing and interview situations as with these tokens, with a small drop in the average N rate in the socializing situation (from 75% to 72%), and no change

Scott Fabius
Kiesling

in the interview situation. However, the meeting situation average drops considerably, from 46% to 33%, and the cluster we find in the socializing and interview activities is now present in the meeting activity as well. The meeting activity also corresponds more closely with variable rule probabilities (except for Waterson). Thus, the reason the meeting activity was so spread out seems to be the influence of *fuckin'*. This finding raises a more interesting question, however: why were the *fuckin'* tokens so influential in the meeting situation? Why did they make up such a great proportion in this situation and not in the socializing situation, where we might think that the 'relaxed' atmosphere would encourage the men to swear more?

[...]

'Vernacular power'

What is the explanation for the differences in (ING) use among these men, who are often assumed to be so homogeneous? Why do Mick and Waterson shift to such a high N value in meetings, when other fraternity members shift in the other direction? I [...] suggest that they are indexing a different kind of powerful alignment role than the other men in the meeting. They are indirectly indexing a hard-working role by directly indexing the physically powerful working-class cultural model. In addition, they directly index the casual camaraderie of the socializing activity types to create a connection to the other fraternity members in the meeting. [...]

But why would working-class men use more vernacular variants in the first place, and value those variants? The answer lies in hegemonic masculinity and the sources of power available to working-class men. Hegemonic masculinity pushes men to have a powerful identity, to construct identities that appear to dominate in some way, either actually or symbolically. Thus, Gal (1992) proposes that the basic process of 'men's language' is symbolic domination. Because working-class men do not have access to economic or structural power, physical power may take its place, especially since their livelihoods often rely on this kind of power. This display, taken to extremes, is known as 'protest masculinity' (introduced by Adler 1956, expanded on by Connell 1995) and is characterized by physical violence. I am proposing that working-class men are drawing on a similar process when they use the vernacular variant more than other groups. Solidarity among these men may be another path of 'resistance' to hierarchical power, but it is nevertheless subject to the strictures of hegemonic masculinity. This interaction between hegemonic masculinity and solidarity leads to what I have termed camaraderie. Physical power and vernacular language therefore become connected through the stereotype of working-class men's identity roles, deeply embedded in the American culture.

This analysis has implications not only for the 'sex pattern,' but for the study of language and identity in general, as well as for perspectives on sociolinguistic style. Most important is the suggestion to realize abstract social values such as prestige, power, and solidarity, which linguists have long found to affect a speaker's style, in more concrete relationships indexed by speakers in conversations – alignment roles. [...]

This view suggests that while identity is a display, it must be understood in terms of social relationships, including potential social relationships a speaker chooses not to identify with. Thus, in the all-male, heterosexual, mostly white fraternity, we cannot say that women, homosexuals, and minority ethnic groups are not relevant. On the contrary, they are central to the men's identity displays. Community relationships are also important, so that the fraternity relationships of member/pledge or older member/ younger member, all of which have proto-typical qualities for the fraternity members, are central to the fraternity men's identities as well. Such a view of the nature of language and society is consistent with sociolinguistic research in the quantitative as well as the qualitative or ethnographic traditions. However, the validity of this view can be tested only by investigation of the interaction among quantitative patterns and highly contextualized uses of linguistic behavior of the kind I have attempted here.

Issues to consider

❏ Is there a phonetic feature in the accent of your own speech community that signals a particular social identity, or a feature that points to an aspiration towards being identified with another, different speech community? Do you yourself adopt such features in order to be identified with a different group? Ask other people around you what they think of your accent (see also A9 and B9).

❏ Kiesling, in this study, aligns the variable pronunciation of (ING) with different situations in which the men have been recorded. Do you know of any similar groups who adopt different styles of pronunciation in different situations?

❏ Social class is a notoriously difficult concept to define, and sociophoneticians have adopted different ways of defining social class in their studies of phonetic speech features. What are advantages and disadvantages of taking the traditional approach of defining social class on the basis of father's occupation? Other researchers have classified the social class of their informants by asking the informants themselves and taking this 'self-definition' as their social class grouping (Milroy 1987). What advantages and disadvantages can you think of for this alternative approach? How else could social class be defined in order to consider the role it plays in relation to the production of different phonetic variants? You should also read D9 to inform your thinking on this issue, as it presents alternatives to a macro social class approach.

THE SEARCH FOR UNITS OF MEANING

D2

The first part of this book (Strands 1 to 5) is organised across the linguistic rank scale from morphology up to discourse. However, this categorisation is merely an analytical convenience: every piece of language consists of elements at most or all of these levels all at once. Furthermore, the categories of sounds, words, phrases, clauses, and so on are not necessarily easily contained or simple to define. For almost every definition of a word, for example, a counter-example or difficult case can usually be imagined.

In this extract, John Sinclair argues for a phrasal approach to the definition of a lexical item (a 'word'). His procedure draws on the use of a concordancing program run on a large corpus of examples of English usage, and he is particularly careful to proceed step by step through his method and argument.

John Sinclair

John Sinclair (reprinted from *Trust the Text: Language, Corpus and Discourse* (2004), London: Routledge, pp. 24–35)

The starting point of the description of meaning in language is the word. This is one of two primitives in language form, the other being the sentence. The sentence is the unit that aligns grammar and discourse, and the word is the unit that aligns grammar and vocabulary. [...]

A glance at any dictionary will confirm the status of the word as the primary unit of lexical meaning. A dictionary lists the words of a language and alongside each one provides an account of the meaning or meanings. Since the common words of a language typically can have several meanings, these are usually listed in separate paragraphs [...] The model is clear – *words* are the units of language but are prone to multiple ambiguity.

The phenomenon attracts a great deal of academic activity, because it has to be accounted for. Most of the explanations are historical, and show the way word forms can coalesce in time, and meanings can specialize and diverge. Theories of meaning arise, with concepts such as 'core meaning' (Carter 1987), and scientific experiments are conducted with the aim of providing evidence to support the theories.

Dictionaries, however, also show that the equation 'word = unit of meaning', while reliable in general, has to be qualified in a few cases. Compounds, for example, typically consist of two words, each of which has an independent existence, but together they make a meaning that is different from the normal putting together of their individual meanings. *Blackbird* is the usual example; a blackbird is a black bird, but not all black birds are blackbirds. In addition, the bigger dictionaries often include a few paragraphs at the end of the entry where a number of idiomatic phrases are listed, with explanations to show that these also claim a meaning in combination that they do not have in simple concatenation [...]. The low prominence of these features, and the almost total absence of provision for them in the grammar, makes it clear that they are considered as marginal phenomena, almost aberrations, exceptions that prove the rules.

I say 'almost total absence' because although the traditional parsing and analysis was quite pure in this respect, the business of language teaching has brought into prominence one type of combination in English that is so common it cannot really be ignored. This is the phrasal verb, the verb plus particle that conjures up an unpredictable meaning; the scourge of the learner. The structure does not fit the model, neither semantically nor grammatically, because a single meaning-selection straddles a major structural boundary. As a result, dictionaries for the learner usually make special provision for phrasal verbs, and grammars for learners make apologies for their very existence.

Besides compounds and phrasal verbs we can mention idioms, fixed phrases, variable phrases, clichés, proverbs, and many technical terms and much jargon, as examples of recognized patterns where the independence of the word is compromised in some way. In conventional descriptions of a language, whether lexical or grammatical, they are tucked away, well off-centre. They seem to be anarchic, individual, unstable, one-off items that just do not fit into a tidy description. Unlike phrases and clauses which fit together in Chinese boxes with labelled bracketing, these spill out all over the place, fit no hierarchical place, and relate in mysterious ways to word meaning. Sometimes the criterion given for identifying phrasal verbs, idioms, etc., is that the meaning is not the same as the sum of the meaning of the constituent words. [. . .]

John Sinclair

a)   none of the words may appear to contribute directly to the meaning of the expression (*bear on* = be relevant to)
b)   some may, while others may not (*to beat someone up*)
c)   each still seems to mean what it normally means (*the rain beats down*).

This last type is usually called a *collocation*, a frequent co-occurrence of words; it does not have a profound effect on the individual meanings of the words, but there is usually at least a slight effect on the meaning, if only to select or confirm the meaning appropriate to the collocation, which may not be the most common meaning. So in 'the rain beats down', the meaning of 'beat' is '[to hit] hard, usually several times or continuously for a period' (Cobuild 1995).

It is thus clear that there are many cases in texts where the independence of the choice of words is compromised, because other patterns cut across them and constrain them. [. . .]

One hypothesis, to be explored [here], is that the notion of a linguistic item can be extended, at least for English, so that units of meaning are expected to be largely phrasal. [. . .] The idea of a word carrying meaning on its own would be relegated to the margins of linguistic interest, in the enumeration of flora and fauna for example.

Part of the supporting argument for this hypothesis is that words cannot remain perpetually independent in their patterning unless they are either very rare or specially protected (for example by being technical terms, if indeed that status offers the protection that is often claimed for it). Otherwise, they begin to retain traces of repeated events in their usage, and expectations of events such as collocations arise. This leads to greater regularity of collocation and this in turn offers a platform for specialization of meaning, for example in compounds. Beyond compounds we can see lexical phrases form, phrases which have to be taken as wholes in their contexts for their distinctive meaning to emerge, but which are prone to variation. [. . .]

In considering the corpus data, we shall begin in an area of patterning that on intuitional grounds should be relevant – the area of very frequent collocations, idioms, fixed phrases and the like. If we are to find evidence of extended units of meaning, it is surely there that we should look. A typical idiom in English is built around *naked eye*. [. . .]

We shall examine in detail the expression *naked eye*. There is no useful interpretation for this phrase based on the 'core' meanings of the two words, e.g. 'unclothed organ of sight', although we can work back from the phrasal meaning, roughly 'without (the) aid (of a telescope or microscope)' and make a metaphorical extension to *naked* which fits the meaning. Notice that, once established, it is dangerously easy to reverse the procedure and assume that the metaphorical extension is obvious. It is not; *naked* in the collocation *naked eye* could equally well mean 'unprotected', 'without eyelids', 'without spectacles, contact lenses, etc.', and the collocation *naked eye* could easily mean 'shocked' (? they stripped in front of the naked eyes of the watchers) or

John Sinclair

'provocative espionage device' (? American use of their naked eye spy satellites has caused Iraq to retaliate), or a dozen other metaphorical extensions of the semantic features of the two words involved.

The data analysed for this study comes from *The Bank of English*, which contained in mid-1995 a total of 211 million words of current English from a wide range of sources. There are 151 instances of *naked eye*, [...]. By inspection of the concordances, it is clear that there is greater consistency of patterning to the left of the collocation than to the right, so we move in our study step by step to the left. [...]

The first position to the left of *naked eye* (designated N-1) is occupied by the word *the*, in 95 per cent of the examples. The deviant examples are explained as the influence of regular features of English – the concord of personal pronouns and the nominalization of noun phrases. Therefore it is established that *the* is an inherent component of the phrase *the naked eye*.

We now turn to position N-2, immediately to the left of *the*. Two words dominate the pattern – *with* and *to*:

... you can see with the naked eye ...
... just visible to the naked eye ...

The other prepositions are *by*, *from*, *as*, *upon* and *than* (though some grammars do not recognize *as* and *than* as prepositions). The total number of prepositions in this position is 136, which is over 90 per cent. The word class 'preposition' is thus an inherent component of the phrase, accounting for over 90 per cent of the cases.

What we have done, in terms of our analysis, is to change our criterion from collocation to *colligation*, the co-occurrence of grammatical choices to account for the greater variation. The pattern observed here is not full colligation, because it is the co-occurrence of a grammatical class (preposition) with a collocating pair, but it is an extremely useful concept at this stage of our investigations.

Roughly 10 per cent of the instances do not have a preposition at N-2. These show what we might consider to be a short form of the phrase, primarily used as the subject or object of a clause, where a preposition would be inappropriate:

... the two form a naked-eye pair ...

The short form is found both in general use and in a semitechnical use [...].

We now consider N-3, and leave on one side the short and technical instances (reducing the total number to 134). It is immediately clear that variations on two words – *see* and *visible* – dominate the picture.

All of these are prominent collocations, restricted to the two word classes 'verb' and 'adjective'. On this occasion colligation, being divided between the two, is not as important as another criterion, that of *semantic preference*. Whatever the word class, whatever the collocation, almost all of the instances with a preposition at N-2 have a word or phrase to do with visibility either at N-3 or nearby. This new criterion is another stage removed from the actual words in the text, just as colligation is one step more abstract than collocation. But it captures more of the patterning than the others.

John Sinclair

Having established a criterion of this kind, we seek to maximise it. Even single occurrences of words can be included so long as they have the selected semantic feature, which is what we are counting. So, among the verbs we find *detect*, *spot*, *spotted*, *appear*, *perceived*, *viewed*, *recognized*, *read*, *studied*, *judged* – and the verb *tell*, which is used in a meaning similar to *detect*.

... you cannot tell if ...

Other adjectives at N-3 are *apparent*, *evident*, *obvious* and *undetectable*, each having a semantic feature of, roughly, 'visibility'. The criterion of semantic preference implies a loosening of syntactic regimentation, and in turn this means that the strict word-counting on which we have based positional statements is not as appropriate as it was earlier. While the majority of 'visibility' indications are to be found at N-3, quite a few are at N-4, and a scattering are even farther away or on the right hand side of the expression. [...]

At this point we draw attention to a concord rule that has been obscured by the step-by-step presentation, which presents the prepositional choice before the semantic one. This rule is a correlation between the 'visibility' choice and the preposition choice, depending on the word class of the semantic preference. Adjectives take *to*, and verbs take *with* in all but a very small number of cases. [...]

We have one more step to take – to look at the selections to the left of N-3 and see if there is any further regularity that might be incorporated into the phrase that we are studying. We must expect that in many cases the concordance line is not long enough, and in a thorough study we would have to look at extended contexts; if

'visibility + preposition + *the* + *naked* + *eye*'

is all one basic lexical choice, then a reasonable context of four or five words on either side would in most cases take us beyond the limit of the printed line. To avoid adducing a great deal of extra evidence, we shall concede at the outset that there are likely to be some indeterminate cases.

It is clear from a superficial glance that there is little or no surface regularity, but closer examination [...] justifies one further element in the structure of a lexical item. We postulate a *semantic prosody* of 'difficulty', which is evident in over 85 per cent of the instances. It may be shown by a word such as *small*, *faint*, *weak*, *difficult* with *see*:

... too faint to be seen with the naked eye ...

and barely, rarely, just with *visible*:

... it is not really visible to the naked eye ...

or by a negative with 'visibility' or *invisible* itself, or it may just be hinted at by a modal verb such as *can* or *could*:

... these could be seen with the naked eye from a helicopter ...

John Sinclair

A semantic prosody (Louw 1993) is attitudinal, and on the pragmatic side of the semantics/pragmatics continuum. It is thus capable of a wide range of realization, because in pragmatic expressions the normal semantic values of the words are not necessarily relevant. But once noticed among the variety of expression, it is immediately clear that the semantic prosody has a leading role to play in the integration of an item with its surroundings. It expresses something close to the 'function' of the item – it shows how the rest of the item is to be interpreted functionally. Without it, the string of words just 'means' – it is not put to use in a viable communication. So in the example here, the attention to visibility and the strange phrase *the naked eye* are interpreted as expressions of some kind of difficulty. [. . .]

Having arrived at the semantic prosody, we have probably come close to the boundary of the lexical item. In any case, with only the short lines of data that are made available for this study, we lack the evidence with which to continue the search. However, we have enough already on which to base the description of a compound lexical item. We shall describe its elements in the unreversed sequence, the textual sequence.

The speaker/writer selects a prosody of difficulty applied to a semantic preference of visibility. The semantic preference controls the collocational and colligational patterns, and is divided into verbs, typically *see*, and adjectives, typically *visible*. With *see*, etc., there is a strong colligation with modals – particularly *can, could* in the expression of difficulty – and with the preposition *with* to link with the final segment. With *visible*, etc., the pattern of collocation is principally with degree adverbs, and the negative morpheme *in-*; the following preposition is *to*. The final component of the item is the *core*, the almost invariable phrase *the naked eye*.

Note that this analysis makes two important observations, which tend to confirm the existence of this compound lexical item:

a   The beginning of the item is very difficult to detect normally, because it is so variable; on the other hand the end is fixed and obvious. But if the analysis is correct, the whole phrase must be seen as the result of a single choice, with no doubt a number of subsidiary internal choices.

b   The initial choice of semantic prosody is the functional choice which links meaning to purpose; all subsequent choices within the lexical item relate back to the prosody.

Here, then, is one model of a lexical item consisting of several words, and with a great deal of internal variation. The variation, however, disappears when the description invokes an appropriate category of abstraction, and despite the variation there is always a clearly preferred selection right down to the actual words. The variations are negligible around the core, and can be explained by the tension between different constructional pressures; further away from the core they become more varied, allowing the phrase to fit in with the previous context, and allowing some more detailed choices to be made. [. . .]

The case for compound lexical items will be made by piling up evidence of the kind illustrated in this chapter, and apparently pervading much of the vocabulary. So strong are the co-occurrence tendencies of words, word classes, meanings and attitudes

John Sinclair

that we must widen our horizons and expect the units of meaning to be much more extensive and varied than is seen in a single word. [...]

Models that arise from corpus-driven studies, like the one proposed here, have a holistic quality that makes them attractive. The numerical analysis of language is aligned closely with the meaningful analysis; lexis and grammar are hardly distinguished, surface and abstract categories are mixed without difficulty. As a result some of the problems of conventional description are much reduced – for example there will be little word-based ambiguity left when this model has been applied thoroughly. Although a great deal of research has to be done to find the units and make the description coherent, the gain for students and users of language should be well worth the effort.

Concordance sample for **naked eye**

agents too small to see with	the naked eye	and so they much preferred
binaries that can be seen with	the naked eye	(very few of these) or through
our galaxy that you can see with	the naked eye	Now to expand our horizons: The
is like viewing the moon with	the naked eye	. You see a disk with some
of thing you could look at with	the naked eye	'Would you like to
it is not really visible to	the naked eye	. About five years ago, a
cannot always be perceived by	the naked eye	and said, 'As I've gotten
even though nothing is visible to	the naked eye	. We should trust our patients
the opening is not visible to	the naked eye	. Typically, the closed
photoaging changes are visible to	the naked eye	. And even more disturbing
little rooftop house. Viewed with	the naked eye	, she was nothing more than a
is visible with	the naked eye	. While stroke path can be with

Issues to consider

❑ What is a word? Try to write down your own definition, and then ask someone else to think of an example that does not fit your definition.

❑ You could select another phrase and apply the same procedure that Sinclair follows in his investigation here. You would need access to a large corpus such as the British National Corpus that Sinclair uses, and you would also need a simple concordance program. Alternatively, a standard Internet search engine will allow you to collect a less systematic but still interesting body of data from texts across the web. Even within a word-processing program, the 'Find' facility will allow you to find a selected phrase in any text file that you have.

❑ Though Sinclair draws in this extract on pragmatics and the notion of intuitive well-formedness, the title of his book (*Trust the Text*) underlines his insistence that properly systematic techniques can reveal holistic, generalised and subconscious features in language by focusing largely upon linguistic data. Consider the practice of corpus linguistics in this respect: what can a corpus technique not be able to show about any aspect of language?

THE SPEECH ACTS OF THE IN-GROUP

In this study, Joan Cutting presents an analysis of the speech acts of an 'in-group' of students. She begins (prior to the excerpt) by noting that most speech act analyses are synchronic 'snapshots' of a moment in time; here she offers a developmental view of the evolution of speech act rules across the academic year.

Joan Cutting   **Joan Cutting** (reprinted from 'The speech acts of the in-group', *Journal of Pragmatics* 33 (2001): 1207–33. © Elsevier 2001).

This developmental study examines the casual conversations of an academic discourse community: students of MSc courses in Applied Linguistics in the University of Edinburgh (UE). It focuses on the 1991–1992 in-group of students of the then Department of Applied Linguistics (DAL) and in particular on six native-speakers of English [...], in order to describe the social rules of the student common room and to show how they change from the moment the students meet until the end of the course. [...]

Analysis of speech acts from the point of view of function showed that whereas in the autumn term, 32% of all conversations contained transactional speech acts, in the spring and summer the level was on average 10%, thus confirming the researcher's impression that common room chat has a mainly interactional function. Presumably, transactional speech acts occur in the autumn because the students are still finding their way about then; dialogues are concerned with negotiations about tasks – who is in whose tutorial group, what a tutorial task consists of, and so on. In the rest of the course, there is less to be negotiated, since they have got all their ways of studying and their support mechanisms established. Analysis also showed that CK [course knowledge] speech acts are less likely to have a transactional function than NCK [non-course knowledge] topics are. [...] Thus, in the spring term, there is practically no transactional talk: that is when CK dialogues are the norm, and CK dialogues then have but 3% of 'talk for getting things done'. The stressful spring term requires rather expressions of in-the-same-boatness and solidarity.

An examination of non-neutral speech acts (to self, to interlocutors and to a third party) showed that 24% of all discourse units contain language overtly expressing a non-neutral attitude, and that, as hypothesised, these speech acts do increase throughout the course (Autumn: 15%, Spring: 25%, Summer: 27%). Thus, it appears that speech acts expressing an attitude are acceptable once the students come back after Christmas; once they get to know each other and the group has gelled, they can express more emotion. This is regardless of topic: it happens across both K areas.

The analysis of each type of non-neutral speech act taken separately suggested more specific social rules, ones that could not have been predicted. In both CK and NCK dialogues, the predominant attitude is 'positive to interlocutors and communication', constituting almost half of all non-neutral speech acts (see Table D3.1). Students know that they must 'be nice to each other', whatever they are talking about. Conversely, 'negative to interlocutors and communication' is three times as likely in NCK dialogues as it is in CK; students know not to risk being negative towards each other in the context of the course.

Table D3.1 Percentage of each non-neutral speech act out of all non-neutral units

Joan Cutting

Speech Act category	NCK	CK
Positive to self	1	8
Negative to self	3	14
Positive to interlocutors/communication	43	43
Negative to interlocutors/communication	19	7
Positive to third party/situation	13	5
Negative to third party/situation	21	24

A longitudinal analysis of the speech act 'positive to interlocutors and communication', taking both K areas together, shows that there is a steady increase throughout
the year (see Table D3.2). [. . .] This significant increase may be indicative of an increased
need to express in-the-same-boatness. The first social rule seems to be '*Express a positive
attitude to your interlocutors and the communication, whatever topic you are talking about, and
especially in the spring and summer terms*'.

The second most frequent non-neutral speech act in both CK and NCK dialogues
is 'negative to third party or situation', and in CK dialogues the rate is only slightly
higher than in NCK (see Table D3.1). Students expect each other to sound negative
about things in general. Conversely, CK dialogues have but a third of the 'positive to
third party or situation' that NCK dialogues have; students know to avoid appearing
pleased with components of the course context. Table D3.1 also shows that CK dialogues
have five times more of the speech act 'negative attitude to self' than NCK dialogues
do. The category is the third densest of CK non-neutral categories. [. . .] Students
know that they are expected to sound negative about the course and their progress
through it.

A longitudinal analysis of all dialogues taking both K areas together showed
that both the speech acts 'negative attitude to self' and 'negative attitude to third
party' peaked in the spring and then dropped in the summer (see Table D3.2). The
increase in all non-neutral speech acts in the spring may be a reflection of the fact
that CK dialogues predominate then, or of the fact that the pressure from the course
increases then. Thus the second social rule seems to be: '*Express a negative attitude
to yourself and to the situation, especially if you are talking about the course, and especially
in the spring term*'.

Table D3.2 Percentage of 'positive to interlocutors', 'negative to self' and
'negative to third party' speech acts out of all units

Term	Positive to interlocutors	Negative to self	Negative to third party
Autumn term	5	2	4
Spring term	9	3	7
Summer term	13	1	4

Joan Cutting

A detailed qualitative analysis of the predominant speech acts within the category 'negative attitude to a situation or third party' in CK dialogues showed that students evaluate negatively the work, books and lecturers. They complain that the revision for the examination is 'a lot of work', that 3,000 words for the project is 'a lot' to write, that there is 'a lot of pressure', and that the main problem is 'time'. They express dissatisfaction with theories, fields of thought and courses about them, saying that they are 'rubbish', as in:

(1) AM: Gram- Grammar Two.
     AM: But it I mean it's it's just (0.5)
     AM: I don't know.
     AM: It's just I don't know.
     AM: Bloody tosh, isn't it?
     CM: Well it's- it's a bit abstract. (1)

[Note: numbers in brackets indicate length of pause, in seconds]. This example shows that negative evaluations are interactive in the sense that if one speaker displays a negative attitude, the other(s) are expected to do the same. The students complain that books are too 'theoretical', and that articles are 'completely useless'. In (2), BM and DM are discussing an article.

(2) BM: It's pretty it's scurrilous isn't it?
     DM: I think it is awful.

Again, BM chooses to talk negatively and DM is expected to echo the sentiments. They evaluate some lecturers in an exaggeratedly negative fashion: one is 'a fanatic', and another 'a complete maniac'.

[...]

The analysis of expressions of a 'negative attitude to self' in CK dialogues showed that the main speech acts in this category are 'criticise yourself', 'express worry', and 'minimise your progress'. Students evaluate themselves and their work negatively, possibly in the expectation that the interlocutor will contradict them or reassure them of the normality of the situation. They say that their 'handwriting is awful', that they are 'no good at memory things', that they 'never get things done on time', that they cannot 'get [their] brains going', that they cannot 'come up with' a point themselves in their project. [...]

If speakers feel that they may have alarmed interlocutors about their good progress, perhaps showing themselves in a good light, they minimise the significance of it by playing it down, as in:

(4) AF: I've got a couple of totally uninformed sort of basically stupid ideas for
          a project.
     DM: What?
     DM: Well what are these yeah what are these ideas then? (1.5)

A qualitative analysis of expressions of a 'positive attitude to interlocutors' shows that the main speech acts in this category are 'empathise', 'console', 'encourage' and

D3

Joan Cutting

'advise'. These occur in response to the negative evaluations of situation and self mentioned above. The students 'empathise' with each other using expressions such as 'I've done that' and 'same here'; they show solidarity by saying that they are in the same boat. [...]

Another response to worried colleagues is to 'console' them; to tell them 'don't worry', that their progress seems fine. This happens mostly in CK. In (5), CM says that he is going to miss the last week of class and seeks the approval of his colleagues; DM reassures him by minimising the problem:

(5) DM: Er it's no big deal.
     DM: By the time you get to the last week you'll have done most of what you need
          to- you'll know what you need to know for the portfolio.
     DM: If you're answering questions anyway (3) shouldn't be a problem (2)

On occasions, the students 'encourage' each other by praising or congratulating. This happens more in CK than in NCK: students tell each other they have done well, or have good arguments and ideas. In (6), DM has just read through BF's project and praises it:

(6) DM: There's nothing (1) there's nothing startling that I can see missing from
          this (2)
     DM: and it's very readable. (1)

[...]

In the summer term, sometimes students who feel close to each other do not respond to colleagues evaluating the situation and themselves negatively by showing empathy at all. By then, they trust each other enough to risk threatening each other's face by offering 'advice' and 'warning' (transactional 'positive to inter-locutor' talk). Thus, in (7), DM fears that he will have difficulty finding a dissertation topic:

(7) DM: Been trying to think of something that might stretch to twenty thousand words.
          (2)
     DM: And is not excruciatingly boring.
     AF: ((Blows nose)) Well you might have to just face that and cope with it. ((sniffs))
     DM: Mm (2)

and AF's response is not 'I've been trying to think of something too' but 'face it and cope with it'. Her advice is softened with the hedge 'well' and the tentative modal 'might'.

Just as students can show a positive attitude to the course if they are using irony and implying a negative attitude, they can show a negative attitude to the interlocutor if they are indulging in a little banter and implying a positive attitude. Teasing colleagues in the context of the course is a risky endeavour and it only occurs in the autumn and the summer when the stress-level is lower (Cutting 1996). In (8), DM expresses contentment that the deadline for a project has been moved forward:

(8) AM: An // extra week.
     DM: // O//h.
     BF: Ah.
     BF: Oh you dosser!
     BF: You're an absolute dosser!
     DM: (heh heh heh) Brilliant=

BF evaluates his attitude negatively, just to tease.

It becomes more obvious that these social rules exist in the common room, when speakers break them and meet with an adverse reaction. Let us start with the first 'social rule': '*Express a positive attitude to your interlocutors and the communication, whatever topic you are talking about, and especially in the spring and summer terms*'.

Speakers rarely go out of their way to worry their colleagues. Thus, when it happens, the tension that it creates is striking. (9) comes from the beginning of the spring term when the pressure has just begun; CM and AM are discussing their revision for the examination:

(9) AM: But things like this linguistics as well.
     AM: You know I don't mi-mind it.
     CM: You still got enough time for that? (0.5)
     AM: There's not a lot of things they can ask.
     AM: Cos we haven't actually done it that deeply have we?
     CM: I've spent the most time right now on all this all this load of er in Language and Linguistics.
     AM: // Yes.
     CM: // Cos I really want to answer that question.
     AM: And I've I've haven't done anything about the Psycholinguistics.
     AM: I haven't done Chomsky.
     AM: Which is (0.5) probably very stupid but you // know.
     CM: // Avoiding Chomsky in Linguistics is// procrastination I think.
     AM: We//ll.
     AM: No em avoiding it in terms of em (1.5) in terms of er I mean obviously in relation to other things you've got to=
     CM: Yeah=
     AM: but not necessarily you know in depth.

AM is evidently nervous about the linguistics revision. He obeys the rule of speaking negatively about oneself: 'and I haven't done Chomsky. Which is (0.5) probably very stupid but you // know'. However, CM makes no attempt to 'console' or 'empathise'. His reaction is to intensify AM's worry: 'You still got enough time for that?' and 'Avoiding Chomsky in Linguistics is// procrastination I think'. These two conflicting utterances (amounting to 'don't do it now' and 'do it now'), co-occurring with a statement that shows himself in a positive light ('I've spent the most time right now on all this all this load of er in Language and Linguistics cos I really want to answer that question'), do not sound as friendly as AF did with her advice in example (7) above. More solidarity and less power could have been expressed with a hedge and a modal, 'Perhaps you might not have time for that now'. Unconsoled, AM is left consoling himself, showing himself a positive attitude, with 'There's not a lot of things they can ask. Cos we haven't actually done it that deeply have we?'. He is thrown into confusion; witness his incoherent 'No em avoiding it in terms of em (1.5) in terms of er I mean obviously in relation to other things you've got to but not necessarily you know in depth'.

When the second social rule of the common room, '*Express a negative attitude to yourself and to the situation, especially if you are talking about the course, and especially in the spring term*', is broken, it meets with an adverse reaction. Starting with evaluations of the course, it would be fair to say that when students realise that they have expressed a positive attitude to the course, they themselves immediately counter-act it with a negative expression. For example, in (10) AM says that the courses 'Linguistics Research' and 'Language and Linguistics' are 'interesting' and that he is 'really quite pleased':

(10)   AM: Cos (0.5) I mean things like Linguistics Research and that stuff in Language and Linguistics.
        AM: It's quite interesting actually.
        AM: I was really quite pleased.
        AM: I mean it's (2) I don't know.
        AM: I'll be glad when it's finished. (1)
        CM: Yeah // it's
        AM: // I'm not really into it. (4)

and then has to add negatively that he will 'be glad when it's finished' and that he is 'not really into it'. If, on the other hand, speakers express a positive attitude to the course and then leave it, this is met with open disagreement, an attitude 'negative towards the interlocutor'. That is to say: if the speaker breaks the rules, the hearers break them too. (11) is an example: CM is overjoyed that the Easter holidays are upon them:

(11)   CM: Do you realise that we have from er March nineteen until (0.5) April the twentieth?
        CM: With nothing to do?
        AM: Nothing // to do!
        FF: // Well got a project to hand in at // em (heh heh)
        AM: // Yes!

There is a group outcry. [...]

The study of speech acts shows general tendencies regardless of personality. Although personality was not studied in depth, an overall global impression of personality in the data was included. BM likes to express negative feelings about third parties and situations; CM tends to show himself in a positive light and deny solidarity and reassurance to his colleagues; DM is the warmest solidarity-giver, guaranteed to express a positive attitude towards his interlocutors; AF goes in for self-deprecation, modestly showing herself in a poor light; and BF most enjoys a little banter with her male colleagues, playfully showing a negative attitude to them. These differences were not great enough to invalidate the overall results: it can be seen that they are not the causes of the changes observed over time. When a calculation was made of the distribution of discourse units spoken by each of the six recordees in each of the three terms, it was found that BM and AF feature less in the spring and summer term recordings; yet they are the ones who are most negative to self and third party, and

Joan Cutting

speech acts expressing a negative attitude to self and third party peak in the spring. It was also found that CM features more in the spring and summer dialogues than he does in the autumn and that he does not go in for expressions of positive attitude to interlocutor; yet the rate of such speech acts increases over the spring and summer. Thus it would seem that the changes are not a reflection of the characteristics of the recordee featuring most in each term. [...]

[...] This article has suggested that the common room dictates rules about the expression of attitudes. The question is finally, *why* do the in-group members follow the rules? The overall function of common room conversations is interactional; students talk to show solidarity. If one accepts that 'individuals shift their speech styles to become more like that of those with whom they are interacting' (Giles and St. Clair 1979: 46), that the speech acts express strategies of rapport and involvement (Tannen 1984), that a show of feeling is a marker of intimacy (Goffman 1971), and that using irony and banter stressing the shared background and values constitutes a positive politeness technique (Brown and Levinson 1987: 124), one could conclude that the students follow the rules in order to cohere with the rest of the group and feel its support. [...]

Issues to consider

❏ Cutting focuses on the speech act rules within a very specific discourse community (see also A9), and suggests that the patterns she observes are primarily indicators of social solidarity. Can you generalise the same sort of patterns by identifying particular speech acts that are used in other discourse communities? Do you recognise the rules and complex applications around the discourse in your own social setting? Based upon Cutting's findings from this MSc student data, consider which of the following factors seems to you to be the most generalisable across different discourse communities: age relationships, occupational status, geographical location, shared group knowledge.

❏ Cutting briefly mentions Brown and Levinson's (1987) positive politeness strategies in the final paragraph when she is summarising how the common room talk between students governs their expression of attitudes. Analyse all data extracts in Cutting's study from the perspective of Brown and Levinson's politeness strategies, focusing first upon the positive politeness strategies outlined in B3. You should then consider if there is any evidence of negative politeness strategies or impoliteness strategies. Place your politeness analysis alongside Cutting's speech act analysis and re-examine the evidence that you have for how the students are building rapport and expressing involvement with one another. You should then consider the overall usefulness of combining a speech act analysis with an analysis of linguistic politeness.

❏ Cutting suggests towards the end of the excerpt that personality type might be a factor in the data, and more tentatively she suggests that the data can indicate broad personality types, at least as far as discursive behaviour goes. The observation illustrates the position of pragmatics between psycholinguistics (A7–D7) and sociolinguistics (A9–D9). Do you think a speech act analysis of the type undertaken by Cutting can be used to discriminate personality types rather than social variables? How would you design a study such as this?

PREFABRICATED EXPRESSIONS IN SPOKEN LANGUAGE

As you will have discovered across Strand 4, the study of syntax ranges from the most theoretical discussions to the most applied forms of linguistics. In this extract, Jenny Cheshire examines closely the argument that syntax is potentially highly innovative and creative, and discovers that everyday discourse is full of phrases and idioms that are like ready-made templates that we bolt together in order to engage in quick conversation. She examines the syntactic role of these *prefabricated expressions* (also called lexical clusters, phraseological units or formulaic sequences), but her discussion retains an applied linguistic focus. Her examples come from transcription data collected in a sociolinguistic study in the southern English town of Reading, and also from large language corpora. It is interesting to read this excerpt alongside the corpus linguistics of Sinclair in D2. Cheshire sets her sociolinguistic approach (termed *variationist* here) against the traditional theoretical *generativist* approach (see also A13).

Jenny Cheshire (reprinted from 'Syntactic variation and spoken language', in L. Cornips and K. Corrigan (eds) *Syntax and Variation: Reconciling the Biological and the Social* (2005), Amsterdam: Benjamins publishers)

Jenny
Cheshire

Many researchers working on spoken language have claimed that linguists tend to over-emphasise the creative aspect of language. There is no doubt that we can produce and understand an infinite number of sentences that we have never heard before but, as Bolinger (1975: 297) pointed out, the fact that we *can* do this does not mean that we *do*. It would be counter-productive in spontaneous face-to-face communication to constantly produce brand new sentences and speakers use prefabricated expressions to help them cope with the demands of fast speech production. These expressions include conversational routines with clear social or cultural functions, such as forms conventionally expressing apologies, thanks, compliments or requests (for example the English request formulae *I wonder if I could/ could you possibly/ can I just*), frequent collocations, like *heavy smoker, white coffee*, 'construction templates' such as *as far as I (can see/know/can make out)*, or sentence builders such as *my point is, I'm a great believer in* (see Crystal 1995: 162ff.; Wray 2002).

Estimates of the proportion of ready-made chunks of unanalysed language in large-scale corpora of spoken language range from 30 per cent (Biber et al. 1999) to 70–90 per cent (see Aijmer 1996: 31). The difference in the estimated proportions reflects the ways in which the chunks are defined. Sometimes researchers rely on subjective identifications of what counts as prefabricated, whilst others give a strict definition on the basis of collocation patterns within a large corpus. For example, Biber et al.'s (1999) analysis of a 40 million word corpus of spoken and written English excludes combinations of less than three words: it therefore excludes recurrent noun and adjective combinations such as *heavy smoker* and recurrent conversational routines like *I'm sorry*. Estimates of the proportion of prefabricated expressions also reflect decisions about how fixed in form an expression must be in order to be considered prefabricated. *How do you do*, for example, is completely frozen and the 'sentence builder' (Crystal 1995: 162) *what I mean is* is capable only of limited alteration (such as *what I really mean is, what I meant to say was*). Some conversational routines have

Jenny Cheshire

greater flexibility; these include, for example, the compliment formula *I (really) like/ love your NP*, where the NP must refer to an item that is culturally approved (Holmes 1995). Aijmer (1996: 217) accounts for the flexibility of certain conversational routines by seeing them as 'mini-grammars' consisting of collocational stems generating a limited set of structures. An example is the expression *to put it another way*: in the London-Lund corpus this could be described as having a stem generating the related discourse forms *putting it*, *put it* and *put*, followed by one of four manner adverbials (*this way*, *like this*, *another way* and *mildly*). The interrogative *how shall I put it* also occurred in the corpus. Aijmer proposes that conversational routines can be arranged along a continuum from completely fixed forms through semi-fixed forms (e.g. *I'm so/really/very sorry*), frame and slot forms (e.g. *could I have X*) to mini-grammars. It is difficult to accommodate mini-grammars within a formal grammar, however, because their output is so constrained.

Even a strict definition of what constitutes a prefabricated expression gives their proportion within a corpus as 30 per cent: a sufficiently high proportion for their existence to be taken seriously. They raise the question of whether spoken language might be better conceptualised as linear and sequential in structure rather than as hierarchical. The idea is pushed to its limits by Sinclair (1991: 68), who predicts that 'lexical hordes' will invade the traditional domain of syntax and lead to its eventual demise. Skehan (1998: 37) takes a more moderate view, suggesting that the production of speech involves improvising on a clause by clause basis, such that speakers use lexical phrases and lexical sentence stems wherever possible in order to minimise processing demands and only as a last resort generate language that is not part of our memorised lexicon. Even a moderate view, however, suggests that when we are analysing spontaneous spoken language it is important to bear in mind that what may appear to be a syntactic construction may instead be a chunk of ready-made memorised language. [. . .]

Independent adverbial phrases in spoken English are a case in point. These appear to be subordinate adverbial clauses in that they are introduced by conjunctions such as *because*, *when*, or *if*, but there is no main clause. Generative theory does not allow for the possibility of unattached adverbial clauses – understandably, since by definition an adverbial clause is subordinate to a main clause (and they may well be overlooked by researchers, since it is not clear that constructions such as these are accessible to our intuitions). However, both Mondorf (2000) and Ford (1993) noted unattached adverbial clauses in their analyses of adverbial clauses in spoken English. Mondorf reported 6 per cent out of the total number of adverbial clauses (259 out of 4462 clauses) and Ford found 3 per cent out of the total number of temporal adverbial clauses (2 out of 63 temporal clauses). Both authors were able to infer a main clause from the surrounding linguistic context, but it is not always possible to do so. McCarthy (1998: 79–82) for example notes clauses introduced by *if* and *cos* (a reduced form of *because*) that occur alone and function as main clauses. I found it equally impossible to infer a main clause for some *when* structures that occurred in a corpus of conversations between 12–16-year-old working-class adolescents in Reading, Berkshire (see Cheshire 1982). Unattached phrases introduced by *when* were relatively frequent in my Reading corpus, accounting for 25 per cent (28) of the 105 *when* clauses. I will discuss these phrases in some detail in order to illustrate the problems they can pose for a variationist analysis.

Two examples of the *when* phrases are indicated by the arrows in (1) and (2). They were uttered with level tones on every syllable except the last: this has a falling tone and is slightly drawled. Interestingly, they were used only by the male adolescents.

(1) (*the boys are talking about one of their teachers, who was married to someone I knew. Jenny (me) was the fieldworker*)

	Nobby:	yeah Miss Threadgold she ain't bad
	Rob:	yeah she. she went camping with us
	Jenny:	yes he told me she'd been camping
→	Nobby:	when we went camping
	Rob:	she's a good laugh
	Jenny:	is she?
	Nobby:	yeah

(2) (*the discussion has been about jobs the girls might consider doing when they leave school*)

	Jenny:	you have to do horrible jobs if you're a nurse .. all the bed pans
	All:	<LAUGHTER>
	Jenny:	have you ever been in hospital?
	Valerie:	[I have
	Christine:	[oh yeah I have
	Valerie:	I got run over by a car
	Christine:	I fell off a gate backwards <LAUGHS> and I was unconscious
→	Tommy:	oi when I .. when I went in hospital just for a little while...
	Valerie:	sshh
	Tommy:	cos my sister and my cousin they bent my arm .. they twisted it right round

A variationist analysis of the *when* phrases would seem in principle to be possible, if we assume one variant to be a *when* clause that is clearly subordinate to a main clause (for example, *when we went camping* in *when we went camping we had a great time*) and another variant to be an unattached *when* clause as in (1) or (2).

The first step in a variationist analysis would then be to establish the discourse function of the lone *when* phrases and the conventional, subordinate, *when* clauses to ensure that they are equivalent in function. One function of conventional initial *when* clauses is explicatory (Ford 1993: 29, 32). Ford found that this was the case when *when* clauses followed a semantically broad term such as *thing* or *then*. In her data the explication occurred within an extended speaker turn. She argued, in fact, that the use of the semantically broad term contributed to the projection of an extended turn. Only four of the lone *when* clauses in the Reading data were explicatory, however. One of these is illustrated in (3): here Rob explains, in answer to a question, how Britt (one of the playground leaders) tries to control her mind. The lone *when* clause does not elaborate a semantically broad term, nor does it project an extended turn, but it does provide a time frame for a specific situation that illustrates Britt's behaviour. In doing so, it clarifies a semantically problematic concept (the idea of controlling

Jenny
Cheshire

your mind) that the emerging discourse has shown to be ambiguous or too vague for present purposes: this was initially unclear to all the participants, as indicated by Rob's *whatever that means* and Nobby's response (*I don't know*) to my question about how this can be done.

(3) Rob: and Britt she's queer = = she's trying to learn to control
      her mind
  Nobby: = yeah =
  Rob: whatever that means
  Jenny: is she?
  Rob: [yeah
  Nobby: [yeah
  Jenny: oh how is she going to what is she doing to con
  Nobby: I don't know
→ Rob: when you look at smoke and that you know fire =
  Jenny: = yeah
  Nobby: she looks at a flame she's. you can look at. she's trying to look at
      a flame until it burns right out
  Jenny: and then w. how does that control your mind?
  Rob: I don't know

The four lone *when* phrases with an explicatory function, then, do share at least one of the functions of subordinate *when* clauses.

  A further function of subordinate adverbial clauses in initial position is to project an extended turn and present background for material that follows. These characteristics contribute to Ford's view that initial adverbial clauses are pivotal points in the development of talk (p. 62). The remaining 21 lone *when* phrases in the Reading corpus share these characteristics. In (2), for example, the other speakers interpret Tommy's lone *when* phrase, prefaced by his attention-getting *oi*, as an indication that he intends to take a projected turn; this is shown by Valerie compliantly telling her younger sister to be quiet. Usually, the extended turns are narratives of personal experience; thus, in (2) Tommy went on to tell the story of his stay in hospital. Both explicatory and pivotal lone *when* phrases, then, share some aspects of the interactional function of conventional adverbial *when* clauses. As mentioned above, there is social variation in that the forms without an accompanying main clause are used only by the male adolescents. These forms might seem, then, to be candidates for a variationist analysis, with a sociolinguistic variable consisting of two variants, one a *when* clause with a main clause, the other a lone *when* construction without a co-occurring main clause.

  However, this approach would miss an important discourse function of the 21 lone *when* constructions that are pivotal in the development of talk. In every case, the narrative that follows the lone *when* phrase concerns events that are familiar to the other speakers, either because they have heard the story before, or because they participated themselves in the events that are recounted. The narrative is a form of joint reminiscing – a discourse event with an important role in reinforcing group

Jenny
Cheshire

membership (Edwards and Middleton 1986). In the Reading playground conversations these narratives were especially significant in the construction and reinforcement of group friendship patterns amongst the male adolescents. The main function of these lone *when* phrases, in other words, is as a story opener, marking the upcoming story as a shared reminiscence. Female adolescents constructed friendships on a more individual basis, telling stories mainly as monologues. Their different narrative style was reflected in their preferred story opener which [...] was a temporal subordinate clause, clearly situating the story in the past (for further details see Cheshire 2000).

When the lone *when* phrases are considered in their full interactional context, it becomes clear that they cannot be analysed as variants of conventional initial *when* clauses, since they are not functionally equivalent. They have a specific discourse function as a story opener marking a shared reminiscence. [...]

An analysis that fits [...] with the data is to see the lone *when* phrases as conversational routines, together with the other story openers marking an upcoming shared reminiscence (such as *what about when, you know when* or *remember when*). As we saw earlier, a conversational routine is a sequence of words that appears to have syntactic structure but that is produced and processed as a more or less prefabricated phrase (Aijmer 1996). The *when* of the lone *when* phrases may be a reduced form of the other *when* phrases in this group of story openers marking shared reminiscences.

The lone *when* phrases used as story openers are not, of course, completely fixed in their form: they differ, therefore, from prefabricated phrases such as *how do you do?* and are more productive than the *to put it* expressions mentioned on p. 222. Yet they have more in common with prefabricated lexicalised forms such as these than with completely new clauses that have been generated by the grammar. They consist of a frame (*when* + NP + VP, with the verb in the past tense) with a fixed intonation contour. The past tense form of the verb distinguishes the story openers from the other, less frequent lone *when* phrases with an explicatory function: in (3), for example, the verb *look* is in the present tense. The words that constitute the NP and the VP are repeated from the preceding discourse and this facilitates their function as a way of taking the floor: thus in (1) Nobby's *went camping* echoes the words of the preceding three turns and in (2) Tommy's *in hospital* echoes the question *have you ever been in hospital?*

What might initially appear to be an instance of syntactic variation, then, is more appropriately seen as a conversational routine with an interactional function in turn-taking and a social function in indexing group solidarity (as we have seen, it is used only by the boys, along with other story openers that mark an upcoming shared reminiscence). It is not entirely fixed in form and conforms more to a phrase generated by a 'mini-grammar'.

Other forms used as story openers in the Reading conversations are better analysed as prefabricated expressions than as constructions generated by the grammar. One such form involves verbal *-s*. This of course is usually considered to be an agreement marker in generative analyses of English and in present-day standard English it does indeed appear to have this function, occurring only on present tense verb forms with third singular subjects. In many present-day non-standard varieties however the distribution of verbal *-s* differs. In Norwich, England, for example, it is variably

Jenny
Cheshire

absent with third person subjects (Trudgill 1974); in Reading it is variably present with non-third person subjects and quasi-categorical with third person subjects (Cheshire 1982), as in several other varieties of British and North American English. It is sometimes assumed that speakers have regularised the present tense paradigm in these vernaculars, so that verbal -s is an agreement marker in these vernaculars also, but many researchers have identified a wider, diverse range of functions for the form, perhaps especially in African-American English. The functions include marking durative aspect (Pitts 1986, Brewer 1986), habitual aspect (Pitts 1986), variably marking the present tense (Schneider 1983) and marking the historic present (Myhill and Harris 1986). [. . .] Most of these studies exclude from the envelope of variation story openers or topic introducers such as *you know* in (4) and (5). In the Reading corpus, as elsewhere, *you know* used in this way is invariable, never taking the -s suffix, unlike *you know* as a lexical verb, as in (6) and (7):

(4)   you know that hill down there? I rode down that with no hands on the handlebars
(5)   you know your mum . . . . you know that bike she had
(6)   you knows him don't you Nod?
(7)   he says to me 'look here and I see if I knows you'

The story opener then, is a prefabricated expression, like the discourse marker *you know* (which performs a range of conversational functions, including adding liveliness to a conversation and constructing solidarity; see, for example, Holmes 1986, Fox Tree and Schrock 2002: 729). It is not certain, however, that all cases of prefabricated expressions have been accounted for in analyses of verbal -s. After all, existential constructions and canonical clause constructions are usually analysed side-by-side, despite their different syntactic derivations (see Corrigan 1997 for discussion). Analyses of verbal -s, whether generativist or variationist, might benefit from a prior discourse analysis aiming to identify all the prefabricated expressions in which verbal -s occurs: this would not only make the analyses more accountable to the data but would also further our understanding of how and why prefabricated expressions develop and their role in grammaticalisation and other kinds of language change.

Issues to consider

❑   You could try to record an extract of your own conversation and then transcribe it to see what proportion of your own speech consists of prefabricated expressions. Can you think of any examples in ordinary conversation in which a prefabricated expression was adapted creatively?

❑   Consider the difficulties that prefabricated expressions pose for second-language learners of English. Drawing on your knowledge of such idioms, think about how you would set about designing a teaching course for such students.

❑   Cheshire's approach here emphasises the social and communicative function of the syntactic forms chosen: it is very much a piece of applied linguistics. However, there are several hints throughout the excerpt that suggest this approach presents a challenge to traditional theoretical syntax too. Can you find these occasions and consider how syntax as a discipline might be affected by a challenge from applied linguistics?

ADVERTISING DISCOURSE

Guy Cook here sets out the principles and effects of connected text. Through his primary focus on the language of advertising, Cook highlights many important areas of text and discourse study. He also illustrates how discourse analysis and pragmatics are heavily interlinked with one another by integrating his consideration of coherence in discourse analysis with the co-operative principle and principles of linguistic politeness, as detailed in B3. Additionally he also shows how spoken discourse can influence written discourse production, demonstrating how the tools of spoken discourse analysis can inform written textual analysis.

Guy Cook (reprinted from *The Discourse of Advertising*, Second edition (2001), London: Routledge)

Guy Cook

Cohesive devices

Cohesion is the term used in discourse analysis to refer to linguistic devices which create links between sentences and clauses. A number of cohesive devices, for example, are present in the words of a television ad for Pretty Polly tights [numbers added for reference ...]:

> In the 1930s one man touched the lives of millions of women. (1) He wasn't a film star or a singer but a scientist. (2) He invented nylon. (3) Yet two years later, beset with doubt, he took his own life. (4) Wallace Carothers dedicated his life to women. (5) Nylon by Wallace Carothers. (6) Nylons by Pretty Polly. (7)

❑ *Repetition* of lexical items. For example, 'women' is repeated in 1 and 5, 'life' in 4 and 5, 'Wallace Carothers' in 5 and 6.

❑ *Sense relations* between lexical items or phrases. For example, 'man' in 1, and 'film star', 'singer', 'scientist' in 2, are all related semantically by a single component of meaning: 'human'.

❑ *Referring expressions* which refer to a unit in another sentence. For example, the noun phrase 'one man' in 1 has the same reference as the chain of referring expressions ('he ... he ... he') in 2, 3 and 4. These pronouns refer back (*anaphorically*) to 'one man', and forward (*cataphorically*) to 'Wallace Carothers', and are continued by 'his' in 5.

❑ *Ellipsis*, in which an omitted unit is recoverable from a previous sentence. There are two instances in this text: 'but øHE øWAS a scientist' in 2, and 'two years later øTHAN øTHE øTIME øHE øINVENTED øNYLON' in 3.

❑ *Conjunctions* (words and phrases which indicate a logical, temporal, causal or exemplifying relationship). The examples in this text – 'but' and 'yet' – are both conjunctions.

All these devices, which can be described without reference to non-linguistic context, give this text cohesion, and help to link the sentences within it together. Yet they do not account entirely for the perception of these sentences as coherent discourse, with meaning and purpose. This can be illustrated, by maintaining the cohesion, but making some other changes.

Guy Cook

In the 1870s one man touched the lives of sixty women. He wasn't a greengrocer or an astronaut but a stationer. He invented the paper clip. Yet two years later, tormented by mosquitoes, he took his own life. Harold Digby dedicated his life to women. The paper clip by Harold Digby. Paper clips by . . .

This passage does not make sense. Only lunatics and linguists invent such texts. But it does reveal a number of factors which establish coherence. So strong is our desire to *make sense* that, if it were encountered outside a book such as this one, the reaction would be to try to do so. As Leech (1981: 7) puts it: 'a speaker of English faced with absurd sentences will strain his interpretative faculty to the utmost to read them meaningfully'. When such attempts fail, and a text remains incoherent (even though the failure may be that of the receiver), its sender, as a last resort, is likely to be described as 'mad'.

What is it then which makes the ad for nylons make sense, while the derived version about the paper clip does not? Firstly, the ad assumes a great deal of cultural knowledge in the receiver. We know that stockings and tights are made of nylon, and that their use is widespread. We know that famous and successful male film stars and singers have female fans; that scientists can be successful too, but are considered less glamorous. We also know that scientists invent things; that the inventor of a successful product, because of patent laws, could become very wealthy; that wealth is desirable. Following from all this, it is surprising and unexplained (hence 'yet') that such a man should commit suicide. This factual gap, which maintains the interest of the text, may also activate a stereotype: the pauper inventor who foolishly sells a patent; the wealthy and successful person who is nevertheless miserable. The quantity of knowledge needed for interpretation is vast, and its boundaries indeterminate. This summary only skims its surface. Each assumption makes further assumptions, and depends on further shared knowledge for interpretation, thus revealing a paradox in the notion of communication as transfer of knowledge: communication can only take place where there is some knowledge in common in the first place. It is impossible to say everything.

The text also establishes connections through surface form. 'Star', 'singer' and 'scientist' alliterate. There are lexical and grammatical parallels:

Subject/NP	VP	Direct Object/NP	
(one man)	(touched)	(the lives (of (millions (of (women)))))	
(he)	(took)	(his own life)	Adverb/PP
(he)	(dedicated)	(his life)	(to women)

suggesting, illogically, that these actions are in some way equivalent. 'Touched' – meaning both to move and to come into physical contact – is a pun. The second sense suggests the contact between nylon and skin. In the last two sentences, which adopt the verbless grammar of a title, parallelism is the ascendant means of connection, for the equivalent position of 'Wallace Carothers' and 'Pretty Polly' suggests that the latter has all the scientific genius, sensitivity, altruism and tragic glamour of the former.

Pragmatic principles and coherence

Coherence is the overall quality of unity and meaning perceived in discourse. Although aided by cohesion, and almost always accompanied by it, it is not created by it (as the incoherent version of the Pretty Polly ad illustrates) but depends upon other pragmatic factors. Before proceeding with a discussion of cohesion, let us consider some of these pragmatic factors, and how they influence the type and density of cohesive ties.

Guy Cook

One of the standard explanations of how addressers organize text and how addressees perceive it as coherent – how in other words a text becomes discourse – is an appeal to theories of *conversational principles*. According to Grice (1975) discourse is interpreted as though the speaker were following four maxims of a *co-operative principle*: to be true, clear, relevant, and as brief or as long as necessary. At times these demands pull in opposite directions, and one may oust another. They may also be flouted to produce a particular effect (irony, for example, flouts the truth maxim). Lakoff (1973) suggests a further *politeness principle*. Speakers follow three further maxims: to avoid imposing, to make their hearer feel good, to give him or her options. The balance between the two principles changes with the purpose of the communication and the relationship between the participants. [...]

Though the co-operative and politeness principles may be a cultural universal, there is considerable cultural variation in their manifestations, or the balance between their demands. Tannen (1984), for example, suggests that some cultures favour a 'high involvement' politeness, making the hearer feel good by taking interest in personal affairs, while others favour a strategy of non-imposition, making the former seem intrusive and the latter unfriendly when the two come into contact. Brown and Levinson (1987) suggest that while every culture recognizes territory on to which the polite person should not trespass without reason or redressive action, the nature of that territory may vary considerably from culture to culture. In different cultures, different emphasis is given to different types of territory: time, property, friendships, bodily functions, expertise, etc. These differences are a further source of cultural misunderstanding.

Neither advertising nor literature can be easily accounted for in terms of conversational principles. The relationship of addresser to addressee, and the purpose of the discourse are far removed from the phatic communication of the bulge. What is the truth, relevance, clarity, brevity or politeness of a novel or poem? The standards against which these questions can be answered are internal rather than external (in *Othello* Iago was lying, yet within a fiction in which all events were untrue) and judgements by external measures can seem quite beside the point. Literature is both true and untrue, relevant and irrelevant, often economic in expression but also, by utilitarian yardsticks, superfluous. The relationship of addresser to addressee is simultaneously one of extreme distance – the author has not met the readers – yet one of extreme intimacy. Like the voice of a friend, the literary voice addresses us, not for some practical or social purpose, but sometimes to understand itself, or for the pleasure of talking. Both the subject matter and the language of literature are often those reserved for intimate relationships, and many people experience a sense of companionship and intimacy with their favourite authors.

Advertising shares – or attempts to share – many of these qualities. Admittedly, it usually has a clearer purpose than literature – to sell – and the information which it gives in pursuit of this aim may be judged by the standards of the co-operative principle for its truth, clarity, brevity and relevance. Yet factual claims and direct persuasion take up less and less space in contemporary ads. Attention is focused away

Guy Cook

from them to a world where questions of truth, relevance and politeness seem as beside the point as they do in literature. As advertising has matured, formidable restrictions have grown up alongside it, imposed by publishers, broadcasters, the law or advertisers' own organizations. If factual claims are untrue, the advertiser is held responsible. Ads are withdrawn, goods are returned; and, because literal untruth is also bad advertising, it is now shunned by advertisers quite as much as by their moralistic critics. Of course, advertisers continue to use deceptive strategies for disguising or avoiding unattractive facts, for presenting descriptions in such a way that the inattentive may miss the bad aspects or imagine good aspects of a product. But these tactics are well known, over-analyzed, and distract attention away from more powerful strategies. In many ads (perfume, chewing gum) there is no truth value to assess (Thompson 1990). In ads where there are 'facts' (about cars, insurance, orange juice) they are often far from the focus of attention.

Economic extravagance: cohesion in ads

Cohesive devices all serve the co-operative principle and vary with the emphasis on its four maxims. Repetition makes co-reference in text clear, though it may be at the expense of brevity; lexical cohesion may add new information economically while also aiding clarity; referring expressions are brief, though they may sacrifice clarity; conjunctions make connections clear, though they also increase length. Broadly speaking, where there is mistrust and/or an accompanying desire to minimize ambiguity, the truth maxim will be elevated over the clarity maxim. (Instruction manuals and legal documents favour repetition over referring expressions, in the belief that the latter, being more ambiguous, are conducive to misunderstandings and the construction of loopholes.) Where there is trust, where connections can be inferred or clarification obtained, brevity may be ascendant. Narrative thus often lacks the repetition, explicit connectives and density of conjunctions of legal and technical prose. Casual conversation is full of ellipsis – although this is balanced by conversation's own peculiar prolixity: apparently meaningless phrases designed to gain or hold turns, signal turn type or topic change, or simply gain the time necessary for the production and processing of speech (Levinson 1983: 284–370). Where there is repetition or lexical cohesion which cannot be accounted for by the co-operative principle, it is often motivated by the politeness principle. An excess of language often indicates a sense of occasion, ceremony, respect or intimacy.

In referring to the product, or spheres it wishes to associate with it, advertising favours repetition over referring expressions [...] One obvious function of repetition is to fix the name of the product in the mind, so that it will come to the lips of the purchaser lost for a name. But repetition of a name is also an index of rank, esteem, intimacy or self-confidence. Consider the repetition of names in ceremonies, prayers, by lovers, or by arrogant individuals who just 'like the sound of their own name'.

Conjunctions are notoriously absurd in ads, and an easy target for analysts obsessed with demonstrating ads' verbal trickery. Their illogicality can pass unnoticed by its sheer blatancy and nerve, as in this US magazine ad. (The picture shows a little girl sitting on a clean carpet. She is feeding her dolly red fruit juice and spilling it.)

Got a life? Gotta ask for Scotchguard.
Her dolly's thirsty and only juice will do. So don't leave the store without buying
a carpet with genuine Scotchguard protection. Nothing protects better or lasts
longer. No wonder Scotchguard products are used to take care of more carpet
than any other brand. So whether you walk on it, sit on it or wear it, make sure
to ask for Scotchguard protection.
There's protection. Then there's Scotchguard protection.

This use of 'so', however, exploits the ambiguity of the word; for, while, in written
discourse, 'so' is often a synonym for 'therefore', in conversation – and the style
of ads is conversational – it is only a filler, which holds or gains the turn for the
speaker. [...]

Conjunctions, then, are used deftly, to jump over illogicalities. The important and
foregrounded fusion of product with user, situation or effect is more usually achieved
through pun, connotation or metaphor, rather than through any logical or sequential
connection in the world.

Lexical cohesion is used to allow fusion between the product name and other
phrases, by treating them as though they were semantically related to it. ('There's
protection. Then there's Scotchguard protection'.) It is a process which generates
verbosity. Although ads pay for space and thus endure a discipline which can lead
to economic and condensed expression, the lexical and phrasal chains in ads often
appear extravagant and unnecessary:

Galaxy Minstrels chocolate
Silk with a polish. The rounded silk of smooth, creamy Galaxy's chocolate dressed
in layer upon layer of chocolate shell. Coat after coat. Creating the softness of silk
against the gentle crispness of chocolate shell. A delicate study in contradictions,
Galaxy Minstrels.

Here there is nothing but the cohesive chain of noun phrases: a seductively indulgent
over-description whose excess iconically represents the luxury of eating the product,
and successfully presents the nouns in each phrase ('silk', 'Galaxy', 'coat') as equivalents,
accruing the qualities of each other.

Pronouns in ads
[...] One of the most distinctive features of advertising is its use of pronouns. In
discourse in general, the third person pronouns may be either *endophoric*, referring to
a noun phrase within the text – as 'he', for example, refers to Carothers in the Pretty
Polly ad – or *exophoric*, referring to someone or something manifest to the participants
from the situation or from their mutual knowledge ('Here he is', for example, on
seeing someone who both sender and receiver are expecting). The first and second
person pronouns are, other than in quoted speech, most usually exophoric. Their
reference is apparently straightforward: 'I' means the addresser; 'you' the addressee.

Certain genres favour certain pronouns: diaries, for example, favour the first
person; written narratives the first or third; prayers the second; scientific discourse
the third – and so on. Ads use all three persons, but in peculiar ways. 'We' is the

Guy Cook

manufacturer; 'I' is often the adviser, the expert, the relator of experiences and motives leading to purchase of the product; 'he/she' is very often the person who did not use the product, distanced by this pronoun, and observed conspiratorially by 'you' and 'I'; but most striking and most frequent, even in narrative, and also most divergent from the uses of other genres, is the ubiquitous use of 'you'.

In face-to-face communication, 'you' assumes knowledge of the individual addressee. In printed and broadcast discourse, however, there are too many addressees for the pronoun, when it is used, to be so personal and particular. Before such use is condemned as false and hypocritical, however, it should be remembered that advertising shares this use of 'you' in displaced and disseminated communication with religious evangelism, official documents, political rhetoric, recipes, lyric poetry and songs. This similarity to the use of 'you' in other genres, however, may blind us to the particularity of 'you' in advertising.

The difference may be brought out by comparison with another genre. In songs, 'you' functions in a number of ways simultaneously. It may refer to many people in the actual and fictional situation. Take, for example,

> Well in my heart you are my darling,
> At my gate you're welcome in,
> At my gate I'll meet you darling,
> If your love I could only win.
>
> (Traditional folk song: *East Virginia*)

This is the plea of one lover to another. 'I' is the addresser (in this song a woman), and 'you' the addressee (in this song a man). But there are at least four ways of achieving specific reference for these pronouns. The receiver of the song may treat the song as half of an overheard dialogue between two other people. 'I' is the singer and 'you' is her lover. Alternatively, a female listener may project herself into the persona of the addresser and hear the song as though it is her own words to her own lover. Alternatively, a male listener may project himself into the persona of the singer's lover and hear the singer addressing him. (I am assuming that listeners are most likely to identify with singers of their own gender.) Lastly, the pronouns of the song can be interpreted as they would be in conversational face-to-face discourse: 'I' = the singer; 'you' = the addressee. The listener, in other words, imagines that the song is addressed to them. (This perhaps is how besotted pop fans like to hear the love songs of their idols!)

In another kind of song, still involving projection into the singer, the words are perceived as an externalization of an internal dialogue in which 'you' refers to the self:

> You load fifteen tons, what do you get?
> Another day older and deeper in debt.
>
> (The blues song: *Fifteen Tons*)

The 'you' of ads, though also departing from conversational use, functions differently from either of these types of song. The tendency to project the self into the 'I' and address somebody else as 'you' is hampered by the frequent absence of 'I' and the clear address to the receiver. The 'you' of ads has a kind of *double exophora* involving reference to someone in the picture (salient because pictures dominate words) and to the receiver's own self (salient because everyone is interested in themselves). The characters of ads sometimes look out of the picture [...] and directly at the receiver, allowing them to take on the role of either addressee or addresser. This double reference, originating in the text, encourages a completion of the triangle which effects a co-reference between the receiver and one of the people in the picture [...]

This dual identity of 'you' is matched by the mysterious identity of the sender, which is not revealed, though sometimes referred to as 'we'. The visual presence of another person (the character) distracts from this absence, creating an illusion that the dialogue is between character and addressee.

Issues to consider

❑ The textual rewriting which Cook produces with the Pretty Polly tights advertisement is an effective way to demonstrate how textual cohesion and also textual coherence work in practice. Select an advertisement from a newspaper or magazine and rewrite it, replacing selected phrases but keeping the overall syntactic structure of the sentences the same, using Cook's 'paper clips' example as a guide. Then, give your new text to an unsuspecting reader and ask them to provide you with an interpretation of what they think it means, getting them to identify particular lexical features in the text. What devices of cohesion and coherence have they identified in an attempt to help them make sense of the text? How has engaging in the process of rewriting enabled you to identify how the cohesion and coherence of written texts work?

❑ Claims as to the power and effectiveness of advertising often originate with advertising agencies themselves, and of course they have a vested interest in convincing businesses that advertising works. Identify, on the one hand, an ad that you think is powerful and effective, and, on the other, an ad that you think is poor or fails in some way. Can you provide a linguistic explanation for why one is successful and the other is not?

❑ What are the differences in the different modes of advertising across newspaper and magazine texts, billboards, radio, television and cinema ads, webpage banners and ads, static and animated ads? Can the different linguistic features of these forms – within the same genre – be analysed to show their different effects?

SOCIALISATION AND GRAMMATICAL DEVELOPMENT

D6

Debates on the acquisition of language have circled around the relative importance of innate factors and various socially conditioned factors. It is clear that humans do have an innate capacity for language; and it is also clear that the specific vocabulary and detailed grammatical patterns acquired by children are shaped by the speech community in which they grow up. The debate has focused on the extent to which the more general grammatical principles and developments are innately configured or socially patterned.

In this extract, Elinor Ochs and Bambi Schieffelin argue that grammatical development must be seen within the context of the ways that different cultures (even cultures within the English-speaking community) socialise language.

Elinor Ochs and Bambi Schieffelin (reprinted from P. Fletcher and B. MacWhinney (eds) *The Handbook of Child Language* (1995), Oxford: Blackwell, pp. 73–94)

The architecture of grammatical development in the talk of young children is the central concern of language acquisition research. The critical task of language acquisition scholarship over the last several decades has been to account for when, how, and why children use and understand grammatical forms over the course of the early period of their lives. Language socialization – the process in which children are socialized both through language and to use language within a community – has been largely examined without regard to the dynamics of grammatical development, focusing, rather, on culturally relevant communicative practices and activities. In this discussion, we reverse this orientation and focus directly on the role of language socialization in the acquisition of grammatical competence. [. . .]

A critical question addressed in acquisition research is whether or not children's grammatical competence is an outcome of children's participation in simplified communicative exchanges designed to facilitate language use and comprehension. Our response to this question is a qualified 'no.' This conclusion is based on the observation that all normal children acquire a measured degree of competence in producing and understanding grammatical constructions in the early years of their lives, yet the ways in which cultures organize communicative exchanges with children varies widely from community to community [. . .]. To explore this phenomenon in a culturally illuminative fashion, we focus on how cultures organize communication directed *to* children (children as addressees) and *by* children (children as speakers).

Cultural organizations of talk to children (addressees)

In all societies, members want to get their intentions across to children. This is a universal propensity of human culture, a prerequisite for the transmission of cultural orientations from one generation to the next. Furthermore, when members set the goal of getting their intentions across to children, they tend to modify their language in similar ways across the world's communities. Adults, older siblings, and others wanting to communicate to infants and small children in many cultures tend to simplify the form and content of their talk to achieve that end. Common simplifications characteristic of speech addressed to children include consonant cluster reduction, reduplication, exaggerated prosodic contours, slowed pace, shorter sentences, syntactically less complex sentences, temporal and spatial orientation to the here-and-now, and repetition and paraphrasing of sentences. [. . .]

How, then, is the goal of communicating intentions to children realized across different communities? While in all communities, children participate as addressees in interactions with others, the developmental point at which they take on this role varies from community to community. In some communities, such as white middle class communities in the United States and Canada, children are given this role starting at birth, when mothers begin to greet and otherwise attempt to converse with their infants (Bloom 1990, Ochs and Schieffelin 1984). Once the goal of communicating intentions to small infants is put into effect, speakers have quite a job on their hands if they hope to be understood and responded to. Indeed, in the case of communicating intentions to newly born infants, caregivers may not only go to great lengths to gain and sustain their attention (e.g. via high pitch, exaggerated intonation), they also may have to voice or do the child's response themselves (Lock 1981, Trevarthen 1979). In other communities, members do not generally set the goal of communicating intentions to children (i.e. wanting children to understand and respond) at quite such an early point in their lives. In a number of societies, infants are not engaged as addressees until they evidence that they can produce recognizable words in the language. [...]

In societies such as these, infants are not singled out as preferred addressees. Rather, they tend to participate in communicative interactions in the role of *overhearers* of nonsimplified conversations between others. This assumes that small children are being socialized in the context of multiparty interactions, the unmarked condition in traditional and many other societies. In many upper middle class households of the United States and Europe, however, small children may pass the day primarily in the presence of a single adult (e.g. mother) and thus may not have the situational opportunity to take on the role of overhearers of nonsimplified conversations. Indeed, the communicative ecology of upper middle class households may be an important factor in organizing young children in the role of addressees. The sole adult in the household is not likely to talk to herself/himself all day long and thus may be situationally predisposed to attempt to recruit a child of whatever age as a communicative partner in meaningful, albeit highly simplified, exchanges.

In those communities where infants and small children are generally not recruited as conversational partners, they still become grammatically competent speakers—hearers, developing linguistic knowledge in a communicative environment full of grammatical complexity and oriented towards competent interlocutors. Some communities have an explicit ideology of language acquisition centered on precisely the idea that children need to hear linguistically *complex* and not simplified speech to become grammatically competent. Kaluli adults were surprised that American parents produced baby talk in the presence of young children and wondered how the children learned to speak proper language (Schieffelin 1990).

In addition to differences in goal setting, cultures also differ in the extent to which they simplify when they do address children. In some communities, such as among the Tamil (Williamson 1979), Inuit (Crago 1988), and working and middle class Americans and Europeans (Cross 1977; Newport, Gleitman, and Gleitman 1977), simplification involves phonological, morphosyntactic, and discourse modifications. In other communities, such as among Samoans (Ochs 1988), working class African-Americans of Trackton (Heath 1983) and Louisiana (Ward 1971), Javanese (Smith-Hefner 1988) and Kaluli (Schieffelin 1990), simplification may be primarily *restricted* to the domain of discourse, and in particular, to self-repetition of an earlier utterance. An important difference between simplification through repetition and simplification through phonological and grammatical adjustments is that the former tends to preserve the integrity of the adult form of the utterance whereas the latter does not. [...]

An interesting possibility is that cultures that simplify at all levels of linguistic structure in talking to children may put children in the role of conversational partners,

**Elinor Ochs
and Bambi
Schieffelin**

i.e. as addressees expected to actively and centrally participate in communicative exchanges, more often than in cultures that simplify primarily through repetition. [...] From the perspective of the working class African-American, Samoans, Kaluli, and Javanese communities studied, members of cultures that rely on widespread simplification are more eager (or perhaps even anxious) for children early in their lives to take on central communicative roles. In these African-American communities and among the Samoans, Javanese, and Kaluli, however, there seems to be less pressure for very young children to assume an active, central role in the social exchanges at hand, but rather a preference for children at this early stage to stay on the sidelines – on the backs of caregivers, or nestled on their laps or hips or alongside – as observers and overhearers.

In summary, if we look across cultures, children who are expected to be active communicators early in life are often likely to be addressed with highly simplified speech and put in the position of conversational partner. On the other hand, children who are expected to actively participate in communicative exchanges somewhat later in their childhood hear predominantly unsimplified speech and are treated as conversational partners less frequently. The upshot of this discussion, however, is that while these children are socialized into different expectations concerning their social role *vis-à-vis* other participants in a social situation and perhaps as well into different cognitive skills (e.g. the role of overhearer may enhance observational skills), *the outcome in terms of the ultimate acquisition of grammatical competence is not substantially different across these two cultural strategies*. In both cases, most children growing up in these cultures are producing and understanding grammatical constructions before their second birthday. In Western Samoa, for example, a child of 19 months was not only producing multimorphemic utterances but using with some skill two phonological registers (Ochs 1985). Kaluli children between 20 and 24 months use imperative and declarative verb forms, first and second person pronouns, locatives, possessives, several forms of negation, and discourse particles (Schieffelin 1986).

Cultural organizations of talk by children (speakers)

An important focus in the controversy over effects of the communicative environment on language acquisition is the extent to which grammatical competence is facilitated by the practice of caregivers verbally reformulating a child's intended message in grammatically correct adult form. This practice is known as *expansion* (Brown et al. 1968). Typically expansions are caregivers' responses to a young child's relatively ambiguous message and function as requests for confirmation or repair initiations (Schegloff, Jefferson, and Sacks 1977). The facilitating effect of expansions is posited on the assumption that children will match an intention that is currently in their consciousness with the adult formulation of the intended message (Brown et al. 1968, McNeill 1970). [...]

Infants and small children universally produce utterances whose sense is not transparent to those present, and universally those copresent respond using one or more of the following strategies: (1) ignore the utterance; (2) indicate to the child that the utterance is unclear (e.g. by claiming nonunderstanding, by directing the child to resay the utterance, by teasing the child for being unclear); (3) present to the child a candidate understanding or reformulation of the utterance (i.e. make a guess).

Elinor Ochs
and Bambi
Schieffelin

However, while children's unintelligibility and responses to it are universal, the preference for strategy (1), (2), or (3) varies across communities for reasons of ideology
and social order. Specifically, communities organize the goal of decoding the intentions
of children in different ways. In some communities, members are keen to disambiguate
aloud what infants and young children might be intending across a wide range of
situations, and in other communities the situations in which members take on this
goal are highly restricted.

To pursue the cultural organization of decoding the intentions of children it
is necessary to unpack some of the assumptions of this end. One assumption that
underlies this end is that children are indeed acting intentionally, the children are the
authors of their utterances. One variable of crosscultural import is the developmental
point at which children are treated as intentional beings who not only vocalize and
gesture but do so to make a communicative point. Another way of considering this
aspect of crosscultural variation is to see cultures as varying in their view of children
as *authors* of messages. In some communities, children are treated as if their gestures
and vocalizations are meaningful and communicative from a very early point in their
infancy (see especially Trevarthen's (1979) analysis of middle class British caregivers
interpreting small infants in this manner). Caregivers in these communities will respond
to the actions of tiny infants as if they were intentionally directed towards them,
and in this way establish the child as an interlocutor (Lock 1981). In middle class
American and European communities, this practice of treating the infant as an author
is the counterpart to treating the infant as addressee in that both roles combined
constitute the infant as conversational partner.

Many of us may take for granted that caregivers and infants interact in this
manner and may find it surprising that in many communities infants are not considered
as authors. Their gestures and vocalizations are not considered by others as intentional
communicative acts. For example, among the Walpiri, before the age of two, '"talk"
by the child is not interpreted as language, and there are no expansions and recasts
of the child's early words' (Bavin 1992: 327). Similarly, among the Inuit, caregivers
rarely responded to the vocal and nonvocal actions of very young children. [...]

Finally, in some communities, members allow for the possibility that children are
speaking intentionally but rather than trying to establish what these intentions might
be, members assign a socially normative meaning to the child's utterance. As noted
earlier, a psycholinguistic argument is that expansions facilitate language acquisition
because they build on a child's personal intentions, matching the child's meaning
to adult message form. In contrast, there is evidence that, in certain communities,
children's personal intentions sometimes take second place to the members' notions
of what is socially appropriate to a situation at hand. For example, Scollon (1982)
reports that Athapaskan adults provide a cultural 'gloss' for the child's unclear utterance,
that is, a socially appropriate rendering that is situationally sensitive, disregarding what
the child might be intending to express.

The use of cultural glosses is far more widespread than might be assumed, in that
adults may impose a cultural gloss on children's gestures and utterances without
recognizing that they are doing so. First words, for example, may reflect and construct
cultural expectations concerning what children want to communicate. In many communities, first words are highly conventionalized. For example, among the Kaluli, the

Elinor Ochs
and Bambi
Schieffelin

words for 'mother' and 'breast' are recognized as everyone's first words. In traditional Samoan communities, the child's first word is part of the curse 'Eat shit!' [...]

It can also be argued that although caregivers in white middle class American, European, and Japanese households are acting on the belief that their expansions capture the intended meaning of the child's utterance, their expansions may similarly reflect their cultural understandings of what children want. [...]

These practices from diverse communities suggest that a primary goal of members is to socialize infants into culturally appropriate persons and this goal may override any goal relating to drawing out and validating the child as an author of a unique personal message. In these situations, other members actively participate in the authorship of messages. Other-authorship of children's utterances is also manifest in prompting practices, wherein members author a culturally appropriate message for the child to repeat back to the author (dyadic interaction) or to a third party (triadic interactions). Extended prompting of this sort is practiced in a wide range of societies, including Kaluli (Schieffelin 1990), Samoan (Ochs 1988), Mexican-American (Eisenberg 1986), white working class American (Miller 1982), Basotho (Demuth 1986), Javanese (Smith-Hefner 1988), and Kwara'ae (Watson-Gegeo and Gegeo 1986). A more extreme version of cultural prevoicing is found in the practice of ventriloquating for preverbal infants, wherein a member speaks as if the infant were speaking and others respond as if this were the case. Kaluli caregivers, for example, hold small infants facing a third party addressee and speak to that addressee in a high pitch nasalized register (without grammatically simplifying utterances). Here the infant is presented as a speaker without being presented as an author.

The many practices that are alternatives to expansions of personalized messages – either ignoring the utterance, indicating unclarity, providing a cultural gloss, prompting, or ventriloquating – socialize the child to accommodate to the social situation at hand. In contrast, attempts to expand the child's intended meaning evidence an accommodation by others to the child. That is, expansions of the sort discussed by psycholinguists reflect a child centered style of socialization (characteristic of the communities of the psycholinguists), whereas the alternative practices reflect a situation centered style of socialization. [...]

Steps to a cultural ecology of grammatical development

A consistent message is that grammatical development cannot be adequately accounted for without serious analysis of the social and cultural milieu of the language acquiring child. We have seen that grammatical development is an outcome of two primary sociocultural contexts: (1) where children participate regularly in socially and culturally organized activities, and (2) where the language(s) being acquired is/are highly valued and children are encouraged to learn it/them.

[...]

Issues to consider

❏   How do you talk to babies and infants? You could try to record examples of adult–child interaction (obviously with their consent) in order to examine the form of the interaction. Can you speculate on the perspective and assumptions that are held by the adult on the basis of what you discover?

❏   Do you agree with the account of socialisation and grammatical development offered by Ochs and Schieffelin, or do you think they have overstated their case? For example, do you think the evidence they cite supports their argument that socialisation plays a large part in grammatical development, given that they also say that all speakers in all societies eventually come to a fully functional version of the grammar?

❏   The cultural groupings mentioned in the extract are defined by ethnicity or by social class. Within your own broad speech community or ethnic grouping, can you discern different attitudes to children and their language behaviour on the basis of social class differences? What about the impact of other social factors such as education level, geographical location, age of parents, and so on?

PROMOTING PERCEPTION

D7

John Field argues here that researchers should pay more attention to the psycho-linguistic processes in second-language listening skills. In particular, he argues that the question of delineating what counts as a lexical segment (a 'word' between word-boundaries) should be informed by auditory phonetics (defined in A1). There is a practical objective behind Field's argument here: he wants to empower second-language teachers by focusing on the skills of phonetics and word-recognition that they already possess, rather than aiming to provide them with more training in schematic and higher-level awareness. Just prior to the extract below, he argues against the simple use of *comprehension* as a measurement of success in listening, since it actually tests interpretation and focuses on the product rather than the process of listening. Instead, he argues for attention to the phonetic processing of listeners.

John Field (reprinted from 'Promoting perception: lexical segmentation in L2 listening' (2003), *ELT Journal* 57/4: 325–34)

John Field

[. . . T]his article discusses what is arguably the commonest perceptual cause of break-down of understanding: namely, *lexical segmentation*, the identification of words in connected speech. The aim is to exemplify how low-level listening problems can be diagnosed by employing the basic knowledge of phonetics which most ELT practitioners possess. The difference is that the knowledge has to be stood on its head, so that we view phonetics not from the perspective of pronunciation practice but through the ears of the listener. Once identified, areas of difficulty can be tackled by means of simple 5-minute exercises; these might be remedial or they might anticipate problems of listening before they occur.

We tend to overlook the fact that pauses in natural speech only occur every 12 syllables or so, which means that, unlike readers, listeners do not have regular indica-tions of where words begin and end. It is remarkable that we manage to separate out words within these 12-syllable chunks as consistently as we do.

John Field

Determining where word boundaries fall is a greater problem for the non-native listener than is generally recognized. A learner with limited English or weak listening skills adopts a strategy of scanning continuous speech for matches between sequences of sounds and items of known vocabulary. In the anxiety to achieve matches, word boundaries are often breached:

Speaker: *went to assist a passenger*.   Student 1 extracts *sister*
Speaker: *the standard the hotel achieves*.   Student 2 extracts: *stand at the hotel*

We are all familiar with this phenomenon of grasping at cross-boundary straws and assuming words to be present which were not intended. (See Voss 1984 for examples.) The 'matching' strategy is a natural and productive one in the early stages of learning. The danger lies not in the strategy itself but in the tendency of students to overlook the tentative nature of the matches they achieve. There is a strong likelihood that Student 1 above will go on to construct a mental model of the text which includes somebody's sister, even to the point of reshaping what comes next, in order to fit her in somehow.

So a first approach to lexical segmentation should demonstrate to learners the need for caution in word boundary allocation. One technique is to dictate ambiguous sequences, then to disambiguate them by adding additional words:

T dictates: *an ice cream* . . .   [Ss write] . . . T continues dictation: *a nice cream dress*
T dictates: *the boxes of* . . .   [Ss write] . . . T continues dictation: *the boxes have
                                      been opened*.

(For more examples, see Gimson 1994: 253.) This may seem a trivial exercise; but it is an effective way of demonstrating to learners that word boundary location may be a matter of guesswork, and that guesses may have to be revised in the light of later evidence.

A strategic approach to the lexical segmentation issue asks how it is that native listeners manage to locate word boundaries so successfully. Simple matching is not the answer. If it were, we would automatically begin a new word after, for example, hearing PORT in *porter* or PORTER in *portable*. The research of Anne Cutler and her associates (Cutler 1990) suggests that native listeners use a *strong-syllable strategy*, based on the premise that each stressed syllable marks the beginning of a new word. This strategy pays dividends. Using a corpus of spoken English, Cutler and Carter (1987) calculated that some 85.6% of all content words in running speech are either mono-syllabic or stressed on the first syllable. The finding ties in with evidence from Hyman (1977) that lexical stress often fulfils a demarcative role. Many of the world's languages have fixed lexical stress, which occurs on the first, the penultimate, or the final syllable of a word, and thus serves as a reliable cue to word boundaries.

From this, one might conclude that it is worthwhile to train learners of English to emulate the segmentation strategy adopted by native listeners. In fact, Cutler takes the view that it is impossible for learners to develop a segmentation routine in L2 which differs from the one used in their first language. However, her reservation refers to responses to the speech signal which are automatic. It does not rule out the possibility that learners make slightly delayed decisions about what they hear, which resemble those of native listeners.

John Field

This, indeed, appears to be what many of them do. Learners show themselves sensitive to rhythmic regularities in the target language, and appear to learn from experience the value of inserting word boundaries before stressed syllables (Field 2001) without being aware of what they have learnt. We should not be too surprised at this finding: infants acquiring English appear to use rhythm in the same serendipitous way to crack the code of connected speech (Jusczyk 1997).

With appropriate training, learners might acquire the technique much faster – though it may be necessary to train their ears to recognize lexical stress if it is marked differently in English from their native language. A challenging piece of authentic text might be played, and learners asked to write down stressed syllables and match them to words they know. Their attention can then be drawn to how many of these syllables initiate words. A similar awareness-raising exercise might involve playing recordings on low volume, and asking learners to transcribe the more salient syllables.

Focusing on stressed syllables in this way not only assists learners to locate boundaries but also draws attention to the fact that, in connected speech, such syllables are 'islands of reliability': louder and longer than unstressed ones. Some researchers (notably, Grosjean and Gee 1987) have even suggested that it is stressed syllables which serve to identify words for native listeners and that weak ones are accorded a different type of attention. On this analysis, our representation of the word *appear* is triggered by the sequence /pɪə/, our representation of *indestructible* by /strʌk/.

If one major cause of segmentation problems is the lack of between-word pauses, a second and equally important one is the way in which the standard citation forms of words are modified when they occur in connected speech. Several different aspects will briefly be considered (reduction, assimilation, elision, resyllabification, and cliticization) and suggestions made for practice. For a detailed account of these phenomena, see Brown 1990.

Words, and even entire phrases, often appear in connected speech in a reduced form. One reason is that speakers economize on effort: for example, they avoid difficult consonant sequences by eliding sounds. Another reason is rhythmic: the patterns of English prosody dictate that certain closed class words such as prepositions, pronouns, and conjunctions are rarely stressed, and indeed that some may appear in a weak form (usually featuring *schwa* [ə]) in these unstressed contexts.

Unstressed syllables are shorter in duration, and less salient than stressed. They are also much less informative, because only two vowels, /ə/ and a shortened form of /ɪ/, predominate. Small wonder therefore that they pose perceptual problems for the foreign-language listener.

Three main types of reduction give rise to segmentation problems: contraction, weak forms, and the chunking of formulaic phrases. It is relatively easy to design a structured programme which introduces the second-language learner to these features *as a listener*. The proposal here is for 5-minute dictation sessions in which the sentences for transcription contain examples of particular types of reduced form.

A start can be made with the relatively simple area of contractions. Here, one goal is to get learners to recognize that the contracted verb is present at all. Assume

John Field

that a class interprets *I've lived in London for 3 years* to imply that I no longer live there. It may well be that they have not understood the implications of this use of the Present Perfect. But the truth may lie at a much lower level: it may be that they have not noticed the presence of the /v/.

Fifty-one function words in English possess alternative weak forms, most of them of high frequency. A second step in the kind of micro-listening programme proposed aims to ensure that the learner is able to recognize these words when they occur in connected speech. Very sensibly, many teachers choose to treat the weak form as the standard one, and the full form as the exception. This encourages the listener to construct a phonological representation which matches what is by far the more frequent form in connected speech. However, learners' expectations of what they will hear are sometimes unduly influenced by exposure to the written language.

It is worthwhile covering the weak forms as comprehensively as possible (perhaps exemplifying four or five at a time). They can be presented again in read-aloud naturalistic sentences for transcription, where they should be given the kind of low prominence that they receive in spontaneous speech. For reference, a list of all 51 forms [grouped by word-class, and homophonous examples], mainly based on Gimson 1994, is provided [here].

word	weak form	word	weak form
a	ə	am	əm
an	ən	are	ə
any	nɪ	be	bɪ
some	səm / sm	been	bɪn
the	ðə	was	wəz
at	ət	were	wə
for	fə	can	kən / kn
from	frəm	could	kəd / kd
of	əv / ə	do	dʊ / də
to	tə	does	dəz / dz
and	ənd / nd / n	had	həd / əd
but	bət	has	həz / əz
as	əz	have	həv / əv
than	ðən / ðn	must	məst
that	ðət	shall	ʃəl / ʃl
who	ʊ hʊ	should	ʃəd / ʃd
there	ðe / ðə (+ r)	will	wəl / əl / l
he	ɪ / hɪ	would	wʊd / wəd / d
her	ə hə	-n't	n
him	ɪm	Saint	sənt / snt
his	ɪz	Sir	sə
I	ʌ	me	mɪ
we	wɪ	she	ʃɪ
them	ðəm / ðm	us	əs
you	jə	your	jə
our	ɑː / ʌ		

Homophonous weak forms

John Field

ə	a / are / of / er	əv	of / have
ən	an / and	əz	as / has
jə	you / your		

When dealing with weak forms, it is important not to lose sight of the fact that we are presenting the material from the point-of-view of the *listener*, and not of the speaker. We also need to bear in mind that several of these forms are homophonous; the listener (whether native or non-native) needs to use syntactic context to distinguish them from each other.

Finally, we should recognize that native speakers often produce high-frequency sequences of words as chunks (Pawley and Syder 1983). These sequences may become very reduced, with phonemes and even whole syllables elided. They are only recognizable as a unit – and, indeed, it seems likely that native listeners store them as a single semantic and phonetic entity. It is good practice to dictate the most common of these formulaic phrases to learners, so that they can process them holistically when they encounter them. Favourites from my own collection are:

/mɔːmɔː/ [= 'more and more']
/naːpmiːm/ [= 'do you know what I mean']

Penny Ur (1984: 46) provides a useful set of reduced sequences which can be used as material for exercises, as does Gimson (1994: 261–2).

It is not just the lack of pauses that makes it difficult to identify words in connected speech. Accommodatory phonological processes affect precisely the points at which the listener needs unambiguous information – namely word beginnings and endings. The most familiar of these processes are assimilation and elision. We tend to think of these phenomena as random, or at least as very complex. However, as [the following] table [drawn from Gimson 1994: 257–60] shows, assimilation is restricted in its operation, and quite systematic.

/n/	→ [m] before [p, b, m]	ten people	→ *tem people*
	→ [ŋ] before [k, g]	ten cars	→ *teng cars*
/t/	→ [p] or a glottal stop before [p, b, m]	that boy	→ *thap boy*
	→ [k] or a glottal stop before [k, g]	that girl	→ *thak girl*
/d/	→ [b] or a glottal stop before [p, b, m]	good play	→ *goob play*
	→ [g] or a glottal stop before [k, g]	good cause	→ *goog cause*
/s/	→ [ʃ] or omitted before [ʃ]	this shirt	→ *thi shirt*
/z/	→ [ʒ] or omitted before [ʃ]	those shoes	→ *tho shoes*
/t, d, s, z/	→ [ʧ, ʤ, ʃ, ʒ] before [j]	right you are	→ *rye chew are*
		did you go	→ *di due go*

It is worth noting that assimilation in English is usually anticipatory, adjusting the *ends* of words in expectation of the sound that follows. The message for the learner is:

John Field

trust the beginnings of English words rather than the ends. The sounds which are most subject to assimilation and elision are final /t/, /d/, and /s/. These, of course, provide many of the inflectional endings in English. Hence the irony of the grammar teacher telling learners to listen out for such endings, when they may be absent in spontaneous speech.

How to deal with the assimilation problem? Again by using dictation. The nine types of assimilation distinguished in [the] table [above] can provide the basis for a programme in which examples are either dictated as two-word sequences, or embedded in simple sentences.

Elision, unfortunately, follows a less consistent pattern than assimilation; but frequent examples such as *didn't* → [dmt] should certainly be practised for recognition in a connected-speech context or pointed out when they occur in a listening passage. We also need to pay special heed to the way complex clusters of consonants are elided:

  next spring → [nek'sprɪŋ]

Awareness of this kind of feature can aid learners in producing these clusters, as well as recognizing what has been omitted.

Over the years, our ears become habituated to the vagaries of English. We rarely notice the effects which rhythm imposes upon words – effects which, for the learner, can considerably heighten the difficulty of recognition. Firstly, there is the process of *resyllabification*, where, in certain circumstances, a syllable-final consonant attaches itself to the following syllable:

  went in → when tin
  made out → may doubt
  (can't) help it → tell pit

What complicates the situation for the listener is that, after resyllabification, words sometimes acquire false boundary cues. Thus, in the *went in* example, the /t/ may well be lightly aspirated, suggesting that it is word-initial. Similarly, in *made out*, the removal of the /d/ from the first word is likely to be accompanied by a lengthening of the diphthong, so that it sounds to all intents and purposes like the open syllable *may*.

Secondly, there is *cliticization*: an effect which results from the way in which natural English speech tends towards a regular stressed-unstressed pattern. The preference of English speakers for the basic SW (strong-weak) foot means that they often attach two words for no reason other than a rhythmic one. This can happen in defiance of syntactic structure (Example 1: 'go to bed'). It can even lead to prefixes getting dislodged and being produced as if they were suffixes (Example 2: 'got excited').

Example 1:

S	W	S	W	→	S	W
gəʊ	tə	'bed	[pause]	→	'gəʊtə	'bed

Example 2:

S	W	S	W	→	S	W
gʊt	ɪk	'sə'ɪt	ɪd	→	'gətɪk	'səɪtɪd

How to handle these effects? They do not really lend themselves, like other segmentation problems, to short 5-minute dictation slots. The best advice is simply to be aware that they exist – and, when you encounter them in a listening text, to play and replay the relevant section to see if learners can puzzle out for themselves the correct distribution of phonemes and/or syllables.

Indeed, that is the message for all the perceptual difficulties described here. The important thing is to be aware of them, and to be prepared to practise them intensively if there are signs that they are preventing learners from identifying familiar words because of the special conditions of connected speech. The value of a signal-based approach of the kind described is that it draws our attention to problems of both perception and comprehension that would otherwise pass unnoticed.

Issues to consider

❏ Compare Field's psycholinguistic perspective with the perspective from morphology and lexicology across Strand 2 of this book. In particular, how does a psycholinguistic definition of what a 'word' is differ from a lexicological definition?

❏ Can you think of other examples that further confirm Field's arguments? Faced with having to explain examples such as these in a second-language classroom, how would you – as the teacher – develop a lesson to allow your students to improve their English?

❏ Do you agree with the implicit argument here that second-language teaching is largely informed by writing rather than speech?

❏ You could record a reading by a native speaker of any short passage (almost any paragraph from this book will do). Transcribe it closely in phonetic notation (see Strand 1) and identify any examples of reduction, assimilation, elision, resyllabification and cliticization of words that you find. Do you think any of your examples would present difficulties in a second-language classroom?

LEXICAL CHANGE

The vast majority of work in historical linguistics has concerned itself with changes in words and their meanings over time. In the following extract, Jeremy Smith examines several cases of lexical change in order to reveal the distinct types of historical development involved. In the passage prior to the excerpt, he outlines his notion of *variational space*: the meanings of a word including the network of its denotative, connotative and metaphorical meanings. A word's variational space is wider and looser than its semantic field, encompassing all of the possible potential directions that words' meanings might take over time.

Jeremy Smith

Jeremy Smith (reprinted from *An Historical Study of English: Function, Form and Change* (1996), London: Routledge, pp. 120–6)

Various labels have been given to the processes [of lexical change], such as 'narrowing' and 'widening' (e.g. Old English *mete* 'food' > Present-Day English *meat*; Old English *bridd* 'young bird' < Present-Day English *bird*), or 'pejoration' and 'amelioration' (e.g. Old English *scitol* 'purgative' beside Present-Day English *shit*, or Old English *prættig* 'sly' beside Present-Day English *pretty*). It is possible to develop some broader terms for the process of change; R.A. Waldron thus distinguishes between *shift* ('modification of an existing linguistic category') and *transfer* ('change to a different category') (see Waldron 1979: 140). It is, however, perhaps not desirable to make a hard-and-fast division between these categories since words can undergo both processes at once. It is better to see them as poles on a cline, marked by the following stages (which need not, incidentally, be in the order listed):

1. The conceptual meaning of a word moves from one part of its variational space to another.
2. One (or more) conceptual or associative meanings of a word within its variational space is (or are) dropped.
3. A word develops a new conceptual or associative meaning and thus extends its variational space.

In the rest of this section, exemplification of these processes is offered, drawing examples from the history of the English lexicon. The sources of evidence in all cases are the *Oxford English Dictionary* (OED), which is the largest repository of historical material yet assembled for the English lexicon, and, for current modern usage, the *Chambers Dictionary* (1993) and the *BBC English Dictionary* (1992). The reasons for choosing the two latter authorities will be made clear as discussion proceeds. It will be observed in the discussion that the categories 1–3 above overlap.

To illustrate category 1, the history of the meaning of the noun *villain* will be examined. The word derives from Old French *ville* '(rural) settlement', and originally the term *villain* simply meant someone who lived in such a place, a peasant. One spelling of the word, *villein*, has been retained by historians of the medieval period with this original, technical sense. But the word nowadays spelt *villain* has undergone a quite radical change of meaning. The definition in the OED of *villain* is as follows:

> Originally a low-born base-minded rustic; a man of ignoble ideas or instincts; in later use an unprincipled or depraved scoundrel; a man naturally disposed to base or criminal actions, or deeply involved in the commission of disgraceful crimes.... A bird (*esp.* a hawk) of a common or inferior character. *Obs.*... A person or animal of a troublesome character in some respect.

The *Chambers Dictionary* (1993), a desk-dictionary which reflects a wide range of Present-Day English usage, gives the following definition:

> a violent, malevolent or unscrupulous evil-doer; the wicked enemy of the hero or heroine in a story or play; playfully, a wretch; a criminal (*slang*); (*orig*) a villein.

Jeremy Smith

The word has plainly lost its older connotations to do with humble birth, and this is confirmed by the *BBC English Dictionary* (1992), which is designed for foreign learners of, and listeners to, the language and is thus careful to give current English usage of the kind such folk are likely to encounter on (for example) the BBC World Service:

> A person who deliberately harms other people or breaks the law is sometimes referred to as a *villain*. . . . The *villain* in a particular situation is the person, group, or country that is held responsible for things going wrong. . . . A *villain* in a play, film, or novel, is an important character who behaves badly and is responsible for many of the bad things that happen.

From this evidence the pattern involved in the history of this word is clear. The original conceptual meaning of *villain* might be expressed in formalist terms as something like [+HUMAN], [+BASE-BORN]; medieval views of society meant that connotations of 'evil-doing' were added to this core meaning. These connotations subsequently became part of the conceptual meaning of the word, and, after that, the original focal or conceptual meaning was dropped, to be later assigned to the related form *villein*. The originally associative meanings of *villain* have thus become the focal or conceptual meaning of the word.

The history of the meaning of *villain* could also, of course, be taken to illustrate category 2 above, in which one or more conceptual or associative meanings of a word within its variational space is dropped; the term *villain* does not in late-twentieth-century usage, as evidenced by the *BBC English Dictionary*, seem to carry with it the connotations of 'baseness of birth' which it had when it was first introduced to the language. However, the history of the verb *thrill* demonstrates the dropping of meaning more obviously, and will be investigated next.

During the history of the English language there seem to have been at least two verbs with the form *thrill*, with distinct etymologies; the link between these two is therefore more a matter of homophony than polysemy [. . .]. One survives only in some varieties, for instance Scots, as *thirl*; related to Old Norse *þræll* 'servant' with subsequent metathesis (i.e. internal exchange of phonetic segments), it has the present-day meaning of 'bind by ties of affection or duty' (see *Concise Scots Dictionary* 1985: 714). Important in its own dialectal area, this usage can be left aside for the purposes of the present discussion, other than to note that *thirl* has now completely replaced older *thrill* with the same meaning; the form *thrill* is in Scots retained for the same range of meanings as those found in Present-Day English.

The other, more common usage is in Present-Day English another metathesised form, this time derived from Old English *þyrlian* 'perforate, pierce, excavate'. *Chambers Dictionary* (1993) gives the following:

> [transitive] to affect with a strong glow or tingle of sense or emotion, now *esp* a feeling of excitement or extreme pleasure; to pierce (*archaic*) – [intransitive] to pass tinglingly; to quiver; to feel a sharp, shivering sensation; (of something sharp) to pierce or penetrate (with *through*) (*archaic*).

Jeremy Smith

OED definitions are split between *thirl* (the older form) and *thrill*; I have conflated and modified some of the definitions for the reader's convenience. First and last dates of general occurrence, as recorded in *OED*, are also given.

1. To pierce, to run through or into (a body) as a sharp-pointed instrument does; to pierce (anything) with such an instrument; to bore a hole in or through; to perforate [*thirl* 1.; also *thrill* 1.] 1000–1661.
2. To pass right through, penetrate, traverse (anything), [*thirl* 2.] 1175–1560.
3. To make a hole in (the earth); to excavate [*thirl* 3.] 1000–1577.
4. Coal mining. To cut through (a wall of coal, etc.) [*thirl* 4.] 1686–1883.
5. To pierce, penetrate (as a sharp instrument) [*thirl* 5.] 1374–1600 (both recorded sixteenth-century uses are from Scottish authors).
6. To pass through or penetrate (*into* or *to* a place or thing) [*thirl* 6.; also *thrill* 2.] 1300–1565.
7. To cause (a lance, dart, or the like) to pass; to dart, hurl (a piercing weapon) [*thrill* 3.] 1609–1646.
8. To pierce, penetrate (as a sound, or an emotion) [*thrill* 4.] 1300–1642.
9. To affect or move with a sudden wave of emotion (*transitive*); to produce a thrill, as an emotion, or anything causing emotion (*intransitive*) [*thrill* 5.] 1590–1874.
10. To send forth or utter tremulously [*thrill* 6.b.] 1647–1868.
11. To move/cause to move tremulously or with vibration [*thrill* 6.a., c] 1776–1878.

Of these definitions, only one survives in common usage as recorded in [the] *BBC English Dictionary* (1992). In this authority the verb is defined in terms of the noun, thus:

> If something gives you a *thrill*, it gives you a sudden feeling of excitement or pleasure.... If something *thrills* you, it gives you a thrill.

The process with regard to this word's change of meaning becomes clear once these various meanings are examined in chronological order. With the exception of the specialist meaning (4), the older meanings (1–7) die out by the middle of the seventeenth century. But during the Middle English period a new meaning appears, meaning 8, which – through metaphor – introduces 'sound' and 'emotion' into the word's variational space. These metaphorical meanings become central (and thus conceptual) to the meaning of the word from the middle of the seventeenth century onwards and the older meanings disappear. Not only has the conceptual meaning of the word changed, but the older conceptual meanings have disappeared altogether from the word's variational space.

    The extension of variational space to take on a new conceptual or associative meaning, category 3 above, like categories 1 and 2, is demonstrated by the history of *thrill*. However, it may be of interest to examine a more recent example of category 3, the extension in meaning undergone by the adjective *gay*. In the case of this word, conceptual meaning has changed in living memory. *Chambers Dictionary* (1993) gives the full range of current meanings:

lively; bright, colourful; playful, merry; pleasure-loving, dissipated (as in *gay dog* a rake) (*archaic*); of loose life, whorish (*obs*); showy; spotted, speckled (*dialect*); in modern use, homosexual (orig *prison slang*); relating to or frequented by homosexuals (as *gay bar*) . . .

Jeremy Smith

However, current usage as reflected in the *BBC English Dictionary* (1992) seems to be to regard the word as almost exclusively to do with homosexual orientation, whereas the wider range of meanings given in *Chambers Dictionary* is now regarded as obsolete:

> A person who is *gay* is homosexual. . . . *Gay* organizations and magazines are for homosexual people. . . . *Gay* also means lively and bright; an old-fashioned use.

OED records *gay* meaning 'homosexual' as a slang expression from 1935, but until the 1960s the quotations cited by *OED* tend to put the word in inverted commas, followed by an explanation; it is clear that the word had not entered common parlance. The association with homosexuality was obviously a secondary meaning for much of the mid-twentieth century since a related verb, *gayed up*, became current in the 1960s as a term of interior decoration without (as far as I am aware) any implication as to the sexual orientation of the designer or occupier of the building in question. However, the evidence of the *BBC English Dictionary* is that the conceptual meaning of this word is now essentially [+HUMAN], [+HOMOSEXUAL], and it seems likely that the older sense – still part of the word's variational space but now becoming obsolete – will eventually drop away entirely.

Internal and external sources of variation

So far, the discussion has been concerned generally with description rather than explanation. Given [my] historiographical concerns [. . .], however, it is now necessary to turn to the means by which the processes described are triggered and, once triggered, regulated. [. . .]

[. . . T]here are three interacting mechanisms of linguistic change: variation, contact and systemic regulation. The sources of variation in the lexicon fall into two categories:

(1) those which derive from the internal resources of a given variety, and
(2) those derived from contact between languages, or between varieties of the same language.

A form which demonstrates the way in which a language's internal resources contribute to the pool of available variation is the adverb *soon*, defined in the *BBC English Dictionary* as follows:

> If something is going to happen *soon*, it will happen after a short time. If something happened *soon* after a particular time or event, it happened a short time after it.

In Old English, the ancestor of this word, *sōna*, meant 'immediately', but in Present-Day English, as witnessed by the *BBC English Dictionary*, it now clearly means 'later on'. Only in the fossil expression *as soon as* does it retain its older sense in Present-Day English.

Jeremy Smith

The process illustrated by the history of *soon* is interesting, because it demonstrates one of the reasons for the appearance of variant meanings within the variational space of a word: they are the natural result of universal human tendencies to expressive overstatement (exaggeration) and understatement. Metaphor, in this context, can be seen as a sub-category of the former. As M.L. Samuels has put it (1972: 53),

> In lexis, overstatement (exaggeration) could be regarded as corresponding to strong-stress phonological variation, and similarly understatement and euphemism would correspond to weak-stress phonological variation. The difference lies in the selection of discrete forms possessing 'stronger' or 'weaker' *semantic* (not phonetic) properties.

These stronger and weaker usages form part of the variational space of a word, and are thus available for later selection.

A minor, but possibly still important, internal source of variation is to do with phonaesthetic associations. Here a good example is the word *gruelling* 'punishing', 'exhausting'. Related to the noun *gruel*, a species of thin porridge, the history of this word demonstrates nicely the way in which phonaesthetic considerations have conditioned a semantic development.

Externally conditioned variation within a lexicon is rather more complex than that described in the last three paragraphs. In one sense, the impact of one language on another, or of one variety on another, is simple: items in one language are copied into another, and interact with those which are already there.

This is not the end of the matter, however, and it is worth making clear the range of types of borrowing which can be distinguished. A precondition for borrowing is that a role must be seen for the alien form in the receiving language. Sometimes this role is to do with the appearance in the receiving culture of a new concept or object with which the resources of the native language are unequipped to deal, for example *chocolate*, ultimately from Nahuatl/Aztec *chocolatl* (although probably immediately a borrowing from Spanish), or *bungalow*, from Gujerati *bangalo*. Hindustani *banglā*, 'belonging to Bengal'. However, that languages can cope with such phenomena from their own internal resources through the processes of word-formation is proved by, for example, German *Fernseher* 'television' (*lit.* 'far-seer').

More important are occasions when a borrowed word and a synonymous or near-synonymous native word — which may or may not be related in etymology — become differentiated in meaning within the borrowing language. Two examples of such processes are:

1. The difference in meaning between Present-Day English *shirt*, *skirt*. In Old English, *scyrte* appears as a gloss for Latin *praetexta*, an outer garment (cf. Lewis and Short 1879: 1435). The Norse cognate of *scyrte* is *skyrta*, and originally the two words were synonyms. However, when the Norse word was borrowed it developed a meaning distinct from the English usage, and *shirt*, *skirt* have been differentiated in meaning ever since.

2.   The difference in meaning between Present-Day English *ox*, *beef*. A similar process
     of differentiation can be seen with these words. The Old English word, *oxa*, was
     originally synonymous with Old French *boef* (cf. Latin *bōs*). The latter was borrowed
     into English as *beef*, but the meaning became narrowed as 'flesh of the ox'.

Jeremy Smith

Both processes 1 and 2 display a differentiation of conceptual meaning; the pairs *shirt*/*skirt*,
ox/*beef* form contrastive groups which could be expressed formalistically. But differentiation can also take place with regard to associative (connotational and metaphorical)
meaning. One good example of this process is to do with register-distinctions between
native vocabulary and French-derived loanwords; it is 'felt' by a speaker of Present-
Day English that a French-derived word such as *commence* is of a 'higher' register than
begin, the latter form being directly descended from Old English.

L. Bloomfield's comment (1933: 394) is relevant to both internally and externally
induced variation: 'where a speaker knows two rival forms, they differ in connotation,
since he has heard them from different persons and under different circumstances'.
As a result synonyms are never exact: the way in which the variational spaces available
to words overlap with each other seems to be an established fact of the nature of the
lexicon, and is the result of the varying nature of contacts between people. When
these contacts take place between the users of different languages, the subsequent
reorganisations seem to be particularly large.

The result of these two processes, externally and internally induced variation,
is that any given language-state, whether individual or group, consists of a mixture of
variant forms. These variants form a pool, rather like the pool of mutations in biological evolution, from which subsequent selection is made. And, just as in biological
evolution, so in linguistic evolution there are factors which condition the kinds of
choices which take place.

Issues to consider

❑   Evaluate the usefulness of Smith's innovative notion of *variational space*. He
    develops the idea here in order to be able to explore the many potentialities
    of historical changes in word-meaning; however, does the notion have a more
    general theoretical usefulness in lexical semantics? Can you think of advantages
    in being able to talk in broad terms about the different sorts of meanings of
    a word; and what are the disadvantages? In other words, is there a synchronic
    value to the notion as well as a diachronic one?

❑   Smith uses close synonymic variations as part of his argument (*shirt*/*skirt*, *beef*/*ox*,
    and so on). Can you find other examples of such divergent cognates (such as
    mutton/*sheep*, or the different US and UK meanings of *gas*, and so on)? Use the
    etymological history provided by the *OED* to investigate when and how these
    meanings diverged, and offer your own speculations as to why they happened.

❑   Can you think of any words in the usage of your own speech community that seem
    currently to be undergoing change? A good source of evidence for such words is
    informal register in casual, transient and everyday discourse, such as notes, phone
    texts, email, voice-messaging, and relaxed chat. Another good source for spotting
    lexical change in progress is to identify which words and phrases are being criticised
    by conservative commentators as evidence for the moral laxity of society.

D9

SOCIAL RELATIONSHIPS AND SOCIAL PRACTICES

The major difficulty of sociolinguistics is the complexity of social facts, including language. Attempts to study the relationship between language and society necessarily involve focusing on particular restricted aspects, delineating social variables such as gender, age or ethnicity from other variables. Inevitably, the holistic integration of the social phenomenon of language is partly or wholly distorted in the process of this analytical convenience. There have been calls from sociolinguists and social theorists for many years not to disregard the complexity of social context. In this excerpt, Lesley Milroy and Matthew Gordon review different attempts to capture the difficult social connections of language. They also argue for a practical, analytical method of proceeding in sociolinguistic investigations.

Lesley Milroy and Matthew Gordon (reprinted from *Sociolinguistics: Method and Interpretation* (2003), Oxford: Blackwell)

Lesley Milroy and Matthew Gordon

The concept of social network

[A]n individual's social network is the aggregate of relationships contracted with others, a boundless web of ties which reaches out through social and geographical space linking many individuals, sometimes remotely. First-order network ties, i.e., a person's direct contacts, are generally the focus of interest. Within the first-order zone it is important, for reasons to be discussed below, to distinguish between 'strong' and 'weak' ties of everyday life – roughly, ties that connect friends or kin as opposed to those that connect acquaintances. Second-order ties are those to whom the link is indirect, and are often an important local resource, enabling persons to access a range of information, goods, and services.

Social network analysis of the kind generally adopted by variationists was developed by social anthropologists mainly during the 1960s and 1970s (see further Milroy 1987; Li Wei 1996; Johnson 1994). Contrary to the assertions of Murray (1993: 162), it is clear from even a cursory reading of the literature that no canonically correct procedure for analyzing social networks can be identified; scholars from many different disciplines employ the concept for a range of theoretical and practical purposes. For example, Johnson's (1994) survey alludes to a wide range of approaches within anthropology that hardly overlap with the largely quantitative modes of analysis described by Cochran and colleagues (1990). This international and interdisciplinary team of scholars is interested in the role of networks in providing support for urban families. Accordingly, their methods are to a great extent driven by a concern with social policy and practice.

Personal social networks are always seen as contextualized within macro-level social frameworks [...]. These frameworks are 'bracketed off' for purely methodological reasons, in order to focus on less abstract modes of analysis capable of accounting more immediately for observed variable behaviors. A fundamental postulate of network analysis is that individuals create personal communities to provide a meaningful framework for solving the problems of daily life (Mitchell 1986: 74). These personal communities are constituted by interpersonal ties of different types and strengths,

Lesley Milroy and Matthew Gordon

and structural relationships between links can vary. Particularly, the persons to whom an individual is linked may also be tied to each other to varying degrees. A further postulate with particular relevance to students of language change (or its converse, language maintenance) is that structural and content differences between networks impinge critically on the way they directly affect individuals. Particularly, if a personal network consists chiefly of strong ties that are also multiplex or many-stranded, and if the network is also relatively dense (i.e., many of those ties are linked to each other), then such a network has the capacity to support its members in both practical and symbolic ways. More negatively, however, such a network type can impose unwanted and stressful constraints on its members. Thus, we come to the basic point of deploying network analysis in variationist research. Networks constituted chiefly of strong (dense and multiplex) ties appear to be supportive of localized linguistic norms, resisting pressures from competing external norms. By the same token, a weakening of these ties produces conditions that are favorable to particular types of language change. Hence, a network analysis can help to explain why a particular community successfully supports a linguistic system that stands in opposition to a legitimized, mainstream set of norms, and why another system might be less focused or more sensitive to external influences.

Social network and community of practice

Individuals engage on a daily basis in a variety of endeavors in multiple personal communities and the people who comprise an individual's personal communities change, as indeed do the everyday problems that such personal communities help to solve. Eckert employs the concept of *community of practice*, an idea related to social network, to locate the interactional sites where social meaning is most clearly indexed by language, and where language variation and social meaning are co-constructed. A community of practice can be defined as an aggregate of people coming together around a particular enterprise (Eckert 2000: 34–5), and in her analysis of the social dynamics of language variation among Detroit adolescents, Eckert focuses on intersecting clusters of individuals engaged in socially relevant enterprises (2000: 171–212). Such clusters constitute gendered subgroups showing an orientation in their social and linguistic practice to the adolescent social categories of jock and burnout which participants themselves construct.

Eckert comments that the construction of such local styles was possible only insofar as individuals were integrated into local networks and so had access to information, the importance of information being particularly clear at the level of clothing style. She points out that

> [c]ertain aspects of linguistic style are also negotiated consciously. I can recall explicit discussions in my own high school crowd of 'cool' ways to say things, generally in the form of imitations of cool people.... But in general, linguistic influence takes place without explicit comment and all the more requires direct access to speakers. The adoption of a way of speaking, like a way of dressing, no doubt requires both access and entitlement to adopt the style of a particular group.
>
> (Eckert 2000: 210–11)

Lesley Milroy
and Matthew
Gordon
Thus, individuals who are well integrated into local networks are socially positioned to access multiple communities of practice. Eckert is here describing very general social mechanisms by which local conventions and norms – of dress, religion, and general behavior, for example – are negotiated and created, and linguistic norms are no exception. Close-knit networks of the kind where this activity takes place are commonly contracted in adolescence. These are the linguistically influential peer groups that are of particular interest to sociolinguists attempting to understand the kinds of language change associated with different points in the life-span (see Kerswill 1996; Kerswill and Williams 2000). However, such norm-supporting (and norm-constructing) networks also flourish in low-status communities in the absence of social and geographical mobility and foster the solidarity ethos associated with the long-term survival of socially disfavored languages and dialects.

The concepts of network and community of practice are thus closely related, and the differences between them are chiefly of method and focus. Network analysis typically deals with the structural and content properties of the ties that constitute *egocentric* personal networks, and seeks to identify ties important to an individual rather than to focus on particular network clusters (such as those contracted at school) independently of a particular individual. Eckert (2000) explains in detail her procedures for identifying the clusters that form the crucial loci of linguistic and social practice in the social world of the high school. Because it does not attend to the identification of particular clusters or the enterprises undertaken by members which, combined, constitute communities of practice, network analysis cannot address the issues of how and where linguistic variants are employed, along with other network-specific behaviors, to construct local social meanings. Rather, it is concerned with how informal social groups are constituted in such a way as to support local norms or, conversely, to facilitate linguistic change. In the following section we flesh out our discussion with details of specific variationist studies that have employed the social network concept.

Social networks and language variation

[...] A network approach is potentially attractive to variationists for several reasons. First, it provides a set of procedures for studying small groups where speakers are not discriminable in terms of any kind of social class index – as, for example, the southeastern United States island communities investigated by Wolfram, Hazen, and Schilling-Estes (1999). Other examples are minority ethnic groups, migrants, rural populations, or populations in non-industrialized societies. A second advantage is that since social network is intrinsically a concept which relates to local practices, it has the potential to elucidate the social dynamics driving language variation and change. Finally, network analysis offers a procedure for dealing with variation between individual speakers, rather than between groups constructed with reference to predetermined social categories. It was employed chiefly for these reasons in a number of other studies carried out in the 1980s and 1990s in many different kinds of community. Examples of such studies are Milroy (1987) in Belfast; Russell (1982) in Mombasa, Kenya; Schmidt (1985) of Australian Aboriginal adolescents; Bortoni-Ricardo (1985) of changes in the language of rural migrants to a Brazilian city; V. Edwards

Lesley Milroy
and Matthew
Gordon

(1986) of the language of British black adolescents; Schooling (1990) of language differences among Melanesians in New Caledonia; Lippi-Green (1989) on dynamics of change in the rural alpine village of Grossdorf, Austria; W. Edwards (1992) of variation in an African American community in inner-city Detroit; and Maher (1996) of the persistence of language differences in the isolated island community of St. Barthélemy, French West Indies. [...]

The Belfast study carried out a detailed quantitative analysis of the relationship between language variation and social network structure. It adapted many of Gumperz's ideas, particularly in its ethnographically oriented fieldwork methods [...] and in its attention to local practices in interpreting sociolinguistic patterns. As first reported by Milroy and Milroy (1978) the language patterns of 46 speakers from three low-status urban working-class communities — Ballymacarrett, Hammer, and Clonard — were examined. Eight phonological variables, all of which were clearly indexical of the Belfast urban speech community, were analyzed in relation to the network structure of individual speakers. In all three communities networks were relatively dense, multiplex, and often kin-based, corresponding to those described by many investigators as characteristic of traditional, long-established communities minimally impacted by social or geographical mobility (see, for example, Young and Wilmott 1962; Cohen 1982). The extent of individuals' use of vernacular variants was found to be strongly influenced by the level of integration into neighborhood networks. The kind of network ties that were locally relevant emerged, in the course of observation, as those of kin, work, friendship, and neighborhood. As discussed by Milroy (1987), a considerable body of anthropological research had already noted the particular importance of ties of these four types. Some of the Belfast participants worked outside the neighborhood and had no local kin and few local ties of friendship, while others were locally linked in all four capacities. Such differences in personal network structure appear to be associated with a range of social and psychological factors, and in the Belfast communities interacted with a number of other variables such as gender, generation cohort, and neighborhood settlement patterns.

A major challenge for researchers is to devise a procedure for characterizing differences in network structure which reflects local social practice, so that, not surprisingly, the studies reviewed in this section all measure social network structure in quite different ways. The Belfast study developed a Network Strength Scale (maximum score, 5) which assessed speakers' network characteristics with reference to various relationships *within the neighborhood* of kin, work, and friendship that had emerged in the course of the fieldwork as significant to participants. Speakers scored one point for each of the following conditions they satisfied:

❑ were members of a high-density, territorially based group (e.g., a bingo or card-playing group, a gang or a football team, or football supporters' club)
❑ had kinship ties with more than two households in the neighborhood
❑ worked in the same place as at least two others from the neighborhood
❑ worked in the same place as at least two others of the same sex from the neighborhood
❑ associated voluntarily with workmates in leisure hours.

Lesley Milroy
and Matthew
Gordon

A series of statistical analyses revealed that the strongest vernacular speakers were generally those whose neighborhood network ties were the strongest, a pattern complicated, as we might expect, by the interaction of other social variables such as age and gender. Milroy (1987) discusses patterns of this kind in Ballymacarrett, where variants of a single variable are examined in relation both to network structure and to gender. Labov's (2001: 331) re-analysis of the Belfast data confirms the patterns reported by Milroy, and he discusses in particular detail interactions between network and gender in Belfast and Philadelphia (2001: 329–56). In both communities network structure affects language quite differently for men and women [. . .].

The relative socioeconomic homogeneity of the inner-city Detroit African American neighborhood studied by Edwards (1992) made social network analysis an attractive procedure for dealing with intra-community linguistic variation, and he operationalized the network concept in accordance with the specifics of local social practice. While the principal factor associated with choice of variant was age, the most important factor distinguishing age-peers of a comparable social and educational background was participation in neighborhood culture. Edwards interpreted such participation as indicative of relative integration into local networks, and measured this integration by means of a Vernacular Culture Index. This was constructed from responses to ten statements which could range from Strongly Disagree (1 point) to Strongly Agree (4 points). Five statements were designed as indicators of the individual's physical integration into the neighborhood and, like the Network Strength Scale used in Belfast, focused on localized interactions with kin, workmates and friends. (e.g., 'Most of my relatives live in this neighborhood or with me'; 'Most of my friends live in this neighborhood'). Convinced of the importance of attitude in accounting for variation, Edwards designed the other five statements to indicate evaluations of the neighborhood and of black/white friendship ties (e.g., 'I would like to remain living in this neighborhood'; 'I do not have white friends with whom I interact frequently').

Quite a different set of indicators of integration into localized networks was relevant to Lippi-Green's (1989) study of language change in progress in Grossdorf, an isolated Austrian Alpine village with 800 inhabitants. Commenting specifically on the unhelpfulness of macro-level concepts such as social class in uncovering the relationship between language variation and social structure, Lippi-Green examined in detail the personal network structures of individuals, constructing a scale that used 16 differentially weighted indicators. Some of these were associated with the familiar domains of work, kin and friendship, while others dealt with more specifically local conditions – such as the number of grandparents familiar to the speaker who were core members of the village, or the involvement of the speaker's employment with the tourism industry. Particularly important were indicators that linked speakers to major family networks in the village. Overall, the best correlate of conservative linguistic behavior was integration into three important networks, including those which involved workplace and exposure to non-local language varieties. However, the subtlety of Lippi-Green's network measurement scale allowed her to examine correlations both with all of it and with some parts of it, revealing among other things gender-specific social trajectories of language change and variation of the kind discussed earlier in this section.

Issues to consider

❑ Using Milroy's scale of 0–5 calculate the strength of the social networks to which you belong, based upon Milroy's conditions to calculate network strength listed as bullet points above. On the basis of your network strength score, categorise the social networks as either 'first order' or 'second order' and on a scale of 'strong' and 'weak'. Draw a sketch of your own social network with dots for people and lines between you and them to show the relationships. Now looking at your diagram, can you identify the most dense and multiplex aspects of your social life? Are you conscious of using different patterns of language in different facets of your social networks?

❑ Critically consider the advantages and disadvantages of the social network approaches taken in Milroy and Milroy's (1978) study of Belfast, Edwards' (1992) study of inner-city Detroit, and Lippi-Green's (1989) study of Grossdorf described in this extract. Consider how the social networks approach has been adapted to suit each of these different geographical locations. Which social networks study do you find most convincing out of these (or other) examples? Why?

❑ In reference to Penelope Eckert's (2000) work on communities of practice, Milroy and Gordon (2003) point to the importance of the interplay between linguistic style and clothing in her observations of adolescents in the Detroit high school where she collected her ethnographic data. They draw attention to Eckert's findings of the critical importance played by the close-knit network strength of groups, the importance of gendered sub-groups and also the enactment of identity categories such as 'jocks' and 'burnouts'. On the basis of these descriptions, discuss reasons why you think adolescence is such a productive life-stage to conduct sociolinguistic studies.

THE DEVELOPMENT OF WORLD ENGLISHES   D10

In this extract from his book on World Englishes, Andy Kirkpatrick sets out some common processes in the evolution of new varieties of English, and he sets out some cautionary observations against treating all new emergences of forms of English as conforming to a predetermined or universal developmental programme. In particular, he draws attention to the political and ideological factors that are usually bound up with questions of language identification, and suggests that empirical investigation rather than theorising from only a few examples is the best way forward.

Andy Kirkpatrick (reprinted from *World Englishes: Implications for International Communication and English Language Teaching* (2007), Cambridge: Cambridge University Press, pp. 30–7)

Andy
Kirkpatrick

Developmental cycles

[...]

Many scholars have suggested the phases or processes through which varieties of English go. I shall not review all of these here, but consider three main proposals and refer to others. The reader will note that scholars agree in many areas and that

Andy
Kirkpatrick

many of the phases identified by one scholar mirror those of another. There are also a number of different terms that refer to the same idea. For example the terms 'exonormative model', 'transported variety' and 'imported variety' refer to the English spoken by the settlers that arrived in a particular country. It is called 'exonormative' because the model originates from outside the place where it is spoken. This is contrasted with an 'endonormative model', that is, a locally grown variety. 'Transported' or 'imported' varieties obviously refer to the varieties spoken by the settlers, as opposed to the varieties spoken by the locals, which are referred to as 'nativised' or 'indigenised' or 'acculturated'. [...] all varieties are actually nativised in the sense that they all reflect the local cultures of their speakers. This term is also used, however, to distinguish the local variety from the transported variety. The process through which an imported variety goes on its way to becoming a local variety is variously referred to as 'nativisation', 'indigenisation', or a combination of 'deculturation' (of the imported variety, as it loses its original cultural roots) and 'acculturation' (of the local variety, as it grows new cultural roots).

Kachru has suggested three phases through which 'non-native institutionalised varieties of English seem to pass' (1992b: 56). The first phase is characterised by 'non-recognition' of the local variety. At this stage the speakers of the local variety are prejudiced against it and believe that some imported native speaker variety is superior and should be the model for language learning in schools. They themselves will strive to speak the imported, exonormative variety and sound like native speakers, while looking down upon those who speak only the local variety.

The second phase sees the existence of the local and imported variety existing side by side. The local variety is now used in a wide number of situations and for a wide range of purposes but is still considered inferior to the imported model.

During the third phase, the local variety becomes recognised as the norm and becomes socially accepted. The local variety becomes the model for language learning in schools. In places where the local variety has become accepted, local people who continue to speak the imported variety can be seen as outsiders or as behaving unnaturally in some way.

Moag (1992) studied the development of a particular variety – Fijian English – and proposed a 'life cycle of non-native Englishes'. He identified five processes, four of which are undergone by all varieties, and a fifth which may only be experienced by some. The first process he called 'transportation'. This is when English arrives in a place where it has not been spoken before and remains to stay. The second process, 'indigenisation', is a relatively long phase during which the new variety of English starts to reflect the local culture and becomes different from the transported variety. The third process, the 'expansion in use' phase, sees the new variety being used in an increasing number of situations and for more and more purposes. This process is also marked by an increase in variation within the local variety. The local variety becomes the local varieties. The fourth phase is marked by the use of the local variety as a language learning model in school. During this phase, local literature in the new variety will be written. Moag calls this fourth phase 'institutionalisation'. The fifth and final phase sees a decline in use. He suggests that the Philippines and Malaysia are examples of countries where the increased official promotion of a local language – Tagalog in the Philippines and Malay in Malaysia – results in a decline in the use of

Andy
Kirkpatrick

the local variety of English. He wonders whether this decline in use might lead to the eventual death of English in these countries, but there is no evidence of that happening. In fact, in the Malaysian context, there has recently been an officially approved and promoted increase in the uses of English.

A more recent and detailed theory for the development of new Englishes comes from Schneider (2003: 233–81). I call it a theory as Schneider hopes, albeit cautiously, that, 'in principle, it should be possible to apply the model to most, ideally all of the Englishes around the globe' (2003: 256).

He agrees with Mufwene (2001) in arguing that 'postcolonial Englishes follow a fundamentally uniform developmental process' (2003: 233). He identifies five phases in this developmental cycle. The first phase he calls the 'foundation' phase. This is when English begins to be used in a country where, previously, English was not spoken. This is typically because English speakers settle in the country.

The second phase he calls 'exonormative stabilisation'. This means that the variety spoken is closely modelled on the variety imported by the settlers. Schneider does distinguish, however, between the variety spoken by the settlers – which he calls the STL strand – and the variety spoken by the local or indigenous people – which he calls the IDG strand. Schneider argues that this phase sees the slow movement of the STL variety towards the local variety and the beginning of the expansion of the IDG variety. He argues that 'what happens during this phase may not be unlike the early stages of some routes leading to creolisation' (2003: 246).

The third phase is the 'nativisation' phase and Schneider considers this to be the most important and dynamic phase. It sees the establishment of a new identity with the coupling of the imported STL and local IDG varieties. This phase 'results in the heaviest effects on the restructuring of the English language itself' (2003: 248), although the restructuring occurs mostly at the level of vocabulary and grammar.

Phase four is the phase of 'endonormative stabilisation', which is when the new variety becomes gradually accepted as the local norm or model. At this stage the local variety is used in a range of formal situations.

Schneider calls the fifth and final phase 'differentiation'. At this stage the new variety has emerged and this new variety reflects local identity and culture. It is also at this stage that more local varieties develop. For example, Schneider suggests that differences between STL and IDG varieties resurface as markers of ethnic identity.

All three scholars have suggested developmental cycles that have their similarities. [...] Basically, the variety spoken by the settlers becomes changed over time through contact with local languages and cultures. The new indigenous variety is initially considered inferior to the original imported one, but gradually it becomes accepted and institutionalised. Once it is accepted and institutionalised, it then develops new varieties.

All three scholars are really addressing the processes that occur in postcolonial societies. But it is possible that new varieties are also developing in what Kachru termed 'expanding circle' countries, where, by definition, there has been no significant settlement of English speakers. It would appear that, in certain circumstances, expanding circle countries can develop their own Englishes without going through the first 'transportation' or 'foundation' phases. The great majority of non-Chinese English speakers in China, for example, are people from the Asian region for whom English

Andy
Kirkpatrick

is not a first language but who use English in China as a *lingua franca*. And, while an exonormative variety is promoted as a model by the Ministry of Education, the sheer scale of the English language learning enterprise means that speakers of exonormative inner-circle models are heard only by the tiniest fraction of Chinese learners of English. The overwhelming majority of learners are being taught by Chinese teachers; and those Chinese learners who are interacting in English with non-Chinese are, in the main, interacting with people from other expanding-circle countries. [...] the increasingly common phenomenon of local teachers + intranational *lingua franca* use is providing an alternative process for the development of new varieties of English.

A slightly different way of looking at the development of Englishes has been proposed by Widdowson (1997, 2003). While agreeing that 'the very fact that English is an international language means that no nation can have custody over it' (2003: 43), Widdowson makes an important distinction between the spread of English and the distribution of English. He argues that English is not so much *distributed* as a set of established encoded forms, unchanged into different domains of use, but rather that it is *spread*, as a virtual language. He sees the two processes as being quite different. 'Distribution implies adoption and conformity. Spread implies adaptation and non-conformity' (1997: 140). Ghanaian and Nigerian Englishes are examples that have resulted from the spread of English. What Ghanaians and Nigerians speak 'is another English, not a variant but a different language' (1997: 141), and he argues that such varieties 'evolve into autonomous languages ultimately to the point of mutual unintelligibility' (1997: 142). He also argues that their developmental processes are different from the development of regional varieties of English within England which are, he claims, 'variants of the same language, alternative actualisations' (1997: 140). In contrast, varieties found in 'far flung regions...have sprung up in a relatively extempore and expedient way in response to the immediate communicative needs of people in different communities with quite different ancestors' (1997: 141).

Widdowson makes a clear distinction between the developmental processes in indigenised Englishes and other Englishes, and his position moves us to a debate on the nature of the new varieties of English and whether they can rightfully be called Englishes or whether they are, as is Widdowson's view, 'autonomous languages'.

Widdowson's position is broadly representative of the views of those who argue that the development of different intranational varieties of English will necessarily result in a range of mutually unintelligible languages, as, for example, French and Italian developed from Latin. Following the distinction between a dialect and a register (Halliday *et al.*, 1964), Widdowson (2003) suggests that nativised local varieties of English can be considered as dialects in that they are primarily concerned with distinct communities. These dialects are 'likely ... to evolve into separate species of language ..., gradually becoming mutually unintelligible' (2003: 53). In contrast, Widdowson argues that the varieties of English used for specific purposes such as banking or commerce can be seen more as registers, that is varieties of language that have developed to 'serve uses *for* language rather than users *of* it' (2003: 54) (italics in original). Universally agreed *registers* of English will thus be used for international communication and *dialects* will be used for local communication and the expression of identity. As suggested by the 'identity–communication continuum', however, I do not see the need to draw a distinction in this way. Rather, I agree with Mufwene and Schneider

Andy
Kirkpatrick

that all varieties of English develop from similar stimuli and through similar processes. All varieties must, on the one hand, reflect the cultural realities of their speakers and, on the other, be adaptable enough to allow international communication. This is as true of Nigerian English(es) as it is of Liverpudlian English. [...]

Intelligibility is thus not a useful criterion for determining whether a variety has become a different language [...] many varieties of British English can be mutually unintelligible. This is especially the case if the motivation of the speaker is to highlight his or her identity. [...] Smith [1992] has long argued that different varieties do not necessarily equate with unintelligibility. In a well-known study conducted in response to the frequently voiced concern over 'the possibility that speakers of different varieties of English will soon become unintelligible to one another' (1992: 75), he argued that this is a natural phenomenon and nothing to worry about. 'Our speech or writing in English needs to be intelligible only to those with whom we wish to communicate in English' (1992: 75). To this I would add that, following the 'identity–communication continuum', our speech or writing in English can be made intelligible to speakers of other varieties of English. [...]

English as an international language or World Englishes?

The political debate over the spread of English centres around two questions: (1) is it due to imperialism or linguicism; or (2) is it due to a genuine desire of people to learn English because it has become so useful and because it can be adapted to suit the cultural norms of the people who speak it? [...]. In a way, this is a debate about one English and many Englishes. Those who see imperialism as the cause argue that it is British and, to an increasingly greater extent, American English, that is being spread across the world. They argue that British and American English necessarily bring with them Anglo-cultural norms and that to learn this English means adopting British and American culture. As Rahman (1999) has argued in the case of Pakistan, English 'acts by distancing people from most indigenous cultural norms' (cited in Phillipson 2002: 17).

There is little doubt that there are people and institutions who see the spread of English as being both commercially and politically extremely important for their own interests. An example of such an institution could be said to be the British Council. A major task of the British Council is to give access to British culture across the world. What better way to do this than to offer access to British English? Hence British Councils across the world have established English language schools. These schools promote a British or native speaker model and language teaching materials published by British publishing houses. However, it is noteworthy that the British Council sees these schools as operating with an overall purpose of building mutually beneficial relationships between people in the UK and other countries.

There is also little doubt that the British government sees great advantage in the spread of English, especially British English and especially in post-communist countries of Eastern Europe and in countries such as China. A senior British politician [and later prime-minister], Gordon Brown, was extolling the virtues of English in a trip to China he made in 2005.

There is also little doubt that certain varieties of English are considered superior in a range of international contexts. Academic publications in the United States and

**Andy
Kirkpatrick**

Britain favour articles written in Anglo varieties and which follow Anglo rhetorical styles. This has led scholars such as Swales (1997), Ammon (2000) and Kandiah (2001) to consider how any possible prejudice against scholars who are either speakers of different varieties of English or who are second language speakers of English can be addressed.

Phillipson's (2002) elegant argument for the linguistic imperialism thesis has won many followers. Needless to say, however, there are many who disagree with his analysis and who argue that, far from being forced upon people unwillingly, English has been actively sought out by people throughout the world (Conrad 1996; Davies 1996; Li 2002; Brutt-Griffler 2002). In their view, people are making sensible and pragmatic choices; they are not being coerced into learning English. And, far from English being a purveyor of Anglo-cultural norms, the development of new varieties of English shows how English can be adapted by its speakers to reflect their cultural norms.

Kandiah (2001) sees both motivations in action and feels that there is an inherent contradiction for people in postcolonial countries. On the one hand, people realise they need to learn English as it is the international language. On the other, they fear that the need to use English in so many situations and for so many functions will threaten their own languages, cultures and ways of thinking. Yet, as Kachru and others have argued, local Englishes reflect local cultures and ways of thinking. Second, many non-Anglo or non-Western ways of thinking have received international attention through English. To take just three examples from Chinese culture, traditional Chinese medicine, the writings on the Art of War by Sun Zi and the tenets of Confucianism are now much better known in the West than in the past, precisely because this Chinese cultural knowledge and these Chinese ways of thinking have been disseminated through English. As Jacques (2005) has argued, with the rise in power of India and China, American and Western values will be contested as never before. It is highly likely that they will be contested through the medium of English.

In closing this chapter, I want to introduce a conundrum that we face in an attempt to standardise and classify World Englishes. We like models and norms. The conundrum that we have to solve is that we are faced with many models all of which are characterised by internal variation. This has been pointed out by Kachru in his call for a 'polymodel' approach to replace a 'monomodel' approach (1992a: 66). A monomodel approach supposes that English is homogenous, a single variety, it is 'English as an international language'. In Kachru's view, this approach ignores the incontrovertible fact that English is actually characterised by variety and variation. A polymodel approach, on the other hand, supposes variability. Kachru lists three types: 'variability related to acquisition; variability related to function; and variability related to the context of situation' (1992a: 66).

By examining the linguistic features of a range of Englishes and the sociocultural contexts in which they operate, I hope to show how the real situation is characterised by variation and variety and that we need to study 'global' English in specific places (Sonntag 2003). While varieties of English go through similar linguistic and developmental processes, the current status and functions of those Englishes can differ markedly. For example, the roles and functions of English differ markedly today even in Malaysia and Singapore, two countries whose historical backgrounds are so closely related that one was actually part of the other at one stage in the past.

Issues to consider

❑ Assess the three different models of development cycles of World Englishes from Kachru, Schneider and Widdowson presented by Kirkpatrick. Which arguments/ models do you find the most convincing? Why?

❑ How useful do you think these models can be if applied to Expanding Circle countries?

❑ Do you agree with Widdowson that 'the very fact that English is an international language means that no nation can have custody over it' (2003: 43)? Consider arguments for and against.

❑ In light of the arguments presented above, what variety of English do you think should be taught in China? Should an 'exonormative' Inner Circle model still be promoted, when the majority of Chinese English speakers may never communicate with 'native', Inner Circle speakers?

❑ Consider your positioning in relation to the linguistic imperialism argument versus the consensus-based, pragmatic choice argument of speakers actively seeking to learn English (as it has become such a useful tool).

SPEECH AND THOUGHT AS POINT OF VIEW

The examples of stylistic analysis presented earlier in Strand 11 have focused on one feature or level of language. However, there are also areas of concern in stylistic study that involve a collection of linguistic elements forming the literary critical feature. For example, the represented world that is constructed with the aid of the text can be explored by examining the naming conventions as noun-phrases, the verb choices, and other narratological factors. Similarly, the literary critical notion of *point of view* in narrative fiction involves the orientational and perspectivising facilities of language. In this extract from his book on point of view, Paul Simpson draws together a systemic-functional approach to transitivity (see the last part of B4) with attention paid to the modality used in literary texts. *Modality* refers to those parts of language which encode the speaker's attitude to the content of their utterance (for example, being certain in 'It is obvious that you are right', being doubtful in 'It is possible you are right', being subjective in 'It appears that you are right', being wishful in 'I hope that you are right', and so on). Simpson aims to demonstrate how detailed stylistic analysis can augment literary criticism.

Paul Simpson (reprinted from *Language, Ideology and Point of View* (1993), London: Routledge, pp. 92–104)

I wish to add one final component to the analytic model [of transitivity . . .]. This component concerns the ways in which agency and causation relate to the processes expressed by the clause, especially those clauses which express material processes. [Compare]

Paul Simpson

(1)   I broke the vase.
(2)   The vase broke.

In relation to both examples, the question might be asked: which participant is affected by the process expressed by the clause? Clearly, it is the vase – in either case, it breaks. Now, in our transitivity framework a standard breakdown of these examples would look like the following:

	ACTOR	PROCESS	GOAL
(1)	I	broke	the vase.

	ACTOR	PROCESS
(2)	The vase	broke.

The problem here is that the vase appears as the GOAL in (1) but as the ACTOR in (2), despite the fact that it is the affected participant in both cases. This is because there is a special set of verbs in English (like *to break*) which can express both patterns, and each pattern is said to bear an *ergative* relationship to the other. To account for this kind of situation it is sometimes useful to isolate one participant that is the key figure in the process and without which the process could not have come into existence. In examples (1) and (2), the vase represents this key participant role and may thus be labelled the MEDIUM, on the basis that it is the medium through which the process comes into existence. In material processes of this sort, the MEDIUM will always be equivalent to the ACTOR in an intransitive (non-goal-directed) clause and the GOAL in a transitive clause. Consider the following examples, which all realize processes which behave in a similar way to that expressed by (1) and (2):

The police exploded the bomb.	The bomb exploded.
The wind shattered the windows.	The windows shattered.
John cooked the rice.	The rice cooked.

According to the criteria noted above, the MEDIUM will be represented by *the bomb*, *the windows* and *the rice* in each pair of examples. However, in each of the examples on the left, there is another participant functioning as an external cause of the process. This participant, which is responsible for engendering the process from outside, may be referred to as the AGENT. The AGENT will thus be equivalent to the ACTOR in goal-directed material processes – as can be seen by the participant function of *the police*, *the wind* and *John* in the left-hand examples. Consequently, these examples display an AGENT + PROCESS + MEDIUM sequence, whilst those on the right simply display a MEDIUM + PROCESS sequence. The ergative interpretation suggested here need only be invoked for the special types of process identified in this section. It forms a useful supplement, an extra layer, to the standard analysis of transitivity which suffices for most purposes. To show how both types of analysis interrelate with one another, here is a 'double' analysis of examples (1) and (2):

Ergative analysis:	AGENT	PROCESS	MEDIUM
Standard analysis:	ACTOR	PROCESS	GOAL
(1)	I	broke	the vase.

Paul Simpson

Ergative analysis:	MEDIUM	PROCESS
Standard analysis:	ACTOR	PROCESS
(2)	The vase	broke.

The ergative interpretation bears an important relation to the system of *voice*. A clause that displays no feature of agency is neither active nor passive but middle (*The bomb exploded*). On the other hand, clauses which display agency can be either active or passive and are therefore non-middle in voice (*The police exploded the bomb*). In non-middle clauses the feature of agency may be *explicit*, as in *The police exploded the bomb* and its passive equivalent *The bomb was exploded by the police*. On the other hand, it may be left *implicit*, through the removal of the optional 'by-' phrase (*The bomb was exploded*). In reaction to clauses which bear implicit agency, one can still ask *Who by?*, whereas in the case of a middle clause (*The bomb exploded*) one cannot.

The system of options available for ergativity and voice have important pragmatic and contextual implications. [...]

At first, it is best to keep the analysis as straightforward as possible. To this effect, I propose to [examine a passage] from Hemingway's [1952] *The Old Man and the Sea* [...]. As you read the passage, ask yourself a question which has become the first principle of a transitivity analysis: who or what does what to whom or what?

> He knelt down and found the tuna under the stern with the gaff and drew it toward him keeping it clear of the coiled lines. Holding the line with his left shoulder again, and bracing on his left hand and arm, he took the tuna off the gaff hook and put the gaff back in place. He put one knee on the fish and cut strips of dark red meat longitudinally from the back of the head to the tail. They were wedge-shaped strips and he cut them from next to the backbone down to the edge of the belly. When he had cut six strips he spread them out on the wood of the bow, wiped his knife on his trousers, and lifted the carcass of the bonito by the tail and dropped it overboard.

Following up the 'who does what' axiom reveals a number of dominant stylistic traits in the passage. Almost invariably, the old man is the 'doer', doing some action to some entity. The clauses in which he features are all in the simple past and are normally arranged in a sequence which reflects the temporal sequence of the events described. They contain virtually no interpretative intrusions by the narrator. In short, they reflect pure [modally] neutral narrative and with a single exception, all express material processes of doing. In all of these material processes, the old man is the ACTOR so the processes are of the *action* type. As nothing 'just happens' to him in any of these clauses, and he is firmly in control of everything he does, then a full description will specify that these clauses express material action processes of *intention*. Here are breakdowns of some typical patterns:

ACTOR	PROCESS		
He	knelt down ...		

ACTOR	PROCESS	GOAL	CIRCUMSTANCES
he	took	the tuna	off the gaff

ACTOR	PROCESS	GOAL	CIRCUMSTANCES
he	cut	them	from next to the backbone

Paul Simpson

Often, the ACTOR role is ellipted when clauses are strung together, although it is still easily inferred through reference to preceding clauses. The symbol ∅ can be used to denote this sort of implicit agency:

ACTOR	PROCESS	[connector]		
He	knelt down	and		

ACTOR	PROCESS	GOAL	CIRCUMSTANCES	[connector]
∅	found	the tuna	under the stern . . .	and . . .

ACTOR	PROCESS	GOAL	CIRCUMSTANCES	
∅	drew	it	toward him	

[...] Of a total of seventeen processes expressed in this paragraph, only one is non-material. This is a relational process which occurs in the first clause of sentence 4. By way of contrast with the dominant material – action – intention pattern, here is a breakdown of this clause:

CARRIER	PROCESS	ATTRIBUTE
They	were	wedge-shaped strips

Although there is not the space to develop a detailed interpretation of the analysis of this paragraph, a few comments are necessary before we move on to our next example. One of the stylistic consequences of the dominant material paradigm, where mental and other processes signifying reflection and deliberation are suppressed, is that it creates a highly 'actional' descriptive framework. Now, in the context of the [novel as a whole, it can be demonstrated . . .] that this type of description alternates systematically with [non-actional] paragraphs of speech and thought presentation. [...]

A further consequence of the brief analysis undertaken here is that it provides a rationale for more coherent judgements about Hemingway's style. All of the material processes identified display an inflexible pattern of transitivity, where the use of the active voice ensures that the ACTOR element always precedes the process. This invariability may simply be another aspect of the stylistic 'flatness' which typifies the [modally] neutral category of point of view. It certainly appears to have eluded many critics writing about Hemingway's style. For instance, in a much-publicized article, Levin remarks of Hemingway that 'in the technical sense, his syntax is weak' and 'his verbs not particularly energetic' [1951: 591]. There is no technical sense in which syntax can be weak or verbs energetic, yet despite the 'pre-linguistic' nature of these remarks it is still possible to see what the critic is getting at. I hope the twin features of modality and transitivity, operating in tandem, will have provided some clearer understanding of the mechanics of Hemingway's prose style.

The second illustration of the stylistic potential of the transitivity model is some-what more complex. The example chosen for analysis is one which displays positively shaded modality with events being mediated, often ironically, through an opinionated speaking voice. Part of the object of the analysis which follows will be to demonstrate how patterns of transitivity enrich this ironic technique.

[T]he opening of John le Carré's spy-novel *The Little Drummer Girl* is [...] concerned broadly with 'the Bad Godesberg incident' – an explosion resulting from a bomb

Paul Simpson

planted in the centre of a diplomatic community by an international terrorist group. This incident forms the nucleus of the first four pages of the novel, although, bizarrely, the actual explosion and its immediate consequences are never engaged with directly for any sustained period. Instead, much of the narrative is concerned with events that took place prior to or subsequent to the explosion. This is supplemented with discursive summaries of the Rhineland weather and tourist-brochure style descriptions of the residences of the diplomatic community. All of this is narrated in the third person with highly modalized language.

There is, however, one point in the sixth paragraph of the novel where the narrative does move closer to its ostensible topic as the effects of the explosion on a school bus are described. As will be seen, description of the direct consequences of the explosion is almost submerged in the generic sentences [...]:

> Somewhere in every bomb explosion there is a miracle, and in this case it was supplied by the American School bus, which had just come and gone again with most of the community's younger children who congregated every schoolday in the turning-circle not fifty metres from the epicentre. By a mercy none of the children had forgotten his homework, none had overslept or shown resistance to education on this Monday morning. So the bus got away on time. The rear windows shattered, the driver went side-winding into the verge, a French girl lost an eye, but essentially the children escaped scot-free, which was afterwards held to be a deliverance. For that also is a feature of such explosions, or at least of their immediate aftermath: a communal, wild urge to celebrate the living, rather than to waste time mourning the dead. The real grief comes later when the shock wears off, usually after several hours, though occasionally less.

Most of the first paragraph either proclaims universal truths in the form of generics ('Somewhere in every bomb explosion there is a miracle') or offers *post hoc* interpretations of the consequences of the explosion ('...but essentially the children escaped scot-free'). There is, however, a sequence of three clauses which intrudes into this framework and offers a direct, if highly condensed, account of the actual effects of the explosion. This sequence begins:

> The rear windows shattered, the driver went side-winding into the verge, a French girl lost an eye...

Like the narrative clauses identified in the paragraph from Hemingway, these clauses are temporally ordered and express material processes. But there the similarity stops. The second and third clauses constitute our first encounter with material action processes of *supervention*. In these clauses, human ACTORS perform the actions involuntarily; the processes seem to 'just happen'. The first clause requires some elaboration. It expresses an *event* process on the basis that it is performed by an inanimate ACTOR. However, the verb 'shatter' expresses one of those special types of process which permits an *ergative* interpretation (see above). Both layers of analysis are captured below:

Paul Simpson

Ergative analysis:	MEDIUM	PROCESS
Standard analysis:	ACTOR	PROCESS
	The rear windows	shattered

This is a particularly salient choice of process here. It was pointed out earlier that non-goal-directed clauses of this sort, which are neither active nor passive, are middle in voice. Consequently, the processes associated with middle clauses normally appear endogenous; that is to say, they are brought about by the single participant associated with them (the MEDIUM) and not by any external AGENT. Alternative representations of this clause would have to specify some sort of agency, either explicitly in the form of active or passive non-middle clauses:

X shattered the rear windows.
The rear windows were shattered by X.

or implicitly, in the form of a passive with the agent deleted:

The rear windows were shattered.

If we consider the three narrative clauses of the original text together, there is the impression that the processes expressed by them are simply self-engendered, uninduced by any external cause. This is odd, given that they depict the violent effects brought about precisely *by* an external cause. The impact of the bomb explosion is further diminished and, for that matter, trivialized, through the syntactic frame which incorporates these three clauses. For instance, each clause is presented in an asyndetic 'listing' fashion without the use of formal connectors. Furthermore, the consequences of the explosion – especially the French girl's loss of an eye – are clearly undermined by the following adversative clause ('but essentially the children escaped scot-free'), the content of which is manifestly at odds with what has gone before. [. . . O]ther descriptions of violence in *The Little Drummer Girl* exhibit similar transitivity patterns. [. . .]

What this brief analysis has sought to demonstrate is how a certain type of transitivity pattern, especially when developed in conjunction with a positively-shaded modality, can function as an ironizing technique. In the le Carré example, this convergence of modality and transitivity served to highlight the persona of the speaking voice whilst distancing the purported central event of the narrative. So, where the physical horror of certain events is suppressed, the opinionated subjectivity of the narrator is foregrounded. The use of the ironic narrative technique has been commented upon by critics of le Carré, one of whom remarks specifically of *The Little Drummer Girl* that

Where explanations seem unnecessary they are given, where a particularly horrifying incident seems to demand the narrator's acknowledgement of that horror, none is forthcoming. Often there is a throwaway matter-of-factness to descriptions or, again, a disturbing faux-naiveté. Such techniques give a cool pathos to parts of the narrative.

(Barley 1986: 162)

Paul Simpson

While endorsing these observations in general terms, I would want to add that a stylistic analysis will go some way towards explaining just why and how such 'throw-away matter-of-factness' and 'cool pathos' is created. Indeed, the rationale behind much modern stylistics is that not only does the use of linguistic models offer greater 'purchase' on texts but that it also provides the basis for comparative analyses of other texts using those same linguistic models. This comparative principle will further underpin the discussion of the final extract in the stylistic part of our transitivity programme.

In order to provide a complete picture of the point of view spectrum, a text which exhibits negative modal shading will be used to round off this section. This will be a short sample of 'Gothic' horror fiction which represents a genre of writing not covered so far and which should be worth exploring in terms of transitivity. In the extract below [. . .], a first-person narrator discovers that he is in the company of a less than personable companion:

> Was It – the dark form with the chain – a creature of this world, or a spectre? And again – more dreadful still – could it be that the corpses of wicked men were forced to rise, and haunt in the body the places where they had wrought their evil deeds? And was such as these my grisly neighbour? The chain faintly rattled. My hair bristled; my eyeballs seemed starting from their sockets; the damps of a great anguish were on my brow. My heart laboured as if I were crushed beneath some vast weight. Sometimes it appeared to stop its frenzied beatings, sometimes its pulsations were fierce and hurried; my breath came short and with extreme difficulty, and I shivered as if with cold; yet I feared to stir. It moved, it moaned, its fetters clanked dismally, the couch creaked and shook.
>
> 'Horror: a true tale', *Blackwoods* 89 (Harwood 1861)

The markers of negative modal shading take the form of epistemic modal verbs ('*could it be*'), modal lexical verbs of perception ('my eyeballs *seemed* starting'; 'it *appeared* to stop') and comparators based on reference to physical stimuli ('My heart laboured *as if* I were crushed'; 'I shivered *as if* with cold'). The ways in which transitivity patterns intersect with this modal shading are interesting. Despite the control that the narrator appears to have over his mental faculties, all suggestions of physical self-control disappear. Material processes of supervention signal the lack of command that the narrator has over, so to speak, his body parts. Here are a few illustrations:

ACTOR	PROCESS	
My hair	bristled	

ACTOR	PROCESS	CIRCUMSTANCES
My eyeballs	seemed starting	from their sockets

ACTOR	PROCESS	
My heart	laboured	

The abject fear which this linguistic strategy is presumably designed to convey is one feature of the extract, but the attempt to convey suspense, I would suggest, relies on another textual feature. This second pattern relates to the transitivity patterns

Paul Simpson

associated with the protagonist's 'grisly neighbour'. If we look closely at the type of process in which the apparition is *directly* involved, all it really does is 'move' (material action) and 'moan' (verbalization?). Of course, there is the suggestion that it is responsible for more 'happenings' than are attributed to it directly. Consider, for instance, the ominous sequence

> The chain faintly rattled.

The process of 'rattling' is one which allows an ergative interpretation. Although it may therefore permit agency, it can still be represented, as it is here, in the form of an agentless, middle clause. In other words, the chain just rattles, and any responsibility for the rattling is left unspecified and must be inferred from the context. Similarly, cause and effect relations are also suppressed in the final three material processes of the extract, where agentless, middle clauses help develop a picture where inanimate objects appear to have a will of their own:

> its fetters clanked dismally, the couch creaked and shook.

This pattern of transitivity squares neatly with the viewing position of the narrator. The apparition's involvement in the movement of inanimate objects, although not perceived directly, is none the less imputed. The spatial point of view established here is therefore very much akin to a cinematographic technique which is employed almost to the point of cliché in horror films. This is the technique where the action is shot from within a darkly lit room. The camera pans towards the door and then brings in the door-handle in extreme close-up. The door-handle turns. Then the door creaks as it begins to open . . . Although certainly not consciously contrived to do so, the sequence of clauses just used to describe the movement of the door in my example exhibits the same type of transitivity pattern as that used in the passage of horror fiction examined above!

The three short analyses undertaken in this section were designed to illustrate the potential of the transitivity model in stylistics. Although this type of analysis will not provide an exhaustive account of a text's meaning, it should at least offer some insights into one important feature of message construction. Furthermore, some of the ways in which transitivity and modality interact have been assessed, and this has, I hope, enriched further our understanding of point of view in narrative fiction.

Issues to consider

❑   In principle, the framework Simpson sets out here can be used to explore the actional and reflective sequences of any literary work, though of course it will be of most interest in those texts in which the transitivity pattern is particularly thematically significant. In the extract above, Simpson uses examples from a literary classic, a spy thriller and a creepy tale; you could use the framework to explore other types of literary works. Can you find any characteristic patterns – in terms of transitivity – associated with particular genres?

❑   Elsewhere in his book, Simpson shows how 'free indirect discourse' – a sort of blend of speech and thought – is used to create a 'dual voice' between character and narrator. He suggests free indirect discourse is the stylistic key to irony. Irony is a tricky problem in stylistics, since it is at least as much a readerly matter as a product inherent in the text. Irony tends to be studied within pragmatics (see B3) in order to capture this contextual dimension. However, there is no question that there are also accompanying stylistic features that encourage an ironic reading. Find a text that is usually considered to be ironic, and try to account for the stylistic features that point a reader to an ironic interpretation. Is free indirect discourse involved, or is the irony carried mainly by other means?

❑   Simpson finds a few examples where his stylistic analysis offers a more systematic and evidential basis for an impression that is articulated by a literary critic (here, Levin and Barley). You can easily find similar literary critical impressions, opinions, assertions and interpretations in discussions of literary works. Focus on one and see if the literary critic was actually onto something by trying to find the proper stylistic evidence to support their position.

QUALITATIVE, QUANTITATIVE AND MIXED METHODS RESEARCH   D12

The extracts from Zoltán Dörnyei's work here present us with a number of important arguments through which we can assess the viability of quantitative, qualitative and mixed method approaches to conducting English language studies. One point which Dörnyei makes early on when talking in general terms about the social sciences is absolutely crucial to your own study of the English language: you are researching people, and therefore any study you conduct will always have to be selective.

In any English language project that you devise, you will need to decide upon the most reliable and valid way to be selective whilst ensuring that you conduct your project in a manner which enables you to gain access to the data you require. Once you have collected your data, you need to ensure that it will enable you to produce a meaningful analysis which answers your research questions/examines your chosen area of study. In any study of the English language which you encounter as a reader/listener, whether it be quantitative, qualitative or mixed method, you need to develop the skills that enable you to consider critically the methodological choices that researchers have made so that you can judge the reliability and validity of their research findings to make an informed assessment on the overall viability of their arguments.

Zoltán Dörnyei (reprinted from *Research Methods in Applied Linguistics* (2007), Oxford: Oxford University Press, pp. 25–46)   Zoltán Dörnyei

The qualitative–quantitative distinction

Although at first sight the difference between qualitative and quantitative data/research appears to be relatively straightforward, the distinction has been the source of a great deal of discussion in the past at every conceivable level of abstraction. Without dwelling

Zoltán Dörnyei

on this issue too long, let me offer a taste of how things can get very complicated when we start discussing the QUAL–QUAN contrast.

To start with, is there really such a contrast? And if so, where exactly does it lie? Richards (2005), for example, points out that the numerical versus non-numerical distinction does not give us clear enough guidelines because qualitative researchers would almost always collect some information in numbers (for example, the age of the participants), and similarly, quantitative researchers usually also collect some non-numerical information (for example, the gender or nationality of the participants). So, as she concludes, 'qualitative and quantitative data do not inhabit different worlds. They are different ways of recording observations of the same world' (p. 36). Arguing in a similar vein, Miles and Huberman (1994) assert that in some sense, all data are qualitative because they refer to 'essences of people, objects and situations' (p. 9); sometimes we convert our raw experiences of the social world into words (i.e. QUAL), at other times into numbers (i.e. QUAN). Therefore, Sandelowski (2003) actually concludes that qualitative research is not clearly distinguishable from quantitative research because there is no consistent manner in which such a comparison can be made.

Even though I agree that QUAL and QUAN are not extremes but rather form a continuum, we still tend to compare them all the time. Why is that? I would suggest that the almost irresistible urge to contrast qualitative and quantitative research goes back to three basic sources of division between the two approaches: (a) an ideological contrast, (b) a contrast in categorization, and (c) a contrast in the perception of individual diversity. Let us look at these contrasts one by one.

Ideological differences

Although scholars in the social sciences (for example, in sociology) have been using both qualitative-like and quantitative-like data since the beginning of the twentieth century, the QUAL–QUAN distinction only emerged after number-based statistical research became dominant in the middle of the twentieth century and some scholars started to challenge this hegemony flying the 'qualitative' banner. [...] Thus, the terms 'qualitative' and 'quantitative' were originally introduced as part of, or rather for the purpose of, an ideological confrontation. In a thoughtful analysis, Schwandt (2000) describes qualitative inquiry in general as a 'reformist movement', uniting a wide variety of scholars who appear to share very little in common except their general distaste for the mainstream quantitative paradigm. As he writes,

> qualitative inquiry is a 'home' for a wide variety of scholars who often are seriously at odds with one another but who share a general rejection of the blend of scientism, foundationalist epistemology, instrumental reasoning, and the philosophical anthropology of disengagement that has marked 'mainstream' social science. (p. 190)

Having been created in the spirit of antagonism, we should not be surprised that the two terms are still often used to represent contrasting views about the world around us.

Contrasting categorizing/coding practices

One thing that is common to every research approach is that the almost limitless information obtainable from the social world around us needs to be reduced to make

Zoltán Dörnyei

it manageable. Researchers typically use 'categories' or 'codes' to structure and shape this information, but this is where the similarities between QUAL and QUAN end. We find that the nature of the categories and the categorization process in QUAL and QUAN are very different. In fact, Bazeley (2003: 414) argues that 'Codes – the way they are generated, what they stand for, and the way they are used – lie at the heart of differences between quantitative and qualitative data and analysis tools'.

Quantitative researchers define the variables they work with well in advance and assign a logical scale of values to them, which can be expressed in numbers. Thus, quantitative research can start a research project with precise *coding tables* for processing the data (for example, within the 'gender' variable, 'male' is to be assigned 1 and 'female' 2). Qualitative researchers also use coding extensively, but the QUAL categories are different in two important ways. First, they are not numerical but verbal, amounting to short textual labels. Second, they are usually not determined a priori but are left open and flexible as long as possible to be able to account for the subtle nuances of meaning uncovered during the process of investigation. For example, if we wanted to draw the boundary between two countries in an unknown terrain, the QUAN approach would be to take the map and after defining the size distribution of the two countries, draw straight lines using a ruler. In contrast, the QUAL approach would resist this top-down decision making but would expect the boundaries to naturally emerge using the inherent geographical properties of the terrain (for example, rivers and mountain ridges).

Different approaches to individual diversity

Most data collected in the social sciences, regardless of whether it is QUAL or QUAN, is related to *people* – what they do, what they are like, what they think or believe in, what they plan to do, etc. Because people differ from each other in the way they perceive, interpret, and remember things, their accounts will show considerable variation across individuals. The problem is that no matter how well-funded our research is, we can never examine all the people whose answers would be relevant to our research question, and therefore we have to face the fact that the final picture unfolding in our research will always be a function of whom we have selected to obtain our data from.

Both QUAL and QUAN researchers acknowledge this link between the specific sample of participants examined and the results obtained by the research, but the two camps consider the issue in a very different light. Quantitative researchers regard the sample-related variation as a problem which needs to be fixed. The QUAN solution is to take a large enough sample in which the idiosyncratic differences associated with the particular individuals are ironed out by the sample size and therefore the pooled results largely reflect the commonalities that exist in the data. Qualitative researchers, on the other hand, question the value of preparing an overall, average description of a larger group of people because in this way we lose the individual stories. They see this as an undesirable reduction process because in QUAL terms the real meaning lies with individual cases who make up our world. Of course, qualitative researchers are not oblivious to the fact that individuals are different, but rather than believing in a higher-level meaning that can be arrived at by summing up individual cases, they hold that there are multiple meanings to discover.

Thus, quantitative researchers follow a 'meaning in the general' strategy, whereas qualitative researchers concentrate on an in-depth understanding of the 'meaning in

Zoltán Dörnyei

the particular'. However, the story does not end here because the 'big number' approach of quantitative researchers has offered an additional bonus for QUAN data analysis, *statistics*. [...]

Statistics versus researcher sensitivity

Once quantitative researchers had gone down the 'meaning in numbers' path, a welcome bonus emerged. Mathematicians have found that if we have a sufficiently big sample size, the characteristics of the people in this group will approach a very special pattern termed 'normal distribution'. This means that within the sample a few people will display very high values, a few others very low ones, with the bulk of the sample centred around the middle or average range. This is the all-important 'bell-shaped curve' [...], and it has been found that the greater the sample, the more 'normal' the distribution and the more regular the curve becomes. [...] What makes this bell-shaped curve so important is that it has unique properties upon which it is possible to build a whole range of mathematical procedures that have led to the development of 'statistics'.

Thus, adopting the 'meaning in numbers' approach has not only offered quantitative researchers a way out of the individual respondent variation dilemma mentioned above, but it has also provided an elaborate set of statistical analytical tools to use to add systematicity to the data analysis phase rather than having to rely on the researcher's subjective interpretations. Thus, quantitative research could eliminate individual variability both at the data collection and the data analysis stages. For many scholars, the major attraction of QUAN is this systematic, 'individual-proof' nature, governed by precise rules and regulations, thus approximating the regularity of the natural sciences.

In contrast, the 'meaning in the particular' approach of qualitative research has not offered any bonus gifts for the analysis phase of qualitative research. Consequently, although qualitative research also applies various data analytical procedures to make the investigations more rigorous and systematic, at the heart of any qualitative analysis is still the researcher's subjective sensitivity, training, and experience. Thus, while no one would deny that by using qualitative methods we can uncover subtle meanings that are inevitably lost in quantitative research, QUAL is linked to two basic sources of variation, associated with the individual respondents and the individual researcher. For many scholars the major attraction of QUAL is exactly this sensitivity to the individual, but we can perhaps start sensing at this point where some of the strong emotions characterizing the QUAL–QUAN debate originate: it is all too easy to present the above contrast as the antagonistic fight between 'callous' versus 'sensitive'; or 'systematic' versus 'fuzzy'; and ultimately, between 'objective' versus 'subjective'. [...]

Three positions regarding the QUAL–QUAN difference: purist, situationalist, and pragmatist

[... T]aking theorizing to the level of abstraction of different worldviews, paradigms, and perspectives can logically lead to proposing what Rossman and Wilson (1985) called a 'purist' approach to research methodology, arguing that the qualitative and quantitative methodologies are mutually exclusive. Interestingly, although there is no shortage of convincing intellectual arguments to justify paradigm incompatibility, most researchers have actually stopped short of claiming the inevitability of this conflict

Zoltán Dörnyei

and, particularly in the past decade, scholars have started to look for some sort of an interface between the two research traditions. Miles and Huberman (1994: 4–5), for example, pointed out that 'In epistemological debates it is tempting to operate at the poles. But in the actual practice of empirical research, we believe that all of us – realists, interpretivists, critical theorists – are closer to the centre, with multiple overlaps'.

Indeed, if we stop treating QUAL and QUAN research in a very general and contrasting manner and focus on the specific research issues at hand, we find that concrete research topics vary greatly in the extent to which they lend themselves to micro- or macro-level analysis. To take an example from my own research, the concept of 'demotivation' appears to be one where a micro-level qualitative investigation can be beneficial in uncovering the subtle personal processes whereby one's enthusiasm is gradually dampened by a number of internal and external demotivating factors (Dörnyei 2001). On the other hand, the process of 'language globalization' can be investigated particularly well from a quantitative macro-perspective, determining for example how Global English impacts the acquisition and use of local languages in various speech communities (Dörnyei et al. 2006). This would suggest that both approaches have value if they are applied in the appropriate research context – a view that has been often referred to as the 'situationalist' approach to research methodology. (See Rossman and Wilson 1985.)

Although the situationalist view accepts the strengths of both research traditions, it still represents an 'either/or' approach. However, we do not necessarily have to stop here. While it is true that particular research questions or topics can be more naturally linked to either QUAL or QUAN methods, in most cases we can also look at the same research question from another angle, using the other approach, thus uncovering new aspects of the issue. For example, when considering student demotivation – which I suggested above can be successfully examined through a qualitative approach – we can also examine how extensive this problem is in our schools or how much impact it has on students' learning achievement, and these questions can be best addressed through quantitative studies. And similarly, even broad trends such as language globalization can be investigated from a micro-perspective by analyzing, for example, the day-to-day process whereby bilingual families in multicultural environments shift towards the use of one or the other language. This indicates that some sort of an integration of the two research methodologies can be beneficial to 'corroborate (provide convergence in findings), elaborate (provide richness and detail), or initiate (offer new interpretations) findings from the other method' (Rossman and Wilson 1985: 627). This is the *pragmatist* position underlying mixed methods research [. . .]

Strengths and weaknesses of mixed methods research

As a result of the growing popularity of mixed methods research, several arguments have been put forward about the value of mixing methods. Let us have a look at the most important ones.

❏   *Increasing the strengths while eliminating the weaknesses*
     The main attraction of mixed methods research has been the fact that by using both QUAL and QUAN approaches researchers can bring out the best of both paradigms, thereby combining quantitative and qualitative research strengths. [. . .] This is

Zoltán Dörnyei

further augmented by the potential that the strengths of one method can be utilized to overcome the weaknesses of another method used in the study. For example, as mentioned earlier, QUAN researchers have seen QUAL research as being too context-specific and employing unrepresentative samples – in a mixed methods study the sampling bias can be cancelled out if the selection of the qualitative participants is based on the results of an initial representative survey. [...] On the other hand, QUAL researchers usually view QUAN research as overly simplistic, decontextualized and reductionist in terms of its generalizations, failing to capture the meanings that actors attach to their lives and circumstances (Brannen 2005) – in a mixed methods study a QUAN phase can be followed by a QUAL component to neutralize this issue by adding depth to the quantitative results and thereby putting flesh on the bones.

❑ *Multi-level analysis of complex issues*
  It has been suggested by many that we can gain a better understanding of a complex phenomenon by converging numeric trends from quantitative data and specific details from qualitative data. Words can be used to add meaning to numbers and numbers can be used to add precision to words. It is easy to think of situations in applied linguistics when we are interested at the same time in both the exact nature (i.e. QUAL) and the distribution (i.e. QUAN) of a phenomenon (for example, why do some teenage boys consider modern language learning 'girlish' and how extensive is this perception?). Mixed methods research is particularly appropriate for such multi-level analyses because it allows investigators to obtain data about both the individual and the broader societal context.

❑ *Improved validity*
  Mixed methods research has a unique potential to produce evidence for the validity of research outcomes through the convergence and corroboration of the findings. [...] Indeed, improving the validity of research has been at the heart of the notion of triangulation ever since its introduction in the 1970s. Corresponding evidence obtained through multiple methods can also increase the generalizability – that is, external validity – of the results.

❑ *Reaching multiple audiences*
  A welcome benefit of combining QUAL and QUAN methods is that the final results are usually acceptable for a larger audience than those of a monomethod study would be. A well-executed mixed methods study has multiple selling points and can offer something to everybody, regardless of the paradigmatic orientation of the person. Of course, there is also the danger that the study might fall through the 'paradigmatic crack' and alienate everybody, but in the current supportive climate this is less likely.

Weaknesses

Mixing qualitative and quantitative methods has come to be seen by many as a forward-pointing and potentially enriching approach, but as Mason (2006) cautions us, the reasoning or logic behind such an assumption is not always as readily expressed as is the sentiment itself. Hesse-Biber and Leavy (2006) go even further when they suggest that the popular belief that the sum may be greater than its parts is not necessarily true. They cite an interview with Janice Morse, who warns about the danger of using mixed methods research as a 'substitute for sharp conceptual thinking and insightful analyses' (p. 334). Indeed, it would be clearly counterproductive to adopt a strategy whereby 'when in doubt, mix methods . . .'.

Hesse-Biber and Leavy (2006) also raise the issue of how well-versed any given researcher can be in both types of methodology, which leads to a critical question: Can more harm than good be done when researchers are not adequately trained in both methods? This is a realistic danger because the vast majority of researchers lack methodological skills to handle both QUAL and QUAN data. And even if we can expect this situation to improve with the growing awareness of mixed methods research, the question still remains: Apart from a relatively small number of unique, methodologically ambidextrous specimen, can we assume that the vision of a multimethodologically savvy new breed of researchers is realistic?

Finally, Maxwell and Loomis (2003) highlight a further issue, the diversity of the possible combinations of different methods, which is, as the scholars argue, far greater than any typology can adequately encompass. One cannot help wondering whether there is really a principled approach to guiding the variety of combinations so that we do not end up with an 'anything goes as long as you mix them' mentality.

Issues to consider

❑   Out of the three approaches to selecting methodologies outlined by Dörnyei, the *purist*, *situationalist* and *pragmatist* approach, which do you find most convincing? Why? Considering the strengths and weaknesses of all three approaches, discuss your individual position on this issue in small groups.

❑   Revisit the methodological decisions that you made as part of the activity you conducted in C12, where you were asked to choose a specific methodological approach in order to conduct an English language project in various contexts:

   ○   Classify your decisions for each of these data collection scenarios as *purist*, *situationalist* or *pragmatist*.

   ○   On the basis of this classification and on the arguments presented by Dörnyei, would you revise the type of methodology(ies) which you selected for your data collection? Why/why not?

❑   Compared with the more traditional quantitative and qualitative paradigms, it is clear that the mixed methods approach is still very much in the process of development. As Dörnyei has shown us, it has many strengths, but there are also weaknesses, and important issues still have to be clarified. Studies of the English language, as a part of empirically based studies within the social sciences, can aid this development. Dörnyei is very much in favour of a mixed methods approach, and he embraces this in his own research. On the basis of the strengths and weaknesses of a mixed methods approach outlined by Dörnyei and on the knowledge you have gained from this strand across the book, how can researchers favouring mixed methods in English language studies ensure that they do not fall foul of the 'anything goes as long as you mix them' mentality to which Dörnyei refers?

D13　**RESEARCHING 'REAL' LANGUAGE**

Writing from a social science perspective, Bob Carter and Alison Sealey take an overview of the way that linguistics as a discipline has developed in the modern era. Their primary principle is the 'applied' nature of any linguistic theorising, and from that position they find the main paradigms in theoretical linguistics disappointing. Developing the notion of linguistic study as inherently and necessarily a matter of *applied linguistics*, they work back from that to a theoretical view of language that is fully contextualised and humanistic. It is a perspective that is shared by the authors of this book.

Bob Carter and Alison Sealey (reprinted from 'Researching "real" language', in B. Carter and C. New (eds) *Making Realism Work* (2004), London: Routledge, pp. 111–30).

Bob Carter and Alison Sealey

The study of language: contemporary debates

Like many of the disciplines whose subject matter is closely concerned with human beings, linguistics has had to struggle for its place in the academy. Its definition as 'the scientific study of language' would seem to be designed partly with this in mind, and traditional linguistics identifies its remit as the provision of a 'grammatical model' of a language, which is an attempt to represent systematically and overtly what the native speaker of that language intuitively knows. Linguistics is routinely acknowledged to overlap with many other disciplines, including psychology, philosophy, anthropology and sociology, and its concerns have included the identification and description of different languages around the world, the history of changes in language through time, the relationship of the sub-systems of language to each other (sounds, units of meaning, vocabulary, syntax) and so on. To some extent, linguistics has needed to distinguish its own field of study from other, cognate areas, and two of the key contributors to the discipline [Saussure and Chomsky] have been important in this respect. They are figures with whose work social scientists are likely to be familiar, [...] because they are concerned with the nature of the real and with stratified accounts of language.

Language as a system

The structuralist Saussure is responsible for positing the distinction between *langue*, the underlying totality of the resources of a language, or the capacity of the grammatical system which is housed in the human brain, and *parole*, the act of language use by an individual in a specific context. Saussure was concerned with the formal properties of the linguistic system which make possible a potentially infinite number of combinations of individual units, according to a system of syntactic categories, each having distinct properties. Saussure's work thus introduces a stratified view of language, one that distinguishes between its actualisation by real speakers in specific social settings and a conception of it as a system of interrelated structures and mutually defining entities. Importantly, this opens up the possibility of an interplay between utterances and these systemic features; meaning, for example, is not only speaker derived, but for Saussure is also partly made possible by the arbitrary relation between signifier and signified.

The generativist Chomsky drew a distinction between *competence* and *performance* which parallels Saussure's *langue/parole*. In an often-quoted passage, he makes clear that linguistics is concerned with idealised representations of what are essentially unobservable mental processes. 'Linguistic theory,' he states:

Bob Carter
and Alison
Sealey

> is concerned primarily with an ideal speaker-listener, in a completely homogeneous speech-community, who knows its language perfectly and is unaffected by such grammatically irrelevant conditions as memory limitations, distractions, shifts of attention or interest, and errors (random or characteristic) in applying his knowledge of the language in actual performance. This seems to me to have been the position of the founders of modern general linguistics, and no cogent reason for modifying it has been offered.
>
> (Chomsky 1965: 3–4)

Empirically observed language production is deemed to be of only marginal interest to this project, and research in this tradition sets greater store by the intuitions of native speakers' judgements as to whether or not a particular construction is grammatical in the language in question.

In both Saussurean and Chomskyan approaches to linguistics, the relation between the structural elements of language and their empirical manifestations in language-in-use is, in our view, rather one-sided. That is, people's actual language behaviour is contingent, 'imprecise' and ephemeral, whereas the systemic features of language are endurable, structured and consistent. These linguists' work thus tends to diminish the role in research of transient, empirically observable language use in favour of the stable, non-observable structural entities which are held to govern or regulate its use by individual speakers, and so encourages a view of *langue* or competence as autonomous entities. With its echoes of older philosophical claims about the distinction between 'appearance' (actual language use) and 'reality' (what underlies or generates actual language use), this is a form of realism from which we would wish to distance ourselves.

[...]

Language, society and human practice

[...] Some approaches [to the study of language and society] constitute language and social structures as discrete, although related, entities or objects of study which can be readily demarcated. The more robust forms of structuralism suggest that meaning is a product of the relationship between signs, and is thus internal to the linguistic system itself. We would reject the disregard of human practice which is implied in this perspective. Archer [1988], too, has exposed the downwards conflationism of Chomskyan linguistics, which reduces the independence of the socio-cultural level to 'its ingenuity in elaborating permutations of the code', denying to its users the potential to make any 'reciprocal contribution to altering the code itself' (1988: 39). On the other hand, the stronger versions of relativism [such as the Sapir-Whorf hypothesis: see B13] suggest that all meanings are indexical: context-bound, and reducible to what human beings say. We would reject in this perspective the implied disregard of the constraints and enablements of language itself. Our position thus lies

D13

**Bob Carter
and Alison
Sealey**

somewhere between these two extremes, recognising the importance of both elements, as the realist language philosophers Devitt and Sterelny also do:

> A word's relation to others in the language – *internal* relations – may often be important to its meaning; for example, the relation of 'pediatrician' to 'doctor'. But a language's relations to the nonlinguistic world – its *external* relations – are always important.
>
> (Devitt and Sterelny 1999: 263)

The conceptualisation of language as a form of human practice is in some senses a materialist position, recognising as it does that human practice in the world has temporal and logical priority over language. That is to say, that the human being comes before language: each individual exists in the world, and has material needs, before having access to language. Desires to do things in the world may precede the acts in which people engage, and precede the language used to accomplish those acts. However, in the linguistically saturated world inhabited by the contemporary human species, there is perpetual interplay between practice and language, with the existence of language representing a quantum leap in the human potential for practice in the world.

Language as a cultural emergent property

The interplay of language and practice to which we have just alluded rests not only on the assertion of the temporal priority of human practice, but also on the stratified social ontology of culture, structure and agency. [... R]ealists claim that the world is not directly produced or constructed by us, but is rather the complex outcome of the interactions between structural contexts and ourselves. They view social relations and structures as emergent properties of social interaction (Archer 1995). Since emergence is a key term [...], we shall take a moment to explore it in more detail.

Emergence refers to the generation of new entities or phenomena from the combination of other entities or phenomena. Because the new entity is emergent from this combination, it possesses certain distinct features, namely: irreducibility to any of its constituent elements; autonomy from any of its constituent elements; ability to interact with any of its constituent elements. Thus languages are emergent products of the engagement of human practice with the material world: they cannot be reduced to any of their constituents (that is, languages are not merely what human beings say, nor are they simply an internal relationship between linguistic signs, nor yet a grammar which is grasped intuitively and is not corrigible by human intervention); they have a partial independence or autonomy both from human beings (we learn a language that pre-exists us) and from the material world (through language people create things, such as stories and characters which have no physical counterpart); and finally, language is itself a practice, capable of enabling people to act upon and modify the world (we do things with language), as well as to act upon themselves and others (language enables us to reflect upon, interpret and make judgements about ourselves and others). In short, we support Archer's description of language as a 'cultural emergent property' (Archer 2000).

**Bob Carter
and Alison
Sealey**

Of course, if language is emergent in the sense outlined above, it is itself capable of combining with other elements in the social world to produce what Archer terms second and third order emergence. Thus, for instance, writing is a technology emerging from the combination of human practice with language. The invention of writing transforms the potentiality of language immeasurably by freeing language from its dependence on human interlocution. This is not a normative statement: we are not saying that literate societies are preferable to oral ones – and in any case few contemporary societies remain completely uninfluenced by the phenomenon of literacy. However, the central (realist) point is that language as a cultural emergent property has powers and properties, and that written language, as a second order emergent property from sound-based verbal economies, possesses a more extensive range of properties and powers. It is important to note, though, that these properties and powers are experienced as constraints and enablements by people only *in their practice* in the world. It is only when individuals or groups try to modify their circumstances, or resist the efforts of others to change them, that the properties of language become causally influential. But the causal influence is mediated through agency, through social interaction.

It follows from this that access to writing does not necessarily entail a restructuring of thought: it is an enablement which exists *in potentia*; its realisation depends on human practice, on people wishing to do things in the world. How people employ writing at any historical moment or conjuncture depends not on writing itself but on the circumstances of its use: the intentions of its users, their respective political and economic influence, their control of military and other resources and so on. To this extent we concur with the characterisation of literacy by Street (1984) as inherently 'ideological', rather than 'autonomous', since literacy is always literacy in use. Literacy is a matter of human practice first and foremost.

Nevertheless, as a second order emergent property, writing is not reducible to its constituents, and retains a *partial* autonomy from them. Amongst the core features of texts is their suitability for travel, especially once technological developments in typography made possible efficient reproduction. This allows texts, in marked contrast to embodied utterances, to move beyond their site of production, thus changing the communicative context dramatically 'both as regards the emitter and as regards the receivers, with consequent implications for the nature of the message' (Goody 1986). Thus one potential of written texts is that they can lead to abstract, analytic thought; by making memory more reliable they enable words to have histories, rituals to have rules, texts to have critics. Writing, as Goody has put it, is the 'technology of the intellect'. Above all, writing establishes an important condition for the development of what Popper (Popper and Eccles 1977) has termed 'World Three', the emergent realm of the products of human consciousness.

The independence of the text, in this sense, makes possible certain transformations of the social and natural world. Constitutions can be written, legal systems can be codified, files can be kept and doctrines can be fought over as a result of writing. Moreover, the effects of writing are cumulative. Ideas, plans and traditions become ever more dense as textual commentary builds upon textual commentary and so place greater and greater pressure on those excluded from access to, and participation in, the ever expanding World Three of human knowledge. Interdiscursivity and intertextuality,

Bob Carter
and Alison
Sealey

both emergent properties of chirographic cultures, permit heightened forms of linguistic reflexivity as well as the commodification of language (Chouliariki and Fairclough 1999).

A [. . .] social constructivist perspective often includes a formulation in which language/discourse and social action are mutually constitutive of each other. However, as Archer has indicated, formulations involving 'mutual constitution' may be associated with 'central conflation', and run the risk of implying temporal conjunction between the two elements, leading to an 'inability to examine the interplay' between them over longer periods of time (Archer 1988: 87). One advantage of an 'emergent property' view of language is that it can free accounts of speakers and the language they produce from the 'eternal present' implied in constructivist descriptions: speakers no longer have to be thought of as simultaneously bringing into being that to which they are responding. Texts (especially written texts) produced by long dead social actors are part of the cultural context within which the current inhabitants of the social world interact. In the next section, we consider further some of the properties of language itself which contemporary research identifies.

Identifying 'the real' in linguistics

It is perhaps unsurprising [. . .] that the notion of 'the real' is important in contemporary debates in the discipline. 'Real language' is particularly salient in dialogue between 'pure' and 'applied' linguists. While the former are likely to claim that 'mainstream' linguistic work is – and should be – mainly concerned with I-language, that is, the cognitive system underlying the ordinary use of language, applied linguists, such as Brumfit, are more inclined to identify their priority as 'the theoretical and empirical investigation of real-world problems in which language is a central issue' (2001: 169). 'Real' is used in this debate with different shades of meaning. For autonomous linguistics, it concerns 'the mechanisms in the underlying linguistic reality which allow us to characterise these expressions [sets of sentences] as well-formed' (Carr 1990: 33). Applied linguists, on the other hand, tend to bring to the fore the 'real' world of sensory experience, so that 'real' can become a near synonym for 'empirical'. The 'real-world' problems with which applied linguistics is concerned include matters of practice and policy, such as teaching foreign languages, producing translations appropriate for specific commercial transactions, or applying knowledge about language in the development of government policies for education.

In this context, 'real language' is either the system 'underlying' actual utterances, making the latter of limited interest to linguists, or it is attested language, words which have actually been spoken by someone somewhere in the context of some socio-communicative purpose. It will be evident that, notwithstanding Chomsky's association with realism via the concept of generative mechanisms, our emergentist position is one which accommodates not only the unobservable systemic features of language, but also attested language use. This is partly because the Chomskyan project has in many ways failed the test of encounters with empirical data. As de Beaugrande puts it, '"generativist" theory-driven procedures preclude the description of adequate data in practice' (1997: 35). Devitt and Sterelny (1999) provide a partial explanation of why this is so. A key criticism which they make of the generative linguists in the Chomskyan tradition is that they conflate two kinds of 'system'. On the one hand,

D13

Bob Carter and Alison Sealey

there is the syntactic structure of linguistic symbols; on the other, there is speakers' ability to manipulate language to produce meanings. What Devitt and Sterelny wish to query is the assumption that these are a single phenomenon, demanding of a single explanation. 'Competence,' they argue, 'together with various other aspects of the speaker's psychology, produce linguistic symbols, but a theory of one is not a theory of the other' (1999: 116–17). Further, they claim that '[t]his conflation of symbol and competence is the first and perhaps the most important problem about current views of competence . . . Why suppose that a grammar explains competence at all?' (p. 167). They prefer to maintain 'a distinction between two sorts of rules, the "structure-rules" governing the products of a competence, and the "processing-rules" governing the production of those products, rules governing the *exercise* of the competence' (p. 171).

Devitt and Sterelny's position makes the enterprise of identifying the neuro-biological dimension of linguistics of far less central importance. They concede (as would we) that linguists' intuitions about grammaticality provide evidence about certain aspects of language, but it is indirect evidence. 'The direct evidence', they continue, 'is provided by the reality itself, the sentences people produce and understand' (p. 183). This position is consistent with that of Pawson, when he says that it is 'utterances [that] have to be the focus of any theoretical discussion of language' (Pawson 1989: 91). A growing number of linguists now take such a position, having recognised that '[l]anguage by itself can be described in "purely linguistic" terms only if it can hold firm and continue to subsist and operate upon its own internal, standing constraints' (de Beaugrande 1997: 36). Evidence suggests that language, as a product of human beings engaged in social interaction, is shaped by much which lies beyond its own internal constraints.

It will be a claim familiar to [our] readers [. . .] that only an acknowledgement of the distinctive properties of culture, structure and agency makes possible consideration of the interplay between them. [. . . W]e would point to the importance of identifying: how the linguistic system itself constrains and enables the communicative intentions of speakers, and, as a cultural emergent property, manifests a partial autonomy from them; how speakers maintain their agential capacity to exercise choice, particularly at the level of situated interaction; and how social structures constrain speakers' choices (which is of central concern in sociolinguistics). [. . .]

[We] require a theoretical perspective able to keep the interplay between the different domains of social life (Layder 1997) always within view, a perspective whose concepts not only reflect agency and structure, but one which also recognises that the effects of agency and structure on social activities and practices are variable and depend upon the relative influence of the different social domains. This, in a nutshell, is the potential offered by recent realist writers for the study of language: an approach which is able to see a role for speakers and their intentions, which acknowledges the weight of history on present action, and which also accommodates the partial autonomy of language.

Issues to consider

❏ Carter and Sealey place idealised forms of linguistic theory (such as Chomskyan linguistics) and relativist forms of linguistics (Sapir-Whorf) as polar opposites, and they then place their own position between these extremes. Do you think this characterisation is fair? Is there a 'middle way' between the two positions? Is it legitimate to arrange linguistics on such a scale?

❑   The 'emergentist' view, according to Carter and Sealey above, regards language as possessing 'irreducibility to any of its constituent elements' and 'autonomy from any of its constituent elements'; it is a holistic and inherently contextualised phenomenon. If this is true, how could we ever engage in analysis at the different levels of the rank-scale, as this book is arranged? It would become illegitimate to study syntax in its own right, or morphology, or phonology. Would this be a problem? What would we lose by ensuring our analyses connected everything with everything else? In short, what would an 'emergentist' linguistics actually look like in practice?

❑   There are many other theoretical approaches to language study that challenge the assumptions of idealised forms of linguistics: cognitive linguistics, integrational linguistics, social semiotics, ethnomethodological approaches within sociolinguistics, corpus linguistic methods within applied linguistics – to name only a few. You could investigate these approaches by following up the Further Reading section at the end of this book.

FURTHER READING

Sounds

The Routledge English Language Introduction (RELI) to phonetics and phonology is Beverley Collins and Inger Mees' (2013) *Practical Phonetics and Phonology: A Resource Book for Students.*

Other good introductions to this field include Knowles (1987) and Odden (2005). Ladefoged (2001) is the classic detailed introductory course. Ashby and Maidment (2005) is a good place to start on the science of phonetics. Foulkes and Docherty (1999) is an excellent collection of sociophonetic studies. Ball and Rahilly (1999) is a good, systematic introduction. Zsiga (2012) is a comprehensive student handbook covering phonetics and phonology.

Words

The RELI book that addresses lexicology is Howard Jackson's (2002) *Grammar and Vocabulary: A Resource Book for Students.*

Aitchison (2002), Jackson and Zé Amvela (2007) are also good, traditional textbooks. The second part of Crystal (2003) deals with English vocabulary. Other good introductions to the study of words are Katamba (1994), Singleton (2000), and the short, readable Halliday and Yallop (2007). Schmitt and McCarthy (1998) provide a teaching perspective. Sinclair (2004) and Carter (2007) are more advanced treatments.

Meanings

The RELI book that addresses meanings is Joan Cutting's (2015) *Pragmatics and Discourse: A Resource Book for Students.*

Cummings (2005) gives a good introductory, multidisciplinary perspective on pragmatics. Thomas (1995) and Grundy (2008) provide entertaining and informative introductory pragmatics texts. Birner (2012) is very good. Harris, Grainger and Mullany (2006) builds upon the political apologies data in C3 if you are interested in investigating this further. Leech (1983) covers a range of introductory areas of pragmatics. Holmes (1995) gives a very useful overview of politeness analysis. Hurford, Heasley and Smith (2007) provides a thorough exploration of semantics study. Cruse (1986) gives a detailed overview of lexical semantics.

Grammar

The RELI book that addresses grammar is Roger Berry's (2012) *English Grammar: A Resource Book for Students.*

Crystal (2004) is a good overall review of grammar. Huddleston and Pullum (2005) is a basic introduction. Sinclair (1990) is a good, usage-based account of English grammar. Greenbaum and Quirk (1990) is probably the standard textbook. Thompson (2004) is the best introduction to functional grammar. Carter and McCarthy (2007) provides a comprehensive guide to modern-day spoken and written English, based upon the Cambridge International Corpus.

Discourse

The RELI book that addresses discourse is also Joan Cutting's (2015) *Pragmatics and Discourse: A Resource Book for Students*. You may also be interested in Paul Simpson and Andrea Mayr's (2009) *Language and Power: A Resource Book for Students* and Alan Durant and Marina Lambrou's (2009) *Language and Media: A Resource Book for Students*.

Introductory-level books on discourse include Cameron (2001), Carter (1997) and Gee (2005). Jaworski and Coupland (2006) is a good advanced collection of papers in discourse analysis. Johnstone (2002) is a more advanced textbook. Cameron (2001) is especially good for spoken language. Schiffrin et al. (2001) is an advanced handbook. Blommaert (2006) is an excellent discussion.

Acquisition

The RELI book that addresses child language acquisition is Jean Stilwell Peccei's (2006) *Child Language: A Resource Book for Students*.

Other good treatments include O'Grady (2005), Foster-Cohen (1999), Lust (2006) and the comprehensive volumes by Bowerman and Levinson (2001) and Gleason and Ratner (2008). See also Clark (2003). There is a handbook by Fletcher and MacWhinney (1996).

Processing

The RELI book that addresses psychological processing is John Field's (2006) *Psycholinguistics: A Resource Book for Students*.

Field (2004) is also a highly readable textbook. A general overview is provided by the accessible Aitchison (2007). Other introductions to psycholinguistics include Garman (2008), Steinberg and Sciarini (2006), Steinberg, Nagata and Aline (2001), Gleason and Ratner (1998), Whitney (1998) and Warren (2012). There is a handbook by Gaskell (2007).

History

The RELI book that addresses the history of English is Dan McIntyre's (2006) *History of English: A Resource Book for Students*.

The classic work is by Baugh and Cable (2012), now in its sixth edition. A more recent perspective is provided by Culpeper (2005a). Smith (2005) is an accessible study, and Smith (1996) is a more advanced though still readable scholarly treatment. Other classics include Strang (1999), which goes in reverse chronological order, Barber (2000) and Freeborn (2006). Fennell (2000) offers a sociolinguistic view of the historical evolution of English.

Society

The RELI book that addresses the field of sociolinguistics is Peter Stockwell's (2007) *Sociolinguistics: A Resource Book for Students*.

Other accessible, lively introductions are Meyerhoff (2006) and Holmes (2008). Mesthrie et al. (2009) also gives comprehensive coverage. Llamas, Mullany and Stockwell (2007) is a good reference work. Coupland and Jaworski (2009) provides a range of up-to-date, informative readings. Wardhaugh (2009) is a more advanced, detailed account.

Globalisation

The RELI book that addresses globalisation is Jennifer Jenkins' (2015) *Global Englishes: A Resource Book for Students*.

Other good, accessible surveys are Mesthrie and Bhatt's (2008) examination of new Englishes and Rubdy and Saraceni's (2006) account. Kirkpatrick (2007) is particularly useful from both a general introductory point of view and an English language teaching perspective. Jenkins (2007) provides an advanced account of English as a lingua franca. Kachru et al. (2009) provides a detailed handbook which covers a wide range of contemporary World Englishes themes. Melchers and Shaw (2011) is a good introduction.

Stylistics

The RELI book that covers stylistics is Paul Simpson's (2014) *Stylistics: A Resource Book for Students*.

The other classic introductions to the field are Short (1996) and Verdonk (2002). The series *From Text to Context* (Verdonk 1993, Verdonk and Weber 1995 and Culpeper, Short and Verdonk 1998) contains collections of articles in stylistics. Toolan (2001) provides a stylistic approach to narrative. Wales (2001) is a glossary and dictionary of the field. Carter and Stockwell (2008) collects classic articles from the last 40 years, and Lambrou and Stockwell (2007) collects recent work in stylistics. There is a handbook by Stockwell and Whiteley (2014).

Methods

The RELI book that covers methods is Alison Sealey's (2010) *Researching English Language: A Resource Book for Students*.

Dörnyei (2007) presents a thorough account of quantitative, qualitative and mixed-methodological approaches as well as an informative discussion on methodological debates. Silverman (2006) is a good guide to follow if conducting qualitative research. Tashakkori and Teddlie (2003) is an advanced account of mixed-methodologies. Milroy (1987) and Cameron (2001) are classic accounts which provide excellent foundations for producing rigorous language studies. Bowern (2008) is an interesting and accessible account of the various stages of conducting linguistic fieldwork.

Theory

The RELI book that addresses the notion of the theory underlying language study is Mark Robson and Peter Stockwell's (2005) *Language in Theory: A Resource Book for Students.*

There are numerous highly advanced, theoretical and philosophical works on language and linguistics. However, good introductions include Wardhaugh (1993), Chapman (2000 and 2006); and Trask and Stockwell (2007).

The English language

Finally, there are numerous introductions to the general field of the English language. Most of them focus on the language up to the level of the sentence, though some also include the levels of discourse, pragmatics, ideology and social aspects as we have covered in this book. The best ones in our opinion are the following: Crystal (2003), Kuiper and Allan (2004), Yule (2006), McGregor (2009), Culpeper et al. (2009); and Jackson and Stockwell (2010).

REFERENCES

Adams, D. (1979) *The Hitchhiker's Guide to the Galaxy*. London: Pan.

Adler, A. (1956) *The Individual Psychology of Alfred Adler: A Systematic Presentation in Selections from his Writings*. New York: Basic Books.

Aijmer, K. (1996) *Conversational Routines in English: Convention and Creativity*. Harlow: Longman.

Aitchison, J. (1997) *The Language Web: The Power and Problem of Words*. Cambridge: Cambridge University Press.

Aitchison, J. (2002) *Words in the Mind: An Introduction to the Mental Lexicon* (third edition). Oxford: Wiley Blackwell.

Aitchison, J. (2007) *The Articulate Mammal: An Introduction to Psycholinguistics* (fourth edition). London: Routledge.

Aldiss, B. (1969) *Barefoot in the Head*. London: Faber & Faber.

Altman, I. and Dalmas, A. (1973) *Social Penetration: The Development of Interpersonal Relationships*. New York: Holt, Rinehart and Winston.

Alvesson, M. and Deetz, S. (2000) *Doing Critical Management Research*. London: Sage.

Ammon, U. (2000) 'Towards more fairness in international English: linguistic rights of non-native speakers?' in R. Phillipson (ed.) *Rights to Language: Equity, Power and Education*, Mahwah: Lawrence Erlbaum Associates, pp. 111–16.

Archer, M. (1988) *Culture and Agency: The Place of Culture in Social Theory*. Cambridge: Cambridge University Press.

Archer, M. (1995) *Realist Social Theory: A Morphogenetic Account*. Cambridge: Cambridge University Press.

Archer, M. (2000) *Being Human: The Problem of Agency*. Cambridge: Cambridge University Press.

Ashby, M. and Maidment, J. (2005) *Introducing Phonetic Science*. Cambridge: Cambridge University Press.

Austin, J.L. (1962) *How to Do Things with Words*. London: Oxford University Press.

Austin, J.L. (1975) *How to Do Things with Words* (second edition). Oxford: Clarendon Press.

Austin, J.P.M. (1990) 'Politeness revisited – the dark side', in A. Bell and J. Holmes (eds) *New Zealand Ways of Speaking English*, Clevedon and Philadelphia: Multilingual Matters, pp. 277–93.

Ball, M. and Rahilly, J. (1999) *Phonetics: The Science of Speech*. London: Arnold.

Banfield, A. (1982) *Unspeakable Sentences*. New York: Routledge & Kegan Paul.

Banville, John (1989) *The Book of Evidence*. London: Minerva.

Barber, C. (2000) *The English Language: A Historical Introduction*. Cambridge: Cambridge University Press.

Barley, T. (1986) *Taking Sides: The Fiction of John Le Carre*. Milton Keynes: Open University Press.

Baugh, A. and Cable, T. (2012) *A History of the English Language* (sixth edition). Abingdon: Routledge.

Bavin, E. (1992) 'The acquisition of Walpiri', in D. Slobin (ed.) *The Crosslinguistic Study of Language Acquisition, Vol 3*, Hillsdale: Lawrence Erlbaum Associates, pp. 309–72.

Bazeley, P. (2003) 'Computerized data analysis for mixed methods research', in A. Tashakkori and C. Teddlie (eds) *Handbook of Mixed Methods in Social and Behavioral Research*, Thousand Oaks: Sage, pp. 385–422.

BBC (1992) *BBC English Dictionary*. London: HarperCollins.

Bell, D. (1994) 'Negotiation in the workplace: the view from a political linguist', in A. Firth (ed.) *The Discourse of Negotiation: Studies of Language in the Workplace*, Oxford: Elsevier Science, pp. 41–58.

Berry, M. (1981) 'Systemic linguistics and discourse analysis: a multi-layered approach to exchange structure', in M. Coulthard and M. Montgomery (eds) *Studies in Discourse Analysis*, London: Routledge and Kegan Paul, pp. 120–45.

Berry, R. (2012) *English Grammar: A Resource Book for Students*. London: Routledge.

Bhatia, T. (2001) 'Language mixing in global advertising', in E. Thumboo (ed.) *The Three Circles of English*, Singapore: Singapore University Press, pp. 195–215.

Bhatia, T. (2006) 'World Englishes in global advertising', in B. Kachru, Y. Kachru and C.L. Nelson (eds) *The Handbook of World Englishes*, Oxford: Blackwell, pp. 601–19.

Biber, D., Johansson, S., Leech, G., Conrad, S. and Finegan, E. (1999) *Longman Grammar of Spoken and Written English*. Harlow: Pearson.

Birner, B. (2012) *Introduction to Pragmatics*. Oxford: Wiley-Blackwell.

Blommaert, J. (2006) *Discourse*. Cambridge: Cambridge University Press.

Bloom, K. (1990) 'Selectivity and early infant vocalization', in J.T. Enns (ed.) *The Development of Attention: Research and Theory*, New York: North-Holland, pp. 121–36.

Bloomfield, L. (1933) *Language*. London: Allen & Unwin.

Bolinger, D. (1975) 'Meaning and memory', *Forum Linguisticum* 1: 2–14.

Bolton, K. (2006) 'World Englishes today', in B. Kachru, Y. Kachru and C.L. Nelson (eds) *The Handbook of World Englishes*, Oxford: Blackwell, pp. 240–69.

Bortoni-Ricardo, S.M. (1985) *The Urbanisation of Rural Dialect Speakers: A Socio-linguistic Study in Brazil*. Cambridge: Cambridge University Press.

Bowerman, M. and Levinson, S. (eds) (2001) *Language Acquisition and Conceptual Development*. Cambridge: Cambridge University Press.

Bowern, C. (2008) *Linguistic Fieldwork: A Practical Guide*. Basingstoke: Palgrave Macmillan.

Brannen, J. (2005) *Mixed Methods Research: A Discussion Paper*. Southampton: ESRC National Centre for Research Methods.

Brewer, J.P. (1986) 'Durative marker or hypercorrection? The case of -*s* in the WPA ex-slave narratives', in M.B. Montgomery and G. Bailey (eds) *Language Variety in the South*, Tuscaloosa: University of Alabama Press, pp. 131–48.

Brown, G. (1990) *Listening to Spoken English* (second edition). Harlow: Longman.

Brown, G. and Yule, G. (1983) *Discourse Analysis*. Cambridge: Cambridge University Press.

Brown, P. and Levinson, S.C. (1987) *Politeness: Some Universals in Language Usage*. Cambridge: Cambridge University Press.

Brown, R., Cazden, C. and Bellugi, U. (1968) 'The child's grammar from i to iii', in J.P. Hill (ed.) *The Second Annual Minnesota Symposium on Child Psychology*, Minneapolis: University of Minnesota Press, pp. 28–73.

Brumfit, C. (2001) *Individual Freedom in Language Teaching: Helping Learners to Develop a Dialect of their Own*. Oxford: Oxford University Press.

Brutt-Griffler, J. (2002) *World English: A Study of its Development*. Clevedon: Multilingual Matters.

Cameron, D. (2001) *Working with Spoken Discourse*. London: Sage.

Carlson, L. (1983) *Dialogue Games*. Dordrecht: Reidel.

Carr, P. (1990) *Linguistic Realities: An Autonomist Metatheory for the Generative Enterprise*. Cambridge: Cambridge University Press.

Carter, R. (1987) *Vocabulary: Applied Linguistic Perspectives*. London: Allen & Unwin.

Carter, R. (1997) *Investigating English Discourse*. London: Routledge.

Carter, R. (2007) *Vocabulary: Applied Linguistic Perspectives* (second edition). London: Routledge.

Carter, R. and McCarthy, M. (2007) *The Cambridge Grammar of English: A Comprehensive Guide*. Cambridge: Cambridge University Press.

Carter, R. and Stockwell, P. (eds) (2008) *The Language and Literature Reader*. Abingdon: Routledge.

Chambers Dictionary (1993) Edinburgh: Chambers Harrap.

Chambers, J. (1995) *Sociolinguistic Theory*. New York: Blackwell.

Chapman, S. (2000) *Philosophy for Linguists: An Introduction*. London: Routledge.

Chapman, S. (2006) *Thinking about Language: Theories of English*. Basingstoke: Palgrave Macmillan.

Cheshire, J. (1982) *Variation in an English Dialect: A Sociolinguistic Study*. Cambridge: Cambridge University Press.

Cheshire, J. (2000) 'The telling or the tale? Narratives and gender in adolescent friendship networks', *Journal of Sociolinguistics* 4: 234–62.

Chomsky, N. (1965) *Aspects of the Theory of Syntax*. Cambridge: MIT Press.

Chouliariki, L. and Fairclough, N. (1999) *Discourse in Late Modernity: Rethinking Critical Discourse Analysis*. Edinburgh: Edinburgh University Press.

Clark, E. (2003) *First Language Acquisition*. Cambridge: Cambridge University Press.

Coates, J. (1995) *Women, Men and Language*. Harlow: Longman.

Coates, J. (1996) *Women Talk*. Oxford: Blackwell.

Coates, J. (1997) 'Competing discourses of femininity', in H. Kotthoff and R. Wodak (eds) *Communicating Gender in Context*, Amsterdam: Benjamins, pp. 285–313.

Cobuild (1995) *The Cobuild English Dictionary*. London: HarperCollins.

Cochran, M., Larner, M., Riley, D., Gunnarsson, L. and Henderson, C. (1990) *Extending Families: The Social Networks of Parents and their Children*. Cambridge: Cambridge University Press.

Cohen, A. (1982) *Belonging*. Manchester: Manchester University Press.

Collins, B. and Mees, I.M. (1991) 'English through Welsh ears: the 1857 pronunciation dictionary of Robert Ioan Prys', in I. Tieken-Boon van Ostade and J. Frankis (eds) *Language Usage and Description*, Amsterdam: Rodopi, pp. 75–90.

Collins, B. and Mees, I.M. (1996) 'Spreading everywhere? How recent a phenomenon is glottalisation in Received Pronunciation?' *English World-Wide* 17: 175–87.

Collins, B., and Mees, I.M. (2013) *Practical Phonetics and Phonology: A Resource Book for Students* (third edition). Abingdon: Routledge.

Concise Scots Dictionary (1985) Aberdeen: Aberdeen University Press.

Connell, R. (1995) *Masculinities*. Berkeley: University of California Press.

Conrad, A. (1996) 'The international role of English: the state of the discussion', in J. Fishman, A. Conrad, and A. Rubal-Lopez (eds) *Post-imperial English*, Berlin: Mouton de Gruyter, pp. 13–36.

Cook, G. (1989) *Discourse*. Oxford: Oxford University Press.

Cook, G. (2001) *The Discourse of Advertising* (second edition). London: Routledge.

Cornips, L. and Corrigan, K. (eds) (2005) *Syntax and Variation: Reconciling the Biological and the Social*. Amsterdam: Benjamins.

Corrigan, K. (1997) *The Syntax of South Armagh English in its Socio-Historical Perspective*. Unpublished dissertation, Dublin: University College Dublin.

Coulthard, M. (1985) *An Introduction to Discourse Analysis*. London: Longman.

Coulthard. M. (2008) 'By their words shall ye know then: On linguistic identity', in C.R. Caldas-Coulthard and R. Iedema (eds) *Identity Trouble: Critical Discourse and Contested Identities*, Basingstoke: Palgrave Macmillan, pp. 143–55.

Coupland, N. (1988) *Dialect in Use: Sociolinguistic Variation in Cardiff English*. Cardiff: University of Wales Press.

Coupland, N. and Jaworski, A. (eds) (2009) *The New Sociolinguistics Reader*. Basingstoke: Palgrave Macmillan.

Coupland, N. and Thomas, A. (1990) (eds) *English in Wales: Diversity, Conflict and Change*. Clevedon: Multilingual Matters.

Crago, M. (1988) *Cultural Context in Communicative Interaction of Inuit Children*. Unpublished dissertation, Montreal: McGill University.

Cross, T. (1977) 'Mothers' speech adjustments: the contribution of selected child listener variables', in C. Ferguson and C. Snow (eds) *Talking to Children: Language Input and Acquisition*, Cambridge: Cambridge University Press, pp. 151–88.

Cruse, D. (1986) *Lexical Semantics*. Cambridge: Cambridge University Press.

Crystal, D. (1995) *The Cambridge Encyclopedia of the English Language*. Cambridge: Cambridge University Press.

Crystal, D. (2003) *The Cambridge Encyclopedia of the English Language* (second edition). Cambridge: Cambridge University Press.

Crystal, D. (2004) *Rediscover Grammar* (second edition). London: Longman.

Culpeper, J. (1996) 'Towards an anatomy of impoliteness', *Journal of Pragmatics* 25: 349–67.

Culpeper, J. (2005a) *History of English* (second edition). London: Routledge.

Culpeper, J. (2005b) 'Impoliteness and entertainment in the television quiz show: The Weakest Link', *Journal of Politeness Research* 1/1: 35–72.

Culpeper, J., Short, M. and Verdonk, P. (eds) (1998) *Exploring the Language of Drama: From Text to Context*. London: Routledge.

Culpeper, J., McEnery, T., Katamba, F., Wodak, R. and Kerswill, P. (2009) *The English Language*. Basingstoke: Palgrave Macmillan.

Cummings, L. (2005) *Pragmatics: A Multidisciplinary Perspective*. Edinburgh: Edinburgh University Press.

Cutler, A. (1990) 'Exploiting prosodic possibilities in speech segmentation', in G.T.M. Altmann (ed.) *Cognitive Models of Speech Processing*, Cambridge: MIT Press, pp. 105–21.

Cutler, A. and Carter, D.M. (1987) 'The predominance of strong initial syllables in the English vocabulary', *Computer Speech and Language* 2: 133–42.

Cutting, J. (1996) *MSc Common Room Casual Conversations: A Lexico-Grammatical Longitudinal Study of a Discourse Community in Formation.* Unpublished dissertation, Edinburgh: University of Edinburgh.

Cutting, J. (1999) 'The implicit grammar of the in-group code', *Applied Linguistics* 20/1: 179–202.

Cutting, J. (2015) *Pragmatics and Discourse: A Resource Book for Students* (third edition). London: Routledge.

Davies, A. (1996) 'Ironising the myth of linguicism', *Journal of Multilingual and Multicultural Development* 17/6: 485–96.

De Beaugrande, R. (1997) *New Foundations for a Science of Text and Discourse: Cognition, Communication, and the Freedom of Access to Knowledge and Society.* Norwood: Ablex.

Demuth, C. (1986) 'Prompting routines in the language socialization of Basotho children', in B. Schieffelin and E. Ochs (eds) *Language Socialization across Cultures*, Cambridge: Cambridge University Press, pp. 51–79.

Devitt, M. and Sterelny, K. (1999) *Language and Reality: An Introduction to the Philosophy of Language.* Oxford: Blackwell.

Dixon, J., Mahoney, B. and Cocks, R. (2002) 'Accents of guilt? Effects of regional accent, race and crime on attributions of guilt', *Journal of Language and Social Psychology* 21: 162–8.

Docherty, G.J., Foulkes, P., Milroy, J., Milroy, L. and Walshaw, D. (1997) 'Descriptive adequacy in phonology: a variationist perspective', *Journal of Linguistics* 33: 275–310.

Dörnyei, Z. (2001) *Teaching and Researching Motivation.* Harlow: Longman.

Dörnyei, Z. (2007) *Research Methods in Applied Linguistics.* Oxford: Oxford University Press.

Dörnyei, Z., Csizér, K. and Németh, N. (2006) *Motivation, Language Attitudes and Globalisation: A Hungarian Perspective.* Clevedon: Multilingual Matters.

Douglas-Cowie, E. (1978) 'Linguistic code-switching in a Northern Irish village: social interaction and social ambition', in P. Trudgill (ed.) *Sociolinguistic Patterns in British English*, London: Edward Arnold, pp. 37–51.

Durant, A. and Lambrou, M. (2009) *Language and Media: A Resource Book for Students.* London: Routledge.

Duranti, A. (1997) *Linguistic Anthropology.* Cambridge: Cambridge University Press.

Duranti, A. and Goodwin, C. (eds) (1992) *Rethinking Context: Language as an Interactive Phenomenon.* Cambridge: Cambridge University Press.

Eades, D. (1992) *Aboriginal English and the Law: Communicating with Aboriginal English Speaking Clients.* Brisbane: Queensland Law Society.

Eckert, P. (2000) *Linguistic Variation as Social Practice.* Oxford: Blackwell.

Eckert, P. (2009) 'Ethnography and the study of variation', in. N. Coupland and A. Jaworski (eds) *The New Sociolinguistics Reader*, Basingstoke: Palgrave Macmillan, pp. 136–57.

Eckert, P. and McConnell-Ginet, S. (1999) 'New generalizations and explanations in language and gender research', *Language in Society* 28/2: 185–201.

Edelsky, C. (1981) 'Who's got the floor?' *Language in Society* 10/3: 383–421.

Edwards, V. (1986) *Language in a Black Community*. Clevedon: Multilingual Matters.

Edwards, W. (1992) 'Sociolinguistic behaviour in a Detroit inner city black neighbourhood', *Language in Society* 21/1: 91–115.

Edwards, J. and Middleton, M. (1986) 'Joint remembering: constructing an account of shared experience through conversational discourse', *Discourse Processes* 9: 423–59.

Eggins, S. and Slade, D. (1997) *Analysing Casual Conversation*. London: Cassell.

Ehrlich, S. (1990) *Point of View: A Linguistic Analysis of Literary Style*. London: Routledge.

Eisenberg, A. (1986) 'Teasing: verbal play in two Mexican homes', in B. Schieffelin and E. Ochs (eds) *Language Socialization across Cultures*, Cambridge: Cambridge University Press, pp. 182–98.

Fairclough, N. (1995) *Critical Discourse Analysis: The Critical Study of Language*. New York: Longman.

Fennell, B. (2000) *A History of English: A Sociolinguistic Approach*. Oxford: Blackwell.

Field, J. (2001) *Lexical Segmentation in First and Foreign Language Listening*. Unpublished dissertation, Cambridge: Cambridge University.

Field, J. (2004) *Psycholinguistics: The Key Concepts*. London: Routledge.

Field, J. (2006) *Psycholinguistics: A Resource Book for Students*. London: Routledge.

Firth, A. (ed.) (1994) *The Discourse of Negotiation: Studies of Language in the Workplace*. Oxford: Elsevier Science.

Firth, A. (1996) 'The discursive accomplishment of normality: on "lingua franca" English and conversation analysis', *Journal of Pragmatics* 26: 237–59.

Fischer, J.L. (1958) 'Social influences on the choices of a linguistic variant', *Word* 14: 47–56.

Fletcher, P. and MacWhinney, B. (eds) (1996) *The Handbook of Child Language*. Oxford: Blackwell.

Ford, C.E. (1993) *Grammar in Interaction: Adverbial Clauses in American English Conversations*. Cambridge: Cambridge University Press.

Foster-Cohen, S. (1999) *An Introduction to Child Language Development*. London: Longman.

Foulkes, P. and Docherty, G. (1999) *Urban Voices: Accent Studies in the British Isles*. London: Arnold

Fox Tree, J.E. and Schrock, J.C. (2002) 'Basic meanings of *You Know* and *I Mean*', *Journal of Pragmatics* 34: 727–47.

Freeborn, D. (2006) *From Old English to Standard English: A Course Book in Language Variations across Time* (third edition). Basingstoke: Palgrave Macmillan.

Gal, S. (1992) 'Language, gender, and power: an anthropological view', in K. Hall, M. Bucholtz and B. Moonwomon (eds) *Locating Power: Proceedings of the Second Berkeley Women and Language Conference*, Berkeley: Berkeley Women and Language Group, pp. 153–61.

Gardner, H. (1974) *The Shattered Mind*. New York: Alfred Knopf.

Garman, M. (2008) *Psycholinguistics*. Cambridge: Cambridge University Press.

Garrett, P. (2007) 'Language attitudes', in C. Llamas, L. Mullany and P. Stockwell (eds) *The Routledge Companion to Sociolinguistics*, Abingdon: Routledge, pp. 116–21.

Gaskell, G. (2007) *The Oxford Handbook of Psycholinguistics*. Oxford: Oxford University Press.

Gauchat, L. (1905) 'L'unité phonétique dans le patois d'une commune', in *Festschrift Heinrich Morf: aus Romanischen Sprachen und Literaturen*. Halle: M. Niemeyer, pp. 175–232.

Gee, J.P. (2005) *An Introduction to Discourse Analysis: Theory and Method*. London: Routledge.

Geertz, C. (1973) *The Interpretation of Cultures*. New York: Basic Books.

Giles, H. (1973) 'Accent mobility: a model and some data', *Anthropological Linguistics* 15: 87–105.

Giles, H. and St. Clair, R. (1979) *Language and Social Psychology*. Oxford: Blackwell.

Gimson, A.C. (1994) *Gimson's Pronunciation of English* (fifth edition). London: Edward Arnold.

Gleason, J. and Ratner, N. (eds) (1998) *Psycholinguistics*. Belmont: Wadsworth.

Gleason, J. and Ratner, N. (2008) *The Development of Language* (seventh edition). London: Pearson.

Goffman, E. (1971) *Relations in Public*. London: Penguin.

Goh, C. (2002) *The Coxford Singlish Dictionary*. Singapore: Angsana.

Goodwin, C. and Goodwin, M.H. (1992) 'Assessments and the construction of context', in A. Duranti, and C. Goodwin (eds) *Rethinking Context: Language as an Interactive Phenomenon*, Cambridge: Cambridge University Press, pp. 147–90.

Goody, J. (1986) *The Logic of Writing and the Organization of Society*. Cambridge: Cambridge University Press.

Greenbaum, S. and Quirk, R. (1990) *A Student's Grammar of the English Language*. Harlow: Longman.

Grice, H.P. (1975) 'Logic and conversation', in P. Cole and J.L. Morgan (eds) *Syntax and Semantics 3: Speech Acts*. New York: Academic Press, pp. 41–58.

Grice, H.P. (1989) *Studies in the Way of Words*. Cambridge: Harvard University Press.

Grosjean, F. and Gee, J.P. (1987) 'Prosodic structure and spoken word recognition', *Cognition* 25: 135–55.

Grundy, P. (2008) *Doing Pragmatics* (third edition). London: Hodder.

Gumperz, J. (1982) *Discourse Strategies*. Cambridge: Cambridge University Press.

Halliday, M.A.K. and Matthiesson, C. (2004) *An Introduction to Functional Grammar* (third edition). London: Arnold.

Halliday, M.A.K. and Yallop, C. (2007) *Lexicology: A Short Introduction*. London: A&C Black.

Halliday, M.A.K., Mcintosh, A. and Strevens, R. (1964) *The Linguistic Sciences and Language Teaching*. London: Longman.

Hammersley, M. (1992) *What's Wrong with Ethnography? Methodological Explorations*. London: Routledge.

Hammersley, M. and Atkinson, P. (1995) *Ethnography: Principles in Practice* (second edition). London: Routledge.

Harris, S., Grainger K. and Mullany, L. (2006) 'The pragmatics of political apologies', *Discourse & Society* 17/6: 715–37.

Harwood, John Berwick (1861) 'Horror: a true tale', *Blackwoods* 89: 64.

Heath, S.B. (1983) *Ways with Words: Language, Life and Work in Communities and Classrooms*. Cambridge: Cambridge University Press.

Hesse-Biber, N.S. and Leavy, P. (2006) *The Practice of Qualitative Research*. Thousand Oaks: Sage.

Holmes, J. (1986) 'Functions of *You Know* in women's and men's speech', *Language in Society* 15: 1–21.

Holmes, J. (1995) *Women, Men and Politeness*. London: Longman.

Holmes, J. (2000) 'Politeness, power and provocation: how humour functions in the workplace', *Discourse Studies* 2/2: 159–85.

Holmes, J. (2008) *An Introduction to Sociolinguistics* (third edition). London: Longman.

Houston, A. (1985) *Continuity and Change in English Morphology: The Variable (ING)*. Unpublished dissertation, Philadelphia: University of Pennsylvania.

Huddleston, R.D. and Pullum, G.K. (2005) *A Student's Introduction to English Grammar*. Cambridge: Cambridge University Press.

Hurford, J.R., Heasley, B. and Smith, M. (2007) *Semantics: A Coursebook*. Cambridge: Cambridge University Press.

Hyman, L.M. (1977) 'On the nature of linguistic stress', in L.M. Hyman (ed.) *Studies in Stress and Accent: Southern California Occasional Papers in Linguistics 4*, Los Angeles: University of Southern California: pp. 37–82.

Hymes, D. (1974) 'Ways of speaking', in R. Bauman and J. Sherzer (eds) *Explorations in the Ethnography of Speaking*, Cambridge: Cambridge University Press, pp. 433–52.

Jackson, H. (2002) *Grammar and Vocabulary: A Resource Book for Students*. Abingdon: Routledge.

Jackson, H. and Zé Amvela, E. (2007) *Words, Meaning and Vocabulary* (second edition). London: Cassell.

Jackson, H. and Stockwell, P. (2010) *An Introduction to the Nature and Functions of Language* (second edition). London: Continuum.

Jacques, M. (2005) 'No monopoly on modernity', *The Guardian Weekly*, Vol. 172, No. 8, 11–17 February, p. 16.

Jaworski, A. and Coupland, N. (eds) (2006) *The Discourse Reader* (second edition). London: Routledge.

Jefferson, G. (2004) 'Glossary of transcript symbols with an Introduction', in G. Lerner (ed.) *Conversation Analysis: Studies from the First Generation*, Amsterdam: Benjamins, pp. 13–31.

Jenkins, J. (2007) *English as a Lingua Franca: Attitude and Identity*. Oxford: Oxford University Press.

Jenkins, J. (2015) *Global Englishes: A Resource Book for Students* (third edition). London: Routledge.

Johnson, J. (1994) 'Anthropological contributions to the study of social networks: a review', in S. Wasserman and J. Galaskiewicz (eds) *Advances in Social Network Analysis: Research in the Social and Behavioural Sciences*, Thousand Oaks: Sage, pp. 113–51.

Johnson, K. (2008) *Quantitative Methods in Linguistics*. Oxford: Wiley Blackwell.

Johnstone, B. (2002) *Discourse Analysis.* Oxford: Blackwell.

Joyce, J. (1922) *Ulysses.* Paris: Sylvia Beach.

Jusczyk, P. (1997) *The Discovery of Spoken Language.* Cambridge: MIT Press.

Kachru, B. (1986) *The Alchemy of English: The Spread, Functions and Models of Non-Native Englishes.* Oxford: Pergamon Press.

Kachru, B. (1992a) 'Teaching World Englishes', in B.B. Kachru (ed.) *The Other Tongue: English across Cultures*, Chicago: Illinois University Press, pp. 355–66.

Kachru, B. (1992b) 'Models for non-native Englishes', in B.B. Kachru (ed.) *The Other Tongue: English across Cultures*, Chicago: Illinois University Press, pp. 48–74.

Kachru, B., Kachru, Y. and Nelson, C.L. (2009) (eds) *The Handbook of World Englishes*, Oxford: Blackwell.

Kandiah, T. (2001) 'Whose meanings? Probing the dialectics of English as a global language', in R.B.H. Goh (ed.) *Ariels – Departures and Returns: A Festschrift for Edwin Thumboo*, Singapore: Oxford University Press, pp. 102–21.

Katamba, F. (1994) *English Words.* London: Routledge.

Kerswill, P. (1996) 'Milton Keynes and dialect leveling in south-eastern British English', in D. Graddol, D. Leith and J. Swann (eds) *English: History, Diversity, Change*, London: Routledge, pp. 292–300.

Kerswill, P. and Williams, A. (2000) 'Creating a new town koine: children and language change in Milton Keynes', *Language in Society* 29: 69–115.

Kirkpatrick, A. (2007) *World Englishes: Implications for International Communication and English Language Teaching.* Cambridge: Cambridge University Press.

Knight, D. (2009) *Backchannelling: Corpus Linguistics and Multimodality.* Unpublished dissertation, Nottingham: University of Nottingham.

Knowles, G. (1987) *Patterns of Spoken English: An Introduction to English.* London: Longman.

Kuiper, K. and Allan, W.S. (2004) *An Introduction to English Language: Word, Sound and Sentence.* Basingstoke: Palgrave Macmillan.

Labov, W. (1966) *The Social Stratification of English in New York City.* Washington: Center for Applied Linguistics.

Labov, W. (1972a) *Language in the Inner City: Studies in the Black English Vernacular.* Philadelphia: University of Pennsylvania Press.

Labov, W. (1972b) 'Introduction', in *Sociolinguistic Patterns*, Philadelphia: University of Pennsylvania Press, pp. xiii–xviii.

Labov, W. (1972c) *Sociolinguistic Patterns.* Philadelphia: University of Pennsylvania Press.

Labov, W. (1994) *Principles of Linguistic Change Volume 1: Internal Factors.* Oxford: Blackwell.

Labov, W. (2001) *Principles of Language Change Volume 2: Social Factors.* Oxford: Blackwell.

Ladefoged, P. (2001) *A Course in Phonetics* (fourth edition). New York: Harcourt.

Lakoff, G. and Johnson, M. (1980) *Metaphors We Live By.* Chicago: University of Chicago Press.

Lakoff, R. (1973) 'The logic of politeness: on minding your p's and q's', *Proceedings of the Ninth Regional Meeting of the Chicago Linguistic Society.*

Lambrou, M. and Stockwell, P. (eds) (2007) *Contemporary Stylistics.* London: Continuum.

Layder, D. (1997) *Modern Social Theory: Key Debates and New Directions*. London: UCL Press.

Le Page, R.B. and Tabouret-Keller, A. (1985) *Acts of Identity*. Cambridge: Cambridge University Press.

Leech, G. (1981) *Semantics* (second edition). Harmondsworth: Penguin.

Leech, G. (1983) *Principles of Pragmatics*. London: Longman.

Leech, G. and Short, M. (1981) *Style in Fiction*. London: Longman.

Leech, G. and Short, M. (2007) *Style in Fiction* (second edition). London: Longman.

Lennon, J. (1965) *A Spaniard in the Works*. London: Jonathan Cape.

Levin, H. (1951) 'Observations on the style of Ernest Hemingway', *Kenyon Review* 13: 581–606.

Levinson, S.C. (1983) *Pragmatics*. Cambridge: Cambridge University Press.

Lewis, C.T. and Short, C. (1879) *A Latin Dictionary*. Oxford: Clarendon Press.

Li, D.C.S. (2002) 'Hong Kong parents' preference for English-medium education: passive victim of imperialism or active agents of pragmatism?' in A. Kirkpatrick (ed.) *Englishes in Asia: Communication, Identity, Power and Education*, Melbourne: Language Australia, pp. 28–62.

Li Wei (1996) 'Network analysis', in H. Goebl, P. Nelde, S. Zdenek and W. Woelck (eds) *Contact Linguistics: A Handbook of Contemporary Research*, Berlin: De Gruyter, pp. 85–102.

Lippi-Green, R. (1989) 'Social network integration and language change in progress in an Alpine rural village', *Language in Society* 18: 213–34.

Lippi-Green, R. (1997) *English with an Accent*. London: Routledge.

Llamas, C. (1999) 'A new methodology: data elicitation for social and regional language variation studies', *Leeds Working Papers in Linguistics and Phonetics* 7: 95–119.

Llamas, C., Mullany, L. and Stockwell, P. (eds) (2007) *The Routledge Companion to Sociolinguistics*. London: Routledge.

Lock, A. (1981) *The Guided Reinvention of Language*. London: Academic Press.

Louw, W.E. (1993) 'Irony in the text or insincerity in the writer? The diagnostic potential of semantic prosodies', in M. Baker, G. Francis and E. Tognini-Bonelli (eds) *Text and Technology*, Amsterdam: Benjamins, pp. 162–76.

Lowry, Malcolm (1933) *Ultramarine*. Harmondsworth: Penguin.

Lowry, Malcolm (1947) *Under the Volcano*. Harmondsworth: Penguin.

Lust, B. (2006) *Child Language: Acquisition and Growth*. Cambridge: Cambridge University Press.

Maher, J. (1996) 'Fisherman, farmers, traders: language and economic history on St Barthélemy, French West Indies', *Language in Society* 25/3: 373–406.

Martin, E. (2006) 'World Englishes in the media', in B. Kachru, Y. Kachru and C.L. Nelson (eds) *The Handbook of World Englishes*, Oxford: Blackwell, pp. 583–600.

Mason, J. (2006) 'Mixing methods in a qualitatively driven way', *Qualitative Research* 6/1: 9–25.

Maxwell, J.A. and Loomis, D.M. (2003) 'Mixed methods design: an alternative approach', in A. Tashakkori and C. Teddlie (eds) *Handbook of Mixed Methods in Social and Behavioral Research*, Thousand Oaks: Sage.

McCarthy, M. (1991) *Discourse Analysis for Language Teachers*. Cambridge: Cambridge University Press.

McCarthy, M. (1998) *Spoken Language and Applied Linguistics*. Cambridge: Cambridge University Press.

McGregor, W. (2009) *Linguistics: An Introduction*. London: Continuum.

McHale, B. (1983) 'Linguistics and poetics revisited', *Poetics Today* 4/1: 17–45.

McIntyre, D. (2006) *History of English: A Resource Book for Students*. London: Routledge.

McNeill, D. (1970) *The Acquisition of Language: The Study of Developmental Psycholinguistics*. New York: Harper and Row.

Mees, I.M. (1983) *The Speech of Cardiff Schoolchildren: A Real-Time Study*. Unpublished dissertation, Leiden: University of Leiden.

Mees, I.M. (1987) 'Glottal stop as a prestigious feature in Cardiff English', *English World-Wide* 8: 25–39.

Mees, I.M. (1990) 'Patterns of sociophonetic variation in the speech of Cardiff schoolchildren', in N. Coupland and A. Thomas (eds) *English in Wales: Diversity, Conflict and Change*, Clevedon: Multilingual Matters, pp. 87–103.

Melchers, G. and Shaw, P. (2011) *World Englishes* (second edition). London: Routledge.

Mesthrie, R. and Bhatt, M. (2008) *World Englishes: The Study of New Linguistic Varieties*. Cambridge: Cambridge University Press.

Mesthrie, R., Swann, J., Deumert, A. and Leap, W. (2009) *Introducing Sociolinguistics* (second edition). Edinburgh: Edinburgh University Press.

Meyerhoff, M. (2006) *Introducing Sociolinguistics*. Abingdon: Routledge.

Miles, M.B. and Huberman. A.M. (1994) *Qualitative Data Analysis* (second edition). Thousand Oaks: Sage.

Miller, P.J. (1982) *Amy, Wendy, and Beth: Learning Language in South Baltimore*. Austin: University of Texas Press.

Mills, S. (2003) *Gender and Politeness*. Cambridge: Cambridge University Press.

Milroy, J. and Milroy, L. (1978) 'Belfast: change and variation in an urban vernacular', in P. Trudgill (ed.) *Sociolinguistic Patterns in British English*, London: Arnold, pp. 19–36.

Milroy, J., Milroy, L. and Hartley, S. (1994) 'Local and supra-local change in British English: the case of glottalisation', *English World-Wide* 15: 1–33.

Milroy, L. (1987) *Language and Social Networks* (second edition). Oxford: Blackwell.

Milroy, L. and Gordon, M. (2003) *Sociolinguistics: Method and Interpretation*. Oxford: Blackwell.

Mitchell, J.C. (1986) 'Network procedures', in D. Frick and H-W. Hoefert (eds) *The Quality of Urban Life,* Berlin: De Gruyter, pp. 73–92.

Moag, R.F. (1992) 'The life cycle of non-native Englishes: a case study', in B.B. Kachru (ed.) *The Other Tongue: English across Cultures*, Chicago: Illinois University Press, pp. 233–44.

Mondorf, B. (2000) *Sex Differences in English Syntax*. Unpublished dissertation, Düsseldorf: Düsseldorf University.

Mufwene, S. (2001) *The Ecology of Language Evolution*. Cambridge: Cambridge University Press.

Murray, S. (1993) 'Network determination of linguistic variables', *American Speech* 68/2: 161–77.

Myhill, J. and Harris, W. (1986) 'The use of the verbal -*s* inflection in BEV', in D. Sankoff (ed.) *Diversity and Diachrony*, Amsterdam: Benjamins, pp. 25–32.

Newport, E.L., Gleitman, H. and Gleitman, L.R. (1977) 'Mother, I'd rather do it myself: some effects and non-effects of maternal speech style', in C. Ferguson and C. Snow (eds) *Talking to Children: Language Input and Acquisition*, Cambridge: Cambridge University Press, pp. 109–50.

Ochs, E. (1982) 'Talking to children in Western Samoa', *Language in Society* 11/1: 77–104.

Ochs, E. (1985) 'Variation and error: a sociolinguistic study of language acquisition in Samoa', in D. Slobin (ed.) *The Crosslinguistic Study of Language Acquisition*, Hillsdale: Lawrence Erlbaum Associates, pp. 783–838.

Ochs, E. (1988) *Culture and Language Development: Language Acquisition and Language Socialization in a Samoan Village*. Cambridge: Cambridge University Press.

Ochs, E. and Schieffelin, B. (1984) 'Language acquisition and socialization: three developmental stories and their implications', in R. Shweder and R. Levine (eds) *Culture Theory: Essays on Mind, Self and Emotion*, New York: Cambridge University Press, pp. 276–320.

Ochs, E., Schegloff, E. and Thompson, S. (eds) (1996) *Interaction and Grammar*. Cambridge: Cambridge University Press.

Odden, D. (2005) *Introducing Phonology*. Cambridge: Cambridge University Press.

OED (2009) World English Dictionaries. Accessed 25 April 2009: http://www.askoxford.com/globalenglish/dictionaries/.

O'Grady, W. (2005) *How Children Learn Language*. Cambridge: Cambridge University Press.

Orwell, G. (1948) *Nineteen Eighty Four*. London: Everyman.

Page, N. (1973) *Speech in the English Novel*. London: Longman.

Pascal, R. (1977) *The Dual Voice*. Manchester: Manchester University Press.

Pawley, A. and Syder, F.H. (1983) 'Two puzzles for linguistic theory', in J. Richards and R. Schmidt (eds) *Language and Communication*, London: Longman, pp. 191–227.

Pawson, R. (1989) *A Measure for Measures: A Manifesto for Empirical Sociology*. London: Routledge.

Peccei, J.S. (2006) *Child Language: A Resource Book for Students*. London: Routledge.

Perakyla, A. (1997) 'Reliability and validity in research based on transcripts', in D. Silverman (ed.) *Qualitative Research: Theory, Method and Practice*, London: Sage, pp. 201–20.

Phillipson, R. (2002) 'Global English and local language policies', in A. Kirkpatrick (ed.) *Englishes in Asia: Communication, Identity, Power and Education*, Melbourne: Language Australia, pp. 7–28.

Pitts, A. (1986) 'Contrastive use of verbal -s in slave narratives', in D. Sankoff (ed.) *Diversity and Diachrony*, Amsterdam: Benjamins, pp. 73–82.

Popper, K. and Eccles, J.C. (1977) *The Self and Its Brain*. Berlin: Springer.

Pye, C. (1992) 'The acquisition of K'iche' Maya', in D. Slobin (ed.) *The Crosslinguistic Study of Language Acquisition*, Hillsdale: Lawrence Erlbaum Associates, pp. 221–308.

Richards, L. (2005) *Handling Qualitative Data: A Practical Guide*. London: Sage.

Rimmon-Kenan, S. (1983) *Narrative Fiction: Contemporary Poetics*. London: Methuen.

Roberts, C. and Sarangi, S. (2003) 'Uptake of discourse research in interprofessional settings: reporting from medical consultancy', *Applied Linguistics* 24/3: 338–59.

Robson, M. and Stockwell, P. (2005) *Language in Theory: A Resource Book for Students*. London: Routledge.

Rosewarne, D. (1984) 'Estuary English', *Times Educational Supplement* 42, 19 October.

Rossman, G.B. and Wilson, B.L. (1985) 'Numbers and words: combining quantitative and qualitative methods in a single large-scale evaluation study', *Evaluation Review* 9/5: 627–43.

Rubdy, R. and Saraceni, M. (2006) *English in the World: Global Rules, Global Roles*. London: Continuum.

Russell, J. (1982) 'Networks and sociolinguistic variation in an African urban setting', in S. Romaine (ed.) *Sociolinguistic Studies in the Speech Community*, London: Edward Arnold, pp. 125–40.

Sacks, H., Schegloff, E. and Jefferson, G. (1974) 'A simplest systematics for the organisation of turn-taking in conversation', *Language* 50: 696–735.

Samuels, M.L. (1972) *Linguistic Evolution, with Special Reference to English*. Cambridge: Cambridge University Press.

Sandelowski, M. (2003) 'Tables or tableaux? The challenges of writing and reading mixed methods studies', in A. Tashakkori and C. Teddlie (eds) *Handbook of Mixed Methods in Social and Behavioral Research*, Thousand Oaks: Sage, pp. 321–50.

Sarangi, S. and Roberts, C. (1999) 'The dynamics of interactional and institutional orders in work-related settings', in S. Sarangi and C. Roberts (eds) *Talk, Work and Institutional Order: Discourse in Medical, Mediation and Management Settings*, Berlin: Mouton de Gruyter, pp. 1–57.

Schachter, S. (1959) *The Psychology of Affiliation: Experimental Studies of the Sources of Gregariousness*. Stanford: Stanford University Press.

Schegloff, E.A., Jefferson, G. and Sacks, H. (1977) 'The preference for self-correction in the organization of repair in conversation', *Language* 53/2: 361–82.

Schieffelin, B. (1986) 'The acquisition of Kaluli', in D. Slobin (ed.) *The Crosslinguistic Study of Language Acquisition*, Hillsdale: Lawrence Erlbaum Associates, pp. 525–94.

Schieffelin, B. (1990) *The Give and Take of Everyday Life: Language Socialization of Kaluli Children*. Cambridge: Cambridge University Press.

Schiffrin, D., Tannen, D. and Hamilton, H.E. (eds) (2001) *Handbook of Discourse Analysis*. Oxford: Blackwell.

Schmidt, A. (1985) *Young Peoples' Djirbal*. Cambridge: Cambridge University Press.

Schmitt, N. and McCarthy, M. (1998) *Vocabulary: Description, Acquisition and Pedagogy*. Cambridge: Cambridge University Press.

Schneider, E.W. (1983) 'The origin of the verbal -*s* in Black English', *American Speech* 58: 99–113.

Schneider, E.W. (2003) 'The dynamics of new Englishes: from identity construction to dialect rebirth', *Language* 79/2: 233–81.

Schooling, S. (1990) *Language Maintenance in Melanesia*. Dallas: SIL.

Schwandt, T.A. (2000) 'Three epistemological stances for qualitative inquiry', in N.K. Denzin and Y.S. Lincoln (eds) *Handbook of Qualitative Research* (second edition), Thousand Oaks: Sage, pp. 183–123.

Scollon, S. (1982) *Reality Set, Socialization and Linguistic Convergence*. Unpublished dissertation, Honolulu: University of Hawaii.

Sealey, A. (2010) *Researching English Language: A Resource Book for Students*. London: Routledge.

Searle, J.R. (1969) *Speech Acts*. Cambridge: Cambridge University Press.

Searle, J.R. (1979) *Expression and Meaning*. Cambridge: Cambridge University Press.

Seidlhofer, B. (2004) 'Research perspectives on teaching English as a lingua franca', *Annual Review of Applied Linguistics* 24: 145–209.

Short, M. (1996) *Exploring the Language of Poems, Plays and Prose*. London: Longman.

Silverman, D. (2000) *Doing Qualitative Research: A Practical Guide*. London: Sage.

Silverman, D. (2004) *Qualitative Research: Theory, Method and Practice* (second edition). London: Sage.

Silverman, D. (2006) *Interpreting Qualitative Data: Methods for Analyzing Talk, Text and Interaction* (third edition). London: Sage.

Simpson, P. (2014) *Stylistics: A Resource Book for Students* (second edition). London: Routledge.

Simpson, P. and Mayr, A. (2009) *Language and Power: A Resource Book for Students*. London: Routledge.

Sinclair, J. (1990) *Collins COBUILD English Grammar*. London: HarperCollins.

Sinclair, J. (1991) *Corpus, Concordance, Collocation*. Oxford: Oxford University Press.

Sinclair, J. (2004) *Trust the Text: Language, Corpus and Discourse*. London: Routledge.

Sinclair. J. and Coulthard, M. (1975) *Toward an Analysis of Discourse*. Oxford: Oxford University Press.

Singleton, D. (2000) *Language and the Lexicon*. London: Arnold.

Skehan, P. (1998) *A Cognitive Approach to Language Learning*. Oxford: Oxford University Press.

Smith, J. (1996) *An Historical Study of English: Function, Form and Change*. London: Routledge.

Smith, J. (2005) *Essentials of Early English* (second edition). London: Routledge.

Smith, L.E. (1992) 'Spread of English and issues of intelligibility', in B.B. Kachru (ed.) *The Other Tongue: English across Cultures*, Chicago: Illinois University Press, pp. 75–90.

Smith-Hefner, B. (1988) 'The linguistic socialization of Javanese children', *Anthropological Linguistics* 30/2: 166–98.

Sonntag, S.K. (2003) *The Local Politics of Global English: Case Studies in Linguistic Globalisation*. Lanham: Lexington Books.

SPAS (2002) The SPAS manifesto. http://www.lumpar.com/s_p_a_s_.htm. Accessed 25 April 2009.

Steinberg, D. and Sciarini, N. (2006) *An Introduction to Psycholinguistics* (second edition). London: Longman.

Steinberg, D., Nagata, H. and Aline, D. (2001) *Psycholinguistics: Language, Mind and World*. London: Longman.

Stephenson, N. (1992) *Snow Crash*. New York: Bantam.

Stockwell, P. (2007) *Sociolinguistics: A Resource Book for Students* (second edition). London: Routledge.

Stockwell, P. and Whiteley, S. (eds) (2014) *The Cambridge Handbook of Stylistics*. Cambridge: Cambridge University Press.

Strang, B. (1999) *A History of English*. London: Pan.

Street, B.V. (1984) *Literacy in Theory and Practice*. Cambridge: Cambridge University Press.

Swales, J. (1990) *Genre Analysis*. Cambridge: Cambridge University Press.

Swales, J. (1997) 'English as Tyrannosaurus Rex', *World Englishes* 16/3: 373–82.

Tannen, D. (1984) *Conversational Style: Analyzing Talk among Friends.* New Jersey: Ablex.

Tannen, D. (1989) *Talking Voices.* Cambridge: Cambridge University Press.

Tashakkori, A. and Teddlie, C. (eds) (2003) *Handbook of Mixed Methods in Social and Behavioral Research.* Thousand Oaks: Sage.

Tench, P. (1990) 'The pronunciation of English in Abercrave', in N. Coupland and A. Thomas (eds) *English in Wales: Diversity, Conflict and Change,* Clevedon: Multilingual Matters, pp. 130–41.

Thomas, J. (1995) *Meaning in Interaction.* London: Longman.

Thompson, G. (2004) *Introducing Functional Grammar* (second edition). London: Arnold.

Thompson, J. (1990) 'Advertising's rationality', in M. Alvarado and J. Thompson (eds) *The Media Reader,* London: British Film Institute, pp. 208–12.

Toolan, M. (2001) *Narrative: A Critical Linguistic Introduction* (second edition). London: Routledge.

Trask, L. (1995) *Language: The Basics.* London: Routledge.

Trask, L. and Stockwell, P. (2007) *Language and Linguistics: The Key Concepts.* London: Routledge.

Trevarthen, C. (1979) 'Communication and co-operation in early infancy: a description of primary intersubjectivity', in M. Bullowa (ed.) *Before Speech,* Cambridge: Cambridge University Press, pp. 321–49.

Trudgill, P. (1972) 'Sex, covert prestige and linguistic change in the urban British English of Norwich', *Language in Society* 1/2: 179–95.

Trudgill, P. (1974) *The Social Differentiation of English in Norwich.* Cambridge: Cambridge University Press.

Ur, P. (1984) *Teaching Listening Comprehension.* Cambridge: Cambridge University Press.

Verdonk, P. (ed.) (1993) *Twentieth Century Poetry: From Text to Context.* London: Routledge.

Verdonk, P. (2002) *Stylistics.* Oxford: Oxford University Press.

Verdonk, P. and Weber, J.-J. (eds) (1995) *Twentieth Century Prose: From Text to Context.* London: Routledge.

Voss, B. (1984) *Slips of the Ear.* Tübingen: Gunter Narr Verlag.

Waldron, R.A. (1979) *Sense and Sense Development* (second edition). London: Deutsch.

Wales, K. (2001) *A Dictionary of Stylistics* (second edition). London: Pearson.

Ward, M. (1971) *Them Children: A Study in Language.* New York: Holt, Rinehart, and Winston.

Wardhaugh, R. (1993) *Investigating Language: Central Problems in Linguistics.* Oxford: Blackwell.

Wardhaugh, R. (2009) *An Introduction to Sociolinguistics* (sixth edition). Oxford: Blackwell.

Warren, P. (2012) *Introducing Psycholinguistics.* Cambridge: Cambridge University Press.

Watson-Gegeo, K. and Gegeo, D. (1986) 'Calling out and repeating routines in the language socialization of Basotho children', in B. Schieffelin and E. Ochs (eds) *Language Socialization across Cultures,* Cambridge: Cambridge University Press, pp. 17–50.

Wells, J.C. (1982) *Accents of English* (3 vols). Cambridge: Cambridge University Press.

Wenger, E. (1998) *Communities of Practice: Learning, Meaning and Identity*. Cambridge: Cambridge University Press.

Wheatcroft, G. (2007) '*Yo, Blair!*': *Tony Blair's Disastrous Premiership*. London: Hutchinson.

Whitney, P. (1998) *The Psychology of Language*. Boston: Houghton Mifflin.

Widdowson, H. (1997) 'EIL, ESL, EFL: Global issues and local interests', *World Englishes*, 16/1: 135–46.

Widdowson, H. (2003) *Defining Issues in English Language Teaching*. Oxford: Oxford University Press.

Williams, C.H. (1990) 'The anglicisation of Wales', in N. Coupland and A. Thomas (eds) *English in Wales: Diversity, Conflict and Change*, Clevedon: Multilingual Matters, pp. 19–47.

Williamson, S.G. (1979) *Tamil Baby Talk: A Cross-Cultural Study*. Unpublished dissertation, Philadelphia: University of Pennsylvania.

Wolfram, W., Hazen, K. and Schilling-Estes, N. (1999) *Dialect Change and Maintenance on the Outer Banks*. Tuscaloosa: University of Alabama Press.

Wray, Alison (2002) *Formulaic Language and the Lexicon*. Cambridge: Cambridge University Press.

Young, M. and Wilmott, P. (1962) *Family and Kinship in East London*. Harmondsworth: Penguin.

Yule, G. (2006) *The Study of Language* (third edition). Cambridge: Cambridge University Press.

Zimmerman, D. and West, C. (1975) 'Sex-roles, interruptions and silences in conversation', in B. Thorne, C. Kramarae and N. Henley (eds) *Language, Gender and Society*, Rowley: Newbury House, pp. 89–101.

Zsiga, E.C. (2012) *The Sounds of Language: An Introduction to Phonetics and Phonology*. Chichester: John Wiley.

GLOSSARIAL INDEX

Keywords (which are in **bold** throughout this book) are indicated here where a definition is provided or the term is used in a context which makes its meaning clear. Other page references are to places in the book where the term is also used.

accent 3, 8, 28, 30, 37, **39**, 61, 65–6, 87, 89, 96, 98–100, 102–3, 108, 112, 122–8, 168, 173, 175, 186, 207
access code **32**
accommodation **100**, 101, 238
accusative **34**, 35–6
acoustic phonetics **2**
acquisition 25–9, 32, 88, 90, 233–7, 262, 275, 286
acrolect **172**
actor 33, **77**, **79**, 264–9
Adams, Douglas 196
address terms **12**, 169
adjacency pair **82**, 83
adjectival phrase (AdjP) **16**, **18**, 20
adjunct **76**, 77–9, 81
adverb **18**, 20, 78, 97, 212, 228, 249
adverbial complement **77**
adverbial phrase (AdvP) 16, **18**, 20, 77, 222
advertising 117, 140, 174–6, 178, 194, 227, 229–33
affix **7**, 26, 30, 32, 130
affricate **5**, 61, 66
agent 28, 76, **77**, 78–9, 159, 178, 264, 268, 270, 283
agreement **18**, 19, 90, 225, 226
Aldiss, Brian 181
alliteration 108, **126**
allophones **3**
all-together-now (ATN) **84**
alveolar 4, **5**, 61–2, 65–6, 108, 200, 202–5
ambiguity 13, 70, 136, 138, 140, 208, 213, 230–1
American 8, 9, 37, 44, 53, 81, 99, 106, 128–9, 157, 166, 168, 173, 176, 200, 206, 210, 226, 235–6, 237, 238, 255, 256, 261–2, 267
anaphora **23**
antonymy **132**
aphasia 30, **158**, 162
apology 13, 73, 134–9, 208, 221, 285
approximant **5**, 61, 62, 65, 109
Arabic 8, 166
articulators 2, 4–5
articulatory phonetics **2**

association 30, 31–2, 66–7, 68, 158, 161, 249, 250
assonance **126**
attribute **79**, **81**, 266, 270
auditory phonetics **2**, 239
auxiliary **17**, 18, 28, 33, 77

babbling **26**, 27
back-formation **9**, 130
Bantu 8
basic level term **69**
basilect **172**
behaver **80**
behavioural process **79**, 80
bilabial **4**, 61–2, 65–6
Blake, William 132–3
borrowing 8, 250
bottom-up processing **30**
bound morpheme 7, 10, 130
Burns, Robert 123–6
Byron, George Gordon 107–8

captioning 89
cardinal vowels **63**, 64
carrier **81**, 266
case 19, 26, 33–4, 36, 144
cataphora **23**
Celtic 8, 33
centralised vowels **64**
Chinese 104, 155, 166, 172, 178, 262–3
circularity **40**, 119
circumstantial attribution 80, **81**
clause **15**, 16–19, 22, 24, 28, 48, 54, 57, 58, 76–80, 82, 87, 90, 103, 105, 141, 207, 208, 210, 222–6, 227, 263–8, 270
clear l **3**
client **79**
cloze-test **31**
codification 43, 44–5, 97, 103–5, 106, 107, 174
cognitive poetics **49**
cognitivism **57**, 58, 116, 117, 197
coherence **21**, 24, 30, 227, 228, 233
cohesion **21**, 22–4, 156, 227–31, 233
collaborative floor **84**
collocation 117, 209–10, 212, 221–2

communication accommodation theory (CAT) **100**
community of practice (CofP) 101, 114, 253–4
competence 26, **56**, 105, 234, 236, 279, 283
complement 18, **76**, 77–8, 79, 80
completor **17**, 20, 97
complex sentence **78**, 87, 234
compound sentence **78**, 87
compounding **8**, 9
concatenation **27**, 208
conceptual metaphor **117**, 118, 197
concordance 207, 210–1, 213
conjunction **18**, 20, 78–9, 90, 140, 156, 222, 227, 230–1, 241, 282
connective **78**, 230
connotation 31, **66**, 68, 107, 133, 173, 176, 231, 247, 251
consonant 4–6, 26, 28, 37, 60–63, 65, 89, 103, 109, 126, 163, 201, 234, 241, 244
constituency **15**, 16–19, 20, 55, 56, 76, 140
contingency **20**, 279
contronymy 67
convergence 37, **100**, 101
conversation analysis (CA) **24**, 48, 81, 85, 87, 112, 119,
cooing **26**
co-operative principle 69, **70**, 71–3, 148, 227, 229, 230
copula 46, 77, **167**,
corpus **103**, 104–5, 107, 207, 209, 213, 221–2, 224, 226, 240
corpus linguistics **103**, 119, 221, 284, 286
corpus stylistics 49
co-text **21**, 23, 47
creole 259
critical age 29
critical discourse analysis (CDA) **25**, 117, 119
Czech 42–3

dative **34**, 35–6
declarative 13, 46, 78, 86, 236
declension 34
deictic expressions **12**, 27, 110, 170
deixis **12**, 22
denotation 9, 11, 31, 65, **66**, 68, 89, 117, 133, 174, 196, 245, 266
dependency 15, **18**, 19, 20,
derivation 3, 7, 10, 18, 30, 46, 90, 150, 226, 228, 246, 247, 249, 251, 278
determiner **16**, 17, 20, 140
determinism 116, 117
deviance 47
diachronic 56, **95**, 251
diacritics **3**, 62
dialect 8, 10, 20, 33, 36–8, **39**, 91, 96–103, 123, 126, 128, 163, 167, 168, 172, 184, 186–7, 189–90, 247, 249, 254, 260

dialect levelling **102**, 103
dictionaries 6, 7, 30–1, 38, 44–5, 66, 97–8, 106–7, 116, 130, 173–4, 208, 246–9, 287
diphthong 6, **62**, 63, 65, 99, 244
direct object 17, 34, 76, **77**, 228
direct speech act **14**, 46, 95
discourse 10, 15, 16, 19, **21**–5, 39, 48, 57–8, 68, 81, 83, 84, 87, 90, 93–4, 104, 111, 148–9, 175, 182, 194, 207–8, 214, 219–26, 227–9, 231–2, 235, 236, 251, 282, 286, 288; advertising 175, 227; free indirect 270–1; online 170, 174; spoken 23, 79, 112, 145–6, 148, 227; text-messaging 144
discourse analysis (DA) **21**, 23–5, 49, 53, 57, 112, 117, 119, 144, 146, 178, 226, 227
discourse deixis **12**
discourse marker **86**, 205, 226
dispreferred response **82**–3
divergence 79, **100**–1
diversity 37, 90, 96, **98**, 272, 273, 277
dominant 41, **48**, 50, 63, 108, 143, 166, 172, 179, 265–6, 272
double negative **103**
duration **6**, 62, 241

echolalia **27**
echolalia **27**
empiricism **119**
endophora **23**, 231
English as a Foreign Language (EFL) **42**
English as a Lingua Franca (ELF) **42**–3, 44, 45, 104–106, 260, 287
English as a Native Language (ENL) **42**, 105
English as a Second Language (ESL) **42**
entry conditions **93**
Estuary English **102**–3,
ethics 54, 112–3, 115, **122**
ethnography **51**, 53–4, 207, 255, 257
ethnography of speaking **24**
exchange structure **24**, 119
exclamatory 46, **78**
existent **81**
existential process 45, 46, 79, 80, **81**, 140–1, 226
exophora **23**, 231, 232
expanding circle 41, **42**, 44, 174–5, 259, 263
eye dialect **123**, 126, 128, 167, 174

face **72**–4, 82, 86, 136, 139, 148, 217
face-threatening act (FTA) **72**–3, 74, 125
falsifiability **55**–6, 119, 120
felicity conditions **13**
fleeting **93**, 110
flout **70**–1
follow-up (IRF) **24**
foregrounding 46, **47**–8, 95, 110, 159, 179, 231, 268

forensic linguistics **144**
formalism 29, 53, **57**, 76, 156, 197, 222, 247, 251, 268, 278
formality 8, 9, 24–5, **38**, 40, 46, 71, 84–5, 90, 92, 101–2, 114, 146, 148–9, 172–3, 189, 192, 259
Foster, Alan Dean 142
free morpheme 7–10, 130
French 8, 12, 36, 68, 96, 126, 132, 143, 164, 166, 169, 246, 251, 255, 260, 267–8
fricative **5**, 61–2, 65–6, 108
functionalism **57**–8, 116, 117, 197

generativism **56**–8, 116, 117, 119, 197, 221, 226, 279, 282
genitive **34**–5, 36
Germanic 8, 12, 33, 36, 100, 166, 250
glides **5**
glottal stop **3**–4, **5**, 60–1, 65, 103, 243
glottalisation 3, 5
goal **77**, **79**, 264–8
grammars **14**, 15–9, 20, 30–1, 37, 38, 39, 44, 49, 56–7, 76, 79–80, 91, 97–8, 104, 117, 158, 196, 208, 210, 213, 222, 225, 228, 239, 244, 259, 280, 283, 285–6
grapheme **6**, 21
great vowel shift 36–7, 89, 96
Greek 8, 12, 78, 110, 155, 166
grok 9
Gujerati 250

hard c **61**
head **16**, 17–8
header **92**–3
Hindustani 250
historical sociolinguistics **38**
holophrastic speech **27**
homogenisation 96, **98**, 99, 256, 262, 279
homonymy **68**, 132, 144
Hungarian 26
hyperbole **71**
hyponymy **67**–8, 132

iconicity **48**, 108, 179, 181
identified **81**
identifier **81**
illocution **13**, 14
illocutionary force **13**–14
illocutionary force-indicating device (IFID) **13**, 134, 135
imperative 13, 27, 46, 55, **78**, 87, 236
implicature **14**, 70–2
impoliteness 71, **73**–5, 82–3, 136, 149, 220
indexicality **12**, 255, 279
indicators 39, **40**, 220, 256
indirect object 34, 76, **77**
indirect speech act **14**, 70–1

infix **7**
inflection **7**, 8, 9–10, 18, 26, 28, 30, **34**–6, 116
initiation (IRF) **24**, 236
initiator **79**
inner circle **42**, 44–5, 105, 175–6, 260, 263
insertion sequence **83**
instrumental header **92**
instrumental schema **92**, 93
intensive attribution 80, **81**
intensive complement **77**, 78
internal conceptualisation header **92**
International Phonetic Alphabet (IPA) 3, 4, 60, 62–4, 122, 124
interrogative 13, 14, 46, **78**, 222
interruption 24, 28, **83**–4, 92, 136, 139
intuition 17, 49, 56, 57, 111, **119**, 130, 180, 209, 213, 222, 278, 279–80, 283
Italian 8, 87, 178, 260

Japanese 8, 42, 54, 166, 176, 238

Kipling, Rudyard 179
kipple 9

labio-dental **5**, 62, 65–6
language acquisition device (LAD) **29**
language attitudes 39, 43, **99**–103, 170–2, 190, 192
language change 33–7, **38**, 39, 41, 44, 51, 55, 56, 95–9, 190, 226, 245–51
language loyalty **65**, 96, 98–100, 102, 167–9, 174
language planning 39, **97**, 172
lateral approximant **5**, 62, 65
Latin 8, 33, 97, 180, 250, 251, 260
le Carré, John 266, 268
lemma **7**, **30**, 32
Lennon, John 161, 180
lexical category **20**
lexical semantics 10, **66**–9, 109, 132, 251, 285
lexicology 6, **7**–9, 10, 48, 178, 180, 245, 285
lexicon **30**–1, 32, 174, 196, 222, 246, 249, 250, 251
light l **3**
lingua franca **42**–5, 104, 105, 106, 260, 287
linguistic context **21**, 222, 227
linguistic relativity **117**
literacy 87–90, 109, 154–5, 281
locale header **92**–3
localisation **30**
locution **13**

Malay 42, 104, 172–3, 175, 258–9, 262
markers **39**–40, 73, 74, 86, 94, 101, 167, 20, 205, 220, 226, 259, 269
material process **79**, 141–3, 263–70

maxims 70–2, 76, 148, 229, 230
McGonagall, William 127–8
mental process 79–**80**, 141–3
meronymy **68**, 132
mesolect **172**
Middle English 9, 10, 36, 248
minimal pairs **3**
mixed method **52**, 53, 193, 271–7
monophthong **62**–3
Monty Python 182
morpheme 7–10, 15, 21, 130, 212, 236
morphology 6, **7**–9, 20, 28, 31–2, 48, 69, 90,
    104, 128, 130, 158, 180, 200, 207, 245, 284
multi-modal communication **112**

narrative 28, 49, 88–93, 95, 154–6, 224–5,
    230–2, 263, 265–8, 270, 287
nasal **5**, 61–2, 65–6, 181, 238
negative 43, 46, **78**, 97, 99, 102, 103, 110,
    211, 212, 214–6, 219, 269
negative face **72**, 73–4, 139
negative politeness **72**, 73–4, 136, 148, 220
neologisms **9**
network building **27**
nominative **34**–5, 36
Non-Regional Pronunciation **65**, **102**
noun 7, 8, 9, **16**–20, 23, 30, 31, 34, 36, 43,
    46, 77, 97, 109, 132, 202, 221, 231, 246,
    248, 250
noun phrase (NP) 11, **16**–20, 77, 94, 109,
    162, 210, 227, 231, 263

object complement **77**
observer's paradox **112**–5, 119, 193, 198
Old English 10, **33**–5, 36, 128–9, 246–7,
    249, 250–1
one-at-a-time (OAT) 83–**4**
organs of speech **2**–5
orthography **3**, 62, 164
Orwell, George 30, 116, 194
outer circle **42**, 45, 103, 174, 175
overlap **83**
overlexicalisation 66–7, 117

packaging **27**
palatal **5**, 61–2, 65
paralinguistic **101**
parallelism **48**, 109, 126, 179, 228
participant observation **51**–3, 111, 193
participant role **79**–80, 264
participants 13, 22, 25, 72, 79–81, 85, 90, **93**,
    113–4, 142, 143, 188–90, 200, 224, 229,
    231, 236, 253, 255, 272–3, 276
performance 26, 53, **56**–7, 73, 82, 83, 94,
    136, 139, 167–8, 197, 279
performative **13**, 56, 134
perlocution **13**–4

Persian 8
person deixis **12**
personal schema **92**
phenomenon **80**
philology **56**
philonymy **68**, 132–3
phoneme **2**–6, 21, 126–7, 243, 245
phonemic transcript **3**, 242
phonetic transcript **3**, 8, 112, 115
phoneticians **2**, 4, 6, 39, 63–5, 122, 126, 128
phonetics **2**–5, 7, 8, 39, 48, 54, 60–1, 64–5,
    87, 88–9, 108–9, 111–2, 122, 123–4,
    126–7, 161, 207, 239, 243, 245, 247,
    250, 285
phonoaesthetics 108, 179–80, 250
phonologists **2**
phonology **2**–5, 7, 9, 15, 26, 39, 44, 48, 49,
    52, 54, 65, 69, 124, 126, 158, 178, 186,
    190, 192, 200–1, 235, 236, 242–3, 250,
    255, 284, 285
phrasal categories 16, 17, **20**, 97, 105, 109,
    207, 208–9, 231
phrase 6, 8, 11, 15, **16**–20, 22, 24, 27, 28,
    37, 49, 53, 55, 56, 68, 77, 87, 98, 117–8,
    130–1, 140, 145, 161, 167–8, 174, 192,
    197, 207, 208–12, 213, 221–5, 227, 230–1,
    233, 241, 243, 251, 265
physical context **21**–2
place deixis **12**
plesionymy **68**, 132–3
politeness 14, 24, 28, 39, 48, 70–5, 82, 86,
    92, 133–9, 148–9, 163, 168, 196, 220, 227,
    229–30, 285
politeness principle **69**, 71–5, 82, 148,
    229–30
polysemy **68**, 132, 247
Portuguese 8
positive face **72**, 73–4
positive politeness **72**, 73, 220
possessive attribution **81**
post-modifier **17**
power 25, **38**, 44, 47, 99–100, 101, 113, 117,
    142, 185, 206, 218, 281
pragmatics **10**–4, 21–2, 24, 28, 39, 43–4, 48,
    49, 52, 69–72, 75, 76, 79, 90, 92, 97, 104,
    111, 134, 148–9, 178, 196, 212–3, 220,
    227, 228–9, 262–3, 265, 271, 285, 288
precondition header **92**
predicate **76**–8, 79, 141
preferred response **82**–3
prefix **7**, 9, 90
pre-modifier **16**, 17, 20, 76
preposition **18**, 27, 31, 97, 105, 117, 202,
    210–1, 212, 241
prepositional phrase (PrepP) 16, **18**, 20,
    145, 197
prescriptivism 56, **98**

prestige 40, **44**, 45, 52, 65, 87, **96**, 97, 98–100, 171–2, 174, 200, 206

priming **32**

pronunciation 8, 28, 36–7, 39–40, 53, 56, 65, 87, 89, 96, 106, 122, 123, 128, 150, 167, 174, 207, 239

props **90**

prototype effect **31**, 69–70, 94

prototypicality 31, 32, **69**, 76, 79, 87, 110, 157

psycholinguistics **29**–32, 91, 119, 220, 237, 239–45, 286

pure vowel **62**

qualifier **17**, 20, 77, 109

qualitative method **50**, 51–3, 111, 193, 207, 216, 271–7

quantitative method 32, **50**–2, 54, 111, 186, 193, 207, 252, 255, 271–7, 287

questionnaires 50–1, 188–192

rank-shift **18**, 77, 80

rapid and anonymous method **52**, 54

Received Pronunciation (RP) **65**, 98, 100

receiver **80**, 228, 231–3, 281

recipient **79**–80

recursion 15, **18**–9, 20

reference 10–2, 13, 23, 79, 90, 92–3, 94, 154, 156, 169, 170, 227, 230, 231–3

referring expression **11**–12, 22, 227, 230

regional variation **38**, 62, 103

relational process 79, **81**, 266

relative pronoun **78**–9, 105

repetition 22, 46, 84, 90, 101, 108, 109, 139, 158, 227, 230, 234, 235–6

resonance 117, 133

response (IRF) **24**, 43, 82–3, 85

results **93**

retronyms **9**

rhoticity **37**, 40, 52–3, 100

Sanskrit 8

Sapir-Whorf hypothesis **116**–7, 194, 279, 283

sayer **80**

schema accretion **93**

schema preservation **93**

schema refreshment **94**

schema reinforcement **93**

schema replacement **94**

schema theory **91**–5

schemas **91**–5, 118, 159–60, 239

schwa **64**, 241

scope 76, 78, **79**

Scottish English 3, 37, 39, 61, 62, 65, 108, 123–4, 127, 248

scribble 88–9

semantic field 28, **188**, 245

semantic prosody 211–2

semantics **10**–14, 22, 32, 48, 49, 57, 66, 76, 79, 128, 178, 181, 212, 251, 285

sense **10**–12, 15, 22, 26, 31, 66, 77, 95, 108–9, 179, 182, 227, 246, 249

sense relation network 186–9

senser **80**–1

sentence 10, **15**–7, 18–20, 21–22, 33–34, 76, 78–9, 88, 90, 144, 173, 208, 221, 222, 227–8, 282, 288

sequence of events **93**, 156

Shakespeare, William 8, 37, 46, 96–7, 141

shortening **8**–9, 97

single floor **84**

Singlish 171–5

situational schema **92**, 93

slots **93**

social deixis **12**

social distance **38**, 41, 100, **128**, 168, 171

social network **41**, 99, 100–1, 170, 171, 252–7

social semiotics **57**, 284

social status 12, **38**, 40

social variation **38**–9, 56, 220, 224, 252, 256

sociolinguist **37**–41, 52, **65**, 99, 102, 115, 168, 170, 175, 186, 200, 220, 252, 254

sociolinguistics 10, **37**–41, 43, 49, 52, 99–100, 101, 112, 128, 167, 169, 170, 172, 186, 190, 206–7, 221, 224, 252, 255, 257, 283, 284, 286, 287

sociophonetician 39, **65**, 122, 200, 207, 285

soft c **61**

solidarity **38**, 100, 101, **128**, 167–8, 171, 206, 214, 217, 218–20, 225, 226, 254

sound parallelism **126**, 127

sound system 2, 62

Spanish 43, 115, 161, 166, 250

speech accommodation theory (SAT) **100**

speech acts 13–4, 28, 69, 70–1, 134, 136, 138–9, 214–20

speech community 28, **40**–1, 66, 99–101, 167, 168, 170, 207, 233, 239, 251, 255, 275, 279

speech style **38**, 40, 100–1, 189, 192, 220

spread **64**–5

Standard English (SE) **97**, 98, 99, 173, 174, 225

standardisation **43**–5, 87, 95–9, 112, 150–1, 171, 262

steady-state vowel **62**

Stephenson, Neal 195

stereotypes **39**–40, 99–100, 102–3, 167–8, 170, 171, 175, 206, 228

stigma 40, 43, **44**, **96**, 99–102

stop 3–4, **5**, 60, 61–2, 65, 103, 109, 243

structuralism **56**–7, 197, 278–9

style 38, 40, **45**–9, 72, 100–1, 133, 144–6, 154, 162–4, 167, 172, 181, 189, 192, 200, 204, 206–7, 220, 225, 231, 253, 257, 262, 266–7

stylistics **45**–9, 107–11, 119, 126, 133, 178–9, 181, 263–9, 270, 271, 287
subject 16, 19, 28, 33, 34, 46, **76**–80, 210, 225–6, 228
subject complement 18, **76**–8, 79, 80
subjunctive **78**
subordinating conjunction **78**, 140
suffix 7, 9, 26, 34, 36, 78, 90, 128
supportive minimal response **85**
Swift, Jonathan 97–8, 162, 180, 186
syllable 28, 36, 46, 89, 108, **126**, 127, 158, 163–4, 223, 239–45
synchronic 56, **95**–6, 214, 251
synonymy **66**–7, 68, 90, 132, 231, 250–1, 282
syntax 15–20, 27, 28, 29–30, 31–2, 36, 39, 45, 48–9, 56–7, 76–81, 104, 109, 110, 117, 139–143, 158, 178–9, 182, 200, 211, 221–2, 225–6, 233, 234–5, 243–4, 266, 268, 278, 283–4
systemic 15, 19, **57**
systemic functional linguistics **25**, 79–81, 117, 249, 263, 278–80, 282

tag question **103**, 105
Tagalog 258
target **80**, 89
tautonymy **68**, 132
terms of endearment **12**
text 9, 12, 15–6, 19, **21**–5, 45, 47–9, 54, 66, 90, 94–5, 96–7, 119, 174, 212, 227–9, 233, 269, 273, 281–2
thick description 51, 53
time deixis **12**
top-down processing **30**
topic 24, 74, 76, 81, **85**–7, 114, 146, 226, 230
topic drift **85**, 87
topic shift **85**–6
tracks **93**
transcript **3**, **22**–3, 84, 111–2, 115, 146, 242
transcription conventions **22**, 112, 146
transition relevance places **82**

transitivity 17, **77**–8, 80, 247, 248, 263–6, 268–70
tree-diagram **17**, 19–20
turn-taking 24, **81**–5, 87, 92, 146, 225

underlexicalisation **67**
unrounded **64**–5

variationism **37**, 221–6, 252–4
velar **5**, 61–2, 65, 200–1
verb 7, 8, 12, **17**, 20, 30–1, 35, 46, 77–8, 128, 167, 208–9, 210–2, 225–6, 248, 264, 267, 269
verb phrase (VP) 16, **17**, 18, 20, 77
verbal process **80**
verbiage **80**
verbification **8**
voiced **4**–5, 61–2, 65–6, 108–9
voiceless **4**–5, 61–2, 65–6, 108
vowel 4, 5–6, 26, 28, 34, 36, 37, 40, 60, 62–5, 89, 96, 103, 122, 126, 128, 200, 241
vowel trapezium **6**, 63–5

Welsh 33, 37, 98
Woolf, Virginia 143
word 3, **6**–10, 15, 26–8, 30–2, 33–4, 36–7, 53, 60–1, 66–8, 88–90, 117, 126, 130, 132, 207–9, 212–3, 239–42, 244–51, 280, 281, 285
word final **61**, 103
word initial **61**, 244
word list 44, **122**, 201
word medial 53, **61**
word-formation 7–9, 250
world Englishes 37, 39, 41–5, 75, 103, 104–7, 171–6, 257–63, 287

xenonymy **68**, 132–3

Yeats, W.B. 182

Zog 91, 94